Crimean Letters
from the 41st (The Welch) Regiment, 1854–56

Major-General
William Allan

Edited by
W. Alister Williams

Crimean Letters from the 41st (The Welch) Regiment, 1854–56
published in Wales in 2011
by
Bridge Books
61 Park Avenue
Wrexham
LL12 7AW

ISBN: 978-1-84494-072-1

A CIP entry for this book is available from the British Library

Cover illustration:
Russian Rifle Pit - now part of the British Advanced Trenches on theleft of the Right Attack, or Gordon's Battery.
Published by Colnaghi, 11 June 1855.
The figures in the print depict men of the 41st (The Welch) Regiment
[The Royal Welsh Museum, Brecon]

Printed and bound by
Gutenberg Press Ltd
Malta

Contents

Introduction

A BRIEF REFERENCE to *My Early Soldiering Days* in *The History of the 41st Regiment* by D.A.N. Lomax (1899) led to a lengthy search and the eventual tracking down of a copy in the United Services Institute Library in Whitehall in mid 1970s. The book fully justified that often misused adjective 'scarce' in the catalogues of antiquarian booksellers. Although published in a case-bound format, with illustrations, *My Early Soldiering Days* had clearly been a limited edition, almost certainly intended solely for the use of family and friends; so much so that few Crimean historians have ever seen a copy. The copy that was used to provide the basis of this book once belonged to Henry Johnston Younger of Benmore and Kilmun, a cousin of Major-General William Allan.

William Allan was one of the few officers of the old 41st Regiment who had served in the Crimea from the start of hostilities right through to the end. His book was published some forty years after the end of the war but can still be regarded as a primary source as it was based upon his letters which he appears to quote verbatim. He was a regular correspondent with his family, sending what were often lengthy and detailed letters describing life in the trenches before Sevastopol. The publication of this edition makes these letters available to the general reader for the first time.

Although all the letters were written in a style that is easy to read, it has been felt necessary to annotate them in order to clarify some of the military terms in common usage at the time, but which now seem archaic, and to identify the numerous officers, friends and relatives who appear throughout the text. These have been recorded in the endnotes with further details in the notes appended at the end of the text.

It was also thought useful to add a nominal roll of the men of the 41st who served in the Crimea. This has been compiled, as accurately as possible, from the Muster Rolls and Crimean Medal Rolls of the 41st Regiment held by the National Archives.

Most of the Crimean War photographs included in the original edition have been inserted here. The quality of some, however, was very poor and these have been substituted by other, better quality images. In addition, a number of new photographs and maps have been included where it is felt they help to tell the story related in the letters or to clarify a particular point. The photographs of individual officers shown on pages 35, 47 and 137 were clearly taken some considerable time after the end of the war and are sourced from a collection in the Welch Regiment archive held at the Royal Welsh Museum, Brecon.

Acknowledgement must be made to a number of individuals and organisations.

Firstly to Jeremy Archer, William Allan's great-grandson, for his detailed and informative account of the Allan family, for providing a copy of the original book from which the text was extracted, for photographs relating to the Allan family, for his detailed checking of the completed work and for numerous suggestions which were incorporated into the text. Colonel Peter Knox, OBE, Chairman of the Crimean War Research Society, for his valuable suggestions and for carefully checking the typescript. The former Welch Regiment Museum in Cardiff and, in particular, the late Lieutenant Bryn Owen, RN, the curator, for granting me access to some of the photographs and background to the story of the 41st Regiment. Major Martin Everett and the staff of the Royal Welsh Museum (Brecon). The Director and staff of the National Archives, Kew.

A linking commentary has been added which provides a background and continuity to the letters of William Allan. This is differentiated from his original work by the use of italics. There are also extensive endnotes which not only add considerably to the information contained in the letters, but also identify most of the individuals and places named.

W. Alister Williams
Wrexham
2011

Note on spelling of names

The spelling of certain names relating to the Crimean War have changed over the years and may cause some confusion to the reader e.g. Sevastopol was usually written as Sebastopol and Woronstov as Woronzoff during the Victorian period and that spelling has been retained throughout the quoted letters, whilst the modern spelling has been used in the commentaries and notes. The 41st Regiment of Foot was also known as The Welch Regiment but the spelling of the title was changed to 'Welsh' after the Cardwell Reforms of the 1870s and remained with that spelling until the 1920s when it reverted to the archaic spelling 'Welch' (the same applied to the 23rd Regiment of Foot, The Royal Welch Fusiliers). The modern successor regiment to both carries the title The Royal Welsh.

The Allan Family of Hillside and Glen

The rise of this branch of the Allan family on the social scale was both swift and unpredictable. In the early eighteenth century the family was living some ten miles east of the city of Edinburgh, in the village of Prestonpans, on the edge of the Firth of Forth in East Lothian. Unfortunately for the genealogist, Allan is a common surname, not only in Scotland as a whole, but particularly in the village of Prestonpans, and its near neighbour, Tranent.

The earliest confirmed patronymic ancestor of Major-General William Allan was a candlemaker in Prestonpans, who shared the same christian name. On 3 July 1740 at Tranent, this William married Helen, the daughter of a fellow candlemaker, Alexander Cowan. According to the Old General Register of Sasines, William Allan prospered, acquiring property in Prestonpans from Margaret, Grizzel and Ann Warden on 8 December 1762.

While candle-making was a modest – though important – trade, William Allan had laid the foundations for his family to progress in the world. His eldest son, Alexander, soon saw that his future did not lie in Prestonpans and he was admitted as a burgess of Edinburgh on 8 April 1772, and as a gild brother on 5 April 1775. Now a member of the merchant classes, he founded Alexander Allan & Co (bankers), of 40 Princes Street and 126 High Street, Edinburgh, a year or so later. The bank prospered and, within a few years, Alexander Allan had become a 'good catch'. On 11 October 1787 in Edinburgh he married Ann, daughter of Thomas Losh, calico printer, of Carlisle, and his wife Ann, daughter of William Nixon. By this time, William Allan was also a man of property. First of all, he bought a substantial town house, at 20 Charlotte Square, Edinburgh, from Major-General Alexander Dixon of Mount Annan. In 1796, he purchased a country estate of 3,500 acres at Glen, near Innerleithen, Peeblesshire from John Plenderleith for £10,500, which equates today to more than £800,000 if measured by the increase in the retail price index – or almost £10 million in terms of the increase in average earnings over the intervening period.

Having acquired the trappings of success, Alexander Allan focused on providing his children with every advantage in life. His two eldest sons, William and Thomas, both followed him as burgesses and gild brothers of Edinburgh. William later became a magistrate, a member of the Council of the Royal Company of Archers and also of the Pitt Club, and served as Lord Provost of Edinburgh 1829–31. Thomas worked with his father at Alexander Allan & Co. and a third son, Alexander, became an advocate and lived long enough to become the 'father' of the Edinburgh bar. The youngest son, George, joined the army, serving with the 18th Light Dragoons and the 5th Fusiliers, and achieving the rank of lieutenant-colonel. During the Crimean War, Lieutenant-Colonel George Allan spent time at both Constantinople and Varna, in Bulgaria, meeting up several times with his nephew, although he never reached the Crimea itself.

Of Alexander and Ann's seven daughters, only five lived to adulthood and, of these, just two married. However, those two found very suitable husbands: the third daughter, Anne, married William Aitchison of Drummore, Musselburgh while the youngest, Matilda, married Robert, son of Thomas Allan of 19 Charlotte Square, Edinburgh and Lauriston Castle. Anne Aitchison's son, William, served with the Scots Fusilier Guards in the Crimea, and the former's correspondence confirms that the two of them met up on several occasions. By such judicious alliances, the Allan family slowly ceased to be 'trade' – and became gentlefolk.

Alexander Allan senior played an important role in the development of Edinburgh's New Town. On 20 December 1785, he purchased the Hillside Estate – comprising a house set in 6 acres, 3 roods and 11 falls of land – situated south and east of Calton Hill, Edinburgh. The land had originally been acquired from the Governors of George Heriot's Hospital and the vendor was James Grant, merchant, of Edinburgh. Between 1821 and 1823, the Hillside Estate was developed by William Henry Playfair as part of the second New Town, the family not only retaining the feu duties, but also acquiring the freehold of a number of houses in Hillside Crescent. Alexander Allan also patronised the great Scottish portraitist, Sir Henry Raeburn, who painted at least three portraits of family members. Unfortunately, the two paintings that remained in the family were sold in 1908 and their current whereabouts are unknown.

On 13 October 1823 at Craigielands in the parish of Kirkpatrick Juxta, Dumfriesshire, Alexander Allan junior married Jamima, only daughter of William Younger, brewer, of Craigielands and his wife Janet (née Hunter). Alexander and Jamima lived at 5 Hillside

The grave of Alexander and Jamima Allan, William's parents, in the Dean Cemetery, Edinburgh.

Crescent, Edinburgh and had five sons, two of whom died in childhood. The eldest, Alexander, was apprenticed to an Edinburgh banker but drowned off New Zealand on 5 September 1862, whilst a passenger in the *Gypsy*, sailing between Napier and Mohaka. The two surviving sons, William and John Younger, both joined the Army. John Younger Allan purchased an ensigncy in the 71st Highlanders on 18 November 1857 and saw active service with the Yusafzai Field Force on the North-West Frontier in 1863, most notably at Crag Piquet. Having retired from the Army in 1873, he stayed in the East Indies, becoming a coffee planter and, later, a merchant and carpet manufacturer at Srinagar in Kashmir. Captain John Younger Allan died in Lahore on 18 May 1918.

Alexander Allan, William's father.

Alexander and Jamima's second son, William, was appointed to an ensigncy in the 41st Regiment of Foot on 12 July 1850, spending his first two years of military service on Zante, in the Ionian Islands, before being advanced to lieutenant on 11 November 1853. He served throughout the campaign in the Crimea, including the Battle of the Alma, the repulse of the sortie of 26 October 1854, the Battle of Inkerman, the assaults on the Redan of 18 June and 8 September 1855, and the siege and fall of Sevastopol. For his services in the campaign he received the English medal with three clasps, the Turkish medal and was created a Knight of the French *Légion d'Honneur*. He 'got his company' on 25 December 1854. After returning from the Crimea, Captain William Allan served with his Regiment in the West Indies for three years, before spending a year supervising the construction of fortifications on the Isle of Wight. After being promoted to major on 18 April 1865, William Allan was placed in charge of four companies of the 41st Foot for the voyage to Calcutta. The following eight years were spent in India, initially at Agra, and later at Mooltan.

On 23 May 1877, Lieutenant-Colonel William Allan succeeded Lieutenant-Colonel Joseph Jordan in command of the 41st Regiment of Foot, with headquarters then at Pembroke Dock in Wales. The next two years were spent in Aldershot where William Allan soon made an impact on military manoeuvres, according to an article published on 6 June 1878:

> Would it not be advisable to give command of our First Army Corps to a General who has led troops in the field? ... The skirmishing of many of the infantry regiments was ludicrous in the extreme, the anxiety of over-zealous subalterns regarding the dressing

Officers of the 41st Regiment of Foot at Mooltan, India, 1872. Major William Allan is seated fourth from the left, middle row, next to the commanding officer, Lieutenant-Colonel Hugh Rowlands, VC, CB. Quartermaster Elliott is standingfifth from the right. It is interesting to note from the absence of medals how few of the officers appear to be Crimean veterans. [The Royal Welsh Museum, Brecon]

and distance of the files being simply puerile. The 41st, under Colonel Allan, showed an excellent example, however, in skirmishing; there was no confusion, very little noise, officers and men seemed to work harmoniously and quietly together; indeed, the 'Welsh' Regiment moved over the Fox Hill as if it knew what it had to do, and meant to do it.

William Allan was promoted to colonel on 7 October 1879, before the 41st Foot sailed for Gibraltar in mid-1880. On 13 March 1881, the battalion sailed for South Africa to reinforce the troops engaged in the Transvaal War. Any hopes that they might have cherished of active service, having trained hard under a battle-experienced leader, were dashed when a peace treaty was signed with the Boers on 23 March 1881. On 1 July 1881, under the terms of the reform of the infantry by Secretary of State for War, Hugh Childers, the 41st Regiment of Foot became the 1st Battalion, The Welch Regiment.

On 15 March 1882, Colonel William Allan handed over command of his Regiment to Lieutenant-Colonel Henry Haydock, making the following farewell address:

> Colonel Allan regrets that circumstances oblige him to take leave and sever himself from the corps in which he has served for more than thirty-one years. In bidding farewell to the regiment whom he will always look upon as the old 41st, he wishes it every success. He thanks the officers, non-commissioned officers, and all for the ready support and willing assistance they have always given him in the duties connected with the Service generally, and the regiment in particular. This support and assistance have made his command during the last five years an easy task and a pleasure.
>
> To the men he expresses his thanks for the cordial and good spirit of discipline they have evinced in upholding the good character and name of the regiment, and the young soldiers for following the examples of their comrades in keeping up the well-known character of the regiment for smartness. Although obliged to retire and resign the honour of the command, Colonel Allan can never forget the regiment that has been his home almost from boyhood, and he will always watch its welfare with the deepest interest. He feels satisfied that if all continue to be animated with the same spirit, they will maintain the old traditions of the 41st wherever duty and fortune may lead them, and that should they be called on in the hour of need and danger to stand by their 'colours', they will uphold the honour of England and the name of the Welch Regiment.

On the outbreak of hostilities in Egypt in August 1882, Colonel William Allan was appointed to the command of the reserve depôt at Alexandria, thus missing out once again on the opportunity for active service. The decisive battle of Tel-el-Kebir took place on 13 September and, on 19 December 1882, William Allan was appointed to the command of the 21st Regimental District, the depôt of the Royal Scots Fusiliers, at

Officers of the Welch Regiment with the regiment's Crimean veterans, Llandaff Cathedral, Cardiff, 16 August 1895. Identified are: Back row (L–R): 7th General Hugh Rowlands, VC; Front row: 3rd Captain D.A.N. Lomax; 4th Major-General William Allan; 6th Lieutenant-Colonel Edward L. Barnwell Lowry; 7th Lieutenant-Colonel John Owen Quirk, DSO. [Welch Regiment Museum, Cardiff]. Also included are Lieutenants Moreland, Prothero; Colonel A.E.W. Goldsmid (OC Regt Dist), Major Banfield (2IC), Major Threshire; Captains Pennefather, Clifford, Lucas, and Gifford; Lieutenants Fitzwilliam, Schoolfield. [The Royal Welsh Museum, Brecon]

Ayr. After five years in that appointment, convention was followed and he retired on half-pay. On 2 December 1889 he was promoted major-general and, on 9 October 1890, was gazetted to the command of British troops in Cyprus, arriving there in early November.

One commentator wrote of his period of command in Cyprus:

> It is with pleasure that one reads the account by two Non Commissioned Officers of the Troödos Camp published in our last issue regarding the entertainment given by General and Mrs Allan to the non-coms and men of the garrison. The kind thoughtfulness of the Officer in Command in providing some pleasurable relaxation for those whose position at Troödos does not afford much chance of amusement, is commendable in the extreme. Thought for the comfort and happiness of those in the ranks of the army, by Officers, do more to bring about that feeling of sympathy and touch between officers and men so much to be appreciated to day. Were more thought and care given by Officers to the comforts and feelings of their men, we should hear less of those accounts of insubordination which have been so frequent of late in the ranks at Home. General Allan is we hear a popular officer with all in Cyprus and the Garrison is to be congratulated on having such an officer in Command.

In the summer of 1893, William Allan and his second wife visited the Crimea from Cyprus, in the company of Lieutenant-General Henry Kent, late of the 77th Regiment of Foot. It was after their visit that Jennie Allan persuaded her husband that 'his old rubbish' was worthy of publication: *My Early Soldiering Days* was privately published and printed at The Edinburgh Press in 1897.

The same year that he revisited the Crimea, General Allan received 'the reward for distinguished service' of £100 per annum. On 6 June 1894, 'age compelled his retirement' from the Army. On 16 August 1895, William Allan was present in Llandaff Cathedral when the Crimean Colours of the 41st Regiment of Foot were deposited there for safe-keeping. That memorable occasion was described in detail in the *Western Mail* of 17 August 1895:

> At this time one became aware for the first time that while we were gazing forward at the lines 78 veterans of the Crimean War had advanced a little towards us from the grand-stand. There appeared quickly among them the distinguished Cambrian hero, General Hugh Rowlands, VC and CB, whose name will be remembered as long as the records of the Battle of Inkerman are read. With him was Major-General Allan. Both wore the uniforms they have adorned by gallant deeds. Their breasts were ablaze with orders and medals, and their cocked hats plumed with white feathers ...
>
> After the Mayor and Corporation of Cardiff had taken their seats in the chancel the regiment marched in and took their seats ... then the regimental band was heard playing outside and they entered and passed up into the chancel and formed in the sides, followed by the guard of the colours or colours' escort, who formed a line on

each side from the chancel to the west doorway, each soldier holding his gun with bayonet fixed at the shoulder. Now General Hugh Rowlands, VC and CB, and Major-General Allan were seen advancing up the cathedral between the files. All present were standing and the most intense stillness prevailed. On the gallant veteran commanders came, and it was noticed that both were in tears. Archdeacon John Griffiths and Archdeacon Bruce received the two flags by their hands from the poles, and then turned round and handed each in succession to Canon Roberts, who laid both on the Communion Table ... Thus came to a close one of the most interesting events ever witnessed in South Wales.

Major-General William Allan

Despite a distinguished military career, William Allan bore on his chest no orders, decorations or campaign medals, other than those that related to the Crimean War. According to a newspaper cutting:

> Much comment among officers in high rank has been made at the services of Major-General William Allan being unnoticed and unrecognised in the recent Birthday Honours. A General Officer, VC, KCB, writes: 'It is a crying shame that an old officer's meritorious services should be so very conspicuously ignored; one who went out to the Crimea and served continuously, and has never been rewarded.'

The 'General Officer' was certainly General Sir Hugh Rowlands, who was in command of the Grenadier Company of the 41st Foot on 5 November 1854. Lieutenant William Allan was the other officer in the Company, which formed the advanced piquet of the 2nd Brigade. Thus the Grenadier Company of the 41st Foot fired the opening shots at the Battle of Inkerman, during which Hugh Rowlands earned the Victoria Cross for helping to save the life of Lieutenant-Colonel William O'Grady (later Sir William) Haly of the 47th Regiment. During the campaign, Hugh Rowlands and William Allan, who shared accommodation during the bitter winter of 1854–5, developed a close bond, which lasted until Rowlands's death on 1 August 1909.

On 8 September 1870 at St John's Episcopal Chapel, Jedburgh, Major William Allan was married to Anne Campbell (Annie), daughter of William Penney, The Hon. Lord Kinloch, judge of the Court of Session of Scotland, of Bonjedward House, Jedburgh and his wife Louisa, daughter of John Campbell of Kinloch, Perthshire. William and Annie had one son, William Louis Campbell, who was born on 6 July 1871 at Pine Tree Lodge, Dalhousie, in the foothills of the Himalayas. Mrs Allan died on 11 February 1876 at the Central Hotel, Cannes and was buried in the Dean

Cemetery, Edinburgh. A bust of her in marble was made by Sir John Steell, Sculptor to the Queen in Scotland, and exhibited in Edinburgh in 1880.

Jennie Allan (née Senior)

On 31 August 1886 at Compton Pauncefoot, Somerset, Colonel William Allan married Jane (Jennie) Husey, third daughter of the Reverend James Senior (later Husey-Hunt), vicar of Compton Pauncefoot 1839–97. They had one son, Alexander (Alec) Claud, who was born on 10 February 1888 at Rosebank, Ayr.

In retirement, William and Jennie Allan lived first at 43 Manor Place, Edinburgh, before moving to Hillside, Bidborough, Kent, though he still retained Scottish domicile. In 1904 William Allan became Colonel of The Welch Regiment, an appointment he retained until his death. On 18 June 1915, he attended a luncheon at the United Service Club to commemorate the 60th anniversary of the Crimean War. Just twelve officers were in attendance, with a further sixteen, being 'prevented, to their deep regret, from attending'. Major-General William Allan died at Bidborough on 12 July 1918, leaving an estate valued at £21,084 13*s* 11*d*. His funeral, with military honours, took place in Edinburgh with the body being conveyed on a gun carriage, preceded by a firing party. The procession attracted considerable attention as it made its way to the Dean Cemetery, where he was buried beside his first wife. His widow lived later at 3 Calverley Park, one of 'a number of edifices suitable to the reception of genteel families', in Tunbridge Wells, and died on 1 June 1939 at 3 Shorncliffe Road, Folkestone.

William Allan's elder son, William, was educated at Wellington College and

William Allan's grave (right) in the Dean Cemetery, Edinburgh. Commemorated on his gravestone are his first wife, Anne, and his son William Louis Campbell Allan. The memorial on the left is for his uncle, Lieutenant-Colonel George Allan.

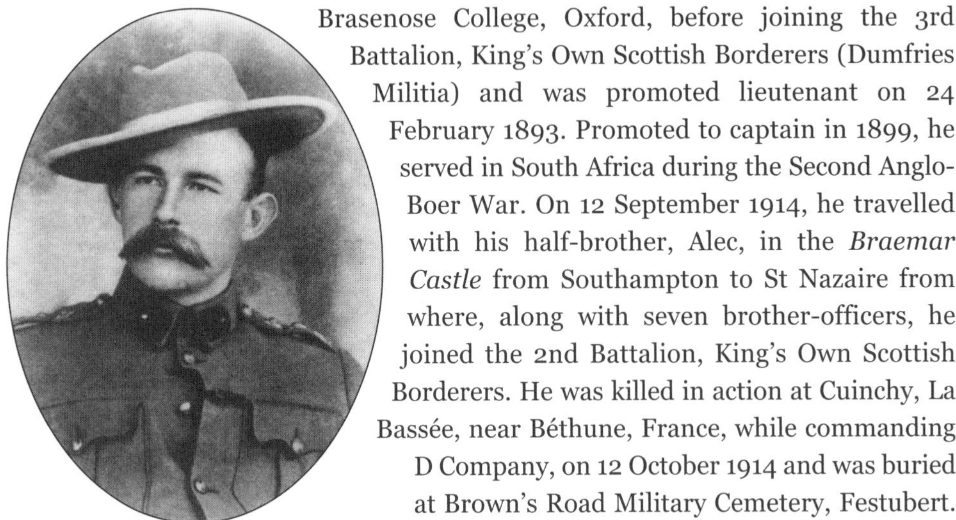

William Louis Campbell Allan

Brasenose College, Oxford, before joining the 3rd Battalion, King's Own Scottish Borderers (Dumfries Militia) and was promoted lieutenant on 24 February 1893. Promoted to captain in 1899, he served in South Africa during the Second Anglo-Boer War. On 12 September 1914, he travelled with his half-brother, Alec, in the *Braemar Castle* from Southampton to St Nazaire from where, along with seven brother-officers, he joined the 2nd Battalion, King's Own Scottish Borderers. He was killed in action at Cuinchy, La Bassée, near Béthune, France, while commanding D Company, on 12 October 1914 and was buried at Brown's Road Military Cemetery, Festubert. The operation during which Major W.L.C. Allan was killed – the advance of II Corps to shorten its lines of communication and close the gap with the French Army on its right – marked the last week of mobile campaigning before trench warfare began.

William Allan's younger son, Alec, was educated at Parkfield, Haywards Heath and later at Rugby, where he was an exact contemporary of the poet, Rupert Brooke, in School Field, W.P. Brooke's House. On 3 June 1906, Alec wrote from Rugby to his mother: 'You are paying too long visits on your friends, you ought to come here and see me as that is a very rare occurrence'. He attended the Royal Military College, Sandhurst, and was commissioned into the Queen's Own Cameron Highlanders on 1 October 1907. He fought in France and Flanders throughout the First World War, commanding 34th Signal Company, Royal Engineers 1915–16 serving as Assistant Director of Signals, 3rd Corps from 20 August 1917 to 8 October 1918. For his wartime services, Alec Allan was awarded a Military Cross on 3 June 1916 and invested as a Companion of the Distinguished Service Order by HRH Prince Arthur of Connaught at the Palace of Holyroodhouse on 4 December 1919. He was also mentioned in despatches on four occasions (14 January 1915; 9 April 1917; 7 April 1918; 8 November 1918).

Alec Allan transferred to The Royal Corps of Signals after the First World War, serving as Chief Signals Officer, Western Command, Chester from 24 May 1929 to 14 August 1933, before retiring from the Army on 14 February 1934. On 15 October 1919 at St Anne's Church, Dunbar, he married Eileen Norah, fourth daughter of Major Peter Marrow, King's Dragoon Guards, of Belhaven Hill, Dunbar and his wife Mary, eldest daughter of Canon Alexander Stewart, Rector of Liverpool. Colonel Alec Allan died on 31 August 1967 at Swallowcliffe Manor, Swallowcliffe, Wiltshire and Eileen Allan died on 26 September 1970 at Birtley House, Bramley, Surrey. They had two sons and two daughters.

Alec and Eileen's elder son, Patrick Alexander William (Pat), was born on 28

August 1920 and educated at Cheltenham College, before being commissioned into The Queen's Own Cameron Highlanders on 22 March 1941. From 15 September 1941, Pat Allan served with C Company of the 2nd Battalion in North Africa, where he was wounded in 1942 and later became a prisoner-of-war. After the war he served on the staff in Singapore 1956–8 during the Malayan Emergency, before retiring in 1959. On 29 May 1948 at Didcot, Oxfordshire, Pat Allan married Stella Mary, daughter of Brigadier Harry Colwell Whitaker, CBE. They had two daughters and he died on 12 June 2003.

Alexander Claud Allan

The family's military connections continued, however: Alec and Eileen's younger daughter, Cynthia Marie, married General Sir John Archer, KCB, OBE, Commander, British Forces, Hong Kong 1976–8, and then Commander-in-Chief, United Kingdom Land Forces 1978–9. Both their sons also joined the Army: I served for ten years with The Dorset Regiment while Simon joined the 10th (Princess Mary's Own) Gurkha Rifles and served a full career.

Jeremy Archer
London
2011

Major-General William Allan
1832–1918

Preface

I HAVE OFTEN BEEN ASKED BY FRIENDS AND OTHERS to collect my husband's letters written to his mother during his early soldiering days, including the Crimean campaign; but in consequence of his objection to having what he calls 'his old rubbish' put into print, I have only recently, and with difficulty, gained his consent.

Naturally, a general officer looks upon his effusions written when a subaltern as 'rubbish,' so I would ask anyone who is good enough to read the following extracts to recollect that they are taken from letters written unreservedly to his parents, and that at the date of their commencement, he was only just emerging from boyhood, although he was soon to learn what war with all its stern realities meant. I would also beg any readers to bear in mind under what trying difficulties some of the letters were penned, though he seldom, if ever, allowed a week to pass without sending a letter home. Being mercifully preserved throughout the campaign, he was able to do more trench work than most others, so I cannot but think that these notes – showing many minor details of his daily life during that eventful period – may prove interesting to others besides his immediate family circle.

Most of the illustrations in the book are from photographs taken at the time of the war, and they are now reproduced for the first time; others we obtained when visiting the Crimea again in 1892 [sic]. It is not easy to describe with what intense interest I went over the old sites and battlefields with my husband, and how glad I am I have had the pleasure of this most interesting and delightful trip before Russian restrictions precluded foreigners from so easily visiting Sebastopol.

J. H. Allan
Edinburgh
1897

1. Malta, Scutari and Varna

When Great Britain declared war on Russia on 28 March 1854, the 41st Regiment of Foot, The Welch Regiment, was stationed on the island of Malta, having arrived there in February 1853 after two years service in the Ionian Islands off the west coast of Greece. The regimental depôt was in Ireland. Traditionally, until the introduction of recruiting and depôt districts by the Regulation of the Forces Act, 1871 (when the 41st became territorially associated with the central and western area of South Wales, with a depot at Maindy Barracks in Cardiff) most British regiments drew recruits from all over the British Isles but particularly from Ireland. Although we cannot easily identify the place of origin of most of the men serving with the 41st between 1854 and 1856, a careful look at the nominal roll will indicate that a large number of recruits had names that, if not necessarily Irish, were of Irish origin. Where the regimental muster rolls do record the place of birth (usually for a man who has been killed or died on active service) the majority appear to have been born in Ireland. As the NCOs and other ranks were drawn from an area which was far beyond the boundaries of Wales, so the officers who served in the regiment were drawn from all over the British Isles, with a high proportion also originating from what might be termed Anglo-Irish gentry. In the 41st Regiment, despite its name being the Welsh Regiment, only two of the officers who served in the Crimea can be confirmed as have originated from Wales, Captains Hugh Rowlands (Caernarfonshire) and Henry Meredith (Denbighshire). William Allan, the author of the letters reproduced here, was a Scotsman who spent all his regimental life in the 41st before moving on to general officer rank.

The army of the 1850s was a very different animal to that which we know today. With 100 regiments of infantry, 27 regiments of cavalry, the Royal Artillery, the Royal Engineers, the Commissariat and the Medical Services, its total strength was rarely more than 150,000 men. Private soldiers enlisted for ten years' service and there was little opportunity for social advancement for the vast majority of experienced soldiers. The British Empire, spread across every continent, placed a high demand for servicemen to provide garrisons and, where necessary, fight colonial wars. To supplement the relatively small numbers of troops available for overseas service, colonies were dependant upon locally-raised forces, ranging from the East India Company's army in the Indian subcontinent to volunteer units in Cape Colony and para-military police forces in Canada. At no time were there more than 50,000 soldiers available for service in Britain and from these forces were drawn to fight regular campaigns in Europe and beyond. If a major conflict erupted it became necessary to rapidly expand the strength of the home-based forces, either by drawing upon volunteers from the locally-based militia and volunteer units or by recruiting men from civilian life. All of this took time and, consequently, Britain rarely had anything more than a small token army available for overseas service in a time of emergency. The government relied upon there being sufficient time to allow for the recruitment of large numbers of men who, after basic training, would supplement those men in the regiments already involved in the fighting. Each regiment was responsible for attracting its own recruits although men were transferred from one regiment to another when the needs of active service required it.

Just as the army itself was deprived of resources during peacetime, in an effort to allow successive governments to balance their budgets, so those organisations that might be termed the 'support services' found themselves struggling to meet the needs of an ever-demanding military hierarchy with a regularly reducing source of funding. When the British Army embarked for Scutari in Turkey in 1854, in support of the Sultan's forces that were at war with Russia, its men were totally unprepared for a campaign fought so far away from their home bases and who were grossly under-equipped. The options available to their commanders were to either delay becoming involved in the war until supplies and new recruits could be brought out from Britain, or fight a short, quick and decisive campaign to defeat the enemy before Russia could fully mobilise her potential vast resources of manpower. Unfortunately, the British generals, many of whom had long outdated experience of actual warfare, chose neither and set out to involve their relatively small forces in support of the Turks almost immediately.

On 3 March 1854, the 41st Regiment was ordered to hold itself in readiness for active service and was brigaded with the 47th and 49th Regiments under the command of Colonel Adams. By 28 March, with the arrival of two companies from Ireland, the regiment had a strength of approximately 850 NCOs and men. The long-serving muskets which had been the mainstay of British infantry regiments were gradually replaced with rifles and the men of the 41st practised on the ranges. On 10 April, the regiment embarked aboard the transport ship Himalaya *and arrived at Scutari near Constantinople five days later, being the first British regiment to arrive in Turkey. On 1 May, the 41st, 47th and 49th were placed in the 3rd Brigade of the 2nd Division under the command of Major-General Sir George de Lacy Evans, KCB. Initially accommodated in the Turkish barracks at Scutari (later to become infamous as the Scutari Military Hospital), the regiment was moved into a tented camp on 3 June.*

By mid May 1854, the Russian forces were laying siege to Silistria in the Danube valley and, following a visit by the British GOC, Lord Raglan, and the French GOC Marshal Saint-Arnaud, it was decided to move forces from Turkey. By July, the 1st, 2nd, 3rd and Light Divisions, as well as some elements of cavalry, had arrived at the Bulgarian port of Varna. The 41st, moved into their camp at Yuskakove on 6 July where, in their impractical service uniforms, they began to suffer under a baking hot sun. The reason for their presence there had already passed as the Russians had raised the siege of Silistria in June and were withdrawing from the Danube region.

Following the destruction of a Russian fleet at Sinope, the Royal Navy had identified the necessity of destroying the naval base at Sevastopol in the Crimea as an essential objective of the war. On 27 June, the British Cabinet approved the overall plan and orders were sent to Lord Raglan to land forces in the Crimea and advance upon, and destroy, the naval installations at Sevastopol.

In the latter part of July, cholera, that scourge of the mid-nineteenth century, arrived at Varna. Brought to the region by the French forces, it quickly spread and men who had yet to fire a shot in anger, or even see an enemy soldier, began to fall victims to the disease in significant numbers. When the orders for operations in the Crimea arrived, the troops began to move out of their disease-infested camps (the 41st were back in Varna by 30 August) and by 6 September all the men, horses and equipment were aboard ships ready to cross the Black Sea. Unfortunately for many, cholera was also an unwelcome and unseen guest waiting to strike down unwitting soldiers. The following morning the fleet sailed for the Crimea.

I BEGAN MY MILITARY CAREER when gazetted to the 41st, the Welch Regiment, on the 12th July 1850, at the age of eighteen, and joined at Cork on the 1st September. The regiment embarked the following February for the Ionian Islands, and was stationed for two years at Zante, when it was ordered to Malta. On the departure of the Service Companies, I, being one of the junior ensigns, was left with the Depôt, and quartered at Westport, Castlebar, Ballinrobe and Boyle.

In June 1853, I left Southampton for foreign service, in the P. & O. S.S. *Ripon*,[1] and landed with my brother ensigns, Swaby[2] and Harriott,[3] at Malta, on the 30th June, after an eventful incident during the voyage, which might have cut short my soldiering on my twenty-first birthday. On the night of the 22nd, having come through the Bay of Biscay, it was reported that we had passed a small boat, on which the officer of the watch, thinking it might be from some wrecked vessel, enquired of the captain if we should stop and hail her, but he received an answer in the negative. Soon after, a second boat came in sight, which caused suspicion that we were too near the coast of Spain. We were carrying sail, and going 11 knots. At 11 p.m., we ensigns, with four others of the 49th, Earle,[4] Corbett,[5] Armstrong,[6] and Corban,[7] had just retired to our cabins, when we suddenly heard a shout from the look-out man, 'Breakers ahead!' followed immediately by the ship's orders, 'Down all sail,' 'Stop her,' 'Back her.' It was a dark and hazy night, but, fortunately for us, the moon appeared from beneath the clouds in time to show the danger into which we were running; a few minutes more and we must have been wrecked. Great excitement and consternation prevailed on board, as, when the vessel was stopped, we could see the breakers in front of us, and a large rock on our starboard quarter. Owing to the thick, foggy weather down Channel, and across the Bay, the ship's officers had failed in taking sights, and it was found the strong current had drifted us 15 miles out of our course. The boats we had seen were fishing-boats. We took some of the men on board to help us out of our difficulty, and put us on our right course again. We had to back out from the shoal of rocks the same way as we had entered, and all felt thankful to have escaped what might have been a great catastrophe.

Fort Ricasoli, Malta, 18th July 1853

I cannot say my first impressions of Malta are very prepossessing; it may be a pleasant place in winter, but at present it is far too hot to be agreeable; with the thermometer standing at 80° at night. The heat at first quite knocked me up, but I am now getting used to it.

It is delightful boating, with a setting sun and a cloudless sky. One is not inclined to walk far in this climate, so rowing is the best exercise one can take. When it gets cooler, I shall hire a horse now and then, and explore the Island. It looks very desolate at present, as there is no grass, and the crops were reaped in May; added to which, the smell of garlic and the ugly women disgust one.

A fine new steamer arrived here yesterday from Southampton, called the *Vedetta*.[8] She is to ply between Malta and Marseilles. She can go 17 knots an hour, and is built for speed to run the French packets off the line. This is a curious place; though on the direct line from India and Constantinople, we never hear any news except through England.

The *Ripon* had no deck cabins except the captain's. Ours was in the front part of the vessel below the first deck. These vessels carry no steerage passengers. We passed too far from Algiers to have a good view of it.

One of the entrances to Valetta is by the Nix Mangiare Steps (i.e. 'nothing to eat'), which gets its name from the number of beggars that are congregated there. From Fort Ricasoli, where I am quartered, to the town, is about a quarter of an hour's row. The nearest route is across the Grand Harbour, where most of the shipping lies, and the fleet also.

To-morrow evening some of the few remaining English have been asked to the Officers' Mess, to a sort of cold collation. I am sorry I cannot be one of the party, as I dine with the General[9] at St Antonio. I should have liked to have made the acquaintance of some people; as yet, I do not know any. There are very few I am told at present in Malta worth knowing. I may meet some ladies at the General's, if it is not a gentlemen's party.

There were great illuminations in the town the other evening in honour of the Virgin Mary, and several processions the next day; two military bands played in front of the palace from nine till midnight.

The strawberries here are now all over. When I first came I had a large plateful every morning at breakfast of the Alpine kind.

Swaby, Harriott and I are going up for our examination at Fort Manoel on Wednesday. I drilled a company this morning, and found I got on swimmingly, but the sun is dreadfully hot even at 6 a.m.

20th July

Last evening I dined at St Antonio. The General is a very nice old fellow. There is no humbug or formality about him, and he received me in such a kind, friendly manner. I had a long chat with him. He says he is going to write to father, and he asked me to drop in some day at 2 p.m. and take a family dinner; or any evening I was riding out in their direction, to come in and have tea and refreshment. We had a very pleasant party at dinner, eighteen in number, no ladies, and almost all redcoats. After dinner we adjourned to the drawing-room, where we met Mrs Jarvis, Miss Jenkins, and Miss Younger. After a cup of tea, we all went out on to the verandah, and enjoyed iced drinks, cigars, etc. What a luxury ice is in this climate!

Returning home in the evening, we had a chapter of accidents; I think the drivers had been indulging too freely at the General's expense. Bush[10] and I were in a carriage together. Shortly after starting, our driver let the reins get under the tail of one of the horses, which made it jib, and nearly sent us against the wall. We had not proceeded much further when the horse kicked over the pole and fell, so we cleared out and got into one of the other conveyances, and after going about a mile, we came upon a carriage lying at the road-side, broken to pieces. The coachman had run into another vehicle, and was thrown off the box, had his arm fractured and head cut. Strickland,[11] of the Commissariat, had his head severely bruised, and two others were more or less hurt. We removed the unfortunate driver into one of the carriages, and drove him to the hospital. I don't think that he is dangerously hurt. There is little doubt that by this time it is reported in the garrison that we were all drunk, having had so many mishaps. We came home at a racing pace; the drivers must all have been a little 'lushey.'

30th July

For more than a week I have been a good deal engaged attending a General Court-Martial. The paymaster of the —th regiment is being tried for making away with public money entrusted to his care; and what with writing, exercises, and studying for my Italian master, my time has been very much taken up. This hot weather is not at all conducive to work. I have now been here exactly a month. The impression I have formed of Malta is not a very delightful one; the thermometer is 87° by day, and 83° at night. I am not yet home-sick, although I fancy there are very few places like 'Merrie Old England.'

The *Indus*[12] is in sight; we expect Captain Bourne[13] by her; he exchanged with Bagot.[14] I am also in hopes that I may hear something of my lieutenancy, as I think Bertram[15] will have to sell, or even if he is allowed to join the Depôt, the change would send Johnston out here, which I do not think would suit the old boy with his family.

Ten days ago, Handcock,[16] Fitzroy,[17] and I were out sailing in the evening; it was blowing pretty fresh, and the sea was high. We went a short distance, then took a tack round by the Quarantine Harbour to Fort Manoel, where the headquarters of the regiment is stationed. On our return home we noticed a boat in our wake. It was by that time becoming dark, and as we were passing Fort St Elmo, a squall caught us, and if Handcock had not let go the sheet, we should have capsized. Hearing a shout, we looked round, and found the sail we had previously seen had disappeared, so we immediately took down our canvas and put about, but the shutters (where the oars are placed) had got so swollen with the wet, that it took us some time to get the oars out. It was nearly a quarter of an hour before we reached the boat, which was keel uppermost. In a minute or two we were much relieved by a Maltese boat coming up alongside of us, with a soldier in it (Private Anderson, of our regiment). He called out that it was Mr Bligh's[18] boat that was upset, and that he had been sailing with him, but Bligh is a first-rate swimmer, and had succeeded in reaching St Elmo point. It was almost a miracle that he was not dashed to pieces against the rocks, there was such a heavy sea. The soldier, who is not a great hand at swimming, was nearly exhausted when he was picked up by the native boatmen. Bligh did not know much about sailing, but he saw us going out, and thought there was no reason why he should not follow. Handcock is an experienced hand, otherwise he would not have found me in his boat that night. It has taught us all a lesson to be more careful in future. I must now go out in my boat and get some rowing exercise. I have not got a sail for her yet, but propose going round to-night to the other harbour to see about it.

1st August

I intended to have despatched this by the *Indus*, but will now post it to-morrow via Marseilles, and trust that it may not be over a quarter of an ounce; if it is, it must wait for the Southampton, as I do not think it is worth 2*s.* 9*d.* I met the General when riding the other evening. I intend going out to St Antonio on Thursday with Bush, and stopping to tea, if they are at home.

Captain Bourne arrived by the *Indus*; we hope to get a step out of him shortly, by showing him the 'dust' (money) that the 17th could not produce. He offered to sell for £700 over regulation, but they could not make it up; Bagot gave him £250, and a free passage to exchange. He will easily get the £700 in this regiment, if he is still anxious to go, and I sincerely trust he may be, as I do not know where to look for my lieutenancy, if he does not sell. Bertram is in for a long spell of sick-leave.

The General Court-Martial wound up its proceedings on Saturday. There is no doubt E—[19] will be cashiered, and it will be fortunate for him if he only receives two years and not transportation. We shall not know the sentence till it has been laid before Her Majesty.

The captain of the *Ripon*, on returning to Southampton, ran down a coal barge, and, I hear, is likely to be suspended for six months. I have not seen anything of the Governor.[20] He does not entertain much at this season, as he lives in the country.

I returned yesterday from my travels (having spent a very pleasant month in Italy), exceedingly delighted with all I have seen. My only regret was having so short a time to see the numerous works of art. However, I visited all the principal sights and ruins, and came back in a French packet, after a boisterous voyage. The Museum at Florence is most interesting; there is a wonderful collection of waxworks there, consisting of wax flowers; the gradual development of the human frame from a skeleton, dissected and put together again, so, that a person, totally unacquainted with anatomy, can easily follow its entire construction; an egg from the day it is laid until the day the chick comes forth; the different stages a moth goes through, several species of fish, and innumerable other animals, all beautifully executed. But there was nothing I was so much struck with, as the wonderful models of the human frame.

The Cathedral at Florence is very beautiful, but before leaving Italy, I was heartily sick of seeing churches. Santa Croce is the finest in Florence. There are so many galleries, with lovely paintings and sculpture to visit and study, that one could well spend a couple of months in Florence. I regretted much that I only had a week to spare there.

The Austrians are hated throughout Tuscany, and the King is in very bad odour; he is at present residing at Pisa. The Tuscans have to pay for the occupation of the Austrian troops. I went by rail through a fertile country from Florence to Siena. The Cathedral is well worth a visit; the marble pavement is of Florentine mosaic, and very rich. The road from Siena to Borne is uninteresting, and surrounded by low volcanic hills; the journey takes thirty-six hours. I remained at Rome ten days, and made the most of my time, seeing all the principal objects. What wonders still remain of ancient Rome! They certainly made monuments and masonry in those days to stand. I had no idea the baths of the Emperors covered such a large area, or that they were on such an extensive scale.

I inspected St Peter's minutely. What an amount of money has been expended on it; 47,000,000 dollars up to 1694. Everything possible has been done in the way of embellishing it, and it is certainly a most splendid edifice. I went up to the ball which can contain sixteen persons. The ascent is easy. A broad winding slope leads nearly to the top, the remainder is by steps. From the upper gallery, there is a fine view of the city and the surrounding country, which is interspersed with grand old remains of palaces, baths, and aqueducts. The best view of the ruins is from the top of the Capitol. Looking down, from there, you have a fine idea of their extent and grandeur. It is a pity to see so many beautiful private palaces going to wreck throughout Italy. Very few of the proprietors, though called Princes, can afford to keep them up; gradually, one by one, they are being sold, and magnificent collections of pictures and sculpture broken up and dispersed. Among the Government galleries there is a deal of rubbish, which is kept because the works are ancient.

The day after my arrival in Rome, Ambrose[21] and Birmingham[22] [sic] of the Buffs, with whom I parted at Naples, arrived, and during my stay I worked hard. It was much pleasanter for me going about with them than being alone. After St Peter's, the finest churches are St John Lateran and St Maria Maggiore. The former is the oldest in Rome, and founded by Constantine. Both the interior and exterior are very grand. In the centre nave are colossal statues of the Apostles. The Chapel of the Corsini family is most magnificent, and decorated by the first painters and sculptors of the age. In the family vault is a group (by Bernini) of Christ, supported by His Mother; it is beautifully cut, and I think equals anything I saw of Michelangelo's by the extensive scale. I am sorry I devoted too much time to the private palaces and churches, as I had not sufficient left to see the Vatican properly, although I was there a whole day and part of another; it is only open to the public on Mondays, but a tip will unclose many a bolt. To see the Palace thoroughly would take a month at least. I believe in Rome one could see something new every day in the year, but the town itself is miserable, and looks dull. It is not a city where I should care to reside long after having seen the sights.

On Sunday I heard the Pope officiate [Pope Pius IX]. His Holiness is a fine-looking old man, but I cannot say much for the cardinals; they are not intelligent looking, and by their appearance one would judge that they were fond of good living. The Pope always dines by himself at the Quirinal Palace (his summer residence). I was shown through his private apartments; they are handsome, but plain. The Chapel adjoining is decorated by Guido.

The journey from Rome to Naples by diligence takes twenty-eight hours. From Capua, there is rail to Naples, and I was glad to avail myself of it, having had quite enough carriage work, which is slow and tedious. The distance by road from Capua is 16 miles, and the diligence takes four and a half hours to do it over, a frightfully bad road. On the journey, the annoyance one meets with from the inspection of passports and baggage is dreadful; it is much worse in the Neapolitan territories than in the others. Five times after crossing the Roman frontier, passports were demanded, and for signing them money is always expected; the system must be a goodly source of revenue to the Governments. On my passport I had more than twenty visas, which cost altogether 45*s*.

The road from Rome is picturesque, and of historical interest. Before reaching Terracino (the frontier station), you pass through the Pontine Marshes, which are more than 30 miles long, over a very dreary and desolate waste, with no habitations, barring a few post stations. The inhabitants are a sickly-looking people. After leaving Terracino, the country becomes very wild and rugged, and in olden times, was much infested with banditti, who took refuge in the mountains. A small place, 'Itri,' Murray[23] mentions as the birthplace of the celebrated brigand, 'Fra Diavolo,' whom the English employed and paid to harass the French towards the end of the last century. Further on, we passed the tomb of Cicero and Gaeta, where the Pope took refuge when he fled from Rome.

A curious incident occurred during my tour! I met Eccles,[24] a late brother ensign, who had left the service, he had been travelling the night before through the Pass of Terracino, when the coach was stopped by bandits, and he and the passengers were robbed of all their valuables. He told me he had lost his watch and about £20, and he was then on his way to consult with the English Consul as to the best means of obtaining the wherewithal to continue his journey.

When at Naples, I visited the Museum, which contains most of the antiquities that have been excavated from the noted cities of Pompeii and Herculaneum. It is very interesting to examine all the different things that have been brought to light, after being buried nearly 2,000 years. Several of the cooking utensils are the same as we use at the present day. Many fine works of marble and bronze have been dug up. How extraordinary it is to see the colour of some of the frescoes, which are nearly as fresh as the day they were painted. The Museum contains many other very fine relics collected from various quarters, besides the things found at Pompeii. The celebrated 'Toro Farnese' is there. To view the rooms is quite in character with everything else the traveller sees in the Neapolitan territories. Money, money, is the cry; every separate room is under the lock and key of a different custodian, who are all appointed by Government, and those people have to give a fixed sum every year to the Treasury. What with passports, examination of baggage, and money extorted for sight-seeing, a good round sum must be added to the revenue.

I was much pleased with Pompeii and Herculaneum. There is not much to be seen at the latter beyond the excavation of the theatre, which, along with the town, was destroyed by the eruption of Vesuvius, and every part filled up by the running lava, which is as hard as stone, so is nothing less than a theatre underground, cut out of the solid rock, the lava having been removed from the interior.

The town of Resina is built on the top of the ancient city of Herculaneum, so when underneath you hear the carriages rolling in the street above you. Pompeii is a great deal more interesting, but nearly everything worth preserving having been taken away to the Museum in Naples, little remains except the walls, and even these are stripped, when a good fresco is discovered. Although the roofs of the houses have fallen in, the side walls remain, and are still very perfect. The rooms are small, and built all much after the same style. The streets are very narrow, with paved footpaths on the sides. The floors of the rooms are mosaic; the finest and most perfect have been removed to the Museum. In the centre of almost all the houses there is a small open court.

Shortly before the eruption, an earthquake threw down many of the public edifices. The appearance of the ruins betokens a city of wealth and grandeur.

There are several temples and two forums. As yet no houses have been discovered which could have been inhabited by the poorer classes. The ground floors were usually shops. The excavations have been going on – off and on – for 100 years, but so slowly that, as yet, only a quarter of the town is uncovered. I believe in future they intend to leave some of the houses as they find them, which will add to the interest of the place.

The weather, when I was at Naples, was wet and hazy, which prevented my making some of the excursions I wished; but the day before I left was lovely, so, with a party of eight, I went to Vesuvius. We drove to Resina, and from there took ponies to the cone of the hill, which is a steep but easy ride. We then dismounted, and began the climb on foot; the first part was the most trying, as it was over very fine ashes, in which one sinks ankle deep, but the upper part is lava, so it is easy enough. There are plenty of guides, who offer to pull you up or carry you in a wicker chair, but I declined all assistance. From the top we had a beautiful view of the Bay and the surrounding country, and we were fortunate in having such a clear day. At present, there is nothing issuing from the crater except sulphureous vapour, and yet the ground is so hot that an egg will boil in the crevices from which the smoke rises. We did not take long to come down the mountain, as the descent is very easy.

I made an excursion to Baie; the view is magnificent on every side. There are many places of interest en route, which have stood since the clays of the Cæsars – ancient temples, baths, and innumerable other ruins. I was surprised to find Naples so large a town; the beggars are swarming, and the filth in the streets shocking, but it is certainly beautifully situated, and must be a delightful winter climate.

No officers are at present allowed leave for England, and we do not know whether we are to go to the West Indies or not. I hope Greece or Constantinople may be our destination. The steamer *Triton*[25] is now towing in quite a fleet of men-of-war, Prussian, Dutch and the *Agamemnon*,[26] five in all. They say that the contractor has an intimation to have supplies ready for 5,000 more troops, along with a large number of Artillery, but it does not do to credit all the reports.

The last news from the East is that there has been a naval engagement [the Battle of Sinope[27]] and that the Turks have got the worst of it. If so, it appears disgraceful that the combined fleet should be on the spot, and not help the Turks; the French I have met say, 'It is England that has prevented them.' I would like to see Aberdeen sent to the right-about, and Palmerston in office, and then we would soon be at it.

The French seem to be trying to get up a row with Naples. The King of Naples has established quarantine on all French vessels, on the plea of cholera, but the truth is, he wishes to throw impediments in the way of the French, English, and Americans entering the country, for they are the only people who speak their minds freely. I could not land at Messina on account of quarantine restrictions.

Johnston[28] has been recommended for the Regimental Adjutancy, but he says he will not take it if it is to interfere with his getting his promised appointment. It is a shame not giving it to some of the younger hands who have applied; Swaby and Rowlands[29] both asked for it, still it is better for the regiment that Johnston should have it for a time to rub the men up. Bertram is talking of selling out and going to New Zealand; if so, and when Balguay[30] is promoted by Tuckey[31] leaving, the Depôt Adjutancy will be vacant, for which I intend applying, as I think I may have a chance, and if I get it, I shall escape at least two years of the West Indies. What do you think of the plan? Pratt[32] and Skipwith[33] are on leave and join the Depôt.

Officers' Guard-Room, 25th December 1853

I quite forgot, when sending off my last, that it was so near the close of the year, and to wish you all a Merry Christmas and a Happy New Year. This day I have had the pleasure of spending on guard, so I cannot say that I have had a very enjoyable Christmas, especially as I had to dine all alone; the officers having agreed that they were all to feed together, none of them could favour me with their company. However, the day has not hung heavy on my hands, as I have had a number of visitors dropping in. You must know that a guard-room is very like a halfway house, which no person can pass without stopping at, so I have had no lack of society. After tattoo, the guard is closed to all visitors, as a precaution against the officer becoming incompetent to perform his duties, which now and then occurred when the —th was here, and open house kept all night.

Captain Hugh Rowlands, c.*1856.*
[W. Alister Williams Collection]

This day's mail from Marseilles brought private information that ships have been taken up to convey several regiments to the Mediterranean, so we may look forward to being under sail for the West Indies in about six weeks. The ships mentioned are the *Canterbury*[34] and *Georgiana*.[35] The passage to Jamaica will not be so pleasant in a freight ship as it was coming here in the *Ripon*.

Yesterday I was lunching at the General's, no one there besides myself. The Army at large has met with a blessing in the resignation of Sir George Brown[36] as Adjutant-General; he has always been averse to anything new, and is very unpopular. There has evidently been a quarrel at the Horse Guards. General Wetherall,[37] the Assistant Adjutant-General has also retired; he was much liked, and will be greatly regretted. I suppose he did not feel grateful for General Cathcart[38] being put over his head. Johnston has lost his interest by the retirement of Brown; he will probably now, poor fellow, not get an appointment. My hopes, with respect to the Depôt Adjutancy, I am afraid, are not likely to be realised, as Johnston told me it was already promised.

Next week we are to have a sham fight. The 41st and 47th are to attack Valetta on the Floriana side, which will be defended by the 49th and 68th. I am not yet acquainted with the entire outline of the engagement; the former succeed in forcing the outer works and beating the defenders back over Floriana to the Porta Reale, then a strong fire opens on us from behind the inner breastworks, and the fortune of the day is changed. It would puzzle a real enemy to establish a footing against such formidable batteries.

The thermometer to-day is 60°, and it is quite cold; in England it would be a hot summer's day. I do not understand how one feels the cold here so much. Some of the officers have fires all day; mine is only lighted in the evening, when I find it very comfortable. Handcock,[39] Harriott,[40] Lawes,[41] and I, with two of the Artillery, rode out last night to hear Midnight Mass at Citta Vecchia. The opera singers being there, the music and singing were very good, and we enjoyed it. The Cathedral looked beautiful with so much silver displayed.

Nevertheless, I do not think it compensated us for the wetting we got riding back, as we were caught in several heavy hailstorms, although we only took a little more than thirty minutes to return, which was sharp work, considering the town is about 7 miles from this. I shall now turn into bed, which I suppose is not quite the thing to do when on guard, but there is no use losing a good night's rest when it can be avoided.

The *Colombo*,[42] a new screw, has made the fastest passage on record from Southampton, viz. seven days and fourteen hours, with six hours' stoppage at Gibraltar. We expect Hunt[43] to be sent home to the Depôt as paymaster instead of Wethered.[44]

Guard House, Malta, 5th February 1854

On the 29th I got my mother's letter of the 23rd, which never failing epistle I look forward to every fortnight with great pleasure. I am on guard to-day. It has been one of great excitement, owing to the arrival of three mails – one from Constantinople and two from Marseilles. The *Caradox*,[45] [sic] a despatch boat, was one. She only remained three hours, and then left for Constantinople; she has on board a French Colonel of Engineers, and General Burgoyne,[46] Inspector of Fortifications. They were on shore for a short time, and took a look at the fortifications of Valetta, and also inspected the 41st in heavy marching order, and afterwards, with the Governor and the Staff, went round the barrack-rooms. The men's kits were laid out. The French Colonel would not believe, when he saw the soldiers' necessaries, that they would all go into the knapsack, so one was packed to convince him. He expressed himself very much taken with the appearance and turn-out of the men, and well he might be, for without partiality, they are a fine body, and if they only had a good chief (like Colonel Adams of the 49th), they would be one of the best regiments in Her Majesty's Service.

It looks very warlike, so many engineers of both nations going to the East. General Burgoyne says we are going to send 30,000 troops. I hope we may have a finger in the pie, and that the 41st may have an opportunity of distinguishing themselves. Although the relief regiments are on the eve of sailing from Cork, it is thought there is little or no chance of our going on to the West Indies, but that the corps coming out will be available as reinforcements. As long as France is on our side, they may withdraw four regiments from Malta. To send 30,000 men would require fifty-five regiments of the same strength as those now serving in the Mediterranean.

I have not yet seen the Queen's Speech, but I hear it mentions an increase to the Army and Navy. If an increase is to take place, the first thing will be to make every regiment 1,000 strong – they are at present 850 – that would only give about 10,000 men. The next thing to be considered would be extra battalions, and they would require more officers. Whatever happens will not do me much good, as those at the head of the lieutenants would be promoted, and they are not for purchase. Handcock[47] has been talking of selling out, but is now wavering; if he does, Richards[48] would get his company.

The *Gazette* to-day mentions that young Carpenter[49] is appointed lieutenant to the *7th*. He now regrets having applied for it, and I hear talks of trying to have it cancelled. It is no promotion for him, as in the 7th he goes to the bottom of twenty-two lieutenants, and if he remained in the 41st, he would probably have been soon a lieutenant, and then he would have had only nine above him for purchase. I hope, if he leaves us, his respected Governor may follow his example; the young one is not a bad fellow, but it is not at all a good thing having a Colonel and his son in the same regiment.

It has been privately intimated to us by the Staff that no regiments go to the West Indies, so we are in great hopes of having a rap at the Russians yet. In a short time our fate must be known.

We had a first-rate party on the 1st inst. at the Maclean's;[50] it was kept up with great spirit till three in the morning. The young ladies are very pleasant and good-looking, one might do worse than take one for a partner for life. I am afraid the agitation of the Scottish National Association will be overlooked, now that there is likely to be something of greater moment.

The garrison theatricals went off very well; there were some clever actors taking part in them. Last week we had another sham fight. One had to imagine a great deal, as we were not allowed to advance or retire except by the roads, owing to the standing crops, which at this season are well advanced. Swaby[51] is painting me in a shell jacket. Although it is only commenced, they say there is a likeness. The next letter you receive may, perhaps, tell something more definite with regard to our movements. Ask father not to forget the Colts revolver; if we are to be sent to the East, it will be hot and rough work.

The Countess of Errol has gone up to Gallipoli with her husband,[52] who is in the Rifles.

Mrs Carpenter, we hear, intends to go with us. I do not think ladies have any business with an army in the field; it is natural that the husbands will not be looking after their proper business.

21st March

My last would inform you that we are not to proceed to the East as soon as we expected; it is thought we may leave early in April. Lord Raglan[53] will inspect the force here before its departure. All the steamers which brought out the different regiments, have left, so at present there is no means of transport for those here. It is conjectured that the regiments now in Malta will form the 2nd Division, not the 1st, and that the other corps that come out will proceed direct to Turkey, without disembarking here, and that then the steamers will return for us, so that within eight days, after landing the first force, the second will have joined them.

Malta presents a very lively appearance just now, with soldiers in various uniforms of the Army – Guards, Highlanders, Rifles, etc., etc. The General has issued an order that officers are to wear uniform in or near the town, which is a great nuisance, as at every yard you meet soldiers, and the trouble of saluting and being saluted is a horrible bore.

I have met a number of friends, three of whom I had not seen since leaving the Grange School.[54] Anstruther,[55] in the Grenadier Guards, Lock,[56] 50th, and Clayhills,[57] 93rd. I am sorry to say, Tillbrook,[58] 50th, is left behind with the skeleton Depôt; Gandy,[59] 28th, and Mark Sprot,[60] 93rd, are also here, and several others whom I know. Mr Scott Elliott[61] arrived on the 13th by the *Valetta*,[62] and brought me the revolver; I have not yet been able to give it a good trial. The Dean and Adams pistols[63] appear to be preferred to Colts;[64] nearly all the officers have brought out the former. Mr Elliott dined with me on Friday. I have not had much time to show the party about, as I've been for the last week engaged with Minié[65] rifle practice. Twenty-six men per company are to be armed with rifles, and it is thought the whole force will receive them.

Yesterday the 3rd, 41st, and 68th, were brigaded together; it was only a short morning's work, but still Mr Elliott and party enjoyed the sight. After it was over, I took them round the fortifications, etc., etc. They have, I think, seen all that is worth visiting here and leave to-morrow for Naples; they say ten days is quite enough of this place, and wish to be in Rome during Holy Week.

Nasmyth[66] has returned from his trip up the Nile; he seems to have derived considerable benefit from it, and intends, as the weather gets warmer, to go to Constantinople. His brother was here the other day, but has returned again to the East. He has three years' leave from India, and is spending it very profitably, receiving £50 a month by corresponding with the *Times*, and giving them an account of what is going on between Turkey and Russia.

The officers who have come out from England are in rather an uncomfortable state, having only been allowed to bring baggage to the amount of 180 *lbs*. for a captain, and 90 *lbs*. for a subaltern, which is certainly precious little, when it includes everything in the way of bedding, portmanteaux, cooking, eating, and washing utensils, etc. When we move, I will try and take my gun with me; Nasmyth has kindly offered to take it, but there is no saying yet whether we are to see Constantinople. Our mess is much larger than usual, many officers of the other regiments come to dinner and breakfast, as they have nothing except their rations.

The 33rd and 93rd are under canvas not far from us in the Ravelin. They are to be inspected to-morrow, and the three battalions of Guards (who are in the lazaretto at Fort Manoel) on Thursday, on the Floriana Parade Ground, so they will have a long march round. Thc 44th, with the two I before mentioned, are the only regiments in tents; the others have all roofs over their heads, and are comfortably put up, considering the accommodation required for the large increase to the garrison.

The hotels and clubs are in great request for dinners. At the latter a *table d'hôte*

Lieut Henry Stratton Bush, 41st Regt.
[The Royal Welsh Museum, Brecon]

Capt Charles Pelgué Bertram, 41st Regt.
[The Royal Welsh Museum, Brecon]

Capt George Robert Fitzroy, 41st Regt.
[The Royal Welsh Museum, Brecon]

Capt Frederick C. Bligh, 41st Regt.
[The Royal Welsh Museum, Brecon]

has been established, at which sometimes sixty sit down, but I hear complaints about the want of attendance, and that after the dinner is over, some have had little or nothing to eat. Everything has risen in price. The poorer classes are complaining much, but some of the tradesmen must be making rapid fortunes; they are working night and day, and yet cannot get through the orders they have received.

The 4th and 77th are hourly expected. The two companies of our Depôt were to leave Dublin on the 11th for Liverpool. We will all be delighted to see them. Pratt[67] and Paterson,[68] late 61st, Lieutenants Wethered[69] and Bertram,[70] and the two junior ensigns, are all that remain. Handcock[71] has gone to England, having sent in his papers. There is a talk of adding another major to each of the regiments composing the expeditionary force, and also another company, making the regiments 1,450.

Since the arrival of the 93rd, I have been out twice riding with Turner.[72] Swaby[73] has finished the likeness he was taking of me; I am not certain that it is very true, but it is good for an amateur, who does not often take up his brush. I will send it home by Mrs Swaby. The *Ripon*, that brought the Guards and afterwards went on to Alexandria, is expected to-night.

8th April

My last was on the 21st. There have been considerable changes since then regarding the expeditionary force, and our turn is likely to be near at hand. The Rifles, with General Brown,[74] embarked on board the *Golden Fleece*[75] on the 30th March; their destination is said to be Gallipoli. Since then the 28th, 44th, 93rd, and part of the 50th have left. The other regiments of the 1st Division are only waiting for the return of the steamers. The *Cambria*,[76] with detachments of the 50th, 33rd and 77th from England, has just cast anchor in the Grand Harbour. The *Himalaya*,[77] with the homeward bound passengers from India, arrived yesterday, she has been detained, and is to be got ready as speedily as possible to take troops; having a very heavy cargo, she will not be in proper order before Tuesday. The *Golden Fleece* and *Emue*[78] are expected from the East immediately. Our orders are to be ready to embark at the shortest notice.

We have received our volunteers, with the exception of twenty-six, whom we should get from the 14th on their arrival, but as they have not yet left Ireland, there is little chance of our seeing them. The draft from our Depôt arrived on the 28th. Northey[79] has a month's leave. Our brigade is composed of the 41st, 47th, and 49th, under Colonel Adams,[80] of the 49th. Every one says it is the finest brigade going up; the reason partly is that we have no recruits, and all our volunteers are trained soldiers.

We have broken up our mess, and the plate, etc., is being packed; my traps are all put up, with the exception of my war-kit. I intend to take a hammock for my bed, as being the most portable; without the blankets it does not weigh 10 *lbs*. What I propose taking will be over 90 *lbs*., the regulation allowance, but as a mule's load is 300 *lbs*., and one mule is allowed to two subalterns, we reckon carrying about 150 *lbs*. each. We do not know yet whether we are to provide our own animals or not. Horses and mules have risen much in price; ponies that could have been got here two months ago for £15, are now £25 and £30; a good mule is £30 and £35. Tailors, saddlers, and tinsmiths are in great request for making pack-saddles, valises, camp canteens, portable beds, etc., besides no end of knick-knacks.

I have been trying my pistol. When I received it, the lock was not in good order, so I had it taken to pieces by our armourer, and it now acts perfectly. I much prefer Deans to Colts for close quarters – which, of course, is the only time a pistol should be used – but for correctness of aim at a distance, the latter is better; almost all the officers belonging to the expeditionary force have invested in Deans.

There has lately been a good deal of excitement owing to the arrival of French troops; their steamers all put into Malta to coal, a number of the officers and men are allowed to disembark. It was a lively sight, seeing a British regiment turn out and line the walls, cheering the steamers as they passed in and out of the harbours. The French returned the compliment, but their shout is not like a British cheer. The first detachment that arrived was accompanied by a General, who is to be second in command, and there was a review of the Guards, 33rd, 93rd, and Rifles. The other day another swell passed through, and there was a second turn-out of all the expeditionary force, excepting the 41st, 47th, and 49th. Some of the officers came into our mess-room to have lunch, and were much surprised at our having so many things to carry about with us, and enquired if we were taking them all to Turkey. They were very pleased with the review. Since writing, we have heard that we are to embark on Monday in the *Himalaya* with the 33rd.

Malta, 8th April

My dear Sir Hector Greig,[81]

I have long intended to despatch a few lines to you, and I must not delay doing so any longer, for fear of finding myself off for the wars before my intention has been executed. I suppose you have seen by the papers that the gallant 41st is under orders to form part of the expeditionary force for Turkey. Our orders are, to hold ourselves in readiness to embark at the shortest notice, at which we are all delighted and in great spirits. What an agreeable change it has been to us, as we were to have sailed for Jamaica this spring.

For some time back Malta has been much enlivened by the passing to and fro of military (French and English), and Valetta has during the last month been swarming with redcoats. It was an unusual sight to see the British regiments turn out and cheer the French as they came into the harbour for coal. The other day the French General, who is to be second in command, passed through. There was a grand review of nearly all the 1st Division on the Floriana Parade Ground. Such a large body of troops had never before been assembled together in Malta, and most probably such a sight will never be witnessed again. The General and his Staff were much taken by the appearance of the men, the Highlanders they said was a splendid corps. A square was formed by the Grenadier Guards and when the French General with his Staff went into the centre, he remarked that he believed it was the first time the French had ever had the honour of entering a British square.

The French troops from Algeria are a very fine lot. During the last few days, several of our regiment have left this; their destination is said to be Gallipoli. The remainder of the 1st Division only await the return of the steamers. The *Himalaya*, with the homeward bound passengers from India, has been stopped to take troops, and some other steamers have arrived to-day, and are to be taken up, so we may expect a move soon, and the sooner the better I shall be pleased. Malta is beginning to get too hot. I cannot say that I have enjoyed my residence here much. Old Ireland, bad as it is, is preferable, but we soldiers are never contented.

The last news from Turkey is supposed to be unfavourable, and the troops are to be hurried on as soon as possible, but at present there is no means of transport from here. There is a contradictory report in Malta that the Turks had entrapped the Russians into crossing the Danube, and had then fallen upon and slaughtered a number of them, but there are so many different rumours, it is impossible to know what to believe. I do not think I can give you much Maltese news that would interest you, as there are very few families now in the Island who were here during your residence. Sir Charles Maclean[82] and his daughters are still here. Sir Lucius Curtis[83] intends returning to England this summer; his daughters have not been in Malta this winter. The society has been rather small, and very few nice young ladies; the Maltese associate very little with the English. San Giuseppe, where you lived, must be a comfortable residence, but I do not know Mr Lushington[84] who is now there. Our present General is very pleasant, and exceedingly liked in the garrison. The Governor is a quiet man, and entertains little at this season. In the summer he lives at Verdala Castle; he has done a good deal to improve the Island. My uncle, Colonel George Allan,[85] I expect here on his way to Constantinople about the 13th inst.

The orders have come out, and I see by them that the 41st with the 33rd embark on Monday afternoon in the *Himalaya*. How fortunate we are getting such a fine large steamer; we shall (at least the men) be very closely packed to stow 1,700 into her. Colonel Adams goes with us. The 47th, 49th, 50th and 77th, go on board the *Indus, Sultan,*[86] *Apollo,*[87] *Cambria* to-morrow, so the whole of the 1st Division, with the exception of the Guards, will be off by Tuesday. There is no saying what may have happened before this day two months [hence]. I hope you may hear that the 41st have distinguished themselves. Our brigade is the 41st, 47th, and 49th, under Colonel Adams[88] of the 49th. Every one here says it is the finest brigade of the lot. We have not a single recruit, our complement being made up by volunteers from the other regiments now in the Malta garrison, who are not going to the East.

All those that are to remain behind are sadly disappointed. I hope the severe winter in England did you no harm; it was a very trying season. It will give me much pleasure to receive a few lines from you at your leisure. I cannot say what my address may be, but 41st Regiment will always find me, as letters will be forwarded. I must say adieu.

Dardanelles, Thursday, 8 a.m., 13th April

I posted a letter on the 9th, the day before we left Malta; it would inform you of our move. Here we are now cutting through the Dardanelles, and expect to reach Gallipoli about noon. We have had a lovely passage – not a wave on the sea, and no sickness on board. This is a capital ship. We weighed anchor at half-past six on Monday evening, and were saluted with no end of cheering from the forts and town. It is now quite a common affair, a regiment leaving for the wars.

The *Emue*, with the 4th Regiment, left soon after us. Before we were out of sight of Malta, the *Himalaya* broke down; the packing round the piston required renewing. We were delayed nearly three hours, which gave the *Emue* a good start. There was a kind of race between the two vessels, as the captain of the *Emue*, before leaving Malta, had said he was confident he could beat the *Himalaya*. We passed her yesterday afternoon, and had great fun chaffing her by signal. She is now astern, but pretty close, having come up with us during the night; we went half speed for three hours, because our pilot did not like to enter the Straits during dark. The entrance is strongly guarded by forts, and the current is very rapid, running 3 knots against us. Before leaving, I called on the General to say good-bye; he wished me all success, and said it was a fine opportunity for us young men, and he only wished his health had allowed him to take part.

14th April

On our arrival at Gallipoli, we were delighted to receive orders from General Brown[89] to proceed to Constantinople, where we have just cast anchor; the appearance of the town is most imposing. We are to occupy the Scutari Barracks, which are on the Asiatic side of the Bosphorus; a thousand Turks are quartered there at present. We are fortunate in being here, for at Gallipoli the regiments are very uncomfortable, encamped on a dreary site. The town there is a poor place, and they have little to eat, and that little very bad. Several of the officers came off to us with haversacks to try and get some additional prog to help their scanty rations. The 4th, 25th, 44th, 50th, 93rd, and Rifles remain at Gallipoli for a few days, and then march to a camp, which is being prepared for them 10 miles off, where they are to throw up a line of entrenchments, and there is some talk of their then going on to Adrianople. The other regiments from home are to land here; the French are to encamp outside the city, about 10 miles off. We expect to remain here for a month or more.

I got leave to go on shore at Gallipoli for an hour, and strolled through some of the French camps, and fraternised with their Algerian troops. The town is built of wood; one or two shells would burn it to the ground; the streets are awfully bad. I did not see any of the native women.

We are lucky dogs being ordered up here, but it is very cold and has been snowing all the morning, with a piercing wind; the thermometer is 21° lower than it was at Malta. The last shave is that the SS [sic] *Furious*[90] went to Odessa, carrying a flag of truce, and was fired at, and that on her lowering a boat, they fired again at that; so she

SS Himalaya, *the ship that transported the 41st Regiment from Malta to Scutari.*

returned to the fleet, and reported the circumstance to the Admiral, who gave orders for the fleet to weigh anchor the next morning for Odessa, to teach them civility.

We have received intimation that officers are to provide their own baggage animals and carry their own tents, which weigh 50 to 60 lbs. Captains are to take their subalterns' canteens. We disembark to-morrow, and occupy the barracks at Scutari. I hope to get on shore after dinner. We are the first arrivals here; the 33rd, you know, are with us.

Camp Scutari, 14th May

We have been here a month, and are no nearer the Russians; we do not know when we are likely to make a move northwards. The *on dit* is that the Light Division proceeds to Varna this week; it consists of the 7th, 23rd, 33rd 19th, 77th, and 88th, with the Rifle Brigade, under the command of General Brown, who has been replaced at Gallipoli by Sir Richard England.[91] The Rifle Brigade, with the 93rd Highlanders, arrived here last week; they have been working at the lines near Gallipoli, which are expected to be completed by the end of the month. The works extend from the Bay of Enos to the Sea of Marmora; the French also have a large force employed on them. These lines of earth-works are being made in case we or the Turks meet with a reverse, and are obliged to retire. A large number of cannon are to be mounted, so they will be very strong, as the neck of land is narrow. No time has yet been named for any part of the force to go to Therapia to commence the lines to cover Constantinople. They will extend 25 miles, but 13 of that is lake, which will only require to be partially fortified to prevent pontooning.

Lord Raglan or some of his Staff, it is said, sail to-night in the *Caradox* [sic] for Varna; but it is impossible to credit all one hears; for instance, one of the shaves that was currently believed in the city was, that Cronstadt was taken, with the loss of 5,000 men and two frigates. The idea of the loss of so many men and only two vessels is ridiculous. One thing I can mention for a fact is, that all the steamers which have brought up troops and stores have orders to remain for some reason or another, and others, now employed in towing the Artillery transports, will arrive in a day or two. About ten large steamers are now lying off Scutari. None of the Cavalry have yet arrived; they and the Artillery will land about 3 miles higher up the Bosphorus, on the Asiatic side. The authorities surely cannot mean that we are all to go from Constantinople into the interior, or why land all on this side and be obliged to re-ship them across to the other, when there are some beautiful barracks near Pera? I think it looks more like a move up to the Black Sea. When on parade on Thursday afternoon, I was delighted at seeing Uncle G[92] and Sylvester L'Amy[93] standing on the square. I have been going about with them a good deal. Last Friday we went and saw the Sultan going to Mosque; he is an insignificant-looking man; he was on horseback, and attended by a number of unmounted officers. The place of worship he attends is close to the palace he is having built near to Torphana. It is not yet completed, though far advanced; the public rooms and the council chamber in it are very fine. The same afternoon we took a caique and rowed to the Sweet Waters of Europe, which is about 4 miles up the Golden Horn. It is a gay sight to see the Turkish ladies turn out in their bright-coloured dresses, and squat down at the edge of the waters. They are all veiled, but some of the veils are very thin, so their features are easily distinguished. The higher classes go about in very peculiar carriages and finely-carved caiques.

Part of the Sultan's harem was present. Friday is their Sunday; they gather there every week during the summer. On Sundays the Sweet Waters is a great resort for the Greeks. Some of the Turkish women are pretty, but for want of exercise, their complexions are pale and sallow, and they dye their eyebrows and nails.

It will be better in future to send letters direct to Constantinople by Trieste or Marseilles. I have moved out of barracks into a tent in the square, and much prefer being under canvas, as the fleas were dreadful in quarters. It was very wet yesterday, but the rain did not come through my tent. Will you ask father to return my name to Cox[94] for purchase, not that I expect to be a captain immediately. I stand fourth on the list, but there is a talk of an augmentation to each of the regiments out here, of one major, three captains, three lieutenants, and three ensigns, and it is said some of the vacancies will be filled up by officers from half pay, few of whom are likely to remain, so when they sell, the promotion will go by purchase. I may, perhaps, soon find myself a captain, though it is improbable that they will give the four companies to officers at present in the regiment. Our Colonel came from Malta with the 30th Regiment. I am going across to Constantinople to see what uncle intends to be about to-day. Government has provided a steamer which runs every two hours.

Scutari, 25th May

Things are now beginning to look a little more like work. The Light Division embark for Varna on the 27th; the Artillery sail to-night. Varna is only sixteen hours by steamer, so before the middle of next week, we expect to be all out of this. A French vessel filled with troops came in this morning; others are shortly expected. Before Monday they say 25,000 allied troops will have disembarked at Varna; a place about 13 miles from the town is talked of as a rendezvous. A magnificent fleet of steamers and transports are at present lying here; it is a grand sight.

The scenery about Stamboul and up the Bosphorus has now become very beautiful; the foliage is fully out, which, contrasted with the wooden houses, gives a fine effect from the water; but the town does not improve on acquaintance. Along the banks of the Bosphorus there is a continued line of habitations; the surrounding country is very barren. I am going up to Therapia to-morrow evening with uncle and S— [Sylvester].[95]

We stop all night, and return by *caique* in the afternoon down the stream; it is much pleasanter going in a *caique* than on a steamer, but it is tedious work rowing up, as the current is very strong in the Bosphorus. Uncle George has been exceedingly kind to me, and has given me everything I require for the campaign, including a capital strong baggage horse, which will also do for riding; besides this, he has fitted me out in first-rate style, with a pack-saddle, saddle-bags, etc, complete, which he brought out with him from London. He has also bestowed on me a strong compact stretcher bed. Sylvester presented me with a bridle and riding-saddle, so altogether, my outfit has not cost me much. I am afraid uncle has deprived himself of things that might be useful to him, should he accompany the army, which he purposes doing, if we are likely to have some real work soon.

The Light Division only left to-day for Varna. They went up in gallant style; nine or ten steamers weighed anchor about the same time. They say the 1st Division is to go before us, so probably we shall not leave until next week. I am just as well pleased that we are to be the last, as this place is preferable to Varna and its neighbourhood, and the other troops will not move forward till we are all together. The last accounts from Schumla are, that Omar Pasha says he will resign if he is not assisted, as he will not stand being defeated, which is certain to occur, if the allies do not advance. It is said that the Russians before Silestria lost 8,000 by a sortie from the garrison.

The loss of the *Tiger*[96] is a great disaster. We hear a parallel case has happened to the *Amphion*[97] in the Baltic. Last Friday week a sad catastrophe occurred to poor Macnish,[98] of the 93rd. About half-past nine o'clock in the evening there was a deluge of rain. Macnish was returning home to his tent with Clayhills;[99] they had to pass a little drain which runs across the road, and which is nearly dry in fine weather, but this evening it was a torrent. The two joined hands, and attempted to cross the water, but the stream took them both off their legs. Clayhills was taken down about 30 yards, then he managed to catch hold of the bank, and succeeded in extricating himself, but poor Macnish was carried out to sea, his body not being found for several days; probably he was stunned or suffocated by the mud. His sword hilt was much dented when it was discovered; I had been talking to both Macnish and Clayhills that same afternoon at the Sweet Waters.

The British camp at Scutari, 1854. The 41st Regiment were billeted in the Turkish Barracks (the large building visible on the skyline) before being moved into the tented camp.

We went and had a look at the Sultan returning from Mosque on Friday, he has not taken the trouble to cross the water to see the English troops. We had a great turn-out on the Queen's Birthday, and gave her three hearty cheers. Our Colonel was thrown from his horse, and severely hurt; he is still laid up, and will not be able to accompany us to Varna if we go soon. I am glad to say that Wethered is to be promoted to his company without purchase, but he is going to leave us afterwards, having been offered the paymastership of the 95th; the regiment is in our Division. We expect a run of promotion by the augmentations, but it is not known whether the steps will go by purchase or not. The whole regiment is to leave the barracks, and be put under canvas in a few days. I am going to pack up all my traps and put the pack-saddle on my horse, and see how he goes along with his load. My next letter may be dated within about 30 miles from the Russians.

Camp Scutari, 9th June

My dear Mother,

I hope you will receive this on the 21st. I cannot allow the mail to go to-morrow without sending you a few lines of good wishes for your birthday! Yesterday I had the pleasure of receiving your letter of the 16th May, along with some other despatches, which, though of rather ancient date, were none the less welcome. It does not do to write to Constantinople via Gibraltar or Malta, as there is no direct communication. Some of the letters were more than a month old.

The Turks are doing wonders; they do not appear to require our assistance. It is reported that the Russians have withdrawn from Silestria, and a rumour is afloat that Sebastopol is the point on which a descent is to be made. Our whole force of Infantry has now arrived. The 42nd disembarked yesterday; the Cavalry and Artillery are joining daily. Four officers of the 4th are here on leave from Gallipoli; they much prefer this quarter. Robertson[100] is among the number, and he says that they want him to settle down at home, but of course he will not retire just now. Poor Gandy[101] of the 28th has broken his leg at the hip joint; he fell from the mast of a vessel, and it is feared he will be a cripple for life. One of the officers of the Artillery had his leg broken by a kick from Brigadier-General Adams'[102] horse, he is doing well. Captain Wallace[103] was killed at Varna the other day by a fall from his horse.

Five days ago, I accompanied the two travellers to the Princes Islands; it was a pleasant day's excursion; the scenery is very pretty. There is a talk of moving the camp a few miles up the Bosphorus to the Giant's Mountain, near Beikos Bay, opposite to Therapia. I forget whether I mentioned having gone up with uncle to Buydkere; it is close to the Black Sea, the view on all sides is beautiful; we took a long walk through the forest of Belgrade.

This morning the regiment received Minié rifles, which, I think, will rather astonish the Russians; the whole force is to be armed with them. The *Himalaya* has arrived with the 5th Dragoon Guards. Nasmyth[104] has come on here from Naples; he talks of returning to Scotland in a few days, so I will send by him some photographic views of Constantinople and the camps. I frequently see Maitland;[105] he went with us to the Princes Islands; he is a very good sort of fellow. We are anxiously waiting for news from England, our latest papers being the 24th, and we expect the *Augmentation Gazette* by the next mail. We are to have another 150 men out here. The regiment is to be increased to 1,400 in all, and have an addition of six officers.

16th June

We are off to Varna to-morrow, per *Medway*,[106] a first-rate steamer; the passage is about fourteen or sixteen hours. The 1st Division has arrived. There is no truth about Silestria having either been taken or the siege raised. Things seem to remain much as they were in that neighbourhood. The Light Division are encamped within a few miles of Varna; they were ordered to Silestria and Schumla, but countermanded after proceeding some distance. They say we shall be hard at it the beginning of next month. Our Cavalry and the French contingent are not all up yet.

Uncle George[107] and Sylvester[108] are heartily tired of Constantinople, and went to Broussa, which is a short distance up the Sea of Marmora, last Tuesday; they are to return on Thursday. I think they will soon now proceed to Varna, as the army has left Scutari. One company of the 49th remains behind to take charge of the stores; at first the order was that two companies were to be detailed, and the second named was Richards' company, to which I have the honour of belonging; he is the junior captain of our regiment. I was in a great state of mind at the idea of being left here, but, happily, it was altered, and I am glad to say we are off for the wars. My address will be 41st Regiment, 2nd Division British Army, Varna.

Nasmyth[109] is on his return home; he took some photographs for me, the one of the camp shows the 41st tents in the centre. The print of Scutari Barracks contains a few tents on the right, overlooking the water, where I was first under canvas; the view from the square is lovely.

Camp Devena Road, 8th July

Since my last we have had two short marches, only about 8 miles each day, which is not a hard morning's work; we started at 5 a.m. and had our tents pitched at 8 a.m. The first day was to Caragoul; now we are about 3 miles in advance of the 1st Division, and 4 from Devena, where the Light Division and Cavalry are; we remain here for some days. Nothing is known about our movements, whether we go to Schumla, Silestria, or retrace our steps, and embark for the Crimea. By all accounts, there is not much for us to do in the Principalities. It is said the Russians have retired on Jassy.

A Council of War was held at Varna two days ago. Omar Pasha[110] and the Admiral were present. I hope Sebastopol is the move; it would be a glorious coup, and do more to finish the war than several battles here. There is a report that the Austrians intend to occupy the Principalities with a large force, which would leave us free to do something else.

This is a delightful place for an encampment, with a beautiful view of the valley, looking towards Varna Bay and the shipping; over the hill there is an extensive view of the Balkan range; the country is hilly and studded with low brushwood. We have all erected arbours to sit in, which are much cooler than our tents. Uncle G[111] and Sylvester[112] are now under canvas at Varna; they have three Turkish tents, and look very comfortable, but the canvas is not as good as ours. I rode into Varna last Wednesday; they were not then quite ready to start, having only succeeded in picking up one good riding animal for uncle, and Sylvester was busy looking out for another. There are plenty of horses, but they are in poor condition; they hope to get a bullock hackerie to carry their baggage; there is a pretty good road to either Schumla or Silestria; they will probably go on direct, and not wait for the army. Uncle wishes, if possible, to go home via the Danube and Vienna. Omar Pasha reviewed the 1st and Light Divisions on his return to Schumla.

Yuskakova Camp, Near Devena, 18th July

I have just written to Wm Aitchison,[113] in answer to a letter received from him. He wishes to know the most useful traps to bring out here; he had received notice that he would most probably have to leave in August. I have advised him not to volunteer to take anybody's place, if this state of inactivity is likely to continue. The general opinion here is, that we shall not move a mile nearer the Danube, but that the Crimea or Anapa is the mark; the transports have orders for six weeks' provisions. Whatever they intend doing this year, the sooner they begin the better, as winter is drawing on apace.

In your letter of the 27th, you ask about the heat. There has been nothing to speak of; this place is a great improvement on Malta, and also on the West Indies, I should fancy; so our regiment has not made a bad hit. This life of inactivity is very weary work. We are still in our old camp, but move a few hundred yards tomorrow to be clear of the bushes; it is thought being so near them is unhealthy, and there is a good deal of dysentery among the troops, but not very bad. There has been heavy rain the last few days, with thunder and lightning. Uncle George and Sylvester remained a couple of days here on their way to Schumla. I accompanied them to their first halting-place, Parvada, which is close to the Balkans.

We are all growing moustaches. The Duke of Cambridge[114] asked Lord Raglan[115] if he would grant the permission in orders. He replied, he would not give orders on the subject, but that he would not say anything against it. General Brown[116] will not allow it in his Division. There is a report that the Russians have burned Bucharest, so we shall not winter there this year. The *Illustrated News* is a great treat out here; I am the only one in the 41st who receives the paper regularly. If the print of Scutari is as like as the one that represented the barrack gate, I think it will be rather difficult for me to point out the window of the room that I lived in; it was on the ground floor, on the left side of the barrack gate, looking up toward the Mosque and village.

This is better encamping ground than Aladeen; there is a beautiful view of the Bay.

Lieut-Col George Carpenter, 41st Regt.
[The Royal Welsh Museum, Brecon]

Maj Lumley Graham, 41st Regt.
[The Royal Welsh Museum, Brecon]

Surgeon Abbott, 41st Regt.
[The Royal Welsh Museum, Brecon]

QM Archibald Elliott, 41st Regt.
[The Royal Welsh Museum, Brecon]

We have no dust here; it was very bad at the other place, having been first occupied by the Light Division. Yesterday and to-day we had races and sports for the men; there will be horse racing next week. We beat the woods the other day with thirty men; one hare and a few doves was the result of the day's sport. There are some pigs in the wood, but we didn't manage to get any.

Yuskakova Camp, 25th July

To My Uncle [George Allan],[117]

I have just received your letter by your express *Bashibazouk*,[118] and was delighted to hear you were put up in such comfortable quarters. The Turks appear to be getting on famously without our assistance. It is just as well that they are not dependent on us, as by all accounts they are not likely to receive any help near the Danube. All the talk is that we embark the first week or so of August for Anapa, and after that is taken, go against the Army in Asia, or perhaps Sebastopol; the Austrians and Turks must look after the Principalities.

At Varna, they are hard at work making fascines and gabions, which looks as if there is something likely to take place soon; they say the fleet will arrive in the Bay on the 28th, and all the transports from the Bosphorus. We are at the same place as when you left us, having only moved 200 yards higher up the hills, to be away from the bushes and the haze that hangs over the camp after sunset. Cholera has been very bad. The last three or four days the camping grounds at Varna and Devena have been changed. The Light Division moved yesterday; they lost seven men the night before, and two prior to that. The French lost sixteen in one day, and several deaths have also occurred in our force at Varna. I believe the 3rd Division were to go to the other side of the lake yesterday.

We received a draft of fifty men this morning; another of one hundred is expected in a few days. I shall then, I fear, be doubled up. I have been fortunate in having had a tent all to myself for so long. Two men of the 95th, who only landed last week, have died; those who have lately arrived from England suffer most. I am thankful to say our camp has been very healthy.

Last week five of our fellows went on leave till the 30th to Schumla and Silestria. I gave Bourne[119] some letters for you; he was to take them to the Consul, if there was no Post Office, as I think perhaps you may have gone to Rustchuk. I was in great hopes that I might have formed one of the party, but the General was scrubby in granting leave to so few. If we are to remain here another fortnight, I may get away in the next batch.

All are heartily sick of this inactivity; it is dreadful being kept so long doing nothing, and having so little to occupy our time; the papers are well scanned, and a great resource. It is difficult to write, when there is so little to mention, and the tents being very hot when the sun shines, so we are driven to the arbours, and there the least puff of wind blows all the papers about, not to say anything of being constantly distracted by the talk and gossip of three or four officers lying on the ground. Some roll themselves up in a quiet corner and try to enjoy a siesta. He is a lucky fellow who can get hold of one of the few stray books, the camp library being very limited.

Yuskakova, 3rd August

Everything here much the same as when I last wrote. I regret to say some of the Divisions have been suffering dreadfully from cholera; the Light have lost four officers, seventy-five men, and three women; it has also been very bad in Varna, our brigade has only lost one man.

Yesterday we buried poor Maule,[120] who was Adjutant-General of this Division. There is now no doubt but that we are to cross the Black Sea, it is said to Sebastopol.

Sir George Brown[121] was last week close off the stronghold, and we hear a landing-place is decided on, and with comparatively little work, we hope to become masters of their fleet, and perhaps the whole place. It is believed if one crown fort on the north side of the harbour is taken, their fleet can be destroyed.

All the regiments are busy making fascines and gabions. We expect to leave this in a few days, but everything is hearsay.

The last *Gazette*, I am afraid, has played the mischief with our promotion; we were in great hopes that the step would go in the regiment, but if we are all alive to enter, on another campaign next spring, there will be a mighty change. Weather at present very unsettled; very hot in the mornings, and cold, with heavy dews, in the evening.

Soombay Camp, 18th August

I suppose you will be expecting to hear from me by this mail to let you know that I am still in the land of the living; as for news, it is scanty, except what is of a sad nature. You will regret deeply to hear of the death of poor Wm. Turner[122] of the 93rd, he died last Saturday morning, and I heard of it in Varna on that day. The funeral took place on Sunday at 6 a.m., I was sorry I was not able to be present. I sent my servant at sunrise to find out the hour, and when he returned it was too late. Colonel Elliott,[123] of the 79th, and he were buried at the same service. The senior Major[124] of the 79th died at Gallipoli on his way to England. We have every reason to be thankful for the good health of our brigade, having had very few cases of cholera or any other sickness. The 93rd have suffered severely, also the Light Division, but I am now happy to say that it is on the decrease. We all think the end of next week will see us out of this horrid country, and I trust that we may never return to it. The preparations for our embarkation are nearly completed, four piers have been constructed on the south side of the Bay, and the large boats for landing are all ready. The Guards, with the 42nd, marched into Varna yesterday, and are to be encamped in a healthy situation for a few days on a hill to the south of the Bay. The remainder of the Highlanders were not able to move for want of transport to carry the sick and the men's packs; they took two days, marching twelve miles; this will show you what a nice state they are in. The 33rd have 200 men unfit for duty, and the 93rd have 175 sick and convalescent.

There are twenty-nine vessels of war in harbour of different nations. Part of the 4th

Division, which is coming, out, have been disembarked at Beikos, a wise move not to bring them up here till they are required. Some of the French Artillery were put on board ship the other day, but cholera broke out, and they were obliged to land them again. The French General, who took the Division up to the Dobrudscha, has committed suicide; he was to have been tried by Court-Martial for losing so many men.

Nearly the whole of Varna was burnt down last week; the fire is still smouldering; a good deal of Government property was lost. There is not a shop left; but you will see the account in the papers. I do not feel up to writing much more, having already written several letters.

Tell Jack[125] to tip me a line when he has nothing better to do, and not to be carried away with the idea of having a red coat on his back; he had better think twice about entering the Army; he can easily find a more comfortable berth, and I should advise him to try and get a more lucrative one. The Army is all very well at home among the lassies, but times change in places like Malta, the West Indies, and an army of no occupation in Turkey. You certainly see something of the world very cheaply, but it has many drawbacks. Honour and glory may be all very fine, but we do not know what that is yet. I hope we may know a little more about it before the middle of next month. To us it seems late to attack Sebastopol, but no one talks of anything else; I rather discredit the taking of Boomarsund[126] before the French troops arrive. It is just as well the editor of the *Illustrated London News* writes the names underneath his illustrations, as we find it rather difficult to make out the place he has depicted where the troops are in camp; some of the prints are, however, good, and the paper is much sought after.

We have no mess, but dine at different hours by companies. Richards[127] and I grub together, there being no ensign with us; a swell dinner consists generally of 3 *lbs.* of rations, a fowl, or a goose now and then; sometimes we wind up with a grand rice pudding; our only drink is brandy and water, a glass of beer is considered a great luxury. I had to borrow this sheet of paper, so don't expect to hear from me again in a hurry.

Soombay Camp, 28th August

I do not feel game to write a letter, so will only send you these few lines to let you know that we are not yet in the breach of Sebastopol, but the time is not far distant. We march for Varna on Thursday, making two days of it, and the men's packs will be carried. The Light Division should be in Varna to-morrow, so on Friday all the troops will be collected there. The Artillery guns are on board, and everything ready in the Bay.

When I was sending off my last letter home, I did not feel very well, and ever since then I have been laid up with country fever. I am now getting on all right, and hope to be able to ride on the march, for if not, I shall have to go in one of those squeaking *arabas*,[128] which will not be pleasant. The change and the sail across the sea will soon

The city and harbour of Sevastopol. This pre-war print clearly shows the size of the harbour and the sophisticated nature of the city before its destruction following the Allied invasion and siege.

set me up. I am a good deal pulled down, and have lost weight, which I do not regret; I hope I may not regain it.

Every[129] has gone home sick, and Northey[130] has sent in his papers; he receives £1,400. Lord Raglan[131] has given him leave, and he is off to-morrow; we did not expect that his resignation would have been accepted.

2. To the Crimea

September 1854

As the Allied fleets sailed across the Black Sea, eventual destination unknown, Lord Raglan, aboard the Caradoc, *went ahead to select a suitable section of the Crimean coast where a landing could be successfully effected. The rocky, steep-cliffed coastline around Sevastopol was totally unsuited to landings from the sea and instead Kalamita Bay, close to the port of Eupatoria, thirty miles to the north of the naval base, was selected and landings commenced there on 14 September and were completed four days later. Midshipman Evelyn Wood, RN (later Field Marshal Sir Evelyn Wood, VC) recorded his memories of the invasion:*

> *[The Crimea] was known to contain a great harbour, and a city with docks, fortifications, and arsenal, but the strength and resources of the enemy, who would oppose us, the nature of the fortifications, and even the topography, except what the map could imperfectly show, lay much in the regions of speculation. It was believed, however, that any Russian force there must be inferior to that of the Allies, that the country would offer no serious impediments to the march and that, with the defeat of the defending army, the place would not long resist the means of attack which would be brought to bear on it. There was no thought of a protracted siege; a landing, a march, a battle, and, after some delay for preliminary bombardment, an assault, were all that made part of the programme.*
>
> *The officers landed in full dress, carrying sword, revolver, greatcoat, and blanket rolled in horseshoe fashion over the shoulder, a water-bottle, some spirits, three days' boiled pork and three days' biscuits. The Rank and File being weak, many still suffering intestinal complaints, it was decided to leave their knapsacks on board, and they were sent to Scutari. Each soldier carried fifty rounds of ammunition, three days' rations, greatcoat and blanket, in which was rolled a pair of boots, socks and forage cap, of the curious pork-pie shape.*

The regiment's strength on this first day in the Crimea was 25 officers and 934 NCOs and men. Captain Hugh Rowlands, OC the Grenadier Company, wrote:

> *We started [at 4pm] and marched four miles, arriving on the ground when it was dark; drizzly rain having fallen for the greater part of the morning, we were wet when we got*

there, and in the middle of the night it came down in torrents, and without fire or anything in the shape of creature comforts we passed a miserable night, lying huddled together in a plowed [sic] field, inches deep in mud. The following morning, luckily, was fine, and when the sun came round we got all right again.

During the second week of October, work began on digging trenches that would gradually move the Allied front closer to the Russian fortifications on the southern side of the city of Sevastopol. These trenches were protected by artillery batteries which would also serve to bombard the enemy positions in preparation for what was hoped would be a glorious and successful assault by the infantry. At this time, the artillery were positioned 1,700 yards from the Malakoff Tower and 1,400 yards from the Great Redan, the two main focus points of the Russian defences. It was firmly believed that no success could be achieved without the destruction or capture of both of these positions.

At 6.30 a.m. on 17 October, the order was given for the bombardment to begin. The British destroyed the Malakoff Tower (but not the Malakoff defences that surrounded it) and a great deal of damage was inflicted on many Russian batteries elsewhere, but all along the front the Russians maintained a regular fire. At 10 a.m. a Russian gunner managed to hit the main French magazine and reduced the French batteries to silence by 10.30. By 11.30, many of the guns in the earthworks around the city had been silenced by the British artillery and by shortly after 3 p.m. *the guns in the Great Redan had been silenced and the defences breached. Sadly, the Allies were in no position to mount an immediate assault.*

But dawn [on the 18 October] had disclosed a new factor in the problem. At nightfall we had looked on works reduced to shapeless heaps, on ruined batteries and disabled guns. Before morning the parapets had been rebuilt, the batteries repaired, and fresh guns from the inexhaustible supplies of the ships and arsenal had occupied the embrasures; and the Allies could now begin to realise how formidable was the opponent who could thus, as chief engineer [Todleben], wield the resources of the place. [A.W. Kinglake, The Invasion of the Crimea*]*

City of London,[1] Varna Bay, 3rd September

My dear Uncle,[2]

I have been disappointed in not receiving intimation of your arrival at Vienna, and am also anxious to hear if you have got all the letters I forwarded.

We were delighted last Tuesday by the receipt of a sudden order to march that afternoon half way to Varna. The following day we encamped near the town, and on the 31st August, 500 of us [Nos 1, 2, 3 and 4 Companies] embarked on board this steamer, under Major Eman;[3] the headquarters are in the *Melbourne*[4] along with the 47th Regiment, Nos. 5 and 6 Companies in the *Harbinger*.[5] We have much the best of it, and plenty of accommodation; our prog is first-rate, which is a great treat after living for five months on tough rations. General Sir de Lacy Evans[6] and Staff are with us; he is a nice old fellow; our grub is perhaps none the worse for his being on board. We expect to leave tomorrow for Baltschick Bay,[7] which is to be the rendezvous. It will be a grand sight, so many men-of-war and transports under sail. Our troops will all have embarked by this evening, Lord Raglan's[8] horses and those of his Staff were put on board to-day. They say the French will be all ready to-morrow. Many of the steamers and transports have left for Baltschick, and are to take in provisions and water there; most probably the final start will be on Tuesday.

The 4th Division is arriving from England, and are all now in the Bay except the 57th, which is coming from Corfu; the 21st arrived this morning from Cork; the Light Cavalry go with us, and the Heavy are to follow. The French have not got transport for more than 25,000 men; the remainder will be brought on afterwards. All our bat horses (*i.e.* officers' baggage animals) are left behind for the present; one officer to a regiment remains to look after them. I luckily escaped by being on the sick-list, and the brick of a doctor said it would be better for me to have a change. The country fever left me very weak and hardly able to walk, but having taken a quantity of quinine, I am nearly well again, and the good feeding on board this ship will set me to rights by the time we reach Sebastopol. Several of our fellows have been laid up with something similar. I may thank my illness for being the means of saving me from being left behind. Richards[9] (my captain) has been detained to look after the baggage animals, and the sick and weakly men of the brigade; he is in a great state of mind at having to do so.

Tuesday, 5th — We are now steaming for Baltschick Bay. Mr Russell,[10] the *Times* Correspondent, is on board; he is a very amusing, clever, and agreeable person.

City of London, anchored off the Crimea 12th September

I posted a letter to Miss Anderson [former governess] before leaving Varna Bay; our expedition took a roundabout course for Sebastopol. We did not leave Varna for Baltschick until the 5th inst.; the force had been collecting there for some days. Our final departure from Baltschick was delayed till the morning of the 7th, when we went off in gallant style, and it was a most magnificent sight to see the different Divisions in their respective lines.

We sail in six lines, the Light Division being the column of direction on the left; the next is the 1st Division, and so on, the Cavalry being on the right. We are convoyed by the men-of-war, the steamers towing the line of battleships and sailing frigates. The different Divisions have five or six steamers, each of which tows two sailing transports. The speed has been very slow, the orders are not to exceed 4 knots an hour, and no Division is allowed to advance in front of the others, so good order is preserved; at night the several lines have a different number of lights, so that we can readily keep our places. Although our speed has been slow, we have beaten the French, and have had to wait for them; they have not the steam transport that we have, a number of their vessels being sailing ones. There has been a good deal of dodging about, but for what reason neither the General nor any of us can make out; instead of steering straight in the direction of Sebastopol, where do you think we have been? We coasted up towards Serpent Island, and were within 49 miles of Odessa, which made us think we were going to have a rap at it.

On the 9th about noon, the ships cast anchor off the Crimea, near Cape Tchoukour, out of sight of land, and remained there till the 11th, when they left at 10 *a.m.*, steering for Cape Eupatoria; we are now lying in that Bay about 5 miles from land, having arrived this evening before dark, so the people on shore must have seen us, and will, I expect, be alarmed lest we disembark in the morning, which I do not think is likely, as we are 55 miles from Sebastopol. It is said that the landing will be about 7 or 9 miles off the harbour, near the Katscha River, but now I must refer back to the 9th. At daybreak, the *Caradox* [sic], with Lord Raglan[11] on board, accompanied by the *Agamemnon* and some other steamers of war, left us, and proceeded towards Sebastopol to reconnoitre, probably to find out the best place to land, and what preparations were being made to receive us. On their return on the 11th we weighed anchor, but nothing transpired; we saw a good many Cossacks on the outlook along the coast, but do not think there will be much opposition to our landing. It is said the fleet can go to within 800 yards of the shore, and sweep a couple of miles of the flat country, and that 2,000 guns will cover our disembarkation; that, I think, will keep the Cossacks of the Don at a respectable distance. It remains to be seen whether the Russians have a sufficient force to risk an engagement; if they do so with anything like equal numbers, they will catch it, I think. The Turkish force is about 12,000 strong, the French 28,000. Our Heavy Cavalry are still at Varna. For the first three days at least, we shall be in a precious plight – no baggage or tents. The men are to disembark with greatcoats, blankets, a shirt, a pair of socks, and boots, and carry three days' rations (the packs are to be left in the transports). The officers will only be able to take a greatcoat, a shirt, a pair of socks, comb, and tooth-brush, with three days' rations. If we have any marching, there is no means of having our baggage or tents brought on, so we may be much more than three days without any covering, or even a blanket.

While lying at anchor on the 9th, I had the pleasure of receiving no end of letters ... among others two from mother, and one from Alexander[12] written just before he sailed for New Zealand.

Wednesday 13th, 2 p.m. – Here we are close off Eupatoria, and the signal, 'Prepare to anchor,' is run up; it looks like having a blaze at the town. We are about 30 miles from Sebastopol by sea, and it must be a good deal more by land. Some of the men-of-war have run in pretty close, and we heard some shots, but from what direction they proceeded, we could not make out. The French, English, and Turkish ensigns have all been run up, and we surely are not likely to meet with opposition. We have been in sight of land all day; it is not an inviting looking country – no trees, but apparently plenty of corn. There are a number of windmills close to the town; and a

Officer, Grenadier Company, 41st Regt. This print clearly illustrates the impractical uniform, complete with tall shako and coatee, that was still being worn at the outbreak of war.

good many of the inhabitants must be Turks, as there are several Minarets.

Good-bye for the present, letters are just signalled for, and the *Caradox* [sic] has gone off with a flag of truce flying.

On 19 September the Allies began their march south, the French and Turks on the right and the British on the left, heading towards Sevastopol some 25–30 miles away. When they reached the small Bulganak river a brief clash occurred between the British and a Russian force which was over in a very short time and the Russians withdrew.

The following day, as the Allies approached the river Alma, a large Russian force was seen to be in position on the high ground ahead and preparations were made for a full-frontal assault. The 41st, being part of the 2nd Division, under the command of their old regimental CO, Lieutenant-General Sir Richard England, began their advance at about 1 p.m. *on the north side of the river, opposite Kourgane Hill. Withdrawing Russian skirmishers set fire to the village of Bourliouk and an artillery battery on the heights forced the regiment to deploy into line. The regiment passed the village on their left and were then ordered to lie down while the divisional artillery fired over their heads. Captain Rowlands later wrote:*

> *The nearer the Alma was approached the more plunging was the fire. I believe all our loss was from artillery, and so plunging was the fire that I saw the head of a rear rank man shot off without touching the front rank man.*

At about 2 p.m.*, the 41st was ordered to move to the right and came under heavy grape-shot fire. They forded the river and advanced through vineyards to the foot of the hills where they reformed. At this point the strong Russian artillery battery which was causing most of the problems encountered by the British, withdrew. The order was then given to 'Fix bayonets!' and the regiment advanced up the slope between Telegraph Tower and the road. Supported by a battery of 2nd Division artillery, the Russians were taken by surprise and, after a short but desperate struggle, elements of their force began to withdraw. After following the enemy for*

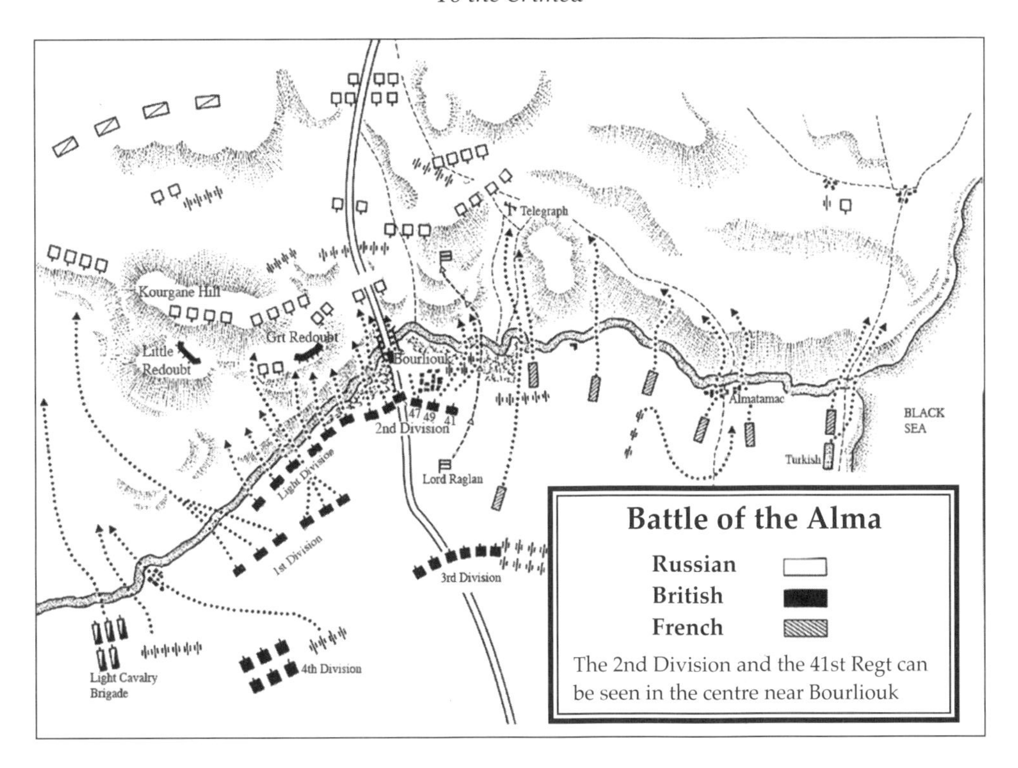

a short distance, the British troops were halted to await a Russian counterattack which never came. The last shot was fired at about 5.30 p.m. *Three companies of the 41st were ordered to mount piquet duty on the right of the front, alongside the French. British casualties at the Alma were 2,002 of whom 27 were from the 41st Regiment (only four of whom were killed).*

Alma, 21st September

I have this moment come off piquet, and hear there is an opportunity of sending a note home, which must be finished in a quarter of an hour. I sent off a hurried line to F from Eupatoria, which I had not time to conclude, as we were parading to see that the rifles were in proper order, when the signal for letters was hoisted. That night we received orders to sail for another point, and landed in the Crimea at 'Old Fort,'[14] in beautiful order, about noon on the 14th. We met with no opposition, and only a few Cossacks were visible. We remained till the 18th, landing Cavalry, Artillery, stores, etc. The weather in the afternoon became unfavourable, there was a heavy surf, which delayed the disembarkation. On the 19th we marched 10 miles, and encountered a Russian force with some guns, so our Horse Artillery and Light Cavalry were ordered up, and after a skirmish, in which we had two casualties, they were sent to the right-about.

Yesterday we had a general engagement [the Battle of the Alma[15]], which lasted some hours; the Russians had a very strong position, but we carried the day, though

I am sorry to say not without very heavy loss. Some of our regiments suffered most severely; I have no time to describe the battle at present; the 41st lost four men killed, and twenty-six wounded; no officers touched. We expect to march to-morrow, and may perhaps meet with a little opposition at another river about 6 miles off, if they have the pluck to light us again. Good troops should have held their position against any amount of men. We land the siege train at the other river; it is thought that all their troops, or nearly so, were out to meet us.

On 23 September, the Allies recommenced their march towards Sevastopol. This delay (during which time they gathered their wounded and buried their dead – including large numbers still being struck down with cholera) was later severely criticised as the armies could have pursued the retreating Russians and perhaps entered Sevastopol almost unopposed. The march reached the river Tchernaya two days later, a position level with Sevastopol, but it was decided to continue southwards to secure a port at the small town of Balaklava which was to serve as the British base of operations for the remainder of the war (the French taking over Kamiesh Bay). On 29 September the 2nd Division's tented camp was established on the high ground to the right of the French camp. The Russian Army, meanwhile, moved out of Sevastopol and positioned itself on the Tchernaya river leaving a garrison of 18,000 soldiers, sailors and trained civilians, under the command of Admiral Kornilov and the senior engineer Colonel Todleben, to prepare the defences of the harbour and city of Sevastopol. On 2 October, all non-combatants were evacuated from the city in anticipation of a siege. On 4 October, the 2nd Division was moved to the extreme right of the British line to a spot overlooking the valley of the Tchernaya and the ruins of Inkerman, a location that was soon to prove to be the most dangerous in the Allied front line.

Balaklava, 28th September

I sent off a hasty scribble on the 21st to say that I was quite well. I had not time to enter into particulars about the action, and I did not wish to cause you any uneasiness, as we expected to have met with a good deal of resistance at the Katscha [river] and the Belbec [river], both of which places they might easily have defended and caused us great loss, but they seem to have retreated hurriedly, and by the accounts we have been able to gather from stragglers, their General could not get the soldiers to meet us again.

We gave them a terrible beating. From the number we buried, it is thought that the Russians had between seven and eight thousand killed and wounded, which is a very heavy loss, considering that they had all the game to themselves till we took the Heights, and then did not the Artillery of our brigade give it them! They had some heavy guns, twenty-four and thirty-two pounders, which was great odds against our nine pounders; we also had the disadvantage of having to climb steep slopes to attack the entrenchments where their guns were posted. You will see by the paper that we had much harder work than the French. Our loss was 2,145 killed and wounded (25 officers killed and 101 wounded), the French 1,443; the old officers say that they never saw such a warmly contested action, and so hot a fire, with the exception of Waterloo. Lord Raglan was highly pleased with the gallantry of our troops, and Sir de Lacy Evans[16] addressed our Division on the 23rd, and said that the Commander of the Forces had especially remarked General Adams'[17] brigade. We crossed the river close to Lord Raglan, and were the first to gain the Heights, which enabled our Artillery to come up and play havoc on their retreating columns. If we had had more Cavalry, we should have taken several thousand prisoners; but our small force was kept on the left, watching the Cossacks, who were strong; they did not attack us.

It is useless giving you a long story, all of which you will have seen in the columns of the *Times* through our friend Russell,[18] the Correspondent, who came from Malta in the *Himalaya* with us, and also to the Crimea in the *City of London*.

We had tents after landing for two nights, but since marching, we have been without them. The weather has fortunately been fine, and all are wonderfully well considering the circumstances; it was rather cold last night. We expect our tents to be landed in a day of two, and are now waiting for the siege train, which is being disembarked at Balaklava Bay. We remained at the Alma a couple of days to bury the dead, and put the wounded on board ship.

On the morning of the 21st it was dreadful to see the result of the previous day's engagement; so many dead and dying on the field was an awful sight. Our wounded were all attended to on the day of the battle, and then the Russians were taken care of. On the 23rd we reached the Katscha, where we expected to have had another engagement. In a house we found about 300 dead Russians, whom we buried. On the 24th we reached the Belbec, which might also have easily been defended.

On the 25th, at Sir John Burgoyne's[19] suggestion, the idea of attacking the star fort on the right of the harbour was abandoned, and we made a flank march round the head of the inlet, through a woody and rough country, descending the Heights [the Mackenzie Heights] by a winding road to the Tchernaya Valley, crossing the river which flows into the harbour by the aqueduct bridge a few miles above the town. It was a very fatiguing march. We started at 10 a.m., and did not reach our bivouac ground, after several halts, till midnight. When crossing the road leading from Sebastopol to Bakshisarai, our Cavalry unexpectedly intercepted the baggage guard of a force of Prince Menschikoff's[20] Army, which had left the town to await the arrival of reinforcements. They captured some carts containing flour, ammunition, and money, and, I hear, a fine Church Service set with diamonds. We certainly deserve to get something, our privations are not a few.

On the 26th the Light Division took the forts that commanded the Bay of Balaklava, and now we are in communication with our ships again. Yesterday we advanced up the Heights to enable Lord Raglan[21] to make a reconnaissance, which was effected

The Heights near Inkerman.

without opposition, and we returned to our old ground.

Mackenzie[22] has been taken prisoner, and I hope we have got some information from him. It is thought that Sebastopol will fall in a week or so, after we go at it. I trust there may not be much bloodshed. Bush[23] is waiting for me to go on board ship, to see if we can pick up anything. My paper is at an end, so excuse this scrawl, I am writing under difficulties on the top of my shako.

Heights Commanding Sebastopol, 3rd October

We have not done much in the fighting line since I sent off my letter of the 28th, but from the great preparations going on, I think there is a bad time coming for the Russians. We have now got our siege guns on the hill, but none are yet in position. Fifty ship guns are being landed, and 1,000 sailors are to work them; they are now encamped close to Balaklava. The French are busy landing their Artillery at a bay near the town [Kamiesh]; there is also a Turkish siege train, if it should be wanted. We shall probably begin to batter away in a few days; the greater part of the forts can be commanded by our heavy guns from the Heights we now occupy. It is expected that it will be easy work to take those on this side of Sebastopol.

The Russian fleet is also commanded from our position; we will most likely require to sink them, as their broadsides would do us great damage. The Russians have sunk some ships across the entrance of the harbour to prevent our fleet getting in. The French left rests on the sea, and our Division, the 2nd, will join their right, it being the left of the English line for the present. The day before yesterday, when I was in the middle of my meagre dinner, a French column passed in front of our camp, exposing themselves to view from the forts; the consequence was that some shot and shell were fired at them. Two of the latter came over our line, and one landed about 20 yards from where I was grubbing, which made us quickly take up our pot and decamp to a distance. Every now and then they are sending a shot at some party or another, but I have not heard of any casualties.

Our Heavy Cavalry disembarked yesterday. I wish they had been present at the battle of the Alma; 20,000 more French have also landed, which will be a good help. Up to this time we have been without tents, except for two nights at our first landing-place; we expect to get them to-night. We have been most fortunate in having fine weather, for if it had been wet, we should have lost a number of men. Since our arrival there have been a few cases of cholera, but the excitement prevents the men from feeling depressed. On the evening of the 28th I received letters and a budget of papers; they are a great treat to us poor fellows, who have nothing to read.

We are still without baggage, as the *City of London* has not made her appearance in the Bay; I wish she would come, as my two pairs of socks are rather the worse for wear. I have just heard from the Colonel that the batteries will be armed to-night, and it is expected with our eighty-seven guns we shall be able to burn their fleet with little trouble. The clergyman attached to our Division had to be left behind at Varna, as he was ill. The Church Service is read on Sundays by one of the senior officers. Glad to hear Uncle G[24] is looking so well after the grilling and rough experience he had here; he should have remained a little longer, and come on with us to the Crimea, and then he would have seen something to repay him for all the discomfort he had to put up with.

This paper I am writing on is taken out of a young lady's music-book. Her father's house (Mr Upton, C.E.[25]) I had the honour of occupying last night when on piquet. We have to thank him for all the trouble that is before us, as he planned the Docks and most of the fortifications.

Inkerman Heights, 12th October

Nothing particular has happened since I last wrote. A good deal of shot and shell has been fired by the enemy, but no material damage done, only one or two men wounded. On the 4th, the 2nd Division moved its position to the extreme right of the line to cover the flank of the army. We are now in a more comfortable place on the slopes looking towards the Tchernaya and Inkerman, and the enemy's forts are further away. We have not yet opened fire from our guns; most of the batteries are nearly complete. It has been a very tedious operation bringing the guns up from Balaklava. You good people in England will be grumbling at the delay, but you can have no idea of the amount of work to be done before everything is ready; you must also bear in mind that the heavy guns that are to be brought into play have to be landed, put together, and dragged up a very steep hill; the distance from the Bay to the batteries is over 6 miles, and it takes thirty-two horses to bring up one of the large guns with a proportion of ammunition.

On the 5th I had an opportunity of going on board the *City of London*, and got some clean clothes, which was a luxury; they were all very civil, and gave us a good lunch, which we poor hungry fellows thoroughly enjoyed. On the 7th I was sent down with fifty pack horses to bring up shot and shell, and I took advantage of the chance to add some stores to our scratch mess. We have now got some of our tents; four officers are together; it is a great thing having a covering over our heads; it was bitterly cold two nights ago, but now I am happy to say it is again milder. I have just been warned to go out with a party to dig, and as they start immediately, I shall have to wind up this sooner than I intended. I saw Colonel Beatson[26] and his brigade-major the other day; the *Bashibasouks*[27] have turned out a great failure; they are now here attached to the force. I lost my revolver the other night, when out patrolling, but I have bought another, which belonged to a poor officer of the 55th, who died from cholera. Must conclude, as the party is falling in. I have now been put into the Grenadier Company.[28]

Inkerman Heights, 13th October

Yesterday afternoon I had only time to write a hurried line before getting ready to go out with a party of 400 men to throw up trenches in front of our batteries; it is the first party of the kind I have been on, and I hope it may be the last, as it is not at all agreeable work digging away in the dark, and being shelled at every now and then. We were so far fortunate that the work had been begun the evening before, so there was some cover. The batteries are nearly completed, and the guns will be put in to-night; it is thought that we shall be ready to open fire on Sunday morning, but such will not be the case, as the ground is rocky and not favourable for the work, and the magazines and traverses, etc., have still to be made. It seems quite providential the few casualties that have occurred, considering the quantity of shot and shell the enemy has fired at us, some of which has dropped right into our camps; I only know of one of the 68th being killed, and a man of the 63rd wounded. In the entrenchments an officer of the 20th was wounded the other day, and I believe up to the present time the losses on our side have been about a dozen, although the Russians have blazed away daily an average of 200 shots.

It may be all very well, men talking about wishing to fight, but I do not believe that, after having once been engaged in a big battle and seeing the horrors of war, they would really wish to do so again; it is very different from the days of yore, when enemies had to encounter each other hand to hand, but now that there are guns which kill at several miles' range, it is very different. We have no excitement at present, as the Russians have it all their own way; a few days hence the aspect of affairs may be changed.

Monday, 16th October — I am on piquet again; the work is hard, and the outpost duties severe. Yesterday was not much like Sunday. I was sent out at 3 a.m. with a party to throw up entrenchments at the twenty-one gun battery, and was at it all day, not getting back to camp till nearly eight in the evening, and my company (now the Grenadiers) had to parade for piquet at 4.30 a.m.; it is twenty-four hours' duty without tents, and we have to keep pretty wide awake. While we were digging, the forts must have fired over 100 shots at the parapet, and not one of them did any damage to the work, or hurt any of the party. Their shell firing was much better than usual; very few of their shells are filled with anything, they only burst. A poor man of the 38th had his leg and arm taken off yesterday, and one of the 49th was killed this morning. Bligh,[29] Dixon,[30] and Stirling[31] joined us last night from Scutari. Barnard[32] and Lockhart[33] are to be sent home; our paymaster Creagh[34] had a medical board yesterday, and will most probably be also sent to England.

You will have seen by the papers that we have had two promotions lately; I am now standing third for purchase; if Sebastopol falls, and I should be spared, I think there is every probability of my becoming a captain in the course of the winter, as many of the officers have had quite enough of this work, and do not like the idea of a campaign in Asia. You can have no notion as to what we have to undergo; we are four and five in a tent, with no more baggage than what we carried on our backs during the march, muddy water to drink. Some of the officers have not even a change of shirt, or socks, and have to get them washed as they best can; and to add to our vexations, we have heard from Scutari that the *City of London* caught fire, and that nearly all the officers' baggage that was left on board was burned. I hope mine may have escaped. The last time I was in her, I, unfortunately, put my watch in my saddle-bags, as I thought I might lose it here. I suppose we shall get some compensation, but it will not repay us for the inconvenience we are put to. I am now nearly walking on my stocking soles, my boots being in such a bad state for want of repair.

Tuesday, 17th October — Yesterday I had a quiet piquet; nothing of any importance took place. At night the embrasures were cut for our guns, and now they are peppering away; they commenced at half-past six, and in less than an hour, silenced nearly all the guns on the top of the Malakoff,[35] which is a strong round tower, and has a commanding position. The allied fleets have not yet come into play; they will very likely soon be in the thick of it. The fire is terrific; I hope the town may not be destroyed; there are some fine buildings which I fear will be reduced to a heap of ruins [the first bombardment of Sebastopol].

After returning from piquet this morning, I was delighted at receiving mother's letter of the 26th, and jumpers. The outward mail should close this evening, but will

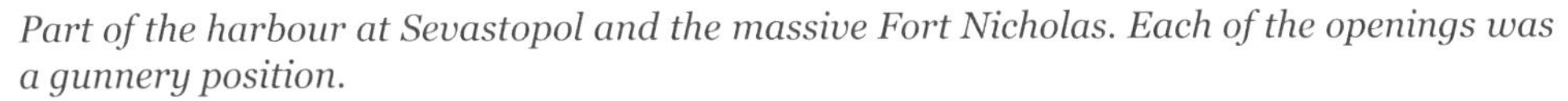

Part of the harbour at Sevastopol and the massive Fort Nicholas. Each of the openings was a gunnery position.

probably be detained to report how the siege is progressing. I will now go up the hill and see the effects of the bombardment.

4.30 p.m. – Things are going on well for us. Rome was not taken in a day, so you must not expect that Sebastopol will be taken in the same time. This has been a quiet day for the Infantry, as the Artillery are attracting most attention. One of our Lancasters[36] has burst, and five magazines have blown up – one English, two French, and Russian. The Round Tower[37] is quite silenced, and several Russian guns in their other works. The French, I fear, have suffered severely by the explosion in their batteries. The fleets came into play about half-past twelve, and are now firing at Forts Constantine,[38] Nicholas,[39] etc.; the latter is on our side of the harbour, which we hope may soon be in possession of the French, who hold the left. There is so much smoke over the town, it is impossible to see what damage has been done to the sea forts, and the lines being so extensive (about 8 miles in length), it is difficult to gain correct information as to what has taken place.

Some nights ago, the Greeks made an attempt to set fire to Balaklava, which, if they had succeeding in doing, would have played the mischief with our stores, and burnt all the shipping; but, fortunately, the conspiracy was discovered, and every one of them sent to the right-about, so the few shops that were being established are closed. I saw Nasmyth[40] the other day; he is now appointed Quarter-Master General for Balaklava.

Since having a cup of tea and a bite of biscuit, I have received my good mother's never-failing epistle; by the same mail there was a letter from Maydwell,[41] wishing to sell out, and wanting £700, but Fitzroy[42] says he must wait till the issue of the siege is determined. If those steps go, I shall be senior; it is of the greatest advantage to get a company as soon as possible.

Wednesday morning, 18th October — The batteries ceased firing during the night; they are now hard at it again. I have just returned from the top of the hill; from this side we can see no damage done to the sea forts. The fleets are lying at their old anchorage.

3. Heights near Inkerman

October–November, 1854

As preparations went ahead for the eventual assault on Sevastopol, the Russians decided to take the initiative. On 25 October, their forces that were encamped in the Tchernaya valley advanced against the British base of operations at Balaklava. A number of false alarms during the previous week had led to Lord Raglan failing to act quickly when news arrived at his headquarters that an enemy force was moving into the valleys before Balaklava. The battle opened at about 6 a.m. and, at first, the Russians had the upper hand, capturing the redoubts on the Causeway Heights. The stand of the 93rd Highlanders, the famous 'Thin Red Line' and the charge of the Heavy Cavalry Brigade halted the advance of the Russian cavalry. At 11 a.m., Lord Raglan gave the famed imprecise order for the British cavalry to try and recover the Causeway Heights, lost earlier that morning in the opening moves of the Russian attack. Lord Lucan, commanding the cavalry, failed to understand what Raglan wished him to do and the resulting charge of the Light Cavalry Brigade secured the place of the Battle of Balaklava in both the minds of the British public and in the annals of historic military blunders. Despite this, the British commanders had achieved some considerable success in the operations of that morning but, sadly, failed to follow them up and secure the overall victory. As a consequence, the Russians were able to quite legitimately claim the battle as their victory. Although they had failed to drive the British out of the Balaklava valleys, they had captured the redoubts on the Causeway Heights and the Woronstov Road. In future, British operations were made much more difficult, being confined to the more westerly area between Balaklava and Sevastopol. Although the Battle of Balaklava does not feature in the official history of the 41st Regiment, a small number of men (six NCOs and 22 men) were on detachment in the area, officially recorded in the muster roll as being 'On command Balaklava'. These helped form what was known as a 'Battalion of Detachments' and earned the men concerned the 'Balaklava' clasp on their Crimean War Medal. As the British breathed a sigh of relief at having escaped from a potentially disastrous situation so relatively lightly, the Russians began operations to follow up on their success.

The following morning, the Russians launched an assault on the British 2nd Division (which included the 41st Regiment) on Home Ridge. At about 12 noon Russian skirmishers were spotted on Cossack Hill. At 1 p.m., the 2nd Division was ordered to be 'ready to turn out at a moment's notice.' An hour later, a Russian force of six battalions and some artillery moved out from Sevastopol and began to climb the slope towards Home Ridge, where the 2nd Division was encamped. The piquets opened fire and maintained their position until their ammunition had expired when they were compelled to withdraw. There followed an exchange of artillery fire during which Lieutenant Harriott of the 41st led forward the Light Company in support of two companies of the 49th Regiment while two further companies of the 41st reinforced the pickets defending the Woronstov Road and Quarry Ravine. The Russians then resumed their advance but were dispersed by artillery fire and four companies of the 41st and 47th Regiments set off in pursuit and the Russians withdrew to Sevastopol. Captain Richards of the 41st wrote:

> *They [the Russians] did very well indeed when opposed to our piquets, who always wear greatcoats; but when we came on in red, and our men yelling like savages, they could stand it no longer. I believe there is something in the colour which frightens them. I do believe we are the kindest enemy in the world. It is wonderful to see the attention our soldiers pay to the wounded Russians; and our surgeons take as much pains with them as with our own.*

In this action, known at the time as the 'Sortie of 26 October' (now called 'Little Inkerman'), the 41st lost one officer who died of wounds (Harriott), one private killed (John Martin) and two died of wounds (John Clough and Daniel Donovan), and eight privates wounded. One senior NCO, Colour-Sergeant Ambrose Madden, was later awarded the Victoria Cross for his action on this day.

Heights near Inkerman, 21st October

This is the fifth day the batteries have been at work. I understand everything is progressing favourably. Each day we silence a number of guns, but the Russians replace them during the night. We shall be obliged to take the place by assault, unfortunately, our batteries cannot reach their shipping, so they will be able to slate us when we advance to take the round fort,[1] which is the key of the position. The fleets have not come into play again since the first day. The ships got rather knocked about on the 17th; the *Rodney*[2] is said to be quite crippled; the *Agamemnon* approached to within 500 yards of Fort Constantine, and suffered less than those that remained 1,200 yards off. The top row of guns on the sea forts was dismantled, but no material damage done to the works. I am afraid the fleet will not aid us much; they may manage to effect an entrance, if we take this side of the harbour.

The other night the Russians attempted to destroy some of the French guns, and nearly succeeded. A party of their sailors was sent out under an officer, who spoke French well, and they passed themselves off as English who had lost their way. They got inside the batteries, and were in the act of spiking the guns, when they were discovered to be Russians. The French then attacked them with their bayonets, which soon made them cut and run, the officer in command being taken prisoner. Each morning we send out some sharp-shooters, who interchange shots with the enemy's marksmen; their officers seem good and plucky. It is becoming monotonous work, playing at long bowls with one another. We have been firing red-hot shot and rockets into the Tower to try and set it on fire, but it being chiefly stone, it does not burn as readily as we could wish. We have blown up four or five of their small magazines.

Lord Dunkillin[3] was taken prisoner yesterday morning; he lost his way in leaving the trenches, and walked into a Russian outpost. Several Poles have given themselves up to us.

Heights Near Inkerman, 27th October

The last two days we have had more excitement than usual. The fiery spirit of the Russians could not any longer brook being shut up in Sebastopol, and being fired on, so, under cover of darkness on Wednesday night, they marched on Balaklava, and early in the morning attempted to take the place, which they nearly succeeded in doing, as the 'Bono Johnnies' [the Turks] retired from the outlying defences without offering much resistance. The Russians attacked, and took the highest redoubt, which commanded No. 2 Redoubt; so the Turks bolted in haste from the others, leaving the cannon (which we had given them to protect the works with) behind them. In trying to retrieve the disaster, we lost over 200 of our Cavalry. The Light Brigade made a most gallant charge up the valley, and cut down a great many Russians, but unfortunately they became exposed to a very heavy cross fire from the enemy's position on the low hills, which caused great havoc amongst the officers and men. I do not know what we can make of the Turks now; it was a pity they were not sent up to the front at first, and made to throw up batteries and trenches. We hear it is proposed to give up Balaklava and draw back to the plateau, where our allies are encamped. Our present position is very extended, and requires a great number of men to defend it, and there is a bay [Kazatch Bay] nearer the left of the French that would answer our purpose as well as Balaklava. The Russians did not succeed in gaining any material advantage, and they must have lost heavily; they had a large force of Cavalry.

On the 26th, when I was on 'The Hay' piquet, on the right of our Division, our left piquets were driven in at 1 p.m. by the Russians, numbering about 8,000 strong.[4] The piquets kept the enemy in check till their ammunition was expended, when they had to fall back on the main body. The enemy came up to within 300 yards of our front line of tents; they were then repulsed and turned, and were followed right down to the valley by our Division. Their loss is supposed to be from 700 to 1,000. The casualties on our side were five officers wounded, ten men killed, and fifty-six wounded. Poor Harriott[5] received a bullet wound, which has fractured the collar-bone. The wound is not considered dangerous, but the doctors have not yet succeeded in extricating the ball. He is off to Scutari, and has asked me to write to his mother, which I have done.

The battlefield of Inkerman. The thick undergrowth which covered much of the battlefield is evident in this 1893 photograph.

Our Division was the only portion of the force engaged. Part of the Guards supported us; it was a very plucky sortie, and they came on like men. Our piquets are firing just now on all sides; it is not yet daylight; there must be something up.

Saturday, 28th, 5 a.m. – I have to go out with a fatigue party immediately to the siege train; we never know what may turn up in the shape of work. Poor Major Powell,[6] 49th Regiment, was shot to-day.

Following Little Inkerman, the days passed without significant incident for the 41st. Their camp was located on the top of Home Ridge which was described in the regimental history:

> *... on a gently sloping piece of ground 1,400 yards wide bounded on the right by the cliffs above the Tchernaya and on the left by Careenage Ravine. From the top of Home Ridge one looked over a hollow some 1,200 yards across to Shell Hill. This hollow was thickly covered with low coppice, strewn throughout with fragments of crag and boulders. The right-hand crest of Home Ridge was continued forward at a right angle for about 500 yards forming what was to be known as the Fore Ridge. In front of the right corner of the latter, and some distance in advance to the right front, stood the abandoned Sandbag Battery ... no more than a wall of earth, several feet thick and 12 paces long, with two embrasures cut into it; the parapet was considerably taller than a man's head, but sloped rapidly at each end.*
>
> *Cutting into Inkerman Ridge and almost bisecting it was the Quarry Ravine. Up this Ravine ran the road to Balaklava ... passing over Home Ridge and through the camp of the 2nd Division. At the point where this road comes out of the Quarry Ravine a wall of loose stones had been made, known as the Barrier.*

Unknown to the Allied forces, in early November the Russians prepared for another assault. Within Sevastopol itself there was a force of some 19,000 infantry with supporting artillery, led by General Soimonoff. On the Heights of Inkerman, on the far side of the Tchernaya river, General Pauloff assembled a second force of 16,000 infantry with supporting artillery, while General Menschikoff had his main army behind the Heights of Inkerman. The plan was for Soimonoff's force to advance undetected from Sevastopol towards Careenage Ravine and assault the Inkerman Ridge from the west. Simultaneously, General Pauloff's force would cross the Tchernaya and assault the Inkerman Ridge from the north and east. Menschikoff would follow through the initial successes of his subordinate commanders with the intention of driving the British off Inkerman Ridge whilst assaults were mounted from the defenders of Sevastopol against the Allied batteries further west. The attack was therefore directed almost entirely against the British 2nd Division which was made up of only 3,000 men. Some 1,400 men of the Light Division were encamped on Victoria Ridge and 1,330 men of the Guards Division were three-quarters of a mile to the rear of the 2nd Division and a mile beyond them were some of the French forces. Further British forces were encamped up to three miles away. If the Russians could achieve the surprise they anticipated, the full force of their attack would be against the 2nd Division. If this comparatively small number of men failed to quickly halt the enemy's advance, there would be little to prevent the Russians achieving their objective.

During the night of 4/5 November the Russians put their plan into action. Marching out from Sevastopol before dawn, Soimonoff's force climbed onto Inkerman Ridge and at 6 a.m. began to form themselves up on the plateau beyond Shell Hill. General Hamley described the morning:

> *The morning was foggy, the ground muddy, and the herbage dank. The mist did not, however, envelop the field. Shell Hill was frequently visible ... it was chiefly in the hollow that the mist lay.*

At 6.30 a.m. Soimonoff's guns opened fire and his infantry approached the northern end of the hollow and attacked the pickets of the 2nd Division made up of 53 men of the Grenadier Company of the 41st and three companies of the 55th; a total of 480 men. Captain Hugh Rowlands, OC the Grenadier Company, later wrote:

> *On the morning of the 5th, I and the company were for outlying piquet ... Colonel Haly, of the 47th, was Field Officer of the day; he gave me my choice of piquets. I selected Cossack Hill (alias Funk Point). When I passed through the night piquet you cannot imagine a more cheerless aspect. Day had scarcely commenced breaking in the East, and a damp cold mist clung to the ground, make objects indistinct, or, rather, imperceptible at a few yards distance. On arriving at Cossack Hill [more generally known as Mount Inkerman], I halted the company about half-way up, and went out to plant sentries about 150 yards over the hill. Having done so I returned to the company, which had just piled arms, and ordered the men to take off their packs, when the sentries commenced firing in a most determined way. I ran up to enquire the cause, when one shouted out that there were columns of Russians close to them. I stood to my arms and advanced in extended order, thinking it was a sortie something like that on the 26th ... On getting on top of the hill, I found myself close upon, very truly, thousands of Russians. I immediately gave an order to retire, which was done for about 200 yards, when I halted on the next bit of high ground [a continuation of Shell Hill] and lay down, quietly waiting for them. Fitzroy, who was in support of me, then came up with the Light Company. His men I likewise extended to reinforce my own. When we retired the Russians came on with the most fiendish yells you can imagine. We commenced firing. To my dismay I found that half the firelocks missed fire, which dispirited the men. At this period the Russian columns opened with their field pieces, pouring in grape and shell. We then got some reinforcements of the 55th and 30th, but were gradually obliged to retire ... I begged and entreated Colonel Haly to allow me to charge, which he did ... and after a little hand-to-hand work we*

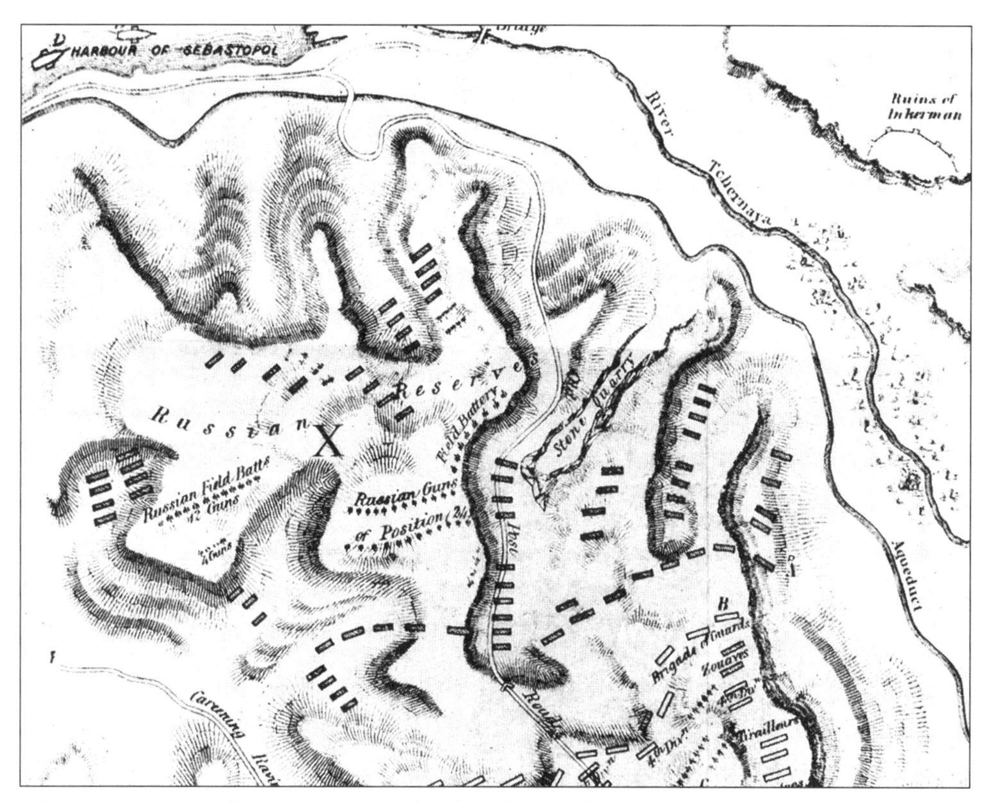

Inkerman, 5 November 1854. X marks the advanced position of the Grenadier Company piquet.

turned them and drove them back about 500 yards, when we were met by a fresh column, who compelled us to retire.

Despite the gallant efforts of the piquets and their reinforcements, the Russians continued to advance, albeit now without the all-important element of surprise. On the left of the 2nd Division's front, five of Soimonoff's battalions were effectively destroyed and the remaining six battalions were defeated on either side of the Sevastopol– Balaklava road.

Pauloff's command had reached the area lying between the west of the Sandbag Battery and the head of Quarry Ravine. As four battalions approached the Barrier, a charge by 200 men of the 30th Regiment drove them back although the remaining five battalions, positioned to the right of the British line were still advancing. Seven companies of the 41st, no more than 525 men, approaching from Fore Ridge, opened fire and drove the 4,000 Russians back, recaptured the Sandbag Battery, and pursued the enemy over the edge of the plateau and down into the valley below. Brigadier-General Adams then ordered the 41st to hold the position around the Sandbag Battery and a message was sent asking for assistance from the other divisions who were, by this time (7.30 a.m.), beginning to arrive on the scene.

At this point, as large formations of Russian troops gathered in the Quarry Ravine and in the valley of the Tchernaya, elements of the Guards Division arrived on the battlefield and the Barrier was recaptured.

Adams and his 400 men were then attacked by 4,000 Russians from Fore Ridge. Two companies of the 41st were placed in front of the Sandbag Battery position to engage the Russian skirmishers and succeeded in driving them back in some disorder. The 41st then charged after the enemy, disappearing into the fog which had again descended over this sector of the battlefield. Eventually, the sheer numbers facing them forced the men of the 41st to pull back and those companies that had remained at the Sandbag Battery position opened with volley fire on the advancing Russians. Three enemy battalions were stopped only to be replaced by three fresh battalions attacking the 41st's flanks. Gradually the defensive position became a confused swirl of small groups of individuals, surrounded by mist, fighting to hold on to their own piece of ground. Few had any idea of any overall strategy or what was happening to their comrades perhaps only a few yards away. Major Eman ordered the recall to be sounded and gradually the battalion reformed. When the Russian artillery turned its attention to this sector of the battlefield the by now significantly-reduced numbers of the 41st, and their comrades in the 49th, withdrew to Mount Head. Their place in the fight for the Sandbag Battery was taken by the Guards.

During the fight for the Sandbag Battery, Lieutenant-Colonel Carpenter, who as Field Officer of the Day had been away from the regiment, returned and was attacked by a number of Russians who dragged him off his horse. Whilst lying wounded on the ground, he was bayoneted in the stomach and clubbed across the mouth. Three soldiers, Thomas Beach (of the 55th), Hurley and Collins (both of the 41st) attempted a rescue and drove off the colonel's assailants. Beach was later awarded the Victoria Cross for this action, Hurley received the DCM and a gratuity of £10 and Collins the Sardinian War Medal. Lieutenant-Colonel Carpenter died the following day.

The battle then degenerated into countless numbers of individual soldiers or small groups of soldiers fighting desperately to gain the upper hand. Some time between 10.30 a.m. and 11 a.m. a large Russian force, estimated at over 6,000 men supported by 100 guns, charged out of the Quarry Ravine and pushed hard against the British centre and left. By this time, the French had arrived and a combined Allied force of nearly 12,000 men faced the near exhausted Russians. For a further two hours men engaged in close combat and by 1 p.m. the enemy had had enough and began to withdraw. Major Goodwyn (later lieutenant-colonel, CO 41st Regiment) recorded his views on the latter stages of the battle, comments that captured the desperate struggle that earned Inkerman the name the 'Soldiers' Battle'. The eventual victory owed little to any strategy laid out by the generals but was rather the result of the tenacious and courageous actions of the junior officers, NCOs and men, each fighting his own individual battle against his own personal enemy:

I gained a high breastwork thrown by us across the road leading to Sebastopol [the

Barrier], and now the most desperate part of the battle began ... I lay down under the breastwork ... After holding the place for about half-an-hour our flanks got turned and the enemy could fire into us from behind. Some wanted still to hold their ground, but many of the soldiers were leaving, and I thought the best thing was to pass the word to 'Retire to the brow of the hill [Home Ridge]', which we did under a tremendous fire of round shot, shell and musketry. Fortunately there was a column of English there, partly formed in reserve. Our running in on them put them in some disorder, which most providentially was stayed by the timely arrival of the 7th Regiment of French Light Infantry ... At last we all stood still ... The Russians appeared bewildered at being so close to us, and it was painfully clear to me that if they carried the brow of the hill, the whole English position was lost, with our camp, magazines, stores, artillery, everything – I was desperate. At last the moment arrived and the word was given. ... We [the officers] all now rushed to the front waving our swords, and I remember begging and entreating the men to charge and to use their bayonets. In a dense mass we charged, but not a moment did they withstand us. After running forward about 50 yards the men again began firing which, at so close a distance, did a great deal of havoc ...

The Russians had sustained 12,000 casualties, the British fewer than 2,500 and the French under 1,000. The 41st lost five officers, four NCOs and 30 privates killed with six officers, ten NCOs and 85 other ranks wounded.

7th November

It is your turn to receive a letter from your soldier brother – I think I may fairly call myself such now, as we are soldiering in real earnest. You will be relieved by seeing my handwriting again, as that horrid telegraph must have caused great anxiety in England by forestalling letters, and reporting our gallant, but dreadful victory of the 5th [the Battle of Inkerman].

On the night of the 4th I was on a working party at Gordon's battery[7] till one o'clock, having been there since four in the afternoon, and after four hours' rest, went out again that morning at half-past five on piquet with Rowlands[8] to the most advanced point, overlooking Sebastopol, and we had just taken up our day position, and posted our sentries, when, about 6 a.m., our left sentries shouted out that 'The Russians are in front.' We had not more than time to get under arms, and extend the main body of the piquet, when shots were exchanged, and the enemy advanced up the slopes in dense masses, preceded by skirmishers, and closely followed by their Artillery, which soon opened upon us with grape and canister. We were compelled to retire, firing till reinforcements reached us from the camp. Our men fought splendidly, and drove the Russians back several times, but they came up in overwhelming numbers, and in the course of the battle nearly got within the lines of our Division; we were just supported in time to prevent part of the enemy's Infantry from gaining the crest of the hill. Most of the Divisions of the British were brought into action during the fight. The fire was very heavy on both sides for several hours, and some of the men expended all their ammunition.

About 11 a.m. a Division of French, commanded by General Bosquet,[9] came to our assistance, and fought most pluckily. During the battle they suffered severely. It is reported by the prisoners from 35,000 to 45,000 attacked us, and that they came from Bucharest ten days ago. The fighting lasted till about 2.30 p.m. – a dreadful Sunday morning's work; the allied loss is supposed to be 2,100. It is difficult to form a correct idea of that of the Russians; it must have been enormous – it is stated from 6,000 to 10,000. Some of their wounded, poor fellows, are still on the ground, and their dead are being buried by cart-loads. I have still a more dreadful tale to tell in the death of five of our officers and six wounded. With the exception of Bush's,[10] the wounds are not severe; he has gone to Scutari, and it is doubtful whether he will lose his arm or not. Johnston's[11] is only a contusion on the heel, Rowlands[12] and Bligh[13] are shot through the right arm, Meredith[14] in the hand, Fitzroy[15] (who was in command of the support piquet) in the leg. In the course of the morning, after we had been engaged some time, Fitzroy came to me and said he had been hit with a spent bullet; soon after I met him again, and he remarked his leg was becoming very stiff, so I told him he had better be off, as the work was getting rather hot for us. When I got back to camp, I heard that he had been shot through the leg, which at the time he was not aware of.

We have to deplore the following killed: our Colonel[16] (who was brought into camp wounded, died yesterday afternoon), Captain Richards,[17] and Lieutenants Swaby,[18] Taylor,[19] and poor Stirling,[20] who was on the sick-list, and came out and joined in the action; he was shot through the head whilst carrying the regimental colour. Richards and Swaby were killed fighting hand-to-hand with the Russians; we fear they were over courageous, and pressed forward too far; they were both cautioned to retire. Swaby said he would not, but would fight to the last. A Russian officer was found lying dead close by him. Richards was near him, and it is reported by the men that he shot one Russian with his revolver, and ran another through with his sword. There is no doubt they behaved rashly in advancing against strong bodies of the enemy, supported only by a few, and a large mass coming down on their flank. The loss in our regiment is 31 killed, 100 wounded, and 15 missing; our brigade is reduced to about 1100, and that of the 1st to 800. The place where our regiment suffered most was in the vicinity of a disused battery,[21] which was erected by us for two 18-pounders to fire across the Inkerman Heights. It is a dreadful reality to think that the two brigades mustered 5,000 bayonets on their arrival at Scutari, and that now they are so reduced. I should indeed be thankful for having been spared to come through such a fearful action with nothing worse than a slight contusion on my head, caused by a wood splinter. Little did we think, when we got up last Sunday morning, that before the sun went down, we should have to lament the loss of so many of our comrades. Of the four officers, Richards[22] Bligh[23] and Bush,[24] that morning sharing my tent, I was the only one left in the evening, the former having been killed, the two latter wounded. Victories may be a matter of great rejoicing at home, but on the battlefield itself they appear very different. The Russians certainly are a set of savages; they stabbed many of our wounded, and to-day they fired on some of our parties who went to bury their dead. Some men of my piquet were in the act of burying a Russian to-day, when one of them was shot, and had his leg broken. I think we are partly to blame for their firing at us in not hoisting a white flag whilst engaged in this duty; they could not be expected to distinguish between a burial party and one sent out to throw up entrenchments. I meant to have written to Swaby's relations, but being on piquet for twenty-four hours has prevented me. Our work will be terribly heavy now; we have only two captains and three subalterns to do all the duty. I am rather seedy, and wish I could have a day's rest. It was bitterly cold for two days. Getting drenched the last evening I was digging in the trenches, I got a chill, and to add to my discomforts, the soles of my boots are quite worn through.

November 8th, 7 a.m. – During the night there was an alarm, but it turned out to be false. We have taken 2,000 prisoners, and 4,000 are dead on the field, so the Russian loss must have been more than 10,000. I am quite done up this morning, and must have a day's rest. Sebastopol will not be taken so easily as was expected. We hope more troops will arrive from France. I am afraid you will find this a dismal epistle, but we are all in low spirits; our messmates are now reduced to five. This morning all the wounded go on board ship.

Russian activity outside the city of Sevastopol declined significantly after the Battle of Inkerman and both sides settled into siege mode, with the Russians strengthening their defences and the Allies making preparations for an assault sometime in the future. Almost immediately, the weather conditions changed and the opposing forces prepared for winter. On 14 November a hurricane hit the region, drowning the Allied positions in torrential rain. Everywhere tents were uprooted and the few possessions the men had were soaked by ever-growing pools of rainwater gathering in the indentations and hollows in the camps. No one was exempt and the hospitals suffered the worst, with the sick and injured losing not only their canvas covers but blankets, clothing and equipment which was scattered across the plateau in every direction. Food supplies for both men and horses were ruined. At sea, 21 ships were destroyed and eight disabled in or near the harbour at Balaklava, almost all of them carrying desperately needed stores. One of these ships, the Prince*, 'contained everything that was most wanted – warlike stores of every description, surgical instruments, guernsey frocks, flannel drawers, woollen stockings and socks, boots, shoes, watch coats; in short all that the foresight of the Government could devise for the equipment and comfort of the troops'. One must recall that before this date, the bulk of the British army in the Crimea had with it only what individual men had been allowed to carry ashore at Calamita Bay in September. Now they had nothing. In the 41st, by 4* p.m. *on the 14 November, only two tents were still standing and the* *officers and men began to scour the area in an effort to make up for their losses. Perhaps never before had the old army adage 'What's not nailed down is mine' been so true.*

Amidst all the chaos in the aftermath of the storm, the 41st's draft of replacements from the depôt at Templedore in Ireland arrived. The six ensigns, two sergeants and 100 men brought the battalion's effective strength up to 18 officers and 300 NCOs and men; a dramatic reduction in the numbers that had landed. The heaviest losses had not been from the actions of the Russians but from disease; many of the regiment were in hospitals nearby but the majority had been transported by sea the 300 miles to Scutari hospital in Turkey. As Sir Edward Hamley wrote:

> *Scutari, the longed for haven, was for weeks the very climax and headquarters of suffering – crammed with misery, overflowing with despair. In those large chambers and long corridors lay thousands of the bravest and most miserable of men. ... Ranged in two rows lay the patients, feet to feet; the tenant of each bed saw his pains reflected in the face of his comrade opposite; fronting each was another victim of war or cold, starvation or pestilence.*

Heights near Inkerman, 12th November

As to-morrow is the day the mail leaves Balaklava, I must try and have a few lines ready to tell you that we have had a week's peace. Matters are in a state of status quo, and we have made up our minds for a winter here, the prospect of which is not very cheering. How often we all think of our dear old homes, and envy you your comfortable firesides, when we poor wretches are told not to make ourselves too comfortable for the night, on the side of a hill, with a cloak and blanket, without a fire. This happens just now with our regiment every third night and day. The piquets are very hard with our reduced numbers, and, unfortunately, the fine weather has broken, and the camp is in a dreadful state of slush. I got quite knocked up, and have been on the sick-list the last three days; but the rest has done me good, and I feel nearly all right again. In a few days we expect a little help by the arrival of six junior officers, who are coming out in the *Jura*,[25] with a draft of 100 men. Last night four companies of the 62nd arrived from Malta; they are to reinforce our position, so that may give us another day off piquet; the 97th are also expected from Greece, the Buffs having left Malta to replace them. We shall be none the worse for an increase to our army after the dreadful losses of the other day, which, I believe, was – 3 generals, 35 officers killed; 106 wounded; 442 men killed; 1,763 wounded. Lord Raglan,[26] in his despatches, estimates the Russian loss about 15,000; the French make it out to be 20,000. Nearly 4,000 have been buried by our parties; the recognised estimate is 1 killed to 5 wounded. Our returns show a larger proportion of killed than that, but we came to very close quarters, and the Russians stabbed some of our wounded. The Grand Dukes Constantine[27] and Michael[28] were present at the battle of Inkerman, having only arrived a day or two before.

We have strengthened our front considerably since the 5th; it was very necessary, as it is a most important position, and one of which the Russians would fain possess themselves; from the crest their guns could sweep most of our camps. You will most likely see in the *Illustrated News* in a few weeks a sketch of the battle; their Correspondent lives in our camp. That was a good print of the Alma which appeared in the number of the 21st October. It is cheering to read in the papers that we were shedding our blood for a grateful country. When in Bulgaria, we used to chaff, and say they would never be satisfied without a large butcher's bill! Alas! it is now an appalling list to look at, and I am afraid it is not yet filled up.

I am sorry to think we may not again see our General, Sir De Lacy Evans,[29] amongst us; he is far from well, and has not strength for the work. He is such a fine old man; he had been sent on board ship for his health a few days before the action, but when he heard an attack had taken place, he came up to join in it, riding a distance of 7 miles, when he was hardly able to sit on horseback. Our Brigadier-General, Adams,[30] was wounded on the 5th, also his aide-de-camp, who was his brother. Maitland,[31] 49th, was sent to Scutari sick some time ago; we do not at present see much of our friends in the other Divisions, as we never know what may turn up if we leave camp. The Highland Brigade is at Balaklava.

There are frequent arrivals of French. Our gallant allies, the Turks, are not of much good; digging is the only thing they are employed at, and it is precious hard work to get them to do that if a shot should chance to come near them. Our tents got dreadfully knocked about the other day by the Russian fire; mine is almost the only whole one left, and it has the seam partly ripped, open. Bourne[32] is now doubled up with me.

I hope Bush may not lose his arm; we have not heard of any of the wounded since their departure. The *City of London* has not yet turned up with the baggage. This bit of paper is another piece of Miss Upton's[33] music-book; their property was not destroyed, but protected by the English, and they were able to remove it to Balaklava, minus a few petty larcenies. Since I have read the character of her father in the *Times*, I regret not having boned a lot of articles; there were some very nice books I had rather a hankering after; my pillage from their house was a pocket-diary, a small flask, and a plate. When writing, if you expect an answer, it may be as well to put a blank sheet in, to make up the weight, as we have not a bookseller round the corner. Is there any little thing you would like particularly out of Sebastopol, as I have every intention of being there some fine morning, though you must not expect much? We have sent to Malta for all their 13-inch mortars, to help us to bring the inhabitants to a little reason; it is getting rather cold work remaining out of doors so long. It should like to see the fleet do something. I have succeeded in replacing my revolver that I lost. I bought one for £4 5*s*.

13th November – After a very wet night, all is quiet this morning.

Inkerman, 17th November

We had a most terrific storm on Tuesday, the 14th, it began about 7 o'clock in the morning. When lying in bed, my tent went 'smash' over my head, and on turning out, a terrible scene presented itself. It was blowing a perfect hurricane, the rain coming down in sheets, and hardly a tent standing in the various camps. It was very dismal to contemplate my house level with the ground, and all my effects exposed to the tempest; luckily one of the doctor's tents stood the gale, and we all huddled into it, and held on by the canvas and pole; it was very cold work. Towards sundown it began to snow, and the wind subsided, so before evening we were able to set up again those tents which had not been blown to ribbons. Many of the men took shelter in the caves on the side of the hill. Fortunately, only a little snow fell, or the road to Balaklava would have been blocked. As it was, it was with the greatest difficulty that the provisions were got up for the next day. The poor horses and animals are in a wretched condition, and the Artillery horses are scarcely able to draw the waggons of ammunition. The catastrophes at sea are frightful, and the loss to the country must be enormous; nine vessels went down off Balaklava, and thirteen off Katscha. The *Prince*[34] sank with all the winter clothing, the telegraph, and £200,000 pay for the troops, and the *Resolute*,[35] with the reserve powder, went down at her anchors. There are wrecks all along the coast, and nearly every ship is more or less damaged. In the harbour at Balaklava the ships got terribly knocked about. Our draft with six ensigns, now all but one lieutenants, had fortunately disembarked the day before the storm.

On the 15th I was sent with a fatigue party to Balaklava to get tents. On the road I met Russell,[36] the *Times* Correspondent; he was not in his usual jovial humour, I suppose the storm had had a depressing effect on his spirits, and it certainly did not tend to raise my own, by his remarking to me that we should very likely all winter in St Petersburg.

The *City of London* has come in, and I am glad to say most of my baggage has escaped the fire, though my little tent, table, and stool are gone; some of the officers have lost everything. The weather is getting colder, and we are much in need of warm clothing. Our batteries fire only very few rounds now every day. The position at Inkerman is now much stronger, and the Russians had better not try us again. There is a talk of hutting the troops. Kingscote[37] is now in my tent, with Bourne;[38] he is a very nice gentlemanly young fellow; he is a nephew of Lord Raglan's;[39] his brother Nigel[40] is on the Staff. The Duke of Cambridge[41] left the army soon after the battle of Inkerman, as he was not well.

27th November

For the last ten days we have done nothing towards the taking of Sebastopol, but it is reported that Lord Raglan[42] is more cheerful, for what reason we don't know, only trust there is a good time coming for us. We have every confidence in our leaders, but it does seem strange that the Russians are allowed to strengthen their positions without being molested. The works round the Tower[43] are stronger than they were on the morning of the 17th October [the first day of the bombardment]. Their men are always very busy working at the Malakoff.[34] I think we gave them a severe lesson the other day, and they will not risk another Inkerman. Our position has been much strengthened with guns and redoubts; if these entrenchments had been thrown up when we first occupied the ground, we should not now have to lament the death of so many of our brave companions. Some French regiments are encamped near us, and are working at the redoubts and batteries. We have begun our hutting, which may be finished by next summer; it is comparatively easy to bring the wood in ships to Balaklava, but the difficulty is in transporting it up to the different encampments; the stone foundations must also be brought from a distance. I do not see much chance of my hut being ready for a long time, as they are being constructed from the left of the line, *i.e.* the Light Company, and I am on the extreme right, so mine will be the last to be put together. A hut will be warmer than a tent, and we can have fires, which will be a great comfort. When there is a spell of wet weather such as we have had since the 14th (the day of the storm), everything becomes damp, and if you budge out of your tent, you are up to your ankles in mud. On the 22nd I was on piquet at the extreme front near Sebastopol, which is called by the soldiers 'Funk Point.'[45]

Many thanks for your kind intention of sending me out a box; the contents will be most acceptable; my socks are rather the worse for wear, and I hope you will send a good pair of warm gloves for night work. The dressing-gown at present will be out of place, but I hope times may improve. I have seldom had my coat off my back since we landed, with the exception of a rub down in the mornings, and that luxury does not take place once in every twenty-four hours. William Aitchison[46] will very likely be sent out sooner than he expected. The affair of the 5th would cause much anxiety in England, and in his regiment many vacancies have occurred. The 97th have arrived, and the 9th came yesterday.

I must wind up now, and warm my toes at the fire before turning in between the blankets. I am for piquet in the morning, so must close this to-night. I have got a waterproof sheet now, which saves me greatly when it is wet on piquet. The duty comes round to our turn every fourth or fifth night. The night after tomorrow I hope to luxuriate in my iron stretcher; I got it up this evening from Balaklava; it will keep me off the ground. Of course we do not indulge in sheets, as we lie down partially clad for fear of a turn-out, though the false alarms are not now so frequent, as the men have become better accustomed to their duties when on piquet.

Cossack Hill Piquet, Inkerman, 7th December

I intended writing you a long letter to tell you I am still in the land of the living, but the mail is going out a day sooner than usual, and I am unexpectedly again on piquet, owing to Skipworth[47] being sick. Yesterday, after returning from a horridly dirty ride to Balaklava, I had the pleasure of receiving a budget of letters. I will try and send William Younger[48] a line some day soon, but at present, work is hard, and after it is over, we do not feel much inclined to take up our pens and scribble letters on our knees, or on the back of a notebook.

This night will be my fourth in the open air out of twelve, pretty severe work, seeing that it has been raining nearly every day since the 9th of last month. The roads are in an awful state; it is wonderful that we can receive supplies from Balaklava; the transport animals are dying fast on the roadside under their loads. Fresh meat has been very scarce this last month; before that we used to get it every other day. We are doing nothing at present, our guns being worn out; fresh ones have arrived, with some very heavy mortars, which I hope may touch up the shipping, but in the present state of the roads, they cannot be brought up. Yesterday, the Russian force in front of Balaklava, under General Liprandi,[49] set fire to their huts at Tchorgoun, and marched off, which I hope may open the Woronzoff Road to us, which has been closed since the battle of Balaklava, and the flight of the Turks. We do not know the reason of the Russians withdrawing, unless the wet weather has rendered it impossible for them to get their provisions. They must have suffered greatly in that low ground; the valley between our heights, and those of Inkerman is all under water.

The sketches you have seen in the papers will have given you a pretty good idea of our position. What a relief it would be to us, if we had another army to invest the north side. I hope strong additions to our force are on the way; the work we have to do is too hard for the men. The intention is to place new batteries on a hill (the Mamelon[50]) approaching the Malakoff.[51] Last night five men of the 55th, not being on the alert, were taken prisoners in one of the advance trenches.

Yesterday two of the Russian steamers went out of the harbour in hopes of catching one of our steamers, but she was wide awake, and soon had her steam up. Shots were exchanged, and on the appearance of one of our larger steamers, Russ very soon sought shelter under their batteries. All our wounded and invalided officers are going home from Scutari with the exception of Rowlands;[52] they are reported as doing well.

17th December

Just returned off piquet, and a precious nasty one too! I find the mail closes in a short time, so I can only send a few lines home with all best wishes for the season. This ought to reach you about the 1st of the New Year. I wish I could be with you all on Christmas Day; we do not expect to have a very joyous one here. How thankful we would be if we could spend it in Sebastopol! If it was only dry, there might be a chance of our getting something done before 1855, but in the present state of weather and roads, matters progress very slowly. When I mounted piquet yesterday morning snow was falling fast; it did not continue long, but left the ground in a slushy state, so there was not much comfort in lying down for a little repose; I hardly got a wink of sleep, and do not feel much in a writing humour. Nothing of any importance has taken place lately; the siege is very monotonous work. We have got some new guns and mortars up; most of the English reinforcements have arrived, and some of the French. Our huts are not getting on very fast towards completion; they will make good cattle-sheds for the Russians after the war is over, which we all hope may soon be the case.

I must end, as it is close on the hour for Church Parade. I was taken aback the other morning when inspecting my company [the Grenadiers] to find three men on parade without boots. On enquiring the reason, they said they had been on fatigue duty the evening before to Balaklava, and as the soles had come off in the mud, they did not see the use of carrying the uppers, and there were no boots big enough to fit them in the small stock the quarter-master had.

When the Colonel[53] came round, he also noticed the peculiar circumstance, and made a great ado to me about it, and said he had never before seen such a thing in the whole course of his soldiering; at which I was rather riled, as I could not provide boots at a moment's notice. However, in the course of the day, I, with difficulty, discovered some large enough in the regimental stores of another brigade.

4. Life in the Trenches

Winter–Spring 1855

For many of the men serving with the 41st Regiment, the winter of 1854–55 was one which they endured in abject misery, suffering from a continuing lack of supplies, inadequate clothing and dreadful weather, conditions that were to be familiar to a future generation manning the trenches of the Western Front in 1914–18. Many have made reference to the American Civil War (1861–65) as the first modern war but this description should really be applied to the Crimea. Whilst the Battle of the Alma had been an engagement straight out of the Napoleonic War, the siege of Sevastopol and the introduction of so many innovations, was a significant step into the future. Not only were the men to fight a lengthy campaign in trenches, they did so under the protection of heavy artillery bombardments, with supplies brought by steam ships and railways, with their activities recorded by designated war correspondents and professional photographers. Everything that the British forces required was brought through the small port of Balaklava and from there by road or (after March) rail to the front line. The soldiers lived in tented encampments behind the front and moved daily to execute their various duties – be they mounting sentries, manning the front line trenches, digging new trenches or lines of communication or assisting with the transportation of supplies. Those who were in the trenches stood ankle- or knee-deep in either mud or snow. Initially, apart from their rifles, which far outclassed the guns supplied to the Russians, they were totally ill-equipped for the demands made upon them. In December, replacement supplies began to arrive for those lost in the hurricane but it was to be mid-January before Lord Raglan could record that 'I believe I may assert that every man in this army has received a second blanket, a jersey frock, flannel drawers and socks, and some kind of winter coat in addition to the ordinary greatcoat.' In February, Captain Rowlands was able to write in a letter home:

> *My rig now, when on piquet, consists of two or three pairs of socks, one over the other. A thick pilot cloth pair of trousers with a piece of red tape down to convert them into regimentals. A thick warm jersey issued to us by Government, a flannel shirt over that. An ordinary mufti waistcoat, and an ordinary pair of high boots, into which I thrust foot, three pairs of socks, thick trousers and all.*

Camp of the 2nd Division before Sevastopol, winter 1854–55.

In January, the French, who had 78,000 men available compared to the 11,000 men fit for duty in the British force, had taken over the right of the Allied position and William Allan led a detachment of the 41st into the trenches for the first time on 23rd of the month. Although this move made it easier for the British to adequately cover the front line, it meant that the men had to march two miles to and from their camp which was still in its original location. Rowlands wrote:

> *I told you in one of my last letters of the French having taken over the Heights of Inkerman. The day they relieved us I was on the left advance, and an officer of the 55th on the right. When they arrived to relieve him, he cautioned them about exposing themselves to the Russian sharpshooters, at which they laughed, and a lot of them jumped up on the parapet for what they called a Cherokee Dance. These were Zouaves, and they had not danced long before four of them were knocked over, which caused them to retreat as sharp as they had got up.*

Towards the end of March, the NCOs and other ranks of the 41st moved into new, purpose-built huts, located closer to the trenches, between the Woronstov Road and Cathcart's Hill, although the officers remained in the tents. As the weather began to improve, so did the circumstances of the troops and parcels which had been longed for during the winter began to arrive to supplement the supplies provided by the government. Sent by families and well-wishers back in Britain, these contained improved clothing paid for by the public following an outcry after the press had revealed the conditions in which the army was existing. The government supplies included an extra uniform for each man and a canvas suit which was to be worn when on trench duty. Within the British camp, the logistical problems were being ironed out following the establishment of the Land Transport Corps in January and many of the soldiers were seconded for service with this new organisation as soon as it was set up in the Crimea.

Service in the trenches during the winter period had meant very little action other than maintaining a careful watch over the Russian defences. Each evening as the men moved into their section of trench, a double line of sentries was sent out into 'No-Man's Land' but for much of the time both sides respected the other and did little to provoke any retaliatory action. The regular bombardments of the Russian defences had been suspended and little progress could be made with advancing the trench system nearer towards Sevastopol because of the frozen, rocky ground. Ahead of the main Russian defences were rifle pits from where occasional exchanges of fire were made and engineers attempted to set and explode mines to break through the enemy's front line.

As the conditions improved in March, the inactivity was broken by the Russians, who launched an assault by 5,000 men against the French trenches, with a smaller attack on the British positions by way of a distraction. As all this went on, preparations were underway to resume the bombardment of Sevastopol in readiness for the infantry assault which would have to be executed if the city was to be captured. As well as the various artillery pieces in the batteries, a new weapon, the mortar, was introduced which could fire over the enemy's defences. On 9 April, the Allies began a ten-day bombardment which reduced much of Sevastopol to rubble. On 15 April, Rowlands wrote:

> *On Sunday evening I went into the trenches. The weather, which had been threatening for the previous day or two, burst about eight o'clock in the evening and lasted, without interruption, until eight on the following evening, when we were relieved. I never saw men suffer more; I know I never did. There we were, paddling about in mud averaging three to eighteen inches in depth. it was worse for us because we were in a new portion of the trench, made the previous day, within fifty yards of the Russians, who had established rifle pits in front of us. They are good marksmen, and appear always to be on the look-out, for directly a particle of a body exposes itself, either through a hole in the gabions or over the parapets, so certain would a bullet lodge either in the object aimed at or somewhere near. I was so glad when morning dawned, for I had scarcely a firelock out of two hundred and fifteen that would go off, so thoroughly were we drenched. If the enemy had come on, we should have been obliged to have depended entirely on our bayonets– no bad things when properly used.*

26th December

I am behind hand with my writing, and must now take this into Balaklava to try and catch the mail, which leaves sooner than usual, although we did not receive early enough intimation of its doing so. I have just written to poor Swaby's[1] father-in-law.[2] I enclose two notes I received from his friends, and also one from Mrs Harriott. You will have seen by the papers the death of poor Harriott;[3] we did not think when he left, he was so seriously wounded; he was hopeful to the last. Rowlands,[4] who is now here, attended on him constantly; I feel much for his poor mother; she wrote in such good spirits about him. Lamont,[5] one of our assistant-surgeons, is very ill with typhoid fever; I am afraid he will not get over it; it is sad being cut off here without a single relation near you.

We passed rather a pleasant Christmas Day yesterday, considering everything; it was a lovely day, with hard frost in the morning. I have knocked up a small kitchen hut, and eight of us dined together in it. Lord Raglan[6] presented Kingscote[7] with a goose, which was a most welcome addition to our rations of fresh meat, which they managed to serve out to the troops for a Christmas dinner, and we had a large pudding (stick-jaw) with currants and raisins, and we did not forget to drink the health of 'the auld folks at home,' in our tot of rum and water.

It is so bitterly cold, I can hardly hold my pen, and my feet are like ice, in spite of the beautiful boots which I received from home two days ago, the postage of which cost 32s; the flannel shirt has also come to hand. I wish I had thought sooner of asking mother to send me a few more things, but we did not expect to be encamped here so long; I want a large waterproof cape to go over the shoulders, and also a very wide waterproof to go outside of one or two coats; some of the fellows have asked me to get half a dozen Shetland shirts, of a dark grey colour. If mother should send out another box, some pots of substantial preserved meats would be most acceptable; so much salt meat is very bad for one, and everything of that kind is an enormous price here.

Government is treating us very well in providing us with fur caps and sheepskin coats, and some underclothing. I see by the despatches that most of us are to have three medals; it has put the troops in good spirits. I hope most of them will be spared to wear them at home; the poor soldiers have earned them dearly, and have had many discomforts. There is a proposal to make a railway from Balaklava to the siege train, which will be a great boon in aiding the transport.

29th December

I rode into Balaklava last Tuesday to catch the mail, but found the steamer was leaving from the Chersonese Bay, so could not send my letter of the 26th inst. A few days ago, I received a note from H. Younger;[8] he is thinking of doing a little business here, and I think it might perhaps be a capital 'spec.' Nothing would give us greater pleasure than to see the ruffians, who charge such exorbitant prices for the common necessaries of life, undersold; 100 per cent, is about their profit. Although beer is not so very dear, it is of a light, inferior quality. Byass (not Bass) sells for 10*d.* a pint bottle, and 1*s.* 6*d.* a quart, porter is 2*s.* a quart. In this cold weather, and the hard work we have, good strong ale would sell well; it is not the officers alone who buy beer, but the whole army.

The soldiers do not know what to do with their money, and give 6*s.* 6*d.* for the very worst description of brandy, which is supplied by the French *vivandières*;[9] it is the vilest kind of *eau de vie*. The prices in Balaklava have been enormous, 1*s.* a pound for brown sugar. I had to pay 3*s.* a pound one day, but there is more competition now, and when the yachts, etc, arrive from England, we hope prices will come down.

Poor Lamont,[10] whom I mentioned as having typhoid fever, is a little better, but so weak, the doctors do not expect him to live. Anderson,[11] our other doctor, was in the same tent, and I am afraid has caught the infection; he was taken to Balaklava this morning, and I hope the change of air will soon restore him to health; he also will be sent onto Scutari. He joined our regiment from the Rifle Brigade at Constantinople, and his absence will make a great blank in our small circle; he is universally liked.

Thank you so much for the sealskin cap and the flannel shirt I received a few days ago; last night on piquet I rejoiced in wearing the former. It was so good of Mr Gott[12] to send me that splendid warm lambskin waistcoat, it is the envy of the whole regiment. The last four days have been fine, which has been a great thing for us, and our camps are comparatively dry.

I am afraid I shall not be able to fulfil my promise about bringing home something from Sebastopol; the 13-inch mortars will probably not leave one stone on the top of another. Peace is all the talk here, and we hope that it may come about; this has been a trying campaign.

12th January 1855

It is a fortnight since I wrote. Owing to the severe weather and hard work, the piquet and trench duties have, since the 3rd inst., been relieved every twelve hours instead of twenty-four. The men are having a rough time of it; some of them have had their toes frost-bitten. The changes in the weather are so rapid – hard frost at night, and heavy thaws during the day – and they have to lie down at night in wet boots, which is very bad for them; at the same time, there is no doubt but that dry, frosty weather is better, for their general health than the damp. They have received several articles of warm clothing, and more comes to hand every day. The officers have now got stoves, but the men's tents, being crowded, will not admit of them.

Since my last letter we have had a heavy fall of snow. The winter months will have passed before the railway is nearly finished; the first detachment of navvies has arrived. The huts may be available for next winter; I am not waiting for them, but have dug down 6½ feet into the ground, and have boarded it over with planks (spoil taken from a Russian house), and have pitched my tent over it, so I have an upper and lower storey. Rowlands[11] and I are going to live together; there will be a fireplace underground and a stove above. I tried the fire this afternoon, but it smoked me out; I hope, however, to improve it.

We have lost poor Anderson[14] and Lamont;[15] the former died on board ship, and the latter of inflammation; he had recovered from the fever. I looked in on the 79th the day I was in Balaklava, and saw Frank Turner;[16] they have easy times of it down there.

You good people at home seem surprised that I could not possess myself of a pair of boots; you forget that I have a large foot, and no one has a second pair, the soldiers at once appropriate the boots of any one killed. Thanks for ordering the long boots, they will be first-rate for piquet. I hear Government is going to give us something in the way of a waterproof, so I hope you have not sent one off; we are very grateful to all you kind people for so many comforts knitted by the fair ladies of the home land.

I am anxious to see the *Augmentation Gazette* to know whether I am a captain, with or without purchase; perhaps Maydwell,[17] having got a Depôt Battalion, will give me a better chance of saving the £1,100; I am afraid they intend bringing in two captains from half-pay.

My mess has knocked up a small hut for the servants to cook in; it is a great protection to them, although it is not altogether water-tight. We have got our horses from Varna; mine is in a wretched condition, I think I shall have to shoot him, he is so weak, and suffering from scurvy. I am looking out for another, being allowed forage for two, as I have charge of a company. I wanted to have bought the horse that belonged to poor Richards,[18] but it was sold whilst I was on piquet.

The works are now nearly all complete, but a large amount of ammunition has still to be brought up, and none of the guns will be placed till all is ready. The engineers do not appear to know much about their business; a battery has just been finished, which has taken two months to construct, and now they say it will not be armed, as it is found to be useless!

23rd January – The French took over our piquet duties at Inkerman on the 21st inst., and now the 2nd Division have to do trench work instead, in front of Gordon's[19] 21-gun battery.

26th January

I was in the trenches all last night, and have had no rest to-day, so will only send you a line to say, 'All's well.'

We are still in our old position, but have now to take duty in the trenches instead of piquet, which adds to our work, as Gordon's battery is a good hour's walk from here; however, I hope we may remain encamped where we are, and not move nearer the other Divisions, as our soldiers have a great advantage in being able to procure firewood close at hand, by rooting up the scrub and brushwood, for fires, cooking, etc. There is a talk of the French taking a hill [the Mamelon,[20] afterwards called by the Russians, the Kamschatka Redoubt] which is nearer the celebrated Round Tower[21] than Gordon's battery; if successful, the allies will be able to throw forward their right, and sap up to the Malakoff,[22] which is the key of the Russian position. This hill is now occupied by the Russian piquets, and not being very far from the Tower, the approach and works when commenced will have to be thrown up with all speed, and held, till completed, at the point of the bayonet. The ground at present is so hard with the long frost, nothing can be done in constructing rapid works. The Russians keep up a continual fire on the French left, the latter seldom return it.

The *Firefly,*[23] *Black Prince*, and the *Loire*[24] are in harbour; each have a box for me. There is now a parcel office established, but the store is not large enough to contain a hundredth part of the articles. Thank Miss Anderson[25] for her kindness in knitting me that comfortable headpiece, and for her congratulations on my promotion. I have had letters from all sides.

Please send some boot-laces, also some small hooks for the front part of the boots; the holes are very inconvenient if the string breaks.

9th February

I have to acknowledge receipt of your letter of the 23rd January; letters are always hailed with joy. The weather has been more favourable of late, and things are looking up. The French to-day brought 1,500 shot and shell into the batteries of Inkerman, which is sufficient ammunition for live guns pounding. Gordon's battery[26] is all but completely armed, and the left attack in working order. Every[27] has got his promotion in two and a half years, without purchase – what a lucky dog! He has not yet been in the Crimea; he was sent home sick from Bulgaria. Poor Hunt[28] has died of consumption.[29]

The railway is getting on, and our regiment is complete in warm clothing. I am glad to say we do not move our position at present. The confusion at Balaklava is not so bad as you appear to think; they are getting on much better now, and chaos is being reduced to order. Our draft of 109 men under Bertram[30] has arrived, so the duty is not so hard. The English Army will not be quite reduced after all to 2000, as the *Times* says! The reports are, however, as a rule, very true. Last week, Rowlands[31] and I walked up to the look-out hill to see what the French were doing since we handed the position over to them; they are engaged making a defensive redoubt, which is to be armed with guns.

19th February

Last mail I received a letter from the bride from Naples. They still think of a trip to the East, but I do not expect they will make it out. I[sabella][32] would create a sensation if seen perambulating the streets of Balaklava; it would require a strongly nerved lady to stand the scenes she would witness between the Inkerman Valley and Balaklava. The other day I took a stroll outside our piquets towards the Tchernaya River with Bertram; it was a revolting sight to find several unburied Russians, who have been lying there throughout the winter. It is curious how callous one becomes to such sights; that which I found very trying after the Alma, I can now look upon without much concern. It is very sad when visiting the sick and wounded in the hospital, to see the ravages the low fever is causing amongst our brave comrades; after a day's illness, they are quite prostrate. We have lately lost a number of our fine old soldiers. Our only remaining surgeon, Abbot,[33] has been sent to Balaklava sick, and also another 'Sawbones' who was attached to us for duty. We have two huts now for the hospital, our sick number at present 160 out of 550.

The weather for the last fortnight has been lovely, and if it will only last a little longer, the British Infantry will still exist as a formidable force; as for the Cavalry and Artillery, they cannot move. The batteries are reduced to about thirty horses out of a complement of 190, and they can only trail their legs into Balaklava to bring up their own forage; the men have to drag the guns and shot into the batteries. In the town Russ gets stronger and stronger everyday. The 'Bono Johnnies' at Eupatoria have retrieved their characters by showing the Russians that they are not to be driven into the sea. Last Saturday they were attacked by a force of about 20,000, which they repulsed with a loss to themselves of 350 killed and wounded, the Russians losing about 2,000; we do not know particulars; the first correct information will be through the *Times*.

I enclose a crocus flower from the battlefield of Inkerman. I hear some snowdrops have also appeared, so we hope the severe weather is nearly over, and that there are signs of Spring.

Meredith[34] has been welcomed home in his county in Denbighshire with the booming of cannon, bells ringing, and triumphal arches; by the accounts in the Chester papers, he has been made rather a fool of.

The Colonel[35] to-day received the articles Mother sent to the regiment; the men are

Capt Henry Warter Meredith, 41st Regt.
[The Royal Welsh Museum, Brecon]

now well off, as heaps of various kinds of warm articles are showering in on them from all quarters. I have got another of my boxes. The sack may be useful if we have any more bivouacking, but I cannot trust myself to make use of it in the trenches in case Russ gives me a poke with his steel some night. They have been very quiet lately, no sorties. The railway progresses slowly, for which we may thank the Duke of Newcastle.[36]

Advanced Trench of Gordon's Battery, 19th February

I find myself again in the trenches, so I have got hold of a pencil, and send you this scrawl to let you know that I am hearty. Have you seen anyone who has been at Glen[37] lately? I hear they are building a new house. What do they think of the improvements?

I have received all my boxes with the exception of the one sent to Lamb[38] at Constantinople; I have had an intimation from him about it, and the fool asks where he is to send it to. I have written to Bourne[39] [at Scutari] to ask him to rescue it out of his clutches; Lamb has retained it a couple of months, which is most aggravating, when I was so badly in need of the articles.

The Russians have thrown up a redoubt in the direction of our old piquet position, near the Careening Creek, to pitch into the new Trench works. Frenchy tried to take it the other night, but, I am sorry to say, did not succeed, and got the worst of it; the Marines did not back up the Zouaves, who behaved gallantly. I have just had a look with the glass at the town; the works are now most formidable. The general opinion is that it will never be taken by assault, but must be invested, and we must lick the army that is in the field.

No. 4 Company are delighted with all the warm things you have sent them in my boxes. The *Cicero*[40] is in harbour, but I have not yet seen any of the ale. We have had beautiful weather lately; the roads are in capital order. It is cold work writing in the trenches, so I must bid *adieu*.

9th March

My last was from Gordon's advanced trench[41] on rather a cold morning; since then we have had spring weather, almost too warm, especially with the clothing in which we now find ourselves clad; we shall soon be looking out for linen jackets, etc.

Exciting news has come to hand of the Czar's death,[42] and also reports of riots in London, but how much of it is true we do not yet know. The Emperor's decease may make great changes in events here. We are speculating on peace; at the same time our preparations are for a grand crash, and we hope to make the place too hot for Rusky. Some think Monday will be our opening day, others say not before the 20th; there is no likelihood of storming the central works. When we succeed in reducing their fire, we shall take the Mamelon Hill[42] and advance our batteries in the right; at present, we cannot do so, as they would be enfiladed. Two miles of railway are finished,[44] and the first stationary engine is being erected, and will be in working order in two or three days; some of the munitions of war are now brought up in the trucks drawn by horses.

General Pennefather[45] has returned, and taken up the command of our Division; he inspected us the other day, and we turned out most creditably. The whole camp was in admiration, and he said it did his heart good to see so fine a regiment, after all the severe work we had under gone. He complimented Colonel Eman[46] and the whole of us, and said that he would take the earliest opportunity of mentioning us to Lord Raglan.[47] It was wonderful to see the way the men manoeuvred; they have not done such a thing since we left Bulgaria, and there are a number of raw recruits in the ranks. If Colonel Eman is spared to go home with the regiment, he will make a name for himself and us; he is a tip-top commanding officer, and thoroughly knows the working of all the departments. The other morning our Artillery rather astonished a little brute of a steamer, that has been always annoying us on the right; we opened a masked battery and caught her napping in supposed security, and put six shots into her, some of them red hot; she disappeared behind the rising ground, and we are not certain whether she is done for or not. Her crew deserted shortly afterwards, which looks as if she went to the bottom. The Russians have sunk another line of booms across the entrance of the harbour.

The other day Turner[48] rode up to see me, and I showed him over the battlefield and the new batteries on the right; he had never been up here before. Yesterday I went to Balaklava with him, and rode over the Heights. I met two more Grange[49] fellows, one meets them in all parts.

I am very glad you are not sending me a shell jacket, I have heaps of everything, and I think my best plan will be, as the weather gets hot, to write to Malta for anything I may want, if it is not to be had here; very likely everything will be plentiful in a short time. A restaurant has been established in the bazaar; all the shopkeepers have been turned out of Balaklava, and they have established themselves in wooden houses about half a mile from the town; it is a great improvement, and there is less confusion.

Inkerman, 19th March

Russ is getting stronger and stronger every day, and as matters stand at present, instead of our hemming them in closer, they have advanced their batteries 400 yards,

Lieut-Col James Eman, 41st Regt. [The Royal Welsh Museum, Brecon]

and taken possession of the hill [Mamelon] in front of the Round Tower,[50] where we intended to have established a battery. If the French cannot succeed better than has been the case lately, the sooner we conclude a dishonourable peace the better! They have fallen considerably in our estimation the last few days; three times they have attempted to take a few sharp-shooters' holes, and each time they have got well thrashed; if they are not equal to doing that, how are they ever to succeed in taking the Tower and its surrounding works? Until these pits are in the possession of the French, we (i.e. the English on the right attack) are not pleasantly situated, as Russ enfilades a good part of our new parallel, and any who pass along run a good chance of being shot, so at present we cannot continue this trench by daylight. We made a good advance last week, but owing to the trench being flanked, it is just now all but useless; when finished, the approaches made by the French from Inkerman will be connected by trench with our right attack or Gordon's battery.[51] On the 14th, the French made their first attempt to take the pits. Russ did not know exactly what was up, and opened fire from all their batteries; the sight was most beautiful. Sebastopol is a grand place to see such like fireworks; you have them in all their splendour and horror. I was going down to the trenches at the time it began, and we all thought we were in for a regular mélée, as we had not been informed of what was to take place. The British officer has no easy task to perform in looking after his soldiers in night attacks; they are sometimes seized with a panic in the darkness; they like to see their way before them, and do not understand fighting behind a parapet.

We are to move our camp shortly to huts that have been constructed in the rear of the 4th Division; it will be a change for the better, being nearer Balaklava. Here the French are close around us, and I cannot say much for the cleanliness displayed in their camp. When the hot weather sets in, the camps will become very disagreeable and unsanitary, from the dust and the remains of dead animals that have been only half buried. The 4th Division had races on the 14th; they were very good, and it was a pleasant meeting. How savage it would make the Russians, if they could have seen us enjoying ourselves.

New Camp near the Windmill, 27th March

I delayed writing my letter yesterday, having had the offer of sending it by Lord Raglan's[52] bag. I do not know what has put it into your heads that we should make a dash at Sebastopol as soon as we heard of the Czar's death; such an attempt would have been madness, and would have cost thousands of lives, and perhaps ended in a total defeat; if you think such a thing was possible, you have but little idea of the strength of the place. Within the last three weeks, Rusky has pushed their works beyond the Malakoff[53] and head of the harbour, and fortified the elevated sites. On the 23rd, a strong sortie was made by them against the centre of our position, but principally on the trenches in front of Gordon's battery,[54] and the French adjoining our right attack. Our loss, I believe, was five officers and forty-two men killed, wounded, and missing; Colonel Kelly[55] 34th, and Lieutenant Montague, [sic] R.E.[56] taken prisoners. The French loss was about 300, and that of the Russians is over 900. On the 24th, there was a flag of truce to bury the dead; I was that day in the trenches, and during the respite, we strolled down to the Russian lines further than they liked; Russ did the same, and we fraternised for a couple of hours, and then as soon as the flag was down, we tried to take each others' lives. The engineers did not lose the opportunity of making a reconnaissance; it was the pleasantest trench duty I had passed. The twenty-four hours' system is now re-established; we are working up towards the Redan,[57] whilst the French are trying to approach the Round Tower.[58] The Russians are defending every inch of ground; there will be some tough work some of these nights, and if they do not increase our army, so as to enable us to send a larger force to guard the trenches, we may get a jolly good licking, and then there will be an outcry in England. Our men are on duty every other day.

This week we have been moving over by companies to the huts on the new ground. The 41st is the first regiment of the Division to change its quarters; the officers' huts will not be put up till all the men are housed. Balaklava has become a wonderful place, and everything is in apple-pie order; the railway is all but finished to the top of the hill, last night the Mussulmen[59] began fighting with the Greeks; pistols and knives were drawn. There is a large number of nondescripts here now, who are employed on the railway, and in erecting store-houses. I send you some violets.

Camp Before Sebastopol, 9th April

To-day has been a lively one in the batteries [the Second Bombardment]. We reopened fire this morning about five o'clock from most of our guns: some are still masked, as the gunners could not do their work, owing to the firing of the sharpshooters from the Russian rifle-pits, which they have connected by trenches.

Our fire has chiefly been directed against the new work [Mamelon[60]] Russ has established on our right front of the Malakoff.[61] We hear it has been completely silenced, but the atmosphere is so thick, it is impossible to see the result from the top of the hill. As we have quite enough of the batteries when on duty – and it must be rather hot work in them to-day – every one has fought shy of having a close view from them, but by the noise it appears the Muscovites have still a good many guns in play.

I do not know for certain if the French have opened all along their left. Rowlands[62] has been in the trenches the last twenty-four hours, so we shall get all the news from

him on his return; poor fellow, he must have been wet to the skin for the last eighteen hours, as he went off without his waterproof. Rusky has been unremitting in his exertions lately, and has established a trench all along our front and the French right.

We hope our allies will soon work round and turn their flank. When the Mamelon is taken, it will greatly facilitate our works; we are now sapping up towards the Redan,[63] which is ticklish work. There are little scrimmages nearly every night on some part of the line. The French, I believe, have to take the Mamelon without our assistance, as their honour is at stake, owing to their late failure in not taking the pits. I suppose it will be done to-morrow or the next night, if the work is silenced. It will be a glorious day when the Round Tower falls; we think that peace will be declared before that day arrives. After the advance on the Mamelon, we must make sharp work of it, as it will be a precious hot place.

We hear a large force of Turks have arrived at Kameish [sic], and are longing for the arrival of the promised regiments from the Mediterranean, etc. The Sardinians are concentrating at Constantinople. The 10th, 12th, and 14th Cavalry from India are in Egypt waiting orders.

You would see in the *Gazette* that Barnard[64] has purchased over four captains, very hard lines for those out here, who have done all the work when he has been kicking his heels at home. When we landed in the Crimea he was left sick on board ship, but for the last five and a half months he has been quite well. Now he is at Malta with Major Pratt,[65] and they are both anxious to hold on there. He writes to Colonel Eman[66] to say that he thinks that he would be more useful looking after the young hands at Malta; he is a great pipe-clay soldier.

Last Saturday the Light Division had races, and at the steeplechase one of the horses fell at the first jump and rolled over his rider, the next horse cleared the fence beautifully, but stumbled over the prostrate horse. Both riders were stunned, but I am happy to say that Thomas,[67] of the Artillery, has nearly recovered, and Captain Shiffner,[68] 34th, is also doing well. The 3rd Division were to have had races to-day, but the weather has been too bad; this is the first out-and-out wet day we have had since the snow disappeared. A Scotch baker has established himself at Balaklava. I have porridge nearly every morning, it is a great treat. An order has been issued that we are all to go about in uniform; it is rather difficult to enforce it with the British officer. The new tunic is now quite common. Buckmaster[69] has a man here taking orders. I have had my measure taken, but it is as well to take the change out of one's old garments as long as the old dress is permitted; I hope to sport my new rig-out in England.

No word yet of either of your boxes; that man Lamb[70] must be a great blackguard. I have shot my horse, and have now got a stoutish pony, which does his work well. I saw Colonel Ainslie[71] the other day. When we go to Balaklava we always hear that it

Facing: 'Russian Rifle Pit – now part of the British Advanced Trenches on the left of the Right Attack, or Gordon's Battery.' Published by Colnaghi, 11 June 1855. The figures in the print represent men of the 41st Regiment. [The Royal Welsh Museum, Brecon]

Camp of the 2nd and Light Divisions before Sevastopol. The 41st Regiment's huts can be seen in the centre distance, although the majority of the army still appears to be accommodated in bell tents. A photograph taken in the spring of 1855.

is to be attacked the next day, but that day never comes off. The truth is, they are so little accustomed to shot and shell, and have nothing to do, so they gossip and retail shaves; they ought to be sent up to the front by way of a change. The other day 300 of the 71st were sent on mules from Balaklava to work in the twenty-one gun battery; they returned by railway; it was altogether rather a novel proceeding in the annals of warfare, and shows how hard up we are for hands to do the work.

The Emperor[72] seems to have given up the idea of paying the Crimea a visit. We are looking for good tidings from the Baltic. I hear the trench party is just coming in.

Tuesday morning, 4.45 a.m. — The news yesterday from the trenches is not very satisfactory, we cannot make out what Russ is about. They did not fire much more than usual from the Round Tower,[73] only from two or three embrasures. If they are short of gunners, they certainly have heaps of guns and also ammunition; perhaps we took them by surprise, yesterday, and they may not have had everything ready. To-day will most likely show; they cannot let us hammer away without replying, or they will find all their guns done up; they knocked over one of ours in the 21-gun battery.[74] We have kept up a slight fire all night, and threw some shells into the town from our heavy mortars. Sir John Burgoyne,[75] commanding the Engineers, has gone home, and been relieved by Sir Harry Jones, R.E.[76]

24th April

There has been a good deal of stir in camp since my last of a fortnight ago. During the bombardment on the 10th our fleet got up steam, but did not engage the sea forts or batteries. The other day I nearly had a great catastrophe to my tent, by the chimney of the stove falling over and setting fire to the canvas; fortunately, it was extinguished without much damage being done. It would not have been a pleasant look-out to have had all my goods and chattels burnt. A telegraph-cable has been laid across the Black Sea, and communication between this and London was opened on the 14th inst.; the line is from St George's Monastery[77] to Varna.

On the 19th the trench party of the 77th Regiment took two Russian rifle-pits in front of our sap;[78] several Russians were killed, and an officer and five men taken prisoners. During the night the Russians attacked and retook one of the pits. Colonel Egerton,[79] and also his Adjutant, Lieutenant Lemprière,[80] 77th, were killed, Captain Trevor,[81] 55th, and Lieutenants Owen[82] and Baynes,[83] R.E., severely wounded. Baynes is a great friend of mine. The next night volunteers from the trench party were called for, and again took the pit, and it was held (in spite of a sortie from the enemy) by the 41st, who, during the twenty-four hours, had nineteen casualties. On the 21st a working party of the 41st, under Rowlands,[84] connected this pit with the Woronzoff ravine.

Yesterday the 3rd Division had some very good races, which had been fixed to take place on the 9th, but had to be postponed on account of the weather. A French officer was successful in winning one of the principal events; Wilkie[85] of the Hussars, as usual, won the steeplechase.

5. On the Offensive

May–July 1855

The second bombardment of Sevastopol ended on 19 April and the men of the 2nd and Light Divisions continued to provide the guards and working parties of the British Right Attack. Gradually, the front line was creeping closer to the Russian positions as men dug communication trenches and, occasionally, captured a forward enemy trench or rifle pit which was quickly reversed and then linked to the existing British trenches. By the end of May, new batteries had been constructed and large stores of ammunition brought up ready for an assault on the Russian positions known as the White Works, the Mamelon (facing the French Left Attack) and the Quarries (in front of the British positions – see sketch map on page 105).

7th May

The last few days we have been living in great expectation. The Highland Brigade and some French regiments sailed on the 4th from Kameish [sic] on secret service, supposed to be against Kertch or the neighbourhood; but much to our disappointment we heard yesterday the expedition has returned along with the fleet, for what reason we do not know [The Emperor Napoleon telegraphed to General Canrobert,[1] and countermanded the expedition]. Making a mess of things seems to be the system of the day – giving orders and counter-orders, thereby giving the Russians previous notice of our intentions, and allowing them sufficient time to collect an army in the field large enough to cope with any that we can bring against them. They now have a very large force at [their] command, and every day they are strengthening their position and fortifications.

We are well pleased with the intelligence in the papers to-day, that the European Conference has broken up without any result, so perhaps that now all prospect of peace is at an end, the Governments may be stirred up to act with decision and vigour. If Austria will act with us, we will yet give our foes in the Crimea a good drubbing before next winter; no one expects to get out of this before that time, and at present it seems that the odds are very much against any of the trench parties returning safe home to Old England. I have just heard that strong reinforcements have arrived in Miss Nightingale,[2] Soyer[3] the cook, and Lola Montes,[4] so perhaps all may yet be well! Our casualties lately have been more severe than usual, owing to Russ having thrown up a trench in front of our attacks, from which they keep up a heavy musketry fire; we

The Genoese Fort and part of the British hospital on the cliffs above the congested port of Balaklava.

have also been making advances against them. Some day we must have a tussle for their trench if Mr *Français* will do the same on the right. For the last week the French have been very plucky and have done great things on the left. One night they took a series of trenches, with eight mortars, and established themselves there. Russ tried the next day to drive them out and got a good licking, with the loss of several hundred men.

On the night of the 5th a party of the 49th were caught napping in our left sap, where the Russian rifle-pit was. Russ came up the ravine, and was among them before they had time to recover from their surprise. The enemy were soon driven out, but the 49th lost three men, and four wounded, and one sergeant missing; altogether, the affair cost us twenty-four. The 30th, who were more to the right in another sap, say that the Russians carried away several of their wounded. We are daily expecting Pratt[5] and Lockhart[6] with fifty men from Malta. The Buffs have arrived, but are detained at Balaklava to supply the place of the Highland regiments; we hope they may come up to our attack, now that the expedition has returned.

Lord and Lady Stratford[7] were here a few days ago. We expect, as the season progresses, that we shall have a great many visitors, though I do not think a camp, especially one such as this, is a fit place for ladies. I must go to dinner, as I am for the reserve trenches to-night; we return to camp at daylight, so I will close this then.

Tuesday, 5 a.m. – We had a quiet night as far as sorties are concerned; a good deal of shelling was kept up on the trenches and working parties. I am now going to turn in and have a short snooze.

22nd May

I am sorry to have to tell you that poor Baynes[8] died from the effects of his wound on the 8th. I rode that day into Balaklava with Peddie,[9] and did a little foraging. The next day I called on and saw Major Green,[10] of the 48th, and afterwards took a ride with Bennet,[11] 33rd. That evening being very dark and wet, the Russians made a sortie against our right attack, but were driven back with loss. The following afternoon, a flag of truce was raised for a quarter of an hour to collect the Russian dead. Twenty-eight were taken in, but many others had been removed under cover of the darkness. I was in the trenches of the right rifle-pit, when a sortie occurred about 10 p.m., but all the line being well prepared, the enemy did not advance far. We had upwards of twenty men killed and wounded, and the reserve force suffered considerably from the shells. On the 11th there was another sortie, this time on our left attack, by three heavy columns. Poor Edwards,[12] of the 68th, was shot, and about twenty-five killed and wounded. Russ retired, leaving one prisoner and five dead in our trenches.

I had no idea Alexander Moncrieff[13] was coming to the Crimea, so I was much surprised when he turned up at our camp on the 12th. I have given him a shake-down in my tent; I took him round in rear of the left and right attacks, batteries, trenches, etc., and showed him our position, and the battlefield of Inkerman, in all of which he took a keen interest, and has been busy with his pencil and brush, taking sketches of various points. He and I rode into Kameish [sic] last week, lunched at a café there, and inspected the extreme left batteries of the French, returning home about 8 p.m., after a pretty hard day's work. The next day we rode to Balaklava, and went over the Heights, called on the 93rd, and came home by Kamara, and saw the Sardinian troops encamped there who appear to be a fine set of soldiers; their strength is about 15,000.

Nearly all the Turks have embarked for Eupatoria. The Buffs have come up to the front, also the 71st and wing of the Rifles; the two former regiments are suffering much from cholera, and have had to change the position of their camp. Yesterday two French officers called on us. General Canrobert[14] has been succeeded in the command of the French troops by General Pélissier.[15] We heard that the reason the expedition returned was owing to General Canrobert having received instructions from France to concentrate his forces.

Omar Pasha[16] has arrived here from Eupatoria, and there has been a Council of War at headquarters, and the expedition has to-day again sailed for Kertch; we hope it will be with better results this time. I was in the trenches on the 18th, when Lord Raglan[17] visited Gordon's battery[18] and advanced work.

31st May

When I was writing to you a fortnight ago, the second expedition had just started, and we had been waiting anxiously for news. Last Sunday morning an order was given to the army to fall in on their respective parades, which caused great speculation in camp as to what it might mean, it being such an unusual occurrence on a Sunday. Great, then, was our delight to receive the welcome tidings that Kertch had been taken without loss on the Queen's Birthday; the news was received with three hearty cheers.

On the evening of the 23rd there was terrific firing all night on the left, near the Quarantine Cemetery, close to the outskirts of the town. The French took some ambuscades, also a trench, which they were unable to hold; their loss was very great. The next night there was again heavy firing of Artillery, and the French succeeded in taking and holding the Russian trench, which is under the walls of the town. During the two nights the French are said to have lost 1500, and the Russians several thousand men. Moncrieff[19] and I rode the next day to the scene of the action; it had been a very severe engagement; we also saw the burial parties employed in their sad duties. He and I made a little expedition on the 25th over the Tchernaya; we joined a French reconnoitring force, but when they withdrew, we still continued to prowl about on our own account, and picked up a few treasures. Moncrieff found a sword and other relics, and I got some more useful articles in the shape of shoemakers' tools, which I stowed away in my saddle-bags for my company's use. After a time we noticed some Cossacks advancing in the distance, and thinking that discretion was the better part of valour on that occasion, we beat a hasty retreat, having thoroughly enjoyed our ride over fresh ground. That evening I was on duty in the right trench next the French; Russ shelled us a good deal from field-pieces.

I have bought a horse from the Land Transport; we drew lots for the animals; mine

Part of the hutted encampment of the British Army above Balaklava, 1855.

seems likely to prove a useful beast; I paid £13 10*s*. for him. I rode him down to Balaklava with Moncrieff, who had also bought a nag, but his steed turned lame for want of shoes, so we left him at Johnston's,[20] the Provost-Marshal. A draft of fifty men has arrived from Malta under command of Lockhart[21] and Johnson.[22] The batteries are now ready for opening.

At 3 p.m. on 6 June all the serviceable batteries opened fire with 544 guns and, by 6 p.m. the following day, all the Russian advanced works had been effectively destroyed and the French were able to occupy the White Works and the Mamelon and the British the Quarries. The Russian front line now comprised the Malakoff and the Great Redan and their linking trenches and barricades.

On 8 June, a large working party of the 41st, under the command of Captain Rowlands and Lieutenant Peddie, was given the difficult task of reversing the captured enemy trenches around the Quarries. This meant raising the parapet on the Russian side of the trench, sealing off all access to the trench from the north and constructing fire steps behind the raised parapet so as to allow guards to mount watch on the enemy positions. When completed, this line of trenches became the British fourth parallel. Captain Rowlands wrote:

> *Our batteries opened suddenly yesterday (6 June) at 3 o'clock and all day today. The Mamelon is completely silenced, and we have just received intelligence that we are to attack the quarries in front of our advanced work and the French are to take the Mamelon at the same time, it may end in our going beyond our present positions and I trust it may, I hate half measures.*
>
> *June 9th. We were successful yesterday in taking the quarries and the French the Mamelon. Both sides lost considerably, particularly the French. The quarries were attacked by 200 of the 49th supported by 300 and 47 of our division and a like number of the Light Division. The general sent for our Colonel and told him he was to furnish the attacking party for the quarries but, unfortunately, we could not muster the number required, most of our fellows being in the trenches. I wish we had been able for the taking was much easier than the holding of them when taken. I was about from six o'clock in the morning until 8 last night. It was fearfully hot, they showered us with grape and round shot. I had on 74 of the 41st with me and I'm happy to say was very fortunate. I had only one killed and three wounded. You cannot form any idea of the sight displayed along our trenches after capturing the quarries which contained a great number of dead, brains scattered about, hands and legs, thin and headless trunks. I saw one of the 79th smashed to pieces by a 32-pounder. He was struck about the centre of the body and the contents dashed all over us. I hope that ere long we'll be in Sebastopol.*

On 12 June an alarm that the Russians were about to assault the British front was quashed by a solitary reconnaissance by Private Thomas McQuade of the 41st and, five days later, the Fourth Bombardment began which all hoped would result in the destruction of both the Malakoff and the Redan and bring to an end the long drawn-out period of trench warfare. During the first day it appeared that both Russian positions had been disabled and that an assault could take place the following day, 18 June, the fortieth anniversary of Waterloo.

8th June

We have been keeping one another pretty lively lately, throwing shot and shell at distant ranges; we have also been treating the town to a few carcasses [bombs] in the hopes of setting fire to the large barracks. Some of our shells burst in our own trenches, and poor Colonel Mundy,[23] 33rd, had one of his arms shattered. On the afternoon of the 6th [the Third Bombardment] our batteries unexpectedly recommenced firing, and continued to do so all night. Lord Raglan[24] that day passed through our camp, and was heartily cheered. I was in my tent at the time, as since my last trench duty I have been rather seedy, with a feverish cold and pain in my back, and in the doctor's hands.

I must now tell you of the exciting events that have been taking place. Our batteries having, been chiefly occupied in trying to silence the Redan,[25] Malakoff[26] and Mamelon,[27] it was decided that we should yesterday seize the quarries and Russian trenches in front of the Redan, and the French attack the Mamelon and redoubts on the right. For our work the Light and 2nd Division were told off to furnish equal numbers, 400 of each as a storming party, 300 more in reserve, and 400 as a working party, all supported by 1200, the usual trench party. The General[28] asked our Colonel[29] to give 200 to storm, but as most of the regiment, including five officers, were then in the trenches, we were not able to find the number, so the honour was given to the 49th in our stead.

Of the 49th party, four of their officers out of the six were wounded. The 62nd Regiment had three officers killed, their two seniors, and another wounded. Our casualties are supposed to be about 40 officers, and 600 men killed and wounded; our chief loss was in holding the ground whilst reversing the trenches and making the necessary communications, but the affair has ended gloriously for the allies. The French did their part of the business rather too well for themselves, as after storming the Mamelon, in their éclat and impetuosity, they followed the retreating Russians to the ditch of the Round Tower,[30] but the enemy being reinforced, managed to get round the French right, and drove them back to their old trenches again, and for a time re-occupied the Mamelon and adjoining trenches, so the attack had to be renewed, which was much more difficult than the first assault, as the works were not at the time held by a strong force. During the night the Russians made several fruitless attempts to retake the quarries and their trenches, supported by their batteries firing round shot and grape. The French are believed to have lost 1,700 killed and wounded, the Russians over 2,000.

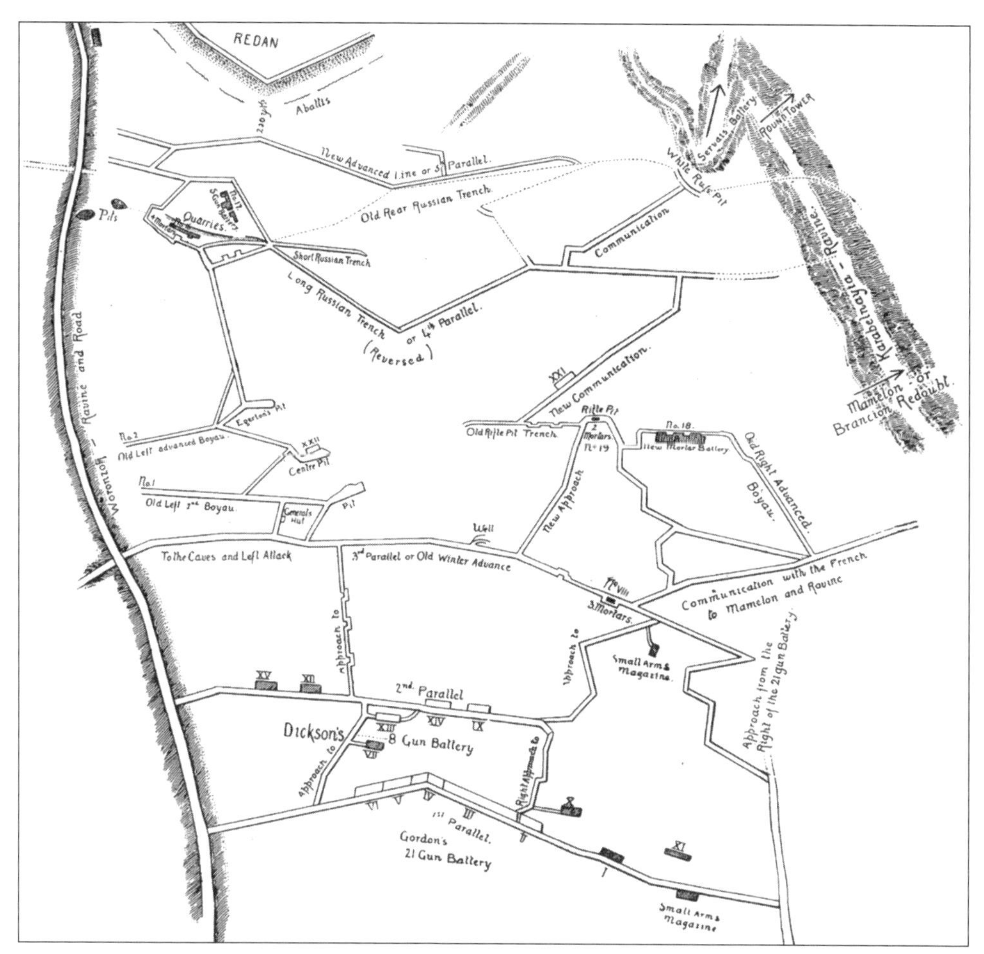

Sketch map showing the British Right Attack trench lines before Sevastopol. The salient of the Great Redan can be seen at the top.

It is reported 62 pieces of cannon and several mortars have been captured. When we from the top of the hill saw the French driven back, we felt dreadfully down in the mouth, but were much relieved when they went at it a second time in gallant style, and maintained their ground, some of them even advanced too far again. The relieved trench party was kept on duty for more than thirty-six hours, and did not return till daylight. Russell,[31] of the *Times*, is at Kertch, so you will not have his report of these doings to rely on.

Friday, 10 p.m. – Rowlands[32] and Peddie[33] have just returned from the trenches in a dreadful state of filth and dirt, having been relieved by Bertram,[34] and four subalterns; they say it is the worst twenty-four hours they ever spent, the Russians were very wroth, and kept pounding the trenches and working parties. Peddie had a man killed close to him by a round shot, but I have told you more than enough of this dreadful slaughter.

This is a quiet night, only a good many shells flying from our side, no musketry, all are repairing damages, etc. I viewed the French attack from the hill, I could not resist the temptation of seeing the fight, although I had no right to leave camp, being under the doctor's treatment, and it is just as well for me that he does not see me at present writing at this late hour. A friend dropped in from the *City of London* to see me, which delayed my doing so before earlier.

The assault on Sevastopol's southern defences was planned to take place immediately after a final bombardment which would further damage the Russian positions and force their men to take cover. Inexplicably, the French GOC, General Pélissier, decided not to order the bombardment and consequently the Russians were in place to defend their positions which had been repaired during the hours of darkness. Despite this, both British and French troops were ordered to advance across the open ground.

Half-an-hour after midnight, the 41st paraded ready to form the vanguard of the storming party that was to capture the Redan. They were to attempt to rush the salient angle of the Russian position whilst men from other divisions positioned themselves on the flanks. Shortly before dawn, the men of the 41st moved into their forward positions facing the Redan, which was about 500 yards away, where they were ordered to lie down and await orders. Throughout this time the men were under enemy artillery fire and sustained a number of casualties. Shortly before 8 a.m. the order to assault the Redan was rescinded and the party withdrew. That night, men of the 41st were ordered into the advanced trench and were involved in the recovery of the wounded.

Camp, 18th June

Having mentioned in my last letter that I was on the sick-list, you will no doubt be anxiously looking for my usual bulletin, especially as long before you receive this, you will have read in the papers an account of this disastrous day: I cannot retire to rest without sending you a line to announce my safety, for it has been far from a second Waterloo. I have not the spirit to enter much into details to-night, and I am very tired after last night and to-day's work; it is enough to say we have all had a most terrible licking, the French are supposed to have lost about 5,000, and we ourselves over 1,000, having gained nothing. The Russian loss is trifling in comparison; we are all dreadfully downcast, and wonder what will be the upshot. There is no firing just now, the Artillery are, however, taking ammunition in to the batteries. Our regiment was to have stormed the salient angle of the Redan,[35] but as the flanking parties did not succeed, we were (luckily for us) not called upon to advance. The 34th have lost a great many of their officers, and out of a force of 200 sailors who carried the ladders, it is said only 20 returned without wounds. How the Russians must crow! The grape and canister played great havoc against the attacking parties. Colonel Goodwyn[36] received

The French trenches and gun batteries before the Malakoff, Sevastopol. The remains of the White Tower of the Malakoff can be seen on the hill in the distance.

a wound in the head, but the peak of his cap saved him. Our regiment had only a few casualties, as we did not leave the trenches. We paraded last night at midnight, and marched down, and occupied the left of our old advanced trench; the French attacked the Round Tower about 4 a.m., and in about half an hour the signal for the advance of the English was given; the assault on the Round Tower did not succeed, so ours was not pushed on. It was an error attacking at dawn, the works should have been bombarded for some hours previous to the advance; it was also a great mistake, our attempting to storm the Redan till the French had taken the Round Tower, as we could not have held the former with the Malakoff[37] still in the possession of the Russians. Our loss on the 8th, including the taking of the quarries and the next twenty-four hours, was about 40 officers, and 500 or 600 men. The next day a truce took place about noon, and lasted till half-past four in the afternoon; Russ occupied the time energetically in repairing damages. My horse, I regret to say, was stolen during the truce.

Soon after the taking of the Mamelon,[38] the Russians evacuated the redoubt on the spur of land on their extreme left, and went off by means of boats. Orders were given to slacken fire on the 10th, and the interval between that date and when our batteries re-opened on the morning of the 17th [the Fourth Bombardment] was employed by the French and us in preparing for a renewal of the siege operations, by mounting guns and mortars in the Mamelon, quarries, and new advanced works. Captain Dawson [39] and Lieutenant R. Lowry, R.E.,[40] were among those killed on the attack of the quarries. Lowry,[41] of the 41st, is a cousin [sic] of the latter; he and I attended the sale of their effects the other day.

The Guards, and also the 93rd, marched up from Balaklava on the 16th, and encamped not far from the position of the 2nd Division in rear of the 1st Royals; I visited several old friends that afternoon.

On 28 June, Lord Raglan died of cholera which had reappeared amongst the army with the advent of hot weather. He was succeeded as GOC by Lieutenant-General Sir James Simpson.

Almost nightly, the 41st furnished working parties to push forward the trenches, consolidate those that were held and repel the enemy attacks. One unidentified witness is recorded in the regimental history:

> *They came on yelling like so many devils, the yells being something between a dog and a cat; they fire away at the same time. The firing is generally very sharp for half-an-hour at the longest, when the Russians shut up and a true British cheer of defiance concludes the performance.*

8th July

I am afraid this will not be a much more cheerful letter than my last, which was written after our failure of the 18th, as, in addition to so many of our brave comrades who were killed on that day, we have now to deplore the loss of our much lamented Commander-in-Chief, Lord Raglan,[42] who died from dysentery on the 28th June. Being in a weak state of health, he took our defeat much to heart. His body is not to be buried in the Crimea, but is being conveyed to England; the funeral service took place at 4 p.m. on the 3rd inst. Just before the procession moved off, when a salute of nineteen guns was being fired, General Pélissier[43] rode up, and placed a piece of forget-me-not on the coffin as a token of regard to our gallant chief; the first part of the road to Kazatch Bay was lined by British troops, the remainder by French.

On the 19th June, the day after our assault, there was a truce to collect the killed and wounded; between four and seven o'clock in the afternoon, the whole army was kept under arms to prevent us going to the front. The Russians are much elated at their success. I was in the trenches the following night, and the men were in good heart, and voluntarily worked in reversing the old Russian trench. There was a large fire in the town near the dockyard creek.

Three thousand men now guard the right attack, and the duty is taken by Divisions; a third of them are withdrawn at daylight from the most advanced position. I was among this number, and on reaching my tent, in the hopes of getting a good snooze, I turned in, but I soon found I had brought back with me from Rusky an enormous quantity of fleas, which proved such hungry and lively companions that I did not get much sleep that morning.

You would be sorry to see the name of Sir John Campbell,[44] and also Colonel Yea,[45] 7th Fusiliers, among the list of those killed. General Pennefather[46] has gone home on account of his health, and General Barnard[47] succeeds him in the command of our Division. There are also other changes on the Staff. General Simpson[48] has assumed command of the army in place of Lord Raglan, General Codrington[49] has replaced Sir George Brown,[50] who has gone to England, and General Estcourt[51] died on the 24th. The French have abandoned the cemetery near the town, which they took lately, as they were losing so many men.

We have had very heavy thunderstorms and torrents of rain, making the constant trench work anything but pleasant; and it has been hard work constructing two new batteries, one near Egerton's rifle-pit[52] for ten guns, and another in continuation of the 8-gun battery.[53] I have bought another horse to replace the one I had stolen, and had a pleasant ride on him to the Sardinian camp, near the Baidar Road, with Bertram.[54] It had formerly belonged to Lieutenant March,[55] [sic] Adjutant of the 33rd, who was shot when running across the open ground.

29th July

On the 13th a party of four of us, Graham,[56] Rowlands,[57] Kingscote[58] and I made a very pleasant expedition to Baidar. We started at half-past two in the morning, and accompanied a French reconnaissance several miles along the road to Yalta, but without encountering any Russian force. The scenery is very fine; after leaving the beautifully wooded pass of Baidar, the road runs along grand precipitous cliffs overhanging the sea. We stopped at a house belonging to a Russian nobleman, and being very thirsty, we were grateful for some Crimean wine which the caretaker was good enough to give us. On our return we lunched under the shade of the trees at Baidar, which was a delightful change from our arid camps.

Now that there is no moon, Russ comes out at night to try and destroy our works, but the attacks lately have not been very vigorous. On the 13th I was in the trenches on the extreme right, next to the French, when they made one of these attacks. I thought they might perhaps look me up, and I was rather in hopes they would, as I think the men I had in charge would have been quite a match for them, especially as I took 100 more, who were working near me, and joined them to my party when the attack began. It was bad luck for me that they did not come nearer; if they had come on, and we had repulsed them, I probably should have been mentioned in the despatches. Some of the despatches are most absurd; if anything extra occurs, the field officer or senior in charge is sure to make the most of it. By the last papers received some officers are mentioned, none of whom fired a shot, and who only occupied the old trenches when the attacking parties took the quarries and trenches.

About a fortnight ago, we were glad to welcome Bligh[59] back from England, also Wavell,[60] who joined from Malta. With our increased number of officers we have been able to enjoy a little more recreation. One day Bligh, Rowlands,[61] and I went to a jolly picnic near the Monastery,[62] chiefly composed of officers of the 2nd Division; the canteen man of the 30th provided the grub; we have also had some cricket. We are making an additional 3-gun battery in the quarries. A Russian shell unfortunately fell in the new mortar emplacement, and set fire to over fifty bombs.

I am glad to say that the pay for the men has arrived at last, and not before it is wanted, as there was very little money in camp. On the 25th we received field allowance for the first time. Major-General Markham,[63] our new General, yesterday inspected the two brigades on their private parades.

6th August

Since I wrote to you we have had more changes among our Generals. General England,[64] the last of the first batch, has gone home, and our Brigadier Lockyer[65] is appointed to Ceylon; Colonel Windham[66] of the Guards gets the vacancy. We are evidently nearing another coup and the sooner the better for ourselves. I was on the trenches the night before last, and such a night! – continual fire from the enemies' batteries from nine in the evening till daylight. Shot after shot at the trenches of our right attack – grape, shot, shell, and 'happy families' or bouquets. The consequence was that there were about fifty casualties, and the working party had to desist after losing Lieutenant Evans[55] and eighteen men of the 55th Regiment in a couple of hours; I was in the short Russian trench, and out of my party of 100 men I lost three. Last night the casualties of the Light Division, I hear, were also very heavy, and to-night much the same game appears to be going on.

It has come to General Simpson's[68] notice that we have lately been blazing away nearly as much ammunition as is brought into the batteries each night, so stringent orders have been given to the Generals on duty in the trenches that they are in the future not to issue directions about the firing, except in the case of a sortie; but the batteries are to be in charge of the Artillery or Naval Commanders. The night I was on the trenches was the first night of our batteries firing so little; the sudden change probably made Russ think we were up to some devilment.

Lieut-Gen Sir Richard England.
Royal Welsh Museum, Brecon

I enclose you a rough sketch [*see page 105*] I have made of our trenches. It is not correct to scale, but will give you some idea of the outline of the trench work, etc. Our nearest trench is about 100 yards from the abattis, and another 100 to the ditch of the Redan.[69] The communications and trenches are nearly all completed, with the exception of about 150 yards from the white Russian pit to the left. Russ had made this pit very substantial with a little ditch in front; it was evidently a place where they kept a body of men; as there are shelters in it, it was of easy access to them from the ravine between the Redan and Malakoff,[70] leading down to the large barracks and the Arsenal. The French are within 60 yards of the little Redan and 150 of the Tower; they cannot bring up their left to encircle the Malakoff without being exposed to an enfilade fire from the Redan. When the French attack, the ravine may aid them in approaching the Servais battery. The abattis in front of them has been quite destroyed by our Artillery fire, so it is not now an obstruction.

Captain Montague,[71] [sic] an Engineer officer, whom you may remember was taken prisoner during the winter, has been released from Odessa, and has just arrived. Perhaps he may be able to give some valuable information, of what he has seen.

On the 3rd, Rowlands[72] and I rode over to the Inkerman Redoubt, near our old camping ground, and round to the north-eastern heights, returning home by the railway. I played in a game of cricket for four or five hours before dinner to-day, but not having had much practice of late, felt rather out of it.

On 16 August the Russians made their last attempt to break the siege by a full scale assault on the French and Sardinian forces in the valley of the Tchernaya but failed to achieve anything. The British were placed on standby but otherwise played no part in this battle

---

17th August

Before this is despatched, you will have heard that the Russians attacked the allied position on the Tchernaya yesterday; it has been a fortunate day for us, and they have paid smartly for their temerity. The battle began about daylight, and it was a hard fight for some hours. In the attack, the enemy succeeded in crossing the river and aqueduct at the Traktir bridge, and some other places, and a few of the men even gained the low hills, upon which the French are encamped. They also drove back the Piedmontese advanced piquets, and established their guns in position there. It is computed that the Russian loss was over 8,000, including 2,000 men taken prisoners; whilst that of the French is comparatively trifling, about 1500; the Piedmontese lost in killed and wounded 200. The Russians hoped to have forced the position, and cut off the Sardinians and Turks, with the French Cavalry, who are encamped between the Tchernaya and Baidar, from the force protecting Balaklava. If they had been successful, they would probably have made an attack from the town on the trenches, to endeavour to destroy the batteries, which they must know are now near completion. After their several defeats, I do not think they will be inclined to try it on again.

This morning at daylight, our batteries, and also some French works near the Mamelon, opened fire, and are still hard at it (4.30 p.m.); the chief object is to detract the line of the forts from our trenches [the Fifth Bombardment].

I met with a misfortune last Wednesday; my scoundrel of a batman bolted with my handbag containing £20 public, and about £5 private money. I discovered my loss on coming off parade, and knowing that he had been in my tent with my saddle about an hour before, I went at once to the stables, but he was not forthcoming. He was last seen in uniform, and on being questioned by one of the bowmen as to where he was going, he said, 'to Balaklava, by the captain's orders.' On learning this, I started immediately for that port with a Sergeant, both of us mounted, and gave the Provost-Marshal the details, and also the police. I left the Sergeant there for a couple of days, and went on to Kameish [sic], and put the *Gendarmerie* [military police] there on the look-out; but as yet nothing has been heard of him or the money. On my return in the evening, I found that he had left some letters, which had been in the bag in the stable. I expect he is either off to Rusky or has succeeded in getting on board some merchant ship.

You will be sorry to hear of a sad accident that has happened to Bertram.[73] He took up his pistol case (with the pistol in the leather pouch lying on the top) to crush some sugar; when doing so, the pistol went off, wounding him badly. The ball was immediately extracted, and I am glad to say he is doing well.

Last night when in the trenches I was wounded in the leg above the knee, but it not being severe, I did not return myself wounded; it was a fortunate escape, as the shell fell close beside me, and I had only time to throw myself flat on the ground when it burst; a piece of the shell cut through the leather ammunition pouch of a man who was near me. I have got a cap which belonged to a Russian General who was killed yesterday at the Tchernaya.

Evening, 7 p.m.— The bombardment has nearly ceased, a shell from the 8-mortar battery has blown up one of the magazines in the Servais battery, exploding also a number of shells, and doing considerable damage. Russ has taken lately to throw shot and shell at long ranges; some of them come into our camps and have killed and wounded several men; as yet none have fallen into our regimental lines, but to-night some have reached the ravine which is only a short distance off. It would not be a pleasant sensation to awake and find a shell with a bright fuse as a companion in one's tent.

31st August

It was this day year that our Division embarked with glad hearts for active service. What sad and also glorious events have happened during the last twelve months, and how few of the brave old lot now remain here above Crimean soil! It is distressing to think of the losses that have resulted from the ambition of the late Czar.

The good news from Sweaborg is cheering, but as yet we do not know whether the success will open the way to Helsingfors, which would be the case if all the batteries are demolished; we may next expect to hear of Revel sharing the same fate. I do not think there is much chance of an attack on Cronstadt this year, for want of vessels of light draught.[74]

You will be very sorry to hear that Lumley Graham[75] has been shot in the right arm; and has had to have it amputated below the elbow-joint. Last Tuesday a very large Russian magazine blew up in the Mamelon,[76] it had only been filled with powder the night before; the damage done has been tremendous, about 150 casualties, and a battery of six guns entirely buried, so much so, that an Artillery officer told me it would be endless work to try and disentomb the guns, and put them in working order again, and that they were not going to attempt it. You will have some idea of the mass of earth thrown out when I mention that the chasm is about 40 feet long by 20 deep, and 25 wide. Graham, Bligh,[77] and I went down on Wednesday forenoon to see the result, and after that, we went poking along in the advanced saps directed against the Malakoff, to see how far they had advanced; it was there that Graham was hit; the same bullet whizzed past me. Part of the trench was enfiladed by the little Redan;[78] it had been thrown up hastily and not completed. The French had warned us of the danger, but like Britishers, we rather pooh-poohed the idea; they have got their saps right up to the abattis, and not far from the ditch. The nights have lately been too bright for much work, but we hope to advance more rapidly now the moon is on the wane.

Last night a sortie was made against a new trench we are attempting to run out of the 5th Parallel towards the salient of the Redan; there being so little depth of soil it progresses slowly. An officer of the 97th has been killed and two others wounded, but not having yet heard full particulars, I am afraid to put the rumours on paper; it is not very creditable that when a sortie occurs, we seem so often to be taken by surprise. This regiment has not been long employed in trench duties, and it is said the working party had taken their belts off which in the most advanced position they should not have done.

The Russians have finished their bridge from Fort Nicholas[79] to the north side, so now they have access across the harbour without the means of boats. The French are fortifying their position on the Tchernaya with trenches and batteries, which will puzzle Mr Russ to take; there is no word at present of an assault; both the French and we are increasing our mortar batteries. I saw James Stewart[80] yesterday looking well. Tillbrook[81] of the 50th has lately come to the Crimea; I called on him the other day, but he was in Balaklava.

Since the Highlanders went to the plains we have had harder work; it is a shame that they should be sent away again from the post of danger, they were only brought up on the 18th June, and we do not see why the Light or 2nd Division should not have had a turn of the easy duties in the valley. We all take for granted that we are in for another Crimean winter, but trust the trench duties will be over before then. The dress bugle has gone for the trench party, so I must hastily say good-night.

6. The Fall of Sevastopol

September 1855

On 5 September the Allied batteries opened what was to prove to be the final bombardment of Sevastopol. Throughout the day and, where possible, the night, front line infantry maintained a steady fire to try and prevent the Russians effecting any repairs to their damaged positions. During the night, Captain Rowlands of the 41st led 20 men out into the open ground and captured a Russian rifle pit. The enemy counter-attacked in force and drove them back. The bombardment continued throughout the next two days. General Codrington selected the men of the 2nd and Light Divisions to lead the British attack on the Redan, which would be launched on 9 September after the French had signalled that they had captured the Malakoff position. Codrington saw the selection of these men, for what was intended to be the final assault, as recognition for the months which they had spent in the forward positions which they knew so well. The Light Division was selected to lead the assault, closely followed by the 2nd Division.

7th September

I send this hasty scrawl to tell you that I am all well in mind and limb. For two days we have been pounding this unfortunate city, and I have just heard that the Light Division parade at 5 p.m. for some duty [the Sixth Bombardment]. It is our Division to-night for trenches, and I am going on, so if anything takes place before the next twenty-four hours, I may have rather an easy berth of it, except for the dust, which is to-day frightful; but we hope this may be the last of the trenches. Captains Every[1] and Lockhart[2] go on with me; the former only arrived in camp yesterday evening with a draft from Malta. The Colonel[3] has posted me to the Light Company.[4] I cannot fancy myself much of a Light Bob, it is better I think to accept of it, as the offer is complimentary, not for the sake of appearance, but for efficiency; the men are the picked soldiers of the regiment, and are even now, after all the cutting up they have had, a very smart lot.

I think Sebastopol has not many days to stand; one of the Russian frigates has just been burnt to the water's edge. I do not believe we shall attack the Redan[5] for the present, but take the Malakoff,[6] which will render the left face of the Redan useless, and let us sap up to the work. Rowlands'[7] name you will probably see in the despatches

for taking a rifle-pit two nights ago; they succeeded in taking it, but Russ came on in force, so he prudently retired with his twenty men. Several officers have been killed in posting sentries near this pit; it was Engineering folly taking it, because we cannot hold it without a trench up to it.[8] Bertram[9] is progressing favourably, and goes home immediately; Graham[10] will shortly follow. Johnston[11] has resigned the appointment of Provost-Marshal on account of his health.

7th September

Before dinner, I closed a hasty note to my dear mother; since then the order for our Division going on trenches has been cancelled. To-morrow we breakfast at 6 a.m., carry two days' rations cooked, and extra ammunition, so I suppose the 18th June is to be enacted over again; I trust on an improved principle, and that we may be successful without much bloodshed; 1,000 men form the storming party, 500 from the Light, and 500 from our Division, the 2nd. We tossed up who should go first, and the Light Division have won the post of honour. Our regiment gives 300 for storming, along with 200 from the 62nd, the 41st also furnishing 100 for working. The other corps have other duties to perform, of which I am ignorant, such as carrying scaling ladders, wool bags, etc. God grant that it may be an honourable day for the allied army, no one dreams of a repulse. Another frigate has been burnt this afternoon. The weather is cool and favourable for the enterprise. It is thought that the French will also make an assault on the left. You may be sure that we shall not attack this time till the fate of the Malakoff is sealed. If I fall in the grand struggle to-morrow, you will some day receive a few of my things, such as my sword, watch, ring, etc.; the other articles will, I suppose, be disposed of as usual.

I must now say *adieu*, and may the Lord shower His blessings on Mother and you, and our dear family, if we are not to meet again on this earth, may we all be re-united in His everlasting kingdom.

Saturday morning, 6.30. a.m. — The cannonading is now very heavy – a beautiful cool morning. If anything happens to me, you had better apply for my vacancy for Jack,[12] and get him into this regiment without purchase, the man waits for letters.

At 12 noon on 9 September, the French stormed the Malakoff, catching the Russians unawares as they changed garrisons (moving the old force out before replacing them with the new in an effort to reduce casualties). Within minutes both the Tricolore and the Union Flag were flying above the Russian position. The ladder parties and storming troops of the Light Division immediately left their trenches and ran the 200–250 yards towards the salient angle of the Redan under heavy fire

Facing: The interior of the Russian defences, looking out towards the Allied trenches. The photograph was taken after the fall of the city and the soldiers in the foreground are French.

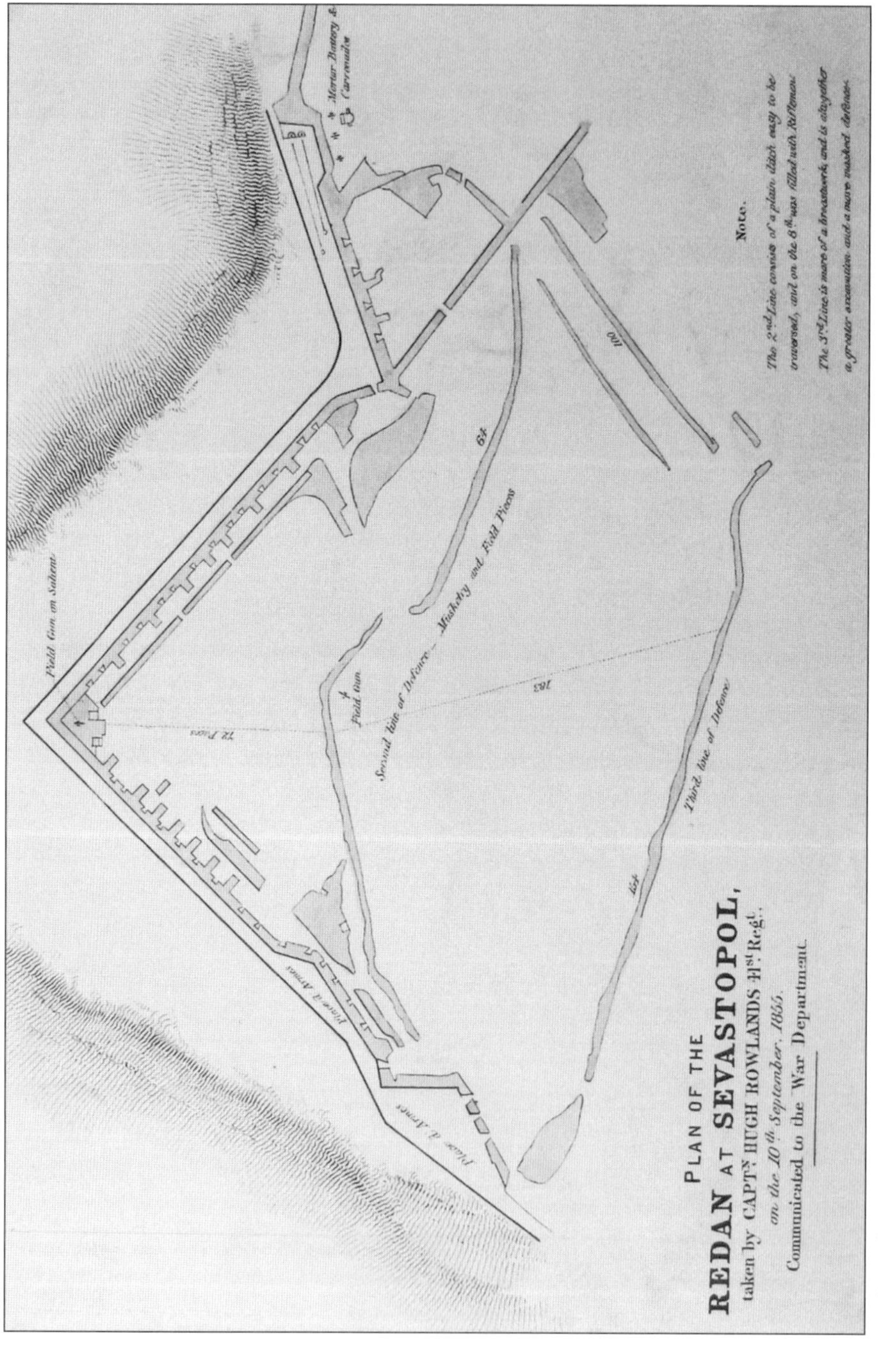

A plan of the Redan, drawn by Captain Hugh Rowlands of the 41st Regiment, 10 September 1855.

Interior of the Russian defences, 1855 showing two of the gun positions. The matted screens above each gun enables the gunners to move about unobserved. Note a similar device, a rope mantelet, fitted around the barrel of the lefthand gun to protect gunners from rifle fire.

from the Russian defenders who had been forewarned by the French attack on the Malakoff. Three hundred men of the 41st, led by the Grenadier Company under the command of Captain Rowlands, and accompanied by Brigadier-General Windham, fixed bayonets and moved out of the trench, followed by the remainder of the regiment's attacking party under the command of Lieutenant-Colonel James Eman. Windham later reported:

> I placed myself with Lieutenant-Colonel Eman, C.B., at the head of the Grenadiers of the 41st regiment, commanded by Captain Rowlands, a fine and gallant young soldier ...
>
> We quickly came to the ditch of the Redan, and passed it, but, owing to the heavy flanking fire and the difficult parallel we had to start from, not in such regular order as could be wished. The same may be said of the 62nd Regiment. They, however, both advanced with courage and resolution, but on crowning the parapet of the Redan got intermixed with Regiments of the Light Division.

The Grenadiers got inside the Redan but only in small groups and, lacking any support, were unable to hold their position and, after about thirty minutes, were pinned down in an exchange of fire with the Russian defenders. After nearly two hours of this form of ineffective combat, the Russians, having been reinforced by men withdrawing from the Malakoff, counter-attacked and drove the British out of *the Redan and back towards their starting point in the trenches. Such was the disappointment at the failure of this second assault on the Redan that many began to search for reasons. Rowlands later wrote to Windham:*

> *I examined a few of the soldiers of the 41st and 62nd Regiments who formed part of the assaulting column on the Redan, and discovered that a general opinion prevailed that the place was mined. There was only one exception, a man of the 41st Regiment (perfectly unknown to me) stated that he thought the men generally had no fear of explosions. Upon being asked the cause of that general clinging to the salient, he replied: 'I consider, Sir, that it was entirely owing to a mixture of Regiments, and that a sufficiently large number of the same Regiment, in officers and men, could not be collected for a simultaneous rush into the place.'*

Despite their success at the Malakoff, the French failed to take their other main objectives, the Little Redan, the Curtain and the Central Bastion. As the badly mauled and depressed Allied soldiers settled back into their trenches, the bombardment recommenced. During the course of the night of 8/9 September, explosions were heard going off behind the Russian lines and fires broke out inside Sevastopol and on the ships in the harbour. At about 1 a.m. a group of volunteers crept out from the Allied lines and made their way towards the Redan to try and ascertain what was happening. When they returned they reported that, save for the dead and the dying, the Redan had been evacuated. As daylight broke over the city, the Allied soldiers entered the Redan and discovered that the Russians had withdrawn across the harbour and that, effectively, the siege was over. When the senior officers discovered the scene of carnage that presented itself inside the Redan, they ordered sentries to be posted to prevent others from entering.

Old Camp, 10th September

How happy I am to be able to say that I have been present at the whole of this memorable siege and fall of Sebastopol, and that by Divine Providence I have been mercifully preserved through all, with hardly a day's sickness; with what a grateful heart I should give thanks to the Almighty for having brought me safely through all the dangers and trials of this severe campaign, when so many of our brave comrades have fallen.

I sent off a hasty note on the evening of Friday to forewarn you of our movements. On Saturday we paraded at 8 a.m., and marched to the right of the quarries, and occupied part of the 5th Parallel, the storming party of the Light Division being opposite to the salient angle; the 300 of the 41st on their right, and 200 of the 62nd touching us. At noon, the French, from their *place d'armes* close to the ditch, sallied out on the Malakoff,[13] and took it quite by surprise, their flag was floating over it in less than a quarter of an hour. It being hoisted was a signal for us to attack the

Interior of the Redan, Sevastopol, looking towards the salient angle from the Russian 'second line' of defence.

Redan,[14] and the French the little Redan;[15] the Light Division went out by companies in line, along with the ladder party; we followed as soon as the ground was vacated, all going over by companies from the same place, as we had no *place d'armes* like the French.

When Rowlands,[16] who was leading the Grenadier Company got up to the parapet of the Redan, he found that the Light Division had quite blocked up the point, at which the ladders were placed, and that very few had entered the interior of the work, and that they were making no progress in the attack. In consequence of this block, the companies and regiments in succession got jumbled up together, and there was a total want of cohesion in the command of the individual companies. Shortly after I reached the ditch and mounted the parapet, a panic seized the men, for no reason whatever that I know of and it was with the greatest difficulty that they were prevented from bolting; a great many succeeded in doing so in spite of the efforts made to reassure them. This action, on their part, of course discouraged the supports before they had left the trenches. There we stood on the salient for an hour and fifty minutes, in a mass of several hundreds, not gaining an inch of ground, and all we could get the men to do, was to pull down the revetment of the ditch and parapet, and fill up the places of the killed and wounded, and it was with the greatest difficulty that they could even be made to do that, they seemed so bewildered at their position, they would not advance five yards to serve any one. It is said in camp to-day, that General Pélissier[17] thought a great deal of the way we fought, so steadily for an hour and fifty minutes; however, that may be, we cannot claim the honour of taking Sebastopol.

It is our only regret in having taken the town, that it can be said that it was the French who did it, which would make it seem as if it were a blot on the bravery of the British soldiery, which is not the case, although from my own experience I have thought that our troops are not, in point of dash and ardour, what they were before the beginning of these confounded trenches. My private opinion is that the British soldier had a very hard, if not an impracticable, duty to perform in storming the salient, when no flank attacks were feasible; the difficulty, after entering the apex of the Redan, was to get the men to extend sufficiently. They were so circumscribed on both sides by the interior, and it was necessary to form a broad front to advance and seize the work, the rear of which was guarded by a trench occupied by the Russians, and from which they poured a deadly and concentrated fire into the assailants, who were crowded together in the angle, and behind the adjoining traverses. It was a fatal mistake subdividing regiments, as both regiments and companies got mixed up together, immediately on crossing the ditch, and general confusion resulted. It must also be remembered that the soldiers had been for months well aware that the place was mined, and that the talk amongst themselves, and which they fully believed, was to the effect that if ever we got into the place they would be blown into the air; I have heard them myself say so over and over again.

Our finale at the Redan was a panic, which seized the front row of our men, and bundled us all into the ditch, and it became a case of *sauve qui peut*. Many men must have been trampled to death, and others wounded; it was fortunate that the ditch had been rendered much more shallow by pulling down the revetment. Rowlands[18] says he feels certain, that by the way his men tried to do their duty, if he had been able to get his company up over the ditch first, they would have followed him in. Rowlands is a brave fellow, but his beauty is for the time being rather spoilt by a grape shot, thrown by the hand, hitting him in the face; four bullets have also cut his clothes and cap; he shot three Russians with his revolver, one after another. I got a lick from a stone thrown by a Russian, and still feel the effects; my jacket was also cut by a bullet.

Our casualties will show you what a sad day it has been for us. Captain Every,[19] who had arrived only two days ago from Malta, was shot in the Redan. He commanded No. 1 [Company] for the first time; he was liked by all, and we were delighted when he rejoined; he volunteered to come up from Malta instead of Harvey.[20] Poor Lockhart[21] was killed in the quarries by a grape shot; he did not belong to the storming party. Kingscote[22] has lost his right hand. Young Maude[23] had a musket ball through his leg.

He [Maude] only arrived at the same time as Every; he was doing duty for the day with my company. Hamilton,[24] the Adjutant, got a graze above the knee; the others are nothing, and should not be entered in the returns. Our casualties are 166, which is heavy out of 300. My present company, No. 4, had twenty wounded and five killed or missing; my late servant, Cuthbert,[25] is one of these; the last that was seen of him was with both his arms broken; he behaved very well. I am very sorry for him. I had parted with him because he had become a little unsteady; latterly he had behaved well, and I had made him a lance-corporal. I had one sergeant killed, and two wounded; the Light Company sergeants were all wounded – not a good prospect for me when I become a Light Bob!

We buried Captains Every[26] and Lockhart[27] to-day, with sad hearts, on Cathcart's Hill, and to-morrow the funeral takes place of our much-lamented and never-to-be-replaced Colonel;[28] he was shot through the chest. He died this morning very peacefully; he will be a dreadful loss to our regiment. I am so sorry for poor Mrs Eman and the children, it will be a great blow to them; they are in Malta. It was only a few days ago, the Colonel[29] read me part of a letter from her, containing a dialogue of the children about their hopes of seeing their father home safe in winter.

Yesterday our regiment was on a piquet guard at the 5th Parallel, rather more agreeable than it was twenty-four hours before. All entrance to the Redan and town was prohibited, and two chains of sentries put to prevent the infraction of the orders, but it was no go to keep every one out, especially officers, who are always the first to break orders of this kind, and who passed the sentries on some pretext or another, such as going on burial parties, or for wood, or other devices; and when once in the Redan, the access to the town was plain sailing.

I got leave from Goodwyn[30] to try my luck, and was not long in effecting my purpose, but I could not find any loot on this side of the creek, and as explosions were taking place every now and then in the suburbs, between Fort Paul[31] and the Malakoff, I was not inclined to pay them a visit on the 'spec' of what I could put in my pocket, or under cover of a pocket-handkerchief (anything seen on you was immediately seized by the sentries). The town is still on fire, and an explosion has this instant taken place; there is hardly a large building left. I went hurriedly through the Redan, and then to the big barrack buildings (which are in ruins), and all about them, then across and up to the rear of the Malakoff, at which I could only have a glance. The ditch is much more formidable than that of the Redan, and I believe the Tower was mined, but the French had obtained possession of it before the Russians could act. I cannot understand how they did not see us assembling in the trenches.

On returning home from our piquet, I got a bell which is to be hung up in our kitchen. I have, to-day, bought some few odds and ends from the French, who have not had such strict regulations as we have, and they are consequently getting many more things than our men. Rowlands[32] will be certain of his brevet, and Skipwith[33] also; they deserve it well. We have no objection to peace now, having got the material guarantee, we hope, without the north side; they have still two or three steamers, but we will settle their hash in a few days. We have taken about 2,000 guns which have never been used. I suppose the Highlanders will have the credit of taking the Redan, because they found it vacated during the night.

17th September

I have just finished a letter to Moncrieff,[34] and can only send a hurried line to ask you to tell I[sabella][35] that she can not visit the Crimea until the harbour is opened to our

The empty and drained dry docks at Sevastopol, 1856 (built under the supervision of the British civil engineer William Upton). In the far distance (centre left) is Fort Nicholas with Fort Constantine beyond. To the right of the pylon are the ruins of Fort Paul with Fort Michael on the right on the far side of the harbour.

fleet, but she can stop at Therapia and let uncle come and gratify his curiosity, and then tell her all about it.

I have picked up a few trashy things from the town; they may, however, be prized in England some day. I will send them home by Kingscote.[36] I have actually got a chair to sit on, and am now writing on a card-table. Prices here are still very exorbitant, especially anything in the grub line.

When exploring Sebastopol and its surrounding works, I was much struck with the indefatigable labour that must have been entailed on the Russian soldier in throwing up and constructing such formidable bomb proof earthworks within their bastions under the skilful direction of their great and renowned Engineer, General Todleben.[37] The Guards on duty were able to take refuge in these bastions from the destructive fire that was hailed upon them from the allied batteries.

The withdrawal from the Malakoff and the Redan, and the movement of the Russian defenders across the harbour, effectively brought the war to an end although the war was to officially continue until the Treaty of Paris was signed on 30 March 1856. Although the Allies only controlled the area of the city south of the harbour, the strategic objective of the war, to render the naval facilities at Sevastopol ineffective had been achieved. The government in London wanted General Simpson and the other Allied commanders to launch a full-scale attack on the Russian field army which was still in its position on the Mackenzie Heights near Inkerman, but no such action was taken. Instead, activity focussed upon the destruction of the Russian defences and facilities in and around the harbour at Sevastopol. At the end of September, a combined force of Allied troops and warships (18,000 French, 17,000 Turks and less than 1500 British) were sent against the town and harbour of Eupatoria, north of Calamita Bay where the Allies had landed in September 1854. This operation was mismanaged and lasted (as far as Britain was concerned) until November. The severe criticism that General Simpson was subjected to, both in the Crimea and in London, led to his resignation on 29 September when he was succeeded as C-in-C of the British forces in the Crimea by General Codrington. In October, an expedition was mounted to Kinburn, a Russian fortress on the tip of a peninsula controlling the Dneiper estuary. Following a naval bombardment the defenders asked for terms.

For the majority of British troops, the period immediately following the fall of Sevastopol meant taking part in various military and engineering operations that would consolidate their position. Many members of the infantry regiments were transferred to the Land Transport Corps and the Army Works Corps and became involved in the construction of roads and improvements to the railway that had been built earlier in the year from Balaklava to the British front-line batteries. Inside Sevastopol, the British destroyed the dry docks and the French destroyed Fort Nicholas.

The British Army spent its second winter in the Crimea under much improved conditions, the construction of hutted encampments having been undertaken the previous spring. Wherever possible, the soldiers found sporting and leisure diversions that helped to pass the time. For the officers, theatrical productions, horse races, cricket matches and tours of the surrounding countryside featured heavily in their correspondence and memoirs.

In December, the Austrian Empire issued Russia with an ultimatum in which it was made clear that, unless the terms of negotiations held in Vienna the previous spring were met, she would join in the war on the side of the Allies. On 16 January 1856, Tsar Alexander II accepted the terms and a peace conference opened in Paris on 25 January which resulted in a ceasefire in the Crimea. The peace treaty was signed in Paris on 30 March and ratified on 27 April.

1st October

Now that the excitement of taking the town is at an end, camp life will become rather monotonous. At present we are engaged preparing our camps for the winter – building little cook-houses, stables for our nags, etc. Last week Fitzroy[38] and I were busy erecting a good building for our ponies, partly of stone, which is very scarce and difficult to get, and partly of wood taken from the houses of Sebastopol. It has to be brought; up on our ponies a distance of 3 miles, and it is a great catch if we can bag a commissariat cart for three or four hours. A few blocks of houses have been told off to each Division from which to procure wood. The Artillery have a great pull over us, as they have their waggons to send to the town. Although we have taken the south side we shall not be comfortably settled in houses this winter. The greater part is a heap of ruins; the only habitable portion is that close to the harbour edge, all of which is commanded from the north side by the Russians, who have thrown up battery upon battery, several of which have, already opened on our fatigue parties and done some damage. There seems to have been some want of foresight on our part, as we are only just beginning to think of building some batteries, which must now be constructed under fire, and all our guns and mortars have been withdrawn from the old batteries, and taken back half way to Balaklava, so when the new works we are building near Fort Paul are completed, the Artillery will have to drag their guns back again, and put them on the harbour front. We have been placed under orders to be in readiness to take the field.

The French, I believe, reconnoitred past Baidar, and found the country impracticable for operations against the enemy. It appears to me it is a great loss of valuable time not undertaking something from Eupatoria before the winter sets in. What is the use of keeping the Cavalry here? They should be doing something, or else have remained on the Bosphorus, as they can be of no use in an entrenched camp.

Road-making and digging drains is the order of the day, the advantage of which will be felt within a couple of months, and prevent us falling into the same plight we

Panoramic view of Sevastopol from the heights near the southern defences. In the distance can be seen the Russian barracks.

Panoramic view of Sevastopol from the heights near the southern defences. Fort Nicholas is located on the nearest headland.

Panoramic view of Sevastopol from the heights near the ruins of the Malakoff.

were in last winter. If ever we return to England we shall be up to all sorts of dodges. I never thought that I should have to earn my bread by breaking stones on the roadside and digging ditches; certainly a military life is a very comprehensive one, and the soldier has to be a Jack-of-all-trades.

Most of our officers are in some way or another preparing a winter establishment. Fitzroy[39] and I are going to share Kingscote's[40] hut, as he is going off next Saturday with Graham[41] and Maude.[42] A hut is not much more comfortable than a tent, but I am in hopes of improving my part of it before the cold weather sets in. Each officer's hut is divided into four rooms, so I have only the one side to look after; Pratt[43] inhabits the other half, and is a natty fellow, so will probably make his side snug. I am going to erect a closed porch with a side entrance, to prevent the wind blowing straight in; the other side I shall build up with bottles, as they are more easily procured than stones. I shall also try if I cannot manage a fireplace; it is much more cheerful than a stove. Fuel to keep the pot boiling will be no easy matter to obtain; last winter we had plenty of roots at Inkerman. Fitzroy[44] is thinking of building a bunk for himself, and if we are doubled up I shall most likely sleep in my tent, and make the hut the sitting-room.

The regiment has put aside one of the Government huts for a reading-room, and it is proposed to try and establish a sort of scratch mess, which will be a great advantage in the long, dreary, winter evenings, and will keep the officers together, so we shall see and know more of the new hands.

In last night's orders it is intimated that we are to have a clasp for Sebastopol, and the regiments are to bear the name on their colours; having the clasp does not show much distinction for the work done in the trenches, as every one who has landed will have it. Who ever set foot in the Crimea before the taking of Sebastopol, if only for twenty-four hours, gets the medal, and if the clasp is given in the same way without restrictions, it will be absurd. The Cavalry have more honours than we have, and I should like to know what they have done towards taking the town! I have now got my medal on my left breast with two clasps; only a small number have yet been received, and they have been given to those who have been here the longest.[45]

It is reported the French have done some dashing thing near Eupatoria, taken five guns and surprised a body of Cavalry. Please instruct Buckmaster[46] to send out my tunic, etc., sharp, as my coatee is falling off my back. Bertram[47] went home to Jersey a week ago. I have a box to send you some day when I can get a good opportunity, but I do not like encumbering Kingscote,[48] who has now only one hand.

Two ensigns[49, 50] joined us the other day rather rarities in this part of the world. Last week I was the only captain left doing duty with the Regiment, but there are now four. Rowlands[51] has succeeded to the brigade majorship, vice poor Rooke,[52] 47th, who has died.

On the 20th September, our Colonel[53] gave an anniversary dinner to the Alma lot; it shows how few there are left of us, when I tell you there were only six present. Yesterday there was another blow-up in the town at the barracks, which are still burning; a poor sentry who was 200 yards off was killed by a stone.

I receive the newspapers you kindly send regularly, and pass them on to the men in hospital, who are delighted with them. I have heard nothing of my batman. The loss falls on myself, as the public money was money due to the men. The scoundrel was a well-conducted, quiet lad, but still waters run deep; he never had a crime recorded against him. I had a note from Moncrieff[54] by the last mail, saying he had sent me a good supply of beer.

19th October

Since I last wrote, William Aitchison[55] has arrived. I was in Balaklava seeing about berths for our poor wounded officers, and heard that the *Ripon* was lying outside the harbour, so I persuaded the boatmen to take me out to her, although it was rather rough; I stayed to dinner, and on going on deck afterwards, discovered that my rowers had made off, and there was no boat to take me on shore, so I had to put up for the night, but I felt rather uncomfortable till I got back to camp, lest I should miss our fellows who were going off that morning, as I had their passage warrants in my possession. However, I managed to get off to shore before breakfast, and was in plenty of time.

The other day W.A.[56] and I had a long ride, and I showed him all over Inkerman and the neighbourhood; we afterwards dined tête-à-tête in his camp. To-day we rode over to the French Guards to see a French officer about a nag that he was thinking of purchasing, but it had been previously sold. The officer was very civil, and took us to his club and gave us beer, and was much pleased when we informed him that the expedition had been successful, and that Kinburn[57] had been taken. You might send me a map to refer to, along with a pocket English Prayer-Book.

You will be sorry to hear of poor Johnston's[58] death; his duty as Provost-Marshal was too hard for him, and broke him down. The last time I saw him he was much altered from what he was before the war; he used to be a strong, hearty-looking man. Not getting the value of his commission will be a great loss to his children.

Mr P—,[59] to whom father gave a note of introduction, called on me about three weeks ago with a captain of one of the ships. After showing them some civility, I escorted them to the right attack, and pointed out the best way for them to see the town. I lent him my telescope, and was surprised he had not returned it; a note, received to-night, explains the reason; when jogging along the road it dropped out of the case, and he lost it; I am very sorry about it as it was a first-rate one, and I have had it throughout the campaign; I got it from poor Nasmyth[60] when at Constantinople. If the box you are sending has not been despatched, you might put in four skins of black leather to line the bottoms and legs of trousers.

I have been rather sold about the occupation of the hut I spoke about, owing to the arrival of more officers, and Dixon,[61] being next senior captain, to me, put in a claim to the Colonel[62] that he was entitled to part of a hut before a subaltern. I am pretty comfortable at present, and am preparing for the winter by building a stone hut with a good fireplace in it, which will be much better than a quarter of a Government hut with a stove in it. It is very difficult now to get a man to work, as all are employed on the roads, etc., so I fear it will be some time before my edifice is finished. I am thinking of piling up wood for the fire in my tent, so you see we hope to be in snugger quarters this winter. We have fitted up a hut as a mess and dining-room.

We are all much disappointed to see by the papers received by this mail that some men who have not done a day's trench duty have been recommended over our heads, all because of their having interest, or being on the Staff. Some of those mentioned have done next to nothing, and have had every night in bed since the siege began, and some of them have hardly ever been under fire. It is very disheartening and unfair to those who have had to endure all the rough and hard work of the campaign.

The Guards are surprised to find that no mention has been made of them, and we are more than astonished how the Highland Division come to be noted in despatches. We are now up at five o'clock each morning to stand to our arms and wait Rusky's attack till broad daylight; it was rather cold this morning: I had my tub and breakfast at half-past seven.

1st November

I have been much engaged this last week road-making – up every morning at 5 a.m., on a working party till 5.30 p.m., breaking stones on the road-side (rather a come-down in the world, but part of a soldier's life). I am happy to say I have completed my last turn for some time to come, I would much sooner do twenty-four hours in the trenches than these road fatigues.

Young Gott[63] is now staying with me; he turned up last Sunday, and I have given him a shake-down, but having been daily on duty since his arrival, I have not been able to go about much with him; the other day he accompanied a party to Baidar, and had a pleasant excursion. He has been travelling for some time in the East, and seems to have had rather a surfeit of sight-seeing; he was present at the bombardment of Kinburn.

I have not yet succeeded in getting my house up, owing to my absence from camp, and when the master is away I find little is done; I hope to have it nearly finished before this lovely weather breaks. I must now to bed as I am up so early in the mornings.

19th November

Having been much occupied with my house lately, I have not been as regular as usual in writing; twice as much work is executed when I am superintending it; but up to this

Facing: Officers of the 41st Regiment in the camp at Sevastopol, May 1856. Back row (L–R): Assistant-Surgeon Gulland; Captain William Allan; Lieutenant Johnson; Lieutenant-Colonel Goodwyn; Captain Page; Brevet-Major Rowlands; Quartermaster Elliott; Captain Bligh. Front row (L–R): Captain Fitzroy; Major Barnard; Surgeon Scott; Captain Harvey.

date I don't think I have allowed more than a fortnight to elapse without sending a few lines homewards. This evening for the first time I am writing beneath the roof of my new habitation, with a cheerful wood fire blazing in the grate; the house is all but finished, but I am waiting for the plaster to dry before sleeping in it. I have just returned from dining with Birmingham[64] [sic] of the Buffs, with whom I travelled during my Italian tour.

Our prospect for this winter is very cheerful compared to the last; we do not expect to have much more to do than to look after our own comforts along with those of the soldiers; drilling in the fine weather will be our chief work.

By telegraph you will have heard of the dreadful explosion the other day. It was appalling; at the moment one thought that either the end of the world had come, or that the whole place was mined. It can never be ascertained how it originated, but gross carelessness must have been the cause of its being so alarming, as shells were thrown more than three-quarters of a mile, which could only have been done by their having been placed on the top or in very close proximity to the powder. No one here has ever before witnessed such a volley of projectiles, the newcomers feel themselves quite entitled to a medal and clasp for the fire they were under! At our distance from the French siege train (over half a mile) we had three huts blown to pieces; wonderful to relate, only one man was killed; the explosion shook houses and displaced articles from the shelves a mile off. It was most fortunate that the windmill, which is used as our powder magazine, did not catch fire. The casualties are estimated at over 400, and the loss of property very great; one of the huts destroyed was occupied as a French hospital.

The last mail brought the long-expected brevet, which in most instances is very judiciously given, but of course there are individual heart-burnings. I can't say I feel altogether satisfied; I have, unfortunately, not yet completed six years' service, and by the regulations an officer cannot be promoted to a brevet majority before he has been that time in the Army. All those who have been promoted have longer service than I have, although our dates as captains are the same, but having been out here the whole time, and gone through everything, as well as having been specially recommended by my commanding officer, should give me an equal, if not a prior claim to some who have received the reward. I feel myself entitled to ask for it, if not at present, at least on the 12th of July, when I shall have completed my six years.

A number of changes have taken place among the heads of our army; General Barnard[65] has now got our Division. I am looking forward anxiously for my boxes, which I know will contain several useful articles. My gun I sent home by Moncrieff.[66] We have not yet succeeded in getting our mess established for want of planking for the roof of the kitchen, but we hope to have it set going before the end of the week.

On the anniversary of Inkerman bonfires were blazing all over the various camps, and reels were kept up to a late hour at night. The weather now looks as if winter will soon set in; at present it is cold and wet, but lately we have had lovely weather. The roads are all but finished, and a locomotive plies along the railway line from Balaklava to the first incline. By to-night's orders we see that the gun-boats have destroyed six rows of corn stacks 2 miles long near Gheisk[67] – not a bad haul! I feel rather loth to quit this comfortable bunk for my miserable tent, but it's getting late, so I must to bed.

3rd December

For the last twelve days I have been rejoicing in my comfortable house; the weather has been very wet and wintry, and we are up to our ankles in Crimean mud. Now we find the advantage of the roads at which we had to toil after the siege operations were over. The working parties are much reduced, but still we are called upon every now and then, but we cannot complain of hard work, as except for the road parties, the army has only to furnish a few guards for the town and the Redan. The Engineers are busy mining the Docks, and will soon be ready to blow them up. Rusky has of late been firing a good deal, but there are very few casualties.

I wrote a letter to our Colonel[68] about my brevet majority, and he has submitted it along with a recommendation from himself; it has gone as far as headquarters for transmission to England. I shall be anxious to know the issue.

Our mess has been going for more than a week, and it succeeds admirably; it is a great improvement from our grubbing by companies, and more sociable. By day the hut is a reading-room and we have a variety of papers; we are going to establish a book club. Messing is optional, but all have joined with the exception of the paymaster and the quarter-master, who rose from the ranks, and do not attend because of the extra expense. I am breakfasting there at present, but when all the good things arrive which I hear are on the way for me, I may be tempted to confine myself to my house in the mornings. I have taken one of my subalterns[69] into my abode; he has not been very well, and I thought it would be a benefit to him to move out of his damp tent till his own edifice is finished, which he is knocking up next to mine.

Byam[70] is ordered home by a medical board; he has disposed of his house for £10; it is not nearly so good as the one I have built; I could get £15 or £20 for mine. The Colonel[71] and Skipwith[72] have got leave till the 29th February, the latter on 'urgent private affairs,' having come into some property. Could you not manage to induce some one to leave me a few thousands which would require my presence in England? We do not think Skipwith will come out again.

I stand well for purchase for my majority, but there is not much use thinking of such a thing when the first action may bowl half of us over. I am going to dine with W.A.[73] to-morrow, if weather permits, but now it is no joke going out in these black wet nights, when there are no cabs to set you down at the door; it is not easy to thread one's way through the different camps in the dark. Last Sunday W—[74] attended our Division kirk, which is a large Government stable [hut] converted into a place of meeting; it was given up by General Windham[75] when he was our Brigadier. It is pouring rain, but as I am brigade captain, I must go and turn out the different guards.

Frazer,[76] the Adjutant, has offered to pay my passage home if I will give up to him

An unidentified officer and NCOs of the 41st Regt in the hutted camp, May 1856. Based upon a Robertson photograph. Note the drum-major on the left (possibly John McNab) and the two drummers (one standing, one lying on the ground).

my house, which offer I accepted, but have since made a compromise with him, as he wishes to have my horse also; so now he is going to give me £50 for the house and horse.

Lieut Edward W.B. Lowry, 41st Regt.
Royal Welsh Museum, Brecon

There was a little difficulty made about my leave at headquarters, as we were short-handed in captains, but Page[77] arrived from Malta, so that was soon squared. Dr Scott,[78] our surgeon, and I arranged to travel together. We secured passage warrants and berths on board the S.S. *Oneida*,[79] and sailed on the 8th December from Balaklava Harbour. We transhipped at Constantinople into the French steamer, *Jourdain*,[80] on the 10th for Marseilles.

There were more than forty officers on board, all bound for dear old England, and a very jovial party we were, every one being in good spirits at the thought of the agreeable change from the dangers and hardships of the past year and a half. Owing to quarantine we could not land at Athens. We reached London in time to spend a Happy Christmas in Scotland with the old folks at home.

William Allan, having served throughout the campaign from the period spent in Varna, to the landing at Calamita Bay, through the battles of the Alma and Inkerman and the entire siege of Sevastopol, was able to travel to Britain on leave in December 1855, returning to Sevastopol in March 1856.

Guards' Camp, Crimea, 7th March

By the above address, you see that I am again located in the Crimea. W. Aitchison[81] has given me a shake-down for to-night; he is looking very hearty. For the present I am living on my friends, and have a bed in Ned Lowry's[82] hut; but hope to get a portion of a hut that is now occupied as an Orderly Room, but which is too near the officers' quarters to be convenient for that purpose. On my return I met with a very warm welcome from all my comrades.

Camp Near Sebastopol, 14th March

My last was from the Guards' camp; since then we have had an improved change in the weather, the snow is entirely gone, and when Fitzroy[83] and I were on the Redan guard yesterday, it was as mild as summer. The Redan works are very much altered; all the guns have been taken out, and fatigue parties are engaged daily in pulling down the parapets to get the wood out of the bomb-proof chambers, where the Russian soldiers had shelter from our fire. The works do the Russians great credit; it is wonderful how they succeeded in getting the massive spars up from the dockyard and arsenal.

The preparations that are going on show the campaign, if the war is continued, will be elsewhere. Balaklava is to be fortified, and piers made at Kazatch Bay. The French are in a wretched state, and are building their hopes on peace; in their camp on the Tchernaya many have been dying.

Major Steward[84] has unexpectedly arrived from Malta. I am still sleeping in Ned Lowry's[85] hut, but I wish I was settled in my own compartment. We are all on the *qui vive* about peace or war, and are looking forward to a telegram deciding the question.

During the armistice, we have been fraternising a little with Rusky; they much appreciate the value they get from the English coin by our purchases. Several officers have been under arrest for transgressing the boundary; the Tchernaya should have been made the line.

Fernoyle, my batman, who deserted and went off with my money, has been heard of in Russia, and my old servant Cuthbert,[86] who was taken prisoner at the Redan, died on the north side from his wound. I have only Fitzroy[87] at present for my subaltern, but I am applying for King,[88] who has come up from Malta. I want a sub who will do work, some of them are very careless young chaps. It was unfortunate that I did not receive the Horse Guards' letter before my departure, offering me my passage back. If I had known that they would have recognised our waiting for the Government steamer, I need not have hurried away. I saw Mrs Swaby[89] in Paris, and also my godson, both looking well.

Owing to my being on duty in the Redan last night, I was unable to dine with W.A.,[90] and attend the Guards' theatricals in the evening, at which General Codrington[91] and some other swells were present.

Camp, Good Friday, 21st March

The post due yesterday has not yet arrived. W.A.[92] is expecting to see in the *Gazette* that he has got his company; the promotion will send him home, there being no vacant company for him here.

Those who landed in the Crimea after the 9th September are crying out because they are not receiving a medal. My name was submitted some time ago to receive the Legion of Honour for my services, but I have not yet heard anything more of it.

Next Monday the Guards' Spring Meeting is to come off on the Tchernaya, for the benefit of the Russians; there will be great fraternising that day. They say General

A group of officers and men of the 41st Regiment in the camp at Sevastopol, May 1856. On the left is the local Crimean goat, 'Billy', which became the regiment's first goat mascot and lived until 1861. Captain Fitzroy is lying on the ground in the centre of the front row. None of the other officers can be positively identified. The figure on the right appears to be a very young boy. This photograph shows the wooden hutments provided for the army during 1855, the variations in the uniforms and the rather dishevelled appearance of the officers at the end of a very unpleasant campaign. The drum in the foreground is one of three captured after the fall of Sevastopol and still held by the regiment.

Luders[93] has entered a horse; a number of exchanges have taken places between us and the Ruskies – generally I think, to the advantage of the latter!

We are longing to know whether there is to be peace, in which every one believes. I have had quite enough of this sort of life, a few months' stay in England is apt to make one very discontented; what I looked upon as a grand mansion in the month of November, I now regard as a wretched hovel!

Sebastopol, 11th April

On receiving the news of peace on the 2nd, a salute of 100 guns was fired. It was very quick intelligence, considering that the telegraph is not at present working between this and Varna. Yesterday's orders allow us to cross the Tchernaya and go into the interior of the Crimea, so parties are being made up for four or five days' excursions. Harvey,[94] Page,[95] and Bligh[96] started this morning. I will not go for a week or more, and by that time I shall have picked up several wrinkles of what is necessary to take with me.

There is a talk of the 41st going to Canada, but the various destinations of the regiments are not yet known. The Mackenzie Heights are strongly fortified, and would have puzzled us to take them by a direct approach. The Russians are encamped there in large numbers, and the forest, where we made the flank march, has all been cut down. Their camps are very dirty, and the appearance of the men slovenly; they don't seem hard up for provisions; they are allowed to go freely about in our camp, and those who have not imbibed too much carry away with them a quantity of tea and sugar, etc., but owing to their predilection for liquor, they are frequently seen afterwards lying on the roadside.

The field allowance being stopped, our men have not now so much money to expend. The Russians go about in their long grey greatcoats; they must be much struck with the clean and smart appearance of our soldiers. We have brigade parades twice a week.

The army is now chiefly employed in collecting the Russian shot from behind the batteries, and taking it to the nearest point of the railway; the quantities are enormous. A year's pay or some prize-money ought to be forthcoming for our doings, or it would be fairer still to have a certain sum for every month's service. Tell M—[97] I have got some crocus roots for her, and marble from the Emperor's steps, with pieces of granite from the docks, and to-day I received a bullet from one of the doctors, to be labelled, 'Taken out of a man's thigh.' Would you like a Russian kitten? Page[98] has promised me his when he leaves.

Now that our mess is broken up, the things you sent me are coming in very useful, both to myself and my friends. Pratt[99] has been laid up for some time with a severe attack of influenza. Fitzroy[100] is promoted, so I must look out for some more subs, and will wait to see what the Depôt boys are like before fixing on another Light Bob. Subs are very scarce with us at present.

25th April

Since my last letter we have had two grand displays; the whole British force was reviewed on the 17th inst. The Russian Staff were present, and were astonished to see such a magnificent display, and so finely equipped an army: the men looked extremely well and healthy, and the Artillery could not have been better turned out even from their stables in England. The country has lavished its money, but now it has a well-appointed young army, and though the French have been dying by scores throughout the winter, our men have been very healthy. We were drawn up in a line of columns on the plateau, near headquarters. The Highlanders did not get back to their camp near Balaklava till about eleven at night. I was not in the ranks, so had a good opportunity of seeing the show, and had some conversation in French with a Russian Staff officer, who expressed his admiration of our troops. Yesterday we had another review of Infantry only, and performed several manoeuvres in the Plains of Balaklava; such a sight will never be seen again. Major Barnard[101] is away for a week, so I am acting major till his return; it is a great pull being mounted.

Four of us have obtained eight days' leave next week, so propose making a trip round by Bakshisarai, Simpheropol, Aloushta, Yalta, Baidar, etc., and we may perhaps go up Tchatir Dagh, if there is not too much snow. The Russian officers have been very civil to those who have been up the country; everything is very expensive, especially forage for horses; we shall take a cart, six horses, and two servants with us.

The 9th, 17th, 39th, 62nd, and 63rd Regiments leave at once for Canada with two batteries of Artillery. These regiments came abroad at the time that we were under orders for the West Indies, so we think there is every chance of our going home. A large portion of the Russian force is leaving the Crimea.

9th May

Since returning from my trip, I have not had time to send a line to say how very much we enjoyed it. We came back delighted with the beautiful scenery and change of air, though our beauty suffered a good deal from the bright sun's rays. I have been spending the greater part of the last few days rambling about in company with W.A.,[102] who leaves to-morrow in the *Melbourne*[103] for England. On Wednesday I dined at his mess, and last night Scott,[104] Fitzroy[105] (Coldstream Guards), and he dined with me I am sending to each of the sisters by him a bracelet from Simpheropol. It is work made in the Caucasus. In the same box you will find some souvenirs of the siege in the shape of blocks of stone and marble, which could be cut for paper weights. The hand grenade may make into an inkstand set on the granite from the docks; there is also a Russian thimble for any old maid who will accept of such a gift.

I have bought some of Robertson's[106] photographs of the town, Redan, etc.; they are much better than Fenton's,[107] and are only 5*s*. each. Fenton was charging £2 for them when I was in Edinburgh.

We are still uncertain with regard to our future destination, but I am glad to say it is not to be Malta. The following corps are detailed, 3rd, 46th, and 68th, Corfu; 1st, 14th,

21st, 28th, 31st, 47th, 48th, 57th, and 71st, Malta; and the 13th, 30th, 55th, 89th, and 92nd, Gibraltar. No regiments are to go to the West Indies at present. General Barnard[108] is to command at Corfu. I wish we were going to the Ionian Islands.

Seven French medals have now been received for our non-commissioned officers and privates; they are the same as those given to the soldiers of the French Army. It is a difficult duty, selecting the proper men to receive them, and will probably cause some dissatisfaction and envy.

Some of our steamships have come into Sebastopol Harbour. One of them ran aground to-day, and it was a long time before they could get her off again.

13th May

I must now give you an outline of our eight days' trip in the country; our party consisted of Scott,[109] Pennefather,[110] Cornwall,[111] and self, a cart and seven horses, of which two were used for the cart; three servants, one to drive the cart, another to ride postillion, and the third to cook, etc. Our baggage was – one bell tent, one piquet ditto, for the servants, a waterproof sheet, and blankets per man, which, with our own kits and forage for ourselves and horses, made a heavy load.

We started on the 29th of last month, having despatched the cart in advance by the Traktir Bridge and Mackenzie's Farm. We baited on the banks of the Belbeck for a couple of hours, and then went on to Bakshisarai where we encamped. It is a poor town, with nothing inviting or interesting about it, and built very much the same as the Turkish villages. We went early to roost after a feed from our larder, having had an enjoyable but fatiguing day. The following morning we were early in the saddle, partaking only of a cup of coffee and biscuits, promising ourselves something more substantial at the Alma; we halted at the river, and had a delicious bathe about 10 a.m., which sharpened our appetites and made the ham rapidly disappear. At 3 p.m. we raised our canvas on the far side of Simpheropol, on the banks of the Salgher, and then had a stroll through the town; we heard a Russian band playing in the gardens, many Rusky officers were present listening to it, and some ladies, but none of them very attractive. A short visit to the capital of the Crimea is quite enough to satisfy one's curiosity, the houses are similar to those that once stood in Sebastopol. All along the road from our camp we found no want of supplies, there being plenty of fresh meat, arid bread, and even some luxuries. The shops and bazaars were all open, and the natives selling their various kinds of merchandise. We were independent of hotels, and returned to our camp for dinner. Next morning, after a bathe and breakfast, we sauntered through the bazaar and purchased some souvenirs; the shopkeepers are making a good thing out of us, and will remember the British officer and his money for some time. Very few French have found their way so far into the interior. We had an early dinner, and then started for Ennis-sala, which is at the foot of the Tchatir Dagh, and had a pleasant ride till dusk, very glad to escape from the constant sight of soldiers with their transport waggons, which were passing incessantly all the way along the route from the Belbeck to Simpheropol. In many parts the road from the interior was half a mile broad, which showed the difficulty the Russians must have had with their transport during the wet months. The main road being entirely cut up in the winter, the waggons must have been nearly axle deep in mud in some parts. There appeared to be no large Depôt of supplies at any place. The horses were in good condition, but the route was marked with the signs of many a dead animal.

We did not go up to the top of the mountain, as we found we had not a day to spare. On the Simpheropol side of the hill there was a battery of Artillery, and on the crest of the Pass, there had been an encampment of troops. Trees were cut down, and laid ready to obstruct the road at a moment's warning, so it was evident the Ruskies thought a landing at Aloushta might be attempted, and were prepared to meet it. A bridge across the ravine had been mined, and the destruction of it would have prevented our Artillery advancing. It would have been difficult to take the Pass, if it had been defended by a few thousand men, although a landing could not have been opposed, as our ship-guns could easily command the beach and the valley.

It is about 7 miles from Aloushta to the Pass, by a steep winding road. The village is a wretched place, chiefly inhabited by Tartars, not a good house in the place, but, luckily, we carried our own habitations about with us.

The next day, the 3rd, we started early, and proceeded along a very good mountain road, with the sea in the distance below us. The ride to Yalta was charming, embracing a diversity of scenery, with fine rocky hills, cultivated valleys, and bold coast line; the road winds along the cliff, and at every turn of the headlands a new prospect opens out to view. Yalta is a beautiful little spot lying at the foot of a lovely valley; there are many country residences interspersed.

We pitched our tents as usual, but finding there was an hotel there, kept by an Englishman and his wife, we availed ourselves of it for dinner. When strolling about waiting for the arrival of our cart, the Commandant asked us to come into his house, and he regaled us bountifully with Crimean wine from Prince Woronzoff's vineyards. I cannot say much for the good quality of the beverage, it is like most country wines, sharp and acid, and requires a little cognac to qualify it. The hotel people have lived in this neighbourhood for fifteen years, Mr Hunt (architect of the Orianda Palace and Prince villa)[112] is an uncle of the manager's wife; they were very civil and obliging, and gave us an excellent dinner, with capital turbot and a round of beef, a vast improvement upon our ration cattle. Everything was so tempting, we agreed to have oysters and a heavy lunch the next day before starting.

Early next morning (as we always availed ourselves of water whenever we had an opportunity), Cornwall,[113] Pennefather,[114] and I had a dip in the sea. Just as Corny and I had finished bathing, Pennefather stepped into the water; a wave took him off his legs, and not being able to swim, he gradually rolled out to sea. He sank twice; seeing this, I rushed in to help him, and when up to my neck, I put out my hand, which he grasped, and I tried to draw him back but failed, and found I was getting out of my depth. I managed to free myself from him, and told him to catch hold of my body, but instead of doing that, he caught me round the neck. Luckily, I had turned my back, so was able to swim on shore with him, but when I got him on land, I had to knock him down before he would let go his hold. He had quite lost his presence of mind, and my neck bore the marks of his claws for some days. I vowed I would never bathe with him again; he all but drowned himself, and very nearly succeeded in doing the same kind office for me.

Before leaving Yalta I paid my respects to the Commandant, and presented him with three bottles of brandy, which was an article he could not procure. As a souvenir, he gave me a tablet of Crimean marble, and also a piece for one of my comrades. The ride from Yalta to Aloupka embraced scenery very much the same as that of the day before, only the views are more confined by the grand cliffs that overhang the road and the sea, and there were more palaces and villas with nicely laid out grounds. About 3 miles from Yalta we passed the palace of Count Potoski, which we visited; it is very handsomely furnished. A few miles further on is the Orianda Palace which belongs to the Queen Dowager, but it has not yet been occupied; it is a fine, noble-looking mansion, and luxuriously fitted up, but the site on which it is built is rather circumscribed. Near Aloupka is the Castle of Prince Woronzoff; we failed to gain admission to see over it, as there was no one about the premises.

In this neighbourhood we found a great difference among the country people, who are Tartars, and in a wretched state of poverty, as the Russians compelled them to part with everything, so that they should be unable to help the allies. There was no meat, eggs, bread, or milk to be bought, and the villagers were only allowed two span of oxen.

During our next day's tramp we had to remain near our cart to be ready to render assistance at some parts of the road which were difficult. We encountered three land-slips, in trying to overpass which many a cart had come to grief, but as we knew that two parties had overcome the obstacle, we were not going to be beaten. When we arrived at the first slip we were rather staggered, but after a good deal of recon-noitring, we discovered a place we thought was practicable, by returning a few hundred yards, and making a cut across the hills higher up.

This we accomplished, the cart and horse only once turning topsy-turvy. At the next slip, by dint of dodging about, and with the aid of a Cossack to lead us over the intricate country, we got over the worst of the day's work, and at the last slip, with careful steering and the help of pick and shovel, we surmounted all our difficulties. We met several parties that clay, who had abandoned the undertaking after many fruitless attempts and upsets, so we felt justly elated at our perseverance and success. It had taken us six hours to accomplish 7 miles! That night we halted among some ruined houses, 6 miles or so from Phoros Pass. The Russians had rendered the road very difficult of passage by hurling large blocks of rocks into it. The road to Phoros is fine wild scenery, but rather dreary looking from the stunted wood and want of cultivation. The next day we rode into camp through Baidar, the valley was looking beautiful, most of the trees just coming into leaf, and the orchards all in full bloom.

The round we had taken made a most delightful eight days' tour, and we returned to camp very sorry it was over. The trouble of packing and pitching the tents, and a certain degree of anxiety attending the cart, gave an additional zest and excitement to the trip. After receiving this you need not write any more to the Crimea, as we expect to start next week for Old England.

16th May

I am sorry that Jack[115] has allowed so much time to pass before going up for his examination, as the reduction of the army is about to take place, which will cause stagnation in all grades, and the Horse Guards will have few or no commissions to give away. The regiments that have gone to Canada and the Mediterranean have sent home the officers that come within the break, and before July the whole reduction will have taken place, which will make an aggregate number of about 900 officers. I would not be at all surprised if Jack is not appointed for six months at least. I have written to Algiers advising him to go home at once and try and pass the examinations in June, and father should use all his interest to have him appointed to a corps that has not been out here, he would have a better prospect of promotion; also, they are all so juvenile here, it would be a very bad school for him. Hongkong would be better for a young fellow than a Crimean regiment on its return to England, with so few old officers to look after the youngsters. There is no chance of Bush[116] getting his majority for some time to come, the Lieutenants will not purchase till the reduction has taken place. We do not know yet if the second Lieutenant-Colonel[117] will be put on half-pay. I wish we could pick out those we liked best to remain in the regiment; we shall lose some very good fellows.

The 46th and 68th embark to-morrow, and some other troops the next day. The French are clearing off sharp. On the return of the transports from Italy, our regiments will quickly disappear, but if England is to be our destination, we shall be one of the last corps to leave. We hope we may embark from Sebastopol Harbour. The huts are being pulled down to be sold, and they have begun to take up the railway, so it will not be long before we leave.

To-day we had races at the Tchernaya, which will be the wind-up of the Crimean sports. General Codrington[118] held a farewell inspection of our Division last Monday. Lord Panmure[119] has issued an Address to the Army, which contains a good deal of *soft sodder*, which is instead of prize-money.

Camp Near Sebastopol, 25th May

A party of us are going to the Alma to-morrow; it will be a long ride of about 50 miles. Barnard,[120] Fitzroy,[121] Scott,[122] Gulland,[123] King,[124] Cornwall,[125] Hall,[126] and self start at six o'clock, and hope to be on the battlefield before eleven a.m., where we will lunch and halt for some hours.

The forces in the Crimea are now rapidly diminishing, and the old 2nd Division no longer exists. The 30th and 55th sailed last Wednesday in the *Great Britain*[127] for Gibraltar, and the 47th are off in two days to their old station, Malta. This week will probably see all the Mediterranean regiments out of the Crimea, and then most likely will come the turn of the Guards and the Light Division for home.

Yesterday being the Queen's Birthday, there was another grand review in the plain of Balaklava, which I hope may be the last, as the summer is rapidly advancing. The French medals were distributed by the Generals to the soldiers of their several Divisions, and then a royal salute was fired, and three cheers for the Queen, ending up with a march past. General Pélissier[128] was present, looking as unhappy on horseback as usual. Seven medals were given to each of the regiments that had been out during the whole of the war. I think, on the whole, the selection of the men in the 41st to receive the medal gave satisfaction, though it was a difficult task to decide. There is no word yet of my Legion of Honour. I believe the names will appear in the *Gazette*, so you will most likely know of it before we do.

Yesterday we had a photographic group of the officers of the regiment taken, also one of the men. I have denuded myself of my beard; shaving has become quite a mania at present, and I, personally, do not think an appendage on the chin is an improvement to an Englishman.

The other day I had a pleasant ride with Barnard[129] and Gulland,[130] to Mangap Kalek by the Choulu Valley, and Aitodor through the Korelas Pass, and home by the Belbec and Mackenzie's Farm. The Russians are clearing away fast, the few that are left are under canvas. Cricket and rounders are now the chief amusement.

26th May

We have had a delightful day at the Alma, the weather was not too warm. Unfortunately, our time being short, we were unable to go over the whole of the position, so confined ourselves chiefly to the French part. Peddie,[131] King,[132] and Hall[133] were late in starting, and did not overtake us. On comparing notes afterwards we found that they did not reach the Alma at all; they went as far as the Katscha, and halted there, believing they were then on the battlefield. Peddie even imagined the vineyard the 41st had passed through, and drew attention to it! They returned to camp quite pleased with their day's excursion, and recounted the principal features of the ground. It turned out, however, that they had only passed two rivers instead of three! They were much disgusted when they discovered their mistake, and got well chaffed about it.

Scott[134] and I were the only two of the party who had been engaged in the fight on the 20th September. I shall try and see the ground again, and inspect the English position more fully.

Pennefather had a letter from Cox & Co., who state the 41st are to return home. We hope to be out of this in about a month, in spite of what Sir Charles Wood[135] says. The land transport will be the last to leave; the removal of that branch of the Service will take a considerable time.

13th June

To-morrow and Sunday will clear out all but four regiments who are to go before us. The 23rd, 33rd, 34th, and one of the Highland regiments go to-morrow, along with two ships of Artillery and one of invalids, and the 90th and 77th go the next day in the Queen, then there will be left the 97th, and three Highland corps, and one wing of the 19th. The *Rodney* is in harbour, and I believe some others, so we may be walked off in a day or two. I hope a transport may fall to our lot, and that we may escape the fetters of a man-of-war. We should be home in a third of the time in a good steam transport. I think father ought to come and meet us on our arrival. To-morrow we are to play the 49th a return match at cricket; the other day they beat us by three wickets.

7. Home

June–September 1856

The 41st Regiment, having been one of the first to arrive in Turkey in 1854, was one of the last regiments to leave the Crimea in July 1856. Allan's misgivings about the regiment's future service were to prove well-founded and in January 1857, the 41st embarked for the West Indies which, because of the poor health conditions prevalent there, was perhaps the most unpopular posting in the British Army.

Sebastopol, 16th June

This is the last letter you will receive from me from the Crimea; this morning the baggage was despatched to Balaklava to be placed on board a tug, and taken round to Kazatch Bay and there transhipped to the *Transit*;[1] about eleven o'clock we will be on board; six companies of the 49th go with us. As the *Transit* has not a good name, we do not expect to make a fast passage; she broke down at the naval review, when the members of the House of Commons were on board, and, like most Government ships, is none of the best. The captain says he will have to stop a day or two at all the different stations to have the engines cleaned. On arrival at Malta I will tip you a line. We do not know at which port in England we are to land, but expect it will be Portsmouth; we are now very uncomfortable, for to-day and to-night we have nothing to bless ourselves with. I hope to see General Ferguson[2] at Gibraltar.

Malta Club, 24th June

Here we are so far *en route* homewards, having had a beautiful passage, the sea being as smooth as a mill-pond; but of course something must go wrong on board a Government steamer, and we will be detained here for two or three days having the engine pipes mended; the last forty-eight hours men have been continually at work pumping out the water; the captain's wife is at Malta, so he will not be inclined to expedite matters. We are all very comfortable on board, but the steward is a horrid old screw. With the least rough weather the *Transit* rolls heavily, so we expect to catch it going through the Bay of Biscay. You may be on the outlook for us on the 10th or 12th, if all goes well. We have overtaken some of the vessels that left before us.

You will have seen that Bertram[3] has been made a brevet-major for his Crimean services; from February till August, he has not been in any battle, or the attack on the 8th September. Poor Bligh[4] was dreadfully sold this morning. An officer of the 49th came on board, and said the senior captain of the 41st had been made a brevet-major, so every one congratulated Bligh on his luck; but the mistake was soon discovered, and caused him great disappointment. We have no room on board for our Depôt, so they have to follow afterwards. Malta seems much the same as ever. Most of us dine this evening with our old chums, the 47th.

HMS *Transit*, off Portland Point, 12th July

When at Malta, where we were detained two days, I posted a few lines home via Marseilles. Our old friends, the 47th, treated us most hospitably, and entertained us during our sojourn. We left [Malta] on the 26th [June], and had a delightful passage to Gibraltar, passing several other regiments that had started two days before us. We arrived early in the-morning and stayed that day and all the next coaling, so had ample time to see the Rock and its vicinity. The first day I went with our Colonel[5] to call on the Governor-General, James Ferguson,[6] but he was not at home. Mrs Jarvis[7] and Miss Jenkins[8] are in England, also Hart[9] the A.D.C. That evening most of us dined with the 30th and 55th, and afterwards went to a ball at the theatre; the ladies were chiefly inhabitants of the Rock, only a few could speak English, but it was very good fun. The assembly was principally composed of officers of the garrison and daughters of the shopkeepers; dancing was continued till an early hour, and as the drawbridges are all up after dark, and the port closed, we accepted the shakedowns that were offered; the few hours' rest I had was at Elton's,[10] 55th. The next day I made an early call on the Governor and saw him and Captain Jarvis;[11] he asked me to lunch and dinner, but I was unable to accept, as I had arranged to ride to Algezares with Dr Scott[12] and the two Johnsons,[13] and we had to be on board by 5 p.m.

After leaving Gibraltar we had a strong head wind and encountered a severe storm, in which we lost our jibboom; we were making so little way the captain decided to put into Vigo to coal, where we remained for thirty-six hours, and landed our bands for the edification of the inhabitants. Some of the officers went to a small ball that was given on board a Spanish warship then in the harbour, I did not go, being quite satisfied with what I had seen of the Spanish beauties at Gibraltar. From Vigo we have had a favourable passage.[14]

HMS *Transit*, Portsmouth Dockyard, 13th July

We disembark at noon to-morrow, and proceed to Aldershot to be temporarily stationed there, as Her Majesty has notified her intention of reviewing us, and then we hope to be sent to some snug quarters. Please select some articles of my home kit, and send them as soon as possible. I do not require my heavy baggage at present, nor the iron bedstead, as I have a wooden stretcher. A pair of sheets, shirts, and some mufti will be useful. I see one of our men has been killed in the riots in Ireland, I hope we may be kept out of that country. This is a wet, disagreeable day, quite like Old

England, and very different from the beautiful blue skies we have left behind; if it clears I am going on shore, and will telegraph to you. Our band played on Sunday, I suppose for the last time for a while, as Sunday bands are now knocked on the head in England. I think it is carrying things too far.

Aldershot, 2nd August

I do not see the least probability of my being in Scotland by September, I wish we were off to our final destination, as no one can get leave till it is decided. We heard that we are likely to remain here longer than we expected; if so, we will start a scratch mess which will be a comfort; at present we are grubbing under difficulties. There is a club about a mile off, and by taking our servants to assist at table we can get a pretty good dinner. I asked the Colonel[15] to-day for another recommendation for a brevet, which he said he would be most happy to give, but I do not live in any great hopes, as they will most probably say they cannot make another captain a brevet-major in the 41st. I propose attending the levee on Tuesday. When I was with the Colonel he asked me who I thought ought to receive the Medjidie, and we selected the following: Captains Lowry,[16] Kingscote,[17] Fitzroy,[18] and Lieutenants Hill[19] and Lowry.[20] The Turkish Order is classed in our regiment as second to the Legion of Honour, which distributes the rewards more generally; in some regiments they have been classed as of equal merit, so the same individual receives both the foreign orders.

You would see in the papers that we have had a row with the German Rifles, which originated in a public-house quarrel between a soldier of our regiment and one of the German Legion; it came to a climax by the latter snatching the medal off the 41st man's coat, throwing it on the ground, and trampling on it, which naturally roused the feelings of the English soldiers. There has been a court of enquiry on the subject, and it has ended with three men of the piquet being confined, who will most likely be tried by Court-Martial for not helping to suppress the row; one of the three used his bayonet. Lieutenant Pack,[21] who was in charge of the piquet is under arrest; he is the junior officer of the regiment; most likely he will get off with a wigging for not having handled his men better, as when doubling up to the fight, he injudiciously gave the word: 'Fix bayonets.'

During the excitement some of the piquet were hit and knocked over with stones, so they charged and made free play with their bayonets. There might have been a more serious row the succeeding night if precautionary measures had not been taken in confining the regiment to camp. When it was on parade, the German Rifles came behind the huts and pelted the Light Company with stones, and it was all Major Barnard[22] and the other officers could do to prevent our men breaking off and charging the assailants.

Some of the men of the 49th and Rifle Brigade agreed, as the 41st were not permitted to leave camp, they would take up the quarrel, which might have led to a serious disturbance, so the Horse Guards thought it advisable to order the German Rifles off to another station.

Dover

On Monday we were glad to leave Aldershot where we had been most uncomfortable, as owing to our being sent there only for a short period, we were unable to establish a mess. The regiment is now under canvas near the citadel, from whence we have a good view overlooking the town and harbour. We are disappointed in not being put into barracks, having had enough of camp life during the last two years; as long as the fine weather lasts it is pleasant enough, but we are still in an unsettled state without a mess, and find it very expensive dining at an hotel every day. However, we hope to hire a house in the town for a temporary measure until we move to Shorncliffe.

I am sending you a copy of the answer to my application. I daresay in the next brevet *Gazette* ten years hence I may receive my brevet, when I am either a live or a dead major. A large batch of ensigns has joined us, we have not seen any such young sparks for many months, as in the Crimea they were quite extinct. I have got my Legion of Honour, it is more decorative than the English medal.

Rowlands[23] is to meet with a most enthusiastic reception on his arrival in Wales, and be presented with a sword of honour, value £160 and £100 to be expended in plate, or any other way he may wish. He is a generous-hearted fellow, and has asked the Committee to give the money to the widows and children of the men in his company who have fallen. I am keeping his horse for him during his absence on leave.

Our Depôt has moved from Ireland to Newport; now that they have come to England, it may be to my advantage to join it, instead of running my neck into the Yellow Jack [Yellow Fever], if we go to the West Indies in the spring. The Colonels of the different regiments were called together this morning to meet the new Brigadier-Generals Cameron,[24] 42nd, and Lord West,[25] late 21st, our chief. General Barnard[26] is commanding this district; we know him very well, as he commanded the 2nd Division in the Crimea.

Colonel Goodwyn[27] says it has been decided that the Highland Brigade is to go to Shorncliffe and our Brigade to remain here. My Colour-Sergeant Davies[28] is about to purchase his discharge from the service; he will be a great loss to me, having been a first-rate non-commissioned officer and accountant. I am giving him a silver watch and chain as a souvenir.

1st September — Our Depôt is on its way to Walmer; it will be pleasant being so near one another, it is only 8 miles from this, so we shall have continual intercourse.

8. In Conclusion

The regiment was in camp at Dover for about a couple of months and then went to Shorncliffe, but I was ordered to join the Depôt at Walmer, where I remained till October 1857, when I embarked for Jamaica to rejoin the headquarters of our regiment, which had left in the spring for that station. We returned to England in 1860, and were quartered at Aldershot for a year, then moved to the Isle of Wight, where the men were employed in constructing a military road between the forts near Freshwater. In 1862 the regiment was sent to the north of England, and I was quartered at Sunderland, I had previously spent several years of my boyhood there at the Grange School.

The 41st was stationed in Glasgow in 1863, and the following spring crossed the Channel to Ireland, and remained at the Curragh Camp and Richmond Barracks, Dublin, till it sailed for India in July 1865. On the 18th April I obtained my majority by purchase, having served more than ten years as a captain.

Our Indian service included three years at Agra, two at Subathoo, and three at Mooltan, during which period I made several shooting trips to Cashmere and the Himalayas, and also visited the principal sights of India; we next proceeded to Aden for fourteen months, returning to England in 1875, when we were again quartered at our old station, Shorncliffe.

I was appointed to the command of the Depôt companies at Milford Haven, and went with them to Cardiff, when the 41st regimental district was formed at that centre. On the 23rd May 1877 I succeeded to the command of the regiment, then stationed at Pembroke Dock. The following year we went to Aldershot, where we were quartered in the Permanent Barracks for two years, and then moved in 1880 to Chatham, but owing to the Afghan War we were suddenly ordered on foreign service to Gibraltar in August of that year, and had been there only a few months when we were sent to Natal on active service against the Boers in March 1881, where I was in command of the troops at Ladysmith, Newcastle, and Moy River, till I completed my five years' command in May 1882. It was with feelings of deep regret that I left the regiment, in which I had spent thirty-two years of my life.

During the Egyptian campaign of that year I was nominated to command the Reserve Depôt at Alexandria, and at the close of it was appointed to the 21st regimental district at Ayr, where I remained five years.

I was promoted to the rank of Major-General on the 2nd December 1889, and selected for the command of the troops in Cyprus, 9th October 1890, until the age clause necessitated my retirement in 1894. Towards the expiration of my soldiering a good service reward was conferred on me.

Epilogue

Mrs William Allan

During the period of my husband's command in Cyprus, he was glad to have the opportunity of gratifying the great desire he had always felt to revisit his old haunts in the Crimea, and go over once more the well remembered camping grounds and the scenes of his early active service.

In May 1893 he obtained a month's leave, and we left for Constantinople, where we remained a few days before crossing the Black Sea.

We met another General Officer who was bent on the same object as ourselves, General Kent,[1] late 77th, and it was with intense interest and pleasure that the two wandered together through Sebastopol and the surrounding country, although it naturally could not but awaken many sad reminiscences to both of them. Up and down the familiar ravines, in and out of the various positions where the old batteries and trenches had formerly been, they tramped once more, often pausing to bring to each other's recollection episodes which had occurred during the campaign, and noting the alterations that had taken place during the forty years which had elapsed.

With the exception of these long walks, I accompanied them on all the expeditions, but owing to the limited steam service between Constantinople and Cyprus, we had only a fortnight at our disposal, which was all too short a time to see and do all that we could have wished.

One of our first excursions was to Inkerman, where the 2nd Division had been encamped; we had passed the site of the Windmill, and were ascending the road which crosses the crest of the hill, when my husband stopped the carriage, remarking: 'This is about the place where my tent was pitched,' so we alighted, and had only walked a short distance, when I heard him exclaim: 'By Jove, this is the very hole we dug!' It is now nearly filled up, but is still deep enough to identify the spot over which he had pitched his tent, and where he and General Rowlands[2] lived together during the dreary winter months of 1854–55.

The battlefield is now covered with scrub and brushwood, and the ground, when I saw it, was thickly carpeted with a variety of small wild flowers similar to those which grow in Syria, presenting altogether a very different aspect from what it must have been when the troops were encamped there. That afternoon we visited the well-known cemetery on Cathcart's Hill, where, in addition to the monuments erected to the officers who were buried there at the time of the war, all the memorial tablets have now been collected from the scattered brigades and Division camps.

We lingered a long time over the graves of those brave soldiers who had fallen for their country, searching for and examining the tombstones for the names of individual friends. The cemetery was at that time well looked after, but we were sorry to hear that the Government intended to discontinue the services of a custodian. We had a delightful day exploring the Redan, Mamelon, Malakoff, etc., but with the exception of a few bullets, we could find nothing to bring away as a memento, as the soil has been turned over too often by regular searchers, who even now earn a livelihood by digging up and selling the lead and iron they discover, so little chance remains for a visitor to pick up anything but broken bottles, of which there is an innumerable supply everywhere, left, as our drosky man took pride in explaining to us by the *Inglese*!

There is a small enclosure in the interior of the Malakoff, in the wall of which a memorial tablet is erected to the French who fell there on 8th September 1855, on which these words are engraved:

Unis par la victoire,
Revues par la mort
Du soldat c'est la gloire
Des braves c'est le sort.

an inscription which appealed to us strongly, as being at once so simple and yet so touching. A caretaker lives in what remains of the Round Tower.

Another day we spent at St George's Monastery, from which there is an extensive view of the cliffs near Balaklava Harbour, against which so many vessels were wrecked in that fatal storm of the 14th November 1854.

Shortly before leaving the Crimea, we made a most enjoyable trip to Yalta, close to which is the Palace of Lavidia [Livadia], the summer residence of the Russian Royal Family. We drove through the Baidar Pass. We also rowed up the Harbour to the Tchernaya Valley and head of the Quarry ravine, returning to Sebastopol by way of the Sandbag Battery, and over the field of Inkerman to the plateau overlooking the scene of the Charge of the Light Brigade. It surprises me that in these days of travel, so few English ladies have visited the Crimea, considering how easily it can be accomplished, as it only takes twenty-four hours in a charming little Russian steamer from Constantinople, and on landing there is a comfortable hotel kept by a Swiss, and called Kist's Hotel; the house is built and the adjoining pleasure-gardens laid out on the site of what was Fort Nicholas. We shall always remember with gratitude the kindness and assistance we received from Mr Grierson, the Belgian Consul, and his wife, Mrs Grierson.

On our arrival the captain of the steamer telephoned to Mr Grierson, who came on board and helped us through the usual annoyance and delay of customs, etc., which we greatly appreciated, as we neither of us knew the Russian language, and during our stay in Sebastopol, he assisted us most kindly in many ways.

Captain Murray, the English Consul, was away from home on duty at Yalta, but on his return we had the pleasure of meeting him, and it is to him that my husband is indebted for the translation of the records of the Russian Memorial Monument of 'The Hundred Thousand.' I should like to give one hint which may prove useful to any person contemplating a visit to Sebastopol, and who cannot speak the Russian language. If they should at any time be hungry and unable to explain what they want, let them pronounce the simple word 'Bosh' and they will be surprised, and I have no doubt pleased, to find served up to them the excellent and familiar old friend, 'Scotch Broth!'

Notes

Chapter 1: Malta, Scutari and Varna

1. PS *Ripon*, a paddle steamer built at Money, Wigram & Son's Blackwall Yard in 1846. She was requisitioned in 1854 for use in the Crimean War. In 1864 she brought General Giuseppe Garibaldi to the United Kingdom for a meeting with Prime Minister Palmerston. In 1870, her engines were sold, and the vessel was converted into a brig for Caird & Co in Greenock.
2. Lieutenant John William Swaby, 41st Regt. Commissioned, 1 October 1850. Killed in Action (hit by a musket ball and nine bayonet wounds), Inkerman, 5 November 1854, aged 24. Married Everilda, daughter of Samuel Bamford Hamer of Hawnby, Yorkshire.
3. Lieutenant Hugh Charles Harriott, 41st Regt. Commissioned, 16 May 1851. Arrived in the Crimea 14 September 1854, present at the Alma. On 26 October 1854, he was in command of the Light Company when the Russian assault known as Little Inkerman began when he was shot through the body (broken collar bone). A brother officer wrote to Mrs Harriott: 'The gallant manner in which your son led his company against a far superior force called forth the admiration of General Adams, commanding the brigade, who has expressed to your son his high opinion of his conduct on this occasion.' Despite this, and probably because Harriott was only in temporary command of his company, Adams omitted his name from his despatch. Died in Scutari Hospital, 8 December 1854.
4. Lieutenant William Earle, 49th Regt. Commissioned, 17 October 1851.
5. Lieutenant Robert Corbet, 49th Regt. Commissioned, 22 November 1850.
6. Lieutenant Arthur Savory Armstrong, 49th Regt. Commissioned, 21 August 1849. Lieutenant, 5 December 1851.
7. Lieutenant William Watts Corban, 49th Regt. Commissioned, 12 July 1850.
8. SS *Vedetta,* a three-masted steam-powered ship.
9. Lieutenant-General Sir James Ferguson, KCB (1787–1865). Commissioned, 18th Regt 1801; transferred 43rd Regt; lieutenant 1804; captain 1806; major 1812; transferred 79th Regt; exchanged 85th Regt; lieutenant-colonel CO 3rd Regt, 16 May 1814. OC 88th Regt; exchanged 52nd Regt; colonel 1830; major-general 1841; lieutenant-general; general 1860. Served Peninsular War (wounded twice) and Walcheren. GOC Malta; Governor and C-in-C Gibraltar 1855. Resigned 1859. CB 1831; KCB 1855; GCB 1860. Died Bath, September 1865.
10. Lieutenant Henry Stratton Bush, 41st Regt. Commissioned, 16 April 1850 (by purchase). Landed in Crimea, 14 September 1854. Wounded severely in the arm at Inkerman, 5 November 1854, sent to Scutari Hospital, 9 November 1854. Returned to Britain. Brevet-major, 7 November 1856. Sardinian Medal, Turkish Medal.
11. Deputy Assistant Commissary General Edward Strickland. Appointed, 26 December 1840.

12. *Indus*, a paddle steamer built by Money, Wigram & Sons, Blackwall, 1847 for the Southampton–Alexandria service. Sold in 1869.
13. Captain Johnson Bourne, 17th Regt. Commissioned (by purchase), 11 January 1839; captain, 19 December 1851. Transferred to 41st Regt, 24 June 1853. Served in the Crimea from 14 September 1854 to 16 February 1885 and returned on 14 June 1855. Retired by the sale of his commission 14 July 1855. Captain 1st Derbyshire Militia. Died in Llandudno, 14 July 1856.
14. Major George Bagot, 41st Regt. Commissioned, 26 July 1835; captain, 4 July 1845; brevet-major, 19 October 1849.
15. Captain Charles Pelgué Bertram, 41st Regt. Born Jersey. Commissioned, 6 February 1847 (by purchase); brevet-major, 6 June 1856. Present at the siege of Sevastopol from February 1855.
16. Captain Hon Richard Handcock, 41st Regt. Born in Athlone on 25 July 1826, the eldest son of 3rd Baron Castlemaine, an Irish peer. Commissioned, 12 April 1844 (by purchase); lieutenant, 3 April 1846 (by purchase); captain, 26 November 1852 (by purchase). Resigned his commission April 1854. Succeeded his father as 4th Baron Castlemaine in 1869. Elected representative peer to the House of Lords 1874. Lord Lieutenant of Westmeath 1889–92. Married Hon Louisa Matilda Harris, daughter of 2nd Baron Harris, 10 February 1857; they had five daughters and three sons. Died Moydrum Castle, 26 April 1892. His uncle, Lieutenant-Colonel the Hon Henry Robert Handcock, 97th Regt, was killed in action at Sevastopol 8 September 1855.
17. Captain George Robert Fitzroy, 41st Regt. Born 1831, the eldest son of Lieutenant-Colonel George Fitzroy and Louisa Harris of Grafton Regis, Northamptonshire. He was the grandson of General Lord Charles Fitzroy and great-grandson of the 3rd Duke of Grafton. Commissioned cornet & sub-lieutenant 2nd Life Guards, 23 November 1849; transferred to 41st Regt, 22 March 1850. Landed in the Crimea, 14 September 1854, present at the battles of the Alma and Inkerman. Severely wounded at Inkerman, 5 November 1854, invalided to Scutari then to Britain aboard HMT *Harbinger*, February 1855. Returned to the Crimea and served during the siege of Sevastopol. Exchanged to the Coldstream Guards as ensign and lieutenant 12 January 1855. Major-general, 1 October 1886; retired 1889. Died 1898.
18. Captain Frederick Cherburgh Bligh, 41st Regt. Born 1829, son of Edward Bligh and Sophia Eversfield of Brittas, County Meath, Ireland. Commissioned, 15 March 1850; brevet major, 26 December 1856. Arrived in Crimea, 15 October 1854. Present at Little Inkerman, 26 October 1854. Severely wounded at Inkerman, 5 November 1854. Sent to Scutari Hospital, 9 November 1854. Returned to the Crimea, 12 July 1855. Present at siege of Sevastopol and storming of the Redan, 8 September 1855. Retired with the rank of major. Justice of the Peace. Married Emily East in 1858. Died 1901. His son, Frederick Arthur Bligh, was a major in the Royal Artillery in the Great War.
19. Unidentified.
20. The Governor of Malta.
21. Captain George James Ambrose, 3rd Regt. Commissioned, 4 July 1845. Captain, 12 October 1852. Brevet-major, 17 July 1855. Arrived in the Crimea in December 1855. Lieutenant-colonel (by purchase), 5 January 1858. Sardinian War Medal.
22. Lieutenant Henry George Charles Burningham, 3rd Regt. Commissioned, 14 March 1851 (by purchase); captain, 31 August 1855 (by purchase). Wounded slightly, 31 August 1855. On the night of 31 August 1855 Captain Ross, while on patrol with Lieutenant Burningham, Sergeant McCabe and a small party of men, encountered a Russian piquet which opened fire. Ross was hit seven times and taken prisoner,

subsequently dying of his wounds. Sergeant McCabe, mortally wounded, was carried back under heavy fire to the trenches by Private Lynch who, for his gallant action, was promoted corporal and awarded the MSM. The rest of the patrol was unhurt, but Burningham was wounded later in the night by a piece of shell. Order of the Medjidie, 5th class. Later transferred to 58th Regt. Major, May 1862.

23. Murray. Unidentified.
24. Eccles. This is almost certainly H. Eccles who was commissioned as an ensign into the 41st Regt on 17 May 1850 and retired on 17 June 1851.
25. HMS *Triton*, an iron paddle-powered sloop, launched in 1846 and sold in 1872.
26. HMS *Agamemnon*, a ship-rigged steam battleship, the first warship to be built with screw propulsion. Built at Woolwich and launched in 1852 (3,102 tons), she was classified as a 2nd rate ship, carrying 91 guns. During the Crimean War, she served as the flagship of Rear-Admiral Lyons in the Black Sea and took part in the bombardment of Sevastopol, 17 October 1854 and the shelling of Fort Kinburn, at the mouth of the Dnieper in 1855. Fitted out to carry 1,250 tons of telegraphic cable for the Atlantic Telegraph Company she made the first attempt to lay a transatlantic telegraph cable in 1857 and 1858. Paid off in 1862 and sold in 1870 when she was broken up.
27. Battle of Sinope, a naval battle which took place on 30 November 1853, off Sinope, in northern Turkey, when the Imperial Russian Navy annihilated a patrol force of Ottoman frigates and corvettes anchored in the harbour.
28. Lieutenant William Johnston, 41st Regt. Commissioned, 30 December 1845; lieutenant, 21 February 1850; captain (without purchase), 9 December 1854; adjutant, 6 January 1854. Wounded severely at Inkerman, 5 November 1854. Provost Marshal at Balaklava, resigned September 1855. Died Balaklava, 8 October 1855. A widower at the time of his death, he had one son and one daughter. His brother was a sergeant-major in the 2nd Battalion, The Rifle Brigade.
29. Captain Hugh Rowlands, 41st Regt. Born 1828, second son of John and Elizabeth Rowlands of Plastirion, Llanrug, Caernarfon. Commissioned, 41st Regt 1849 (by purchase); lieutenant (by purchase), 21 April 1851; captain (Grenadier Company), 24 August 1854 (by purchase). Landed Crimea, 14 September 1854. Present at Alma, Little Inkerman, Inkerman (severely wounded in the arm). Evacuated to Scutari Hospital, 9 November 1854. Returned Crimea, 18 December 1854. Present during the siege of Sevastopol, assault on the Quarries, 5 September 1855, led assault party to capture Russian rifle pit (MiD), both assaults on the Redan (senior officer inside the Redan, 8 September 1855) wounded. Town Major Sevastopol, 1855; Brigade Major 2nd Brigade, 2nd Division, 1855–6. Brevet-major, 1856. Returned to Britain aboard HMT *Transit*, July 1856. Crimea Medal with three clasps; Legion of Honour (France); Order of the Medjidie (5th Class); Turkish Medal. Victoria Cross (for action at Inkerman 5 November 1854). Lieutenant-colonel, OC 41st Regt, 23 March 1866. Commandant of the Transvaal, July 1879. Local brigadier-general, Lower Tugela, Zululand, 1879. Lieutenant of the Tower of London, 21 June 1893. General, 16 October 1894. Retired, 6 May 1896. Married Isabella Jane Barrow, 2 November 1866 (son, Major Hugh Barrow Rowlands, Suffolk Regt and King's African Rifles, died of wounds, Somaliland 1903). JP, DL Caernarfonshire. Died 1909.
30. Captain Charles Yelverton Balguay, 41st Regt. Born 1827, son of John Balguay of Duffield Park, Derbyshire, Recorder of Derby. Commissioned 41st Regt (by purchase), 14 May 1847; lieutenant (by purchase), 3 May 1850; captain (by purchase), 30.12.53. Exchanged into 42nd Regt. Retired, 24 April 1855. Married Lucy Adela, daughter of Colonel Caulfield, 2 August 1854, two daughters, one son.

Adjutant 1st Derbyshire Militia, May 1855. Hon Major and Adjutant 1st Volunteer Battalion Sherwood Foresters until retirement. Died, 29 October 1900 at Fairfax, Hampton Hill, Middlesex.

31. Major Charles Timothy Tuckey, 41st Regt. Commissioned (by purchase), 28 June 1839; captain, 3 November 1840 (by purchase); major, 3 November 1846. He served in the 1st Afghan War. Retired 30 December 1854.
32. Captain Robert Pratt, 41st Regt. Commissioned, 16 June 1837. Promoted major (without purchase), 29 December 1854; brevet lieutenant-colonel, 2 November 1855. Served Afghanistan and Crimea. Wounded slightly during the final attack on the Redan, 8 September 1855. Transferred to 23rd Regt as lieutenant-colonel, 27 March 1857. Served Indian Mutiny, 1857–8. Lieutenant-general, 25 June 1881. CB. Married Phoebe Hester Jane, 4 May 1861. Died, 1886.
33. Captain George Skipwith, 41st Regt. Commissioned (by purchase), 25 October 1847; brevet major, 2 November 1855. Served Crimea from September 1854, present at Alma, Little Inkerman, Inkerman and siege of Sevastopol. Medical leave of absence, 28 November 1855–29 February 1856; unattached half pay. *Legion d'honneur,* 1856. Appointed major 97th Regt from half pay, 25 August 1857.
34. *Canterbury,* a 681-ton sailing ship, built at Sunderland in 1851. She was requisitioned for service during the Crimean War.
35. *Georgiana.* Unidentified ship.
36. Lieutenant-General Sir George Brown, GCB, KH (1790–1865). Born in Elgin, Scotland. Commissioned 43rd (Monmouthshire) Regt, 1806. Saw active service in the Mediterranean and at Copenhagen, 1806 and 1807, in the Peninsular War (severely wounded at Talavera) and in the War of 1812 in America (severely wounded at Bladensburg). KH (1831). Adjutant-General to the forces, 1850–3. Lieutenant-general, 1852. Colonel 77th Regt, 1851–4; KCB (1852). Colonel 7th Regt, 1854–5; Colonel 32nd Regt, 1863–5; Colonel Rifle Brigade, 1863–5. GOC the Light Division, Crimea, 1854–55. Present at the battle of the Alma (horse shot under him), Inkerman (wounded), commanded the expedition to Kertch, 1855. Invalided home 1855. KCB (1852). C-in-C Ireland March 1860–March 1865.
37. Major-General Sir George Augustus Wetherall, GCB (1788–1868). Royal Military College. Commissioned, 1803. Served Cape of Good Hope and Java. Military secretary to C-in-C Madras, 1822–5; deputy judge advocate general, India, 1826. Served Canada, 1837–8. CB. Adjutant-General, 1854–60. Governor RMA Sandhurst, 1860–8. Colonel 84th Regiment, 1854. KCB, 1856. Lieutenant-general 1857. GCB, 1865. Died, 1868.
38. Major-General Sir George Cathcart, GCB (1794–1854). Born in Renfrewshire, son of the 1st Earl Cathcart. Commissioned into the Life Guards, 1810. He saw service in the War of 1812 and against France 1813–14. ADC to FM the Duke of Wellington 1815. Deputy-Lieutenant Tower of London, 1846, major-general (1851). A British representative at the Congress of Vienna. Governor of the Cape of Good Hope, 1852–3. Adjutant-General to the Forces, 1853. GOC of the 4th Division, Crimea 1854. He was killed at the battle of Inkerman, 5 November 1854.
39. Lieutenant William Lawes, 41st Regt. Commissioned, 10 April 1849; lieutenant, 22 October 1850 (by purchase). Retired 1855. Captain West York Rifle Regiment of Militia, 19 January 1855–October 1860.
40. SS *Colombo* a screw-powered passenger ship built in Britain in 1853. She was wrecked on the Minicoy Reef, Laccadive Islands (India) on 19 November 1862.
41. Captain William Hunt, 41st Regt. Commissioned, 14 January 1848 (by purchase); lieutenant, 25 August 1846; captain, 6 November 1854. Adjutant. Died at Ballyduff, Co. Tipperary, Ireland, 10 January 1855.

42. Captain Edwin Robert Wethered, 41st Regt. Commissioned, 5 August 1842 (by purchase); lieutenant, 24 May 1844; captain, 6 June 1854. Transferred to 95th Regt as paymaster, 1855. Hon Captain, 30 June 1864. Paymaster Royal Artillery. Staff Paymaster, 1878.
43. Error by William Allan, this vessel was HMS *Caradoc,* a steam-powered, paddle-driven gunboat launched in 1847. She transported Lord Raglan to the Crimea in 1854 and, when he died in 1855, brought his body back to Britain. Broken up 1870.
44. Lieutenant-General Sir John Fox Burgoyne, Bart, GCB (1782–1870). The eldest son of General 'Gentleman Johnny' John Burgoyne of American War of Independence fame, born in 1782. Commissioned into the Royal Engineers, and first saw service in the Mediterranean in 1800. Present at the retreat on Corunna, and assisted in laying Sir John Moore in the grave. Served in Wellington's Peninsula campaign, attaining the rank of colonel. Commanding engineer New Orleans expedition, 1812. Chairman of the Board of Public Works in Ireland; Inspector General of Fortifications (1845), member of the Irish Famine Commission of 1847. Sent to Constantinople (1854) to report on the measures necessary for the defence of the Ottoman Empire. On outbreak of Crimean War was appointed lieutenant-general and supervised the landing of troops in the Crimea. Present at the Alma, Balaklava and Inkerman, and conducted the siege operations before Sevastopol until March 1855, when he was recalled to England. Colonel Commandant of the Royal Engineers. Field Marshal. Constable of the Tower of London, 1865; Lord Lieutenant and *Custos Rotulorum* of the Tower Hamlets. Died in London, 1871.
45. Captain Hon Richard Handcock, 41st Regt. 16*n,* p.158.
46. Captain Edwin Richards, 41st Regt. Eldest son of Captain Edwin Richards, RN, of Ravindon House, County Carlow. Commissioned, 23 February 1849; lieutenant (by purchase), 27 December 1850; captain 28 March 1854 (by purchase). Killed in action at Inkerman, 5 November 1854.
47. Lieutenant George William Wallace Carpenter, 7th Regt. Born Marylebone, *c.*1835, only son of Lieutenant-Colonel George Carpenter, CO 41st Regt. Commissioned from RMC into 41st Regt, 17 June 1851 (by purchase). Exchanged into 7th Regt as lieutenant, 27 January 1854 (by purchase). Severely wounded at the Alma, 1854. Captain, 12 January 1855 (by purchase); major, 13 May 1859 (by purchase); retired, 22 January 1864. Conservative candidate for Berwick, 1868 (not elected). Reserve of Officers, 2-in-C Corps of Cyclists. Married Mrs Maud Elliott, December, 1881. Keen yachtsman and patron of music and drama. Resided at 28 Ashley Place, Westminster. Died, 21 November 1889.
48. Maclean – unidentified.
49. Lieutenant John William Swaby, 41st Regt. 2*n,* p.157.
50. Field Marshal Fitzroy Henry James Somerset, 1st Baron Raglan (1788–1855). Born Badminton, Gloucestershire, eighth son of Henry Somerset, 5th Duke of Beaufort and Elizabeth Boscawen. Commissioned 4th Light Dragoons, 1804; brevet-major, 1811. Staff officer to Sir Arthur Wellesley (later Lord Wellington, later the Duke of Wellington) to Copenhagen (1807) and Portugal (1808). ADC and military secretary to Wellesley throughout the Peninsular War (wounded Busaco, 1810); distinguished himself at Ciudad Rodrigo (1812) and Badajoz (1812); secretary to Wellington when British Ambasssador to France (1814–5); ADC Duke of Wellington (1815), wounded at Waterloo (right arm amputated); MP for Truro, 1818–20 and 1826–9. Master-General of the Ordnance, 1852–5. Created 1st Baron Raglan 1852. Privy Counsellor. General, 1854. GOC British Expeditionary Force to Turkey and the Crimea 1854–5. Field Marshal December, 1854. Died, 29 June 1855.

54. William Allan was a pupil at the Grange School, Sunderland, which was opened by Scotsman James Cowan in 1822. In 1830, with about 50 boarders and 50 day boys, the school moved into the mansion called the Grange from which it took its name. It quickly acquired a reputation for academic excellence but Cowan was forced to close following a tragic swimming accident in 1845 in which one master and three boys died. The school continued under new ownership until its closure in 1853.
55. Ensign & Lieutenant Robert Anstruther, Grenadier Guards. Commissioned 21 January 1853.
56. Captain Andrew Campbell Knox Lock, 50th Regt. Commissioned, 25 December 1850.
57. Ensign James Menzies Clayhills, 93rd Regt. Commssioned, 23 November 1852.
58. Captain Philip Limborch Tillbrook, 50th Regt. Commissioned, 16 November 1849.
59. Possibly Ensign William Gandy, 44th Regt. Commissioned, 18 April 1851.
60. Lieutenant Mark George Sprot, 93rd Regt. Commissioned, 15 October 1850 (by purchase); captain, 29 December 1854.
61. Lieutenant Scott Elliott, 79th Regt. Commissioned (by purchase), 5 April 1831; lieutenant-colonel, 24 December 1852 (by purchase).
62. SS *Valetta*. Details unknown.
63. Introduced at the Great Exhibition of 1851, the .436 Dean & Adams was a British five-shot percussion revolver with a spurless hammer, the first with a solid frame. The revolver's external hammer cocked itself when the trigger was pulled thereby enabling it to be fired more rapidly than other contemporary single-action revolvers which had to be manually cocked prior to each shot.
64. The Colt revolver purchased by many British officers was the Colt 1851 Navy, a cap and ball revolver, which was engraved with a scene from the Texas Navy's victory of Campeche in 1843 (hence it being known as the 'Navy' revolver). This was the standard sidearm used in the American West and during the American Civil War.
65. The Minié rifle was developed in 1849 following the invention of the Minié ball by the French Army captains, Minié and Delvigne. The rifle allowed rapid muzzle-loading rifles to be used as a mass battlefield weapon. The 1851 Pattern, used by the British Army from 1851–5, fired a conical-cylindrical soft-lead bullet, that was slightly smaller than the barrel bore. The bullet had three exterior grease-filled grooves and a conical hollow in its base. The expanding gases formed by firing pushed on the base of the bullet, deforming it so that it engaged the rifling thereby providing a spin which improved accuracy, increased the range and cleaned the barrel.
66. Brevet-Major Charles Nasmyth. Formerly of the Bombay Artillery, he was the eldest son of Robert Nasmyth, FRCS, of Edinburgh. Commissioned into the Bombay Artillery, 12 December 1845. He returned to Europe on sick leave in 1853 and was sent to Omar Pasha's camp as the correspondent of the *Times* newspaper from where he was sent as a correspondent to Silistria in the Danube basin arriving shortly before it was invested by the Russians on 28 March 1854. Lieutenant Nasmyth and Captain James Butler played key roles in the defence of Silistria which 'probably saved the allies from a campaign amidst the marshes of the Danube.' He received the thanks of both the British and Turkish governments and the Turkish Gold Medal and granted the Freedom of the City of Edinburgh. Brevet-majority and a transfer from the East India Company Army on 11 September 1854. Staff officer to Lord Raglan and ADC to Sir John Burgoyne. He was sent home on the grounds of ill health in November 1854. Died France, 2 June 1861. The historian Kinglake wrote that he was 'a man of quiet and gentle manners and so free from vanity so free from all idea of self-gratulation that it seemed as though he

were unconscious of having stood as he did in the path of the Czar and had really omitted to think of the share which he had had in changing the face of events.'

67. Captain Robert Pratt, 41st Regt, 32*n,* p.160.
68. Paterson – unidentified.
69. Captain Edwin Robert Wethered, 41st Regt, 42*n,* p.161.
70. Captain Charles Pelgué Bertram, 41st Regt, 15*n,* p.158.
71. Captain Hon. Richard Handcock, 41st Regt, 16*n,* p.158.
72. Lieutenant William Turner, 93rd Regt. Commissioned, 17 September 1850 (by purchase); lieutenant, 25 June 1852.
73. Lieutenant John William Swaby, 41st Regt, 2*n,* p.157.
74. Lieutenant-General Sir George Brown, GCB, KH, 36*n,* p.160.
75. SS *Golden Fleece*, a 1,850 ton ship built by C.J. Mare & Co of Blackwell and launched in 1853, she was operated by the General Screw Steam Shipping Co on the Southampton–Alexandria service which was withdrawn in 1855 and the ship was chartered to the government for use as a troop transport. She eventually foundered in Penarth Roads in 1869.
76. SS *Cambria,* built by Lairds and launched in 1848, this 590 ton passenger ship was sold to the London & North Western Railway Co in 1859.
77. HMT *Himalaya*, built by C. J. Mare & Sons, Blackwall, 1852, for the Southampton–Alexandria service. Sold to the Government for use as a troopship in 1854. Taken out of servce and used as a hulk, 1895. Sunk in Portland harbour by German bombers, 1940.
78. *Emue,* built by Robert Napier & Sons, Glasgow, 1854, for the Australasian Pacific Mail Steam Packet Co but acquired by Cunard Line in 1854. Converted to sailing ship, and renamed *Winchester,* 1876. Lost in the Malacca Strait, 1880.
79. Augustus J. W. Northey, 41st Regt. Eldest son of Colonel Lewis Augustus Northey of Llangwathan, Pembrokeshire. Commissioned (by purchase) 51st Regt, 14 July 1837; lieutenant, 3 July 1840; captain (by purchase), 27 September 1844. Exchanged into 41st Regt, 8 September 1846; major (by purchase), 27 December 1850. Resigned his commission, 1856. Married Louisa Sophia St George, 14 June 1853. DL, JP. Farmer of Wyngron, Narbeth, Pembrokeshire. Died, 29 June 1890.
80. Colonel Henry William Adams, 49th Regt. Commissioned, 31 July 1823; brevet lieutenant-colonel, 13 March 1840; lieutenant-colonel, 12 April 1844; colonel, 11 November 1851; brigadier-general, 21 February 1854. Reward for Particular Service. CB, 1841.
81. Sir Hector Greig, KCMG, Superintendent of Quarantine, Malta. Chief Secretary, Malta, 1837–47.
82. Colonel Sir Charles Fitzroy MacLean, Bart (1798–1883). Commissioned Scots Fusilier Guards, 1816. CO 81st Regiment (1831–9). Military Secretary, Gibraltar. Colonel 13th Light Dragoons. Retired 1846. 9th Baronet of Duart and Morven, 25th Chief of Clan McLean.
83. Admiral Sir Lucius Curtis, Bart, KCB (1786–1869). Later Admiral of the Fleet.
84. Almost certainly Henry Lushington (1812–55), Chief Secretary, Malta.
85. Lieutenant-Colonel George Allan, former CO 5th Regt. of Foot. He was the uncle of William Allan.
86. HMS *Sultan*, a 74-gun ship of the line, was built by Dudman at Deptford Wharf. She was launched in 1807 and became a receiving ship in 1860. Broken up in 1864.
87. HMS *Apollo*, a 38-gun, fifth-rate frigate was built by George Parsons at Bursledon. Launched in 1805, she was used as a troop ship from 1846 until broken up in 1856.

88. Colonel Henry William Adams, 49th Regt, 79*n,* p.163.
89. Lieutenant-General Sir George Brown, GCB, KH, 36*n,* p.160.
90. This appears to have been an error on Allan's part. This ship was actually HMS *Furious,* a 16-gun paddle-steamer, built at Portsmouth Dockyard by Miller & Ravenhill. She was launched in 1850 and became a hulk at Portsmouth in 1867. Broken up 1884.
91. Lieutenant-General Sir Richard England, KCB (1793–1883). Born in Detroit, Michigan, Upper Canada, the son of General Sir Richard England. Commissioned 14th Regt, 25 February 1808; captain 60th Regt, 11 July 1811; captain 12th Regt, 1812; major 75th Regt, 4 September 1823; lieutenant-colonel 75th Regt, 29 October 1825; lieutenant-colonel 41st Regt, 10 July 1837; colonel 41st Regt, 20 April 1861; general 6 July 1863. He saw service at Walcheren (1809), Sicily (1810–11), Canada (1812), Cape Colony (1833). KCB (1843). GOC 3rd Division during the Crimean campaign. Retired 1877. Described as 'a man of meagre talent and reputation'.
92. Lieutenant-Colonel George Allan, 84*n,* p.163.
93. Sylvester L'Amy. A friend of the Allan family from Edinburgh. He was a former member of the Hon East India Company Service, he served in the Stirlingshire Militia (rising to the rank of colonel). Married to Margaret Sinclair Scott (1863). He died in London in 1898 and was a posthumous benefactor of hospitals in Edinburgh and London.
94. In 1758, Field Marshal the Rt Hon John, Viscount Ligonier, Commander-in-Chief of His Majesty's Forces, appointed his secretary, Richard Cox, as agent to pay his troops. Other regiments followed suit and Cox & Company was formed to act as bankers for virtually the whole army by the end of the Napoleonic Wars.
95. Sylvester L'Amy, 92*n,* p.164.
96. HMS *Tiger,* a wooden-hulled paddle sloop was launched in 1849 and reclassified as a frigate in 1852. Under the command of Captain H.W. Giffard, she ran aground in fog 450 yards off shore near Odessa on 12 May 1854 and was surrendered to the Russians after coming under fire from the shore which set her ablaze.
97. HMS *Amphion,* a 30-gun (later 36-gun), wooden-hulled screw frigate, originally ordered as a sail-powered ship, but later re-ordered as a prototype steam-powered vessel. Built at Woolwich, she was launched in 1846. She was broken up in 1863.
98. Lieutenant William Lear Macnish, 93rd Regt. Commissioned, 28 August 1846; lieutenant, 18 June 1852.
99. Ensign James Clayhills, 93rd Regt.
100. Lieutenant & Adjutant Patrick Robertson, 4th Regt. Commissioned, 7 April 1848. Served Cape Mounted Rifles, Cape Colony 1850–1 (medal), OC Armstrong's Horse. Promoted, 5 December 1851, adjutant, 16 September 1851. Crimea (MinD 22 November 1854). Brevet major, 17 July 1855.
101. Possibly Lieutenant William Gandy, 44th Regt, 58*n,* p.162.
102. Colonel Henry William Adams, 49th Regt, 79*n,* p.163.
103. Captain Albany French Wallace, 7th Regt. Commissioned, 26 Regt 22 February 1839; lieutenant, 29 December 1840; captain, 1 October 1847. Exchanged into 7th Regt, 1 December 1848. A report in *Reynold's Newspaper* of 25 June 1854 stated: 'I am sorry to say that we have had another fatal accident occur at the camp here, to one of the officers of the 7th, Captain Wallace. He was out yesterday evening exercising a newly-purchased horse, when the animal stumbled and fell, pitching

poor Wallace on his head with great force. In spite of all that surgical skill could avail, he remained unconscious, and died in the course of a few hours. As is unfortunately nearly always the case in these melancholy accidents, the deceased was one of the most popular and accomplished officers of his regiment.'

104. Brevet-Major Charles Nasmyth, 65*n,* p.162.
105. Captain William Whitaker Maitland, 49th Regt. Commissioned (by purchase), 16 May 1845; lieutenant, 15 December 1848; captain, 3 February 1854.
106. SS *Medway,* a steam-powered ship launched 1841 for the Royal Mail Packet Company. In 1854 she was requisitioned as a transport vessel for the Crimean War. Scrapped in 1861.
107. Lieutenant-Colonel George Allan, 84*n,* p.163.
108. Sylvester L'Amy, 92*n,* p.164.
109. Brevet-Major Charles Nasmyth, 65*n,* p.162.
110. General Omar Pasha Latas (1806–71). Born Mihajlo Latas, in what is now Croatia, in 1806, the son of Petar Latas, an Austrian army officer. Educated at a military school, he joined the Ogulin Regiment before fleeing to Bosnia in 1823 to escape prosecution for embezzlement. After converting to Islam, he changed his name to Omar. Appointed a lecturer at the Turkish Military Academy and, with the rank of major, became ADC to General Chrzanowski who was in the process of re-organising the Ottoman Army. Promoted to colonel (1839), he held a series of important commands: military governor of Constantinople, OC suppression of a rebellion in Syria (1840), military governor of Lebanon (1842) and OC Ottoman forces during the Albanian rebellion (1843), the Kurdistan rebellion (1846), in Moldavia and Wallachia (1848), and the Bosnian rebellion (1851) and Montenegro (1852). On the outbreak of hostilities with the Russian Empire in 1853, he was given a senior command and defeated the Russians at Oltenta (1853) and defended Silistria and captured Bucharest (1854). He was then given the command of the Turkish forces in the Crimea and defeated the Russians at Eupatoria. Governor of Baghdad, 1857. Field-marshal. In 1867, he commanded Turkish forces in Crete and was appointed Minister of War two years later. He died in 1871.
111. Lieutenant-Colonel George Allan, 84*n,* p.163.
112. Sylvester L'Amy, 92*n,* p.164.
113. Captain William Aitchison, first cousin of William Allan, the son of William and Anne Aitchison of Musselburgh. Commissioned Scots Fusilier Guards, 2 October 1846; captain 24 May 1850; captain (2nd Battalion) 25 March 1856; lieutenant-colonel. He saw active service in the Crimea.
114. HRH Prince George William Frederick Charles, 2nd Duke of Cambridge, KG, KT, KP, GCB, GCH, GCSI, GCMG, GCIE, GCVO, KStJ, ADC (1819–1904). Born in Germany in 1819, he was the grandson of King George III. Served for a short period in the Hanoverian Army, then commissioned as a colonel in the British Army. Inspector of Cavalry 1852–4. GOC 3rd Division in the Crimean campaign. Lieutenant-general June 1854. Present at Alma, Balaklava, Inkerman and the siege of Sevastopol. Returned to Britain on grounds of ill-health, 1855. C-in-C Britsh Army, 5 July 1856. Resigned, 1895.
115. Field Marshal Lord Raglan, 50*n,* p.161.
116. Lieutenant-General Sir George Brown, GCB, KH, 36*n,* p.160.
117. Lieutenant-Colonel George Allan, 84*n,* p.163.
118. *Bashi-bazouks* were Turkish irregular soldiers, usually mercenaries.
119. Captain Johnson Bourne, 17th Regt, 13*n,* p.158.

120. Lieutenant-Colonel Hon Lauderdale Maule, Adjutant-General, 2nd Division. Born in 1807, the second son of Lord Panmure, he was commissioned into the 39th Regt, 24 August 1825. Captain 95th Regt, 1835. Captain 79th Regt, 1835. Major, 1840. Lieutenant-colonel, CO 79th Regt ,1842. Retired half-pay 1852. Appointed Surveyor-General of Ordnance 1853 and AAG 1854. DL Forfarshire 1850. MP Forfarshire 1852–4. Died of cholera 1 August 1854.
121. Lieutenant-General Sir George Brown, GCB, KH, 36*n,* p.160.
122. Lieutenant William Turner, 93rd Regt, 71*n,* p.163.
123. Lieutenant-Colonel Edmund James Elliott, 79th Regt.
124. The senior major of the 79th Regt was possibly James Ferguson.
125. Captain John Younger Allan (1838–1918). The younger brother of William Allan. Commissioned 71st Highlanders in 1857. Saw active service Yusafzai Field Force, 1863. Retired 1873. Coffee planter, merchant and carpet manufacturer at Srinagar in Kashmir. Died Lahore, India, 17 May 1918.
126. The battle of Boomarsund was a naval action fought in August 1854 by Anglo-French forces against a Russian fortress on the Aland Islands in the Baltic Sea.
127. Captain Edwin Richards, 41st Regt, 46*n,* p.161.
128. *Arabas* were Turkish horse-drawn carriages.
129. Captain Edward Every, 41st Regt. Born c.1834, second son of Henry Every of Ouseley Lodge, Old Windsor. Commissioned, 9 July 1852. Went home sick, August 1854. Returned to the Crimea and was killed in action during the final attack on the Redan, 8 September 1855.
130. Major Augustus J. W. Northey, 41st Regt, 78*n,* p.164.
131. Field Marshal Lord Raglan, 50*n,* p.163.

Chapter 2: To the Crimea

1. *City of London,* launched in 1844 for the Aberdeen Steam Navigation Company, this 1,067-ton paddle-powered ship was requisitioned for service as a transport in the Crimean War. In 1869, she was converted to screw propulsion and was sold to George Russell of London in 1871. Scrapped in 1887.
2. Lieutenant-Colonel George Allan, 84*n,* p.163.
3. Major James Eman, 41st Regt. Born c.1817, Cork. Commissioned, 25 March 1836. Served Afghan War 1842. Landed in the Crimea 14 September 1854. Present at battles of the Alma, Little Inkerman, Inkerman and the siege of Sevastopol. Lieutenant-colonel (on the death of Lieutenant-Colonel Carpenter) 6 November 1854. Shot through the lung during the assault on the Redan, 8 September 1855 (Mentioned in Despatches). Died of wounds, 9 September 1855. 'He was engaged in every action, showing the same singular calmness and bravery, and in the surprise of Inkerman greatly distinguished himself by the skilful way in which he handled the piquets.' CB. Buried Cathcart Hill Cemetery. Married to Anna Maria Bowes, he had two daughters and one son.
4. SS *Melbourne* (also known as HMS *Greenock*), a 1,450-ton combined sail and steam-powered ship, built at Greenock for the Australian Royal Mail Steam Company, which had been awarded the first Australian steamship mail contract by the British government two years earlier. Taken over for use as a transport/hospital ship during the Crimean War. She later became the first steam and sailing ship to be fully equipped as a floating hospital rather than an ambulance ship during operations in China in 1860.
5. SS *Harbinger,* originally HMS *Recruit*, a 12-gun iron sailing brig built by the Thames Ironworks and

Shipbuilding Company, the first iron vessel built for the Royal Navy, she was launched in 1846. Sold back to her builders in 1849, she was sold to the General Screw Steam Shipping Company and converted into a screw steamer and renamed SS *Harbinger* in 1852.

6. General Sir George de Lacy Evans, GCB, MP (1787–1870). Born in Moig, County Limerick, Ireland. Entered the British Army in 1806 as a volunteer and was commissioned 22nd Regt in 1807. Served India. Exchanged 3rd Light Dragoons. Served Peninsular War, War of 1812 and the Waterloo campaign of 1815. Commanded the British Legion which volunteered to fight for Isabella II of Spain in the First Carlist War. GOC 2nd Division of the British Army during the Crimean campaign. Member of Parliament for Rye (1830 and 1831–2) and for Westminster (1833–41 and 1846–65).
7. Baltschick Bay is located in the Black Sea, off the coast of Bulgaria, near the city of Varna.
8. Field Marshal Lord Raglan, 50*n,* p.161.
9. Captain Edwin Richards, 41st Regt, 46*n,* p.161.
10. William Howard Russell (1820–1907), an Irish-born reporter with the *Times* newspaper, who spent twenty-two months as a war correspondent covering the Crimean campaign from the first landings in September 1854 until December 1855. His despatches led to a public outcry about the condition of the Army in the Crimea. He later covered the latter part of the Indian Mutiny, the American Civil War and the Franco-Prussian War. He founded the influential journal the *Army & Navy Gazette* and was knighted in 1895.
11. Field Marshal Lord Raglan, 50*n,* p.161.
12. Alexander Allan (1830–62), elder brother of William Allan.
13. Unidentified.
14. Old Fort is a reference to the Genoese fort located beyond the Salt Lake, about one mile south of the landing beach at Calamita Bay.
15. Battle of the Alma, 20 September 1854. The first significant land action of the Crimean campaign.
16. General Sir George de Lacy Evans, GCB, MP, 6*n,* p.166.
17. Brigadier-General Henry William Adams, 79*n,* p.163.
18. William Howard Russell, 10*n,* p.167.
19. Lieutenant-General Sir John Burgoyne, GCB, 44*n,* p.161.
20. Prince Alexander Sergeievich Menschikoff (1787–1869). He began his career as attaché to the embassy at Vienna in 1809 and became a close associate of Czar Alexander I and accompanied him throughout his campaigns against Napoleon. Menschikoff was appointed acting general quartermaster of the General Staff 1817. In 1823, he was transferred to the ministry of foreign affairs. Menshikov retired from army service in 1824 when he was appointed head of the Naval Headquarters and appointed a cabinet minister by Czar Nicholas I. He distinguished himself at the Siege of Varna and in 1830 and was made a member of the State Council. In 1831, Menshikov held the post of Governor-General of Finland. In 1853, he was sent on a special mission to Constantinople and was appointed C-in-C of both land and sea forces on the outbreak of the Crimean War. He personally commanded the Russian army at the battles of the Alma and Inkerman where he displayed a lack of talent and was removed from his command on 15 February 1855 and replaced by Prince Michael Dmitrievich Gorchakov. Between December 1855 and April 1856, he held the post of Governor General of Kronstadt and then retired. He died in 1869.
21. Field Marshal Lord Raglan, 50*n,* p.161.

22. Allan's reference to Mackenzie being taken prisoner suggests that the area of MacKenzie's Farm and Mackenzie's Heights actually had an occupier named Mackenzie. In reality, the name almost certainly came from Thomas Mackenzie, the son of a Scottish Jacobite, who was born in Archangel in 1740. Like his father (Rear-Admiral Thomas MacKenzie), he served in the Imperial Russian Navy, saw action at the Battle of Chesma in 1770 and rose to command the Black Sea Squadron based in the Crimea. MacKenzie played a role in establishing Sevastopol as the headquarters of the Russian Black Sea Fleet. He died in 1786 and his will mentioned that he owned several farms in the area.
23. Lieutenant Henry Stratton Bush, 41st Regt, 10*n*, p.157.
24. Lieutenant-Colonel George Allan, 84*n*, p.163.
25. An English civil engineer, William Upton, had settled in the Sevastopol area where he had worked on the harbour prior to the outbreak of war. 'All other works sink into insignificance at Sevastopol before those projected and accomplished by Colonel Upton, under immense engineering difficulties. They consist of a great fitting basin into which open five dry docks ... above the level of the sea and the ships are floated into them by locks of which there are three, having a rise of ten feet each.
    To supply the basin and thence the canal, the water is brought eleven miles by a beautiful aqueduct of stone ... [which] passes at one part, through an excavated tunnel 900 feet long. Mr William Upton superintended the engineering department and the work was achieved with perfect success.' *The Times*, 1 September 1854.
26. Colonel William Fergusson Beatson, Bengal Army. Inspector-General of Cavalry in India, on special service in Turkey and the Crimea to raise a body of 4,000 irregular Turkish cavalry from the *bashi-bazouks*, which was to have British officers. He was given the local rank of major-general and the Turkish title of His Excellency Shemsi Pasha.
27. Bashibasouks,
28. The Grenadier Company was positioned on the right of the regimental line. It was traditionally made up of the tallest men in the regiment and was regarded as something of an elite unit. In October 1854, the Grenadier Company of the 41st Regt was commanded by Captain Hugh Rowlands.
29. Captain Frederick Cherburgh Bligh, 41st Regt, 18*n*, p.158.
30. Captain Frederick Ball Dixon, 41st Regt. Commissioned, 21 January 1853; captain, 16 March 1855. Served at Little Inkerman, Inkerman and Sevastopol, wounded during the action in the Quarries, 8 September 1855 (wounded, Mentioned in Despatches).
31. Lieutenant John Stirling, 41st Regt. Born *c.*1836, the youngest son of John Stirling of St Andrews, Scotland. Commissioned, 30 December 1853; lieutenant (by purchase), 25 August 1854. Sick at Scutari, October 1854. Killed in action (aged 18 years) when shot through the left temple at Inkerman, 5 November 1854, while carrying the Regimental Colour.
32. Major Robert Cary Barnard, 41st Regt. Born *c.* 1828 in Cheltenham. Commissioned, 19 March 1847. Lieutenant and adjutant until 6 January 1854. Sick at Scutari, October 1854, sick leave to Malta, November 1854. Major (by purchase), 9 March 1855. Returned to Britain aboard HMT *Transit*, July 1856. Retired. Married Mary Julia, daughter of staff surgeon Reade, 8 October 1856 and later Anne. Four daughters and one son. Died Leckhampton, Gloucestershire, 1906.
33. Captain James Augustus Lockhart, 41st Regt. Born *c.*1834, the eldest son of James Lockhart of Sheffield House, Hampshire and Lanhams, Essex. Commissioned (by purchase), 13 May 1853; lieutenant, 3 May 1853; captain, 6 June 1854. Carried the Queen's Colour on landing at Scutari. Sick at Scutari,

September 1854, sent on home leave, October 1854, aboard transport *Libertas*. Killed in action during the final attack on the Redan, 8 September 1855 when he was hit in the head by grape shot.

34. Paymaster Thomas Miller Creagh, 41st Regt. Appointed, 8 December 1848.
35. The Malakoff was the major Russian defensive work on the south side of Sevastopol. It formed the focus of the Allied siege activities and its capture was the main objective of the French forces during the siege.
36. The Lancaster gun was a 68lb, rifled, muzzle-loaded artillery piece, designed by Charles William Lancaster (1820–78) which had an oval bore. It was first used during the Crimean War.
37. The Round Tower, a large stone-built circular structure, was the central feature of the Malakoff, the principal Russian defence position to the south of Sevastopol.
38. Fort Constantine was a large, naval defensive tower guarding the north side of the entrance to Sevastopol harbour.
39. Fort Nicholas was a large fortress on the southern side of Sevastopol harbour which guarded one of the docks.
40. Brevet-Major Charles Nasmyth, 65*n*, p.162.
41. Major Henry Law Maydwell, 41st Regt. Commissioned 82nd Regt, 21 August 1835; exchanged into 41st Regt (vice Tatton), 29 September 1843. Present at civil disturbances in Bristol, June 1844. Served Cape Colony as military secretary to the Commander-in-Chief, Sir Harry Smith, GCB (Mentioned in Despatches), 1850–2. Brevet-major, 31 May 1853. Sent on half pay to Britain on health grounds, August 1854. Appointed a major to serve in a Provisional Depot Battalion, Preston, December 1854. Brevet lieutenant-colonel; colonel, 28 November 1862. AQMG Northern District. Died 1879. Married to Fanny, he had four daughters and one son.
42. Captain George Robert Fitzroy, 41st Regt, 17*n*, p.158.

3. Heights of Inkerman

1. The Round Fort – see Round Tower, 36*n*, p.169.
2. HMS *Rodney*, built in Pembroke Dock and launched 1833, 2,590 tons, 2nd Rate, with 92 guns. Served in the Mediterranean and Baltic during the Crimean War. Converted to screw power in 1860 she was the last unarmoured battleship to serve in the Royal Navy. Broken up in 1884.
3. Ulick Canning de Burgh, Lord Dunkellin. Born 1827, was the eldest son of Ulick de Burgh, 1st Marquess of Clanricarde, and the Hon Harriet, daughter of George Canning. Lieutenant-Colonel in the Coldstream Guards. ADC to the Lord Lieutenant of Ireland 1846–52 and State Steward to the Lord Lieutenant, 1852–4. He served in the Crimean War and was taken prisoner during the siege of Sevastopol. In 1856 Dunkellin was Military Secretary to the Viceroy of India, his uncle Lord Canning. He sat as Member of Parliament for Galway Borough, 1857–65 and County Galway, 1865–7. He died in London, 16 August 1867.
4. Often known as the 'Sortie of 26 October', this short battle is now better known as Little Inkerman.
5. Lieutenant Hugh Charles Harriott, 41st Regt, 3*n*, p.157.
6. Major Charles Thomas Powell, 49th Regt. Served in the 1843 Scinde campaign under Sir Robert Napier, present at battles of Meeanee and Hyderabad. Served Crimea, present at Alma and Inkerman. Killed when shot through the head at Inkerman, 5 November 1854. His brother, Commander Powell, RN, commanded HMS *Vesuvius* and a shore battery during the siege of Sevastopol.

7. Gordon's Battery (also known as the Crown Battery) was the 21-gun battery constructed for the bombardment of Sevastopol, positioned on the Right Attack. It was named after Captain John William Gordon (1805–70), Royal Engineers (commissioned 1823). He was present at the Alma and Inkerman and was appointed director of the Right Attack during the early days of the siege of Sevastopol. Brevet-major 12 December 1854. He later commanded all the Royal Engineers until the arrival of Sir Harry Jones in early 1854. Severely wounded, 22 March 1855. Brevet lieutenant-colonel, 24 April 1855. He commanded the Royal Engineers on the Kertch expedition. CB, ADC to Queen Victoria, KCB. Major-general.
8. Captain Hugh Rowlands, 41st Regt, who was later awarded the Victoria Cross for this action, the citation for which reads: 'For having rescued Colonel Haly of the 47th Regiment from Russian soldiers, Colonel Haly having been wounded and surrounded by them, and for gallant exertions in holding the ground occupied by his advanced piquet against the enemy, at the commencement of the battle of Inkerman' *London Gazette*, 24 February 1857 (see also 29*n*, p.159 & 22*n*, p.190).
9. General Pierre Bosquet (1810–61). Commissioned into the artillery in 1833, he first saw service in Algeria. Major-general, 1853. Served Crimean campaign, present at Alma and Inkerman. His corps occupied the right attack before Sevastopol and he personally led his force in the attack on the Mamelon, 7 June 1855, and the successful assault of 8 September (severely wounded). Created a senator and Marshal of France, GCB, Grand Cross of the Legion of Honour and Order of the Medjidie, 1st Class. He is best remembered for having said of the Charge of the Light Brigade *'C'est magnifique, mais ce n'est pas la guerre: c'est de la folie.'*
10. Lieutenant Henry Stratton Bush, 41st Regt, 10*n*, p.157.
11. Captain William Johnston, 41st Regt, 28*n*, p.159.
12. Captain Hugh Rowlands, 41st Regt, 29*n*, p.159.
13. Captain Frederick Cherburgh Bligh, 41st Regt, 18*n*, p.158.
14. Brevet-Major Henry Warter Meredith, 41st Regt. Son of Henry Warter Meredith and Elizabeth Lowry (daughter of the African explorer Mungo Park) of Pentrebychan, Wrexham. Royal Military College. Commssioned, 6 June 1845 (by purchase); lieutenant, 3 November 1846 (by purchase); captain, 25 June 1852 (by purchase); brevet-major, 12 December 1854. He landed in the Crimea on 14 September 1854 and was present at the battles of the Alma, Little Inkerman, Inkerman (wounded slightly in the hand). Embarked for Scutari Hospital, 9 November 1854, did not return to the Crimea. Crimea Medal with 3 clasps, Order of the Medjidie (5th Class), Turkish Medal. Married Sophia Henrietta Jones-Parry of Llwyn Onn, Wrexham in 1855, one son one daughter. Lieutenant-colonel, 7 March 1862. High Sheriff of Denbighshire, 1886. Died 1901.
15. Captain George Robert Fitzroy, 41st Regt, 17*n*, p.158.
16. Lieutenant-Colonel George Carpenter, 41st Regt. Born 1801, the only son of General George Carpenter, Great Cumberland Place, London, he was descended from Lieutenant-General Lord George Carpenter (1657–1731), Baron of Killaghy, Viscount Callingford and the Earl of Tyrconnel, and Lord George Carpenter (1788–1812) 3rd Earl of Tyrconnell, Viscount Carlingford (who served against Napoleon in Russia). Commissioned 53rd Regt, 27 December 1818; captain, 41st Regt, 9 July 1829 (from half-pay). Served in India, 1830–4 and 1838 (does not appear to have served in the 1st Afghan War); lieutenant-colonel, CO, 41st Regt, 27 December 1850. Landed in the Crimea, 14 September 1854. Present at battle of the Alma (horse shot under him) and Little Inkerman. Died, 6 November 1854, of the wounds he

received at Inkerman. The newspaper reports recorded that 'his death was an honour to his country and family, but a deep disgrace to the Russians.' It would appear that he, despite being severely wounded (shot in the thigh) and out of the action, was attacked several more times (bayoneted in the stomach and clubbed in the face) by Russian soldiers. His last words were reputed to have been 'Cover my head, I am going to sleep'. Buried Cathcart Hill Cemetery.

17. Captain Edwin Richards, 41st Regt. A family friend, Henry George Donovan of the 33rd Regt, wrote to the Richards family on 7 November 1854. ' Eddy's company was sent out to strengthen the picket; but before he advanced far he was surrounded by Russians. Refusing to yield himself a prisoner, he shot four of his opponents and killed two with his sword – thus dying the noblest and most glorious death a man could die, without pain; shot through the body and stabbed by several bayonet wounds, he suffered no pain, as death must have been instantaneous. He was buried with four other officers ... the next morning.' 46*n,* p.161.
18. Lieutenant John William Swaby, 41st Regt, 2*n,* p.157.
19. Lieutenant Alfred Taylor, 41st Regt. Commissioned, 17 January 1851. He was killed in action at Inkerman, 5 November 1854. Son of Smith Taylor, Esq, of Corballis, Drogheda, Ireland.
20. Lieutenant John Stirling, 41st Regt. 30*n,* p.168.
21. The Sandbag Battery, an abandoned artillery position, was located on Fore Ridge, on the Heights above Inkerman, close to the camp of the 2nd Division. It comprised a wall of earth, approximately twelve paces long, with two embrasures. It was held by the 41st Regt and the Guards during the battle of Inkerman.
22. Captain Edwin Richards, 41st Regt, 46*n,* p.161.
23. Captain Frederick Cherburgh Bligh, 41st Regt, 18*n,* p.158.
24. Lieutenant Henry Stratton Bush, 41st Regt, 10*n,* p.157.
25. SS *Jura* (2,241 tons), built 1853 at Glasgow for the Cunard company and chartered for use as a transport vessel during the Crimean War. Later operated in the Mediterranean and the North Atlantic. Wrecked in the Mersey estuary, 3 November 1864.
26. Field Marshal Fitzroy Henry James Somerset, 1st Baron Raglan, 50*n,* p.161.
27. Grand Duke Constantine Mikhailovich (1827–92), second son of Czar Nicholas I of Russia. He first saw action in 1849 during the campaign against the Austrians in Hungary for which he was awarded the Cross of St George for bravery. In 1853, he was appointed General-Admiral of the Imperial Navy and head of the Department of the Imperial Navy, charged with reforming the Russian navy. He served on the committee which brought about the emancipation of the Russian serfs in 1861. He was made Viceroy of Poland in 1862 where he was wounded in an assassination attempt. He resigned in 1863 but continued to serve in various offices of state in Russia.
28. Grand Duke Michael Mikhailovich (1832–1909), fourth son of Czar Nicholas I of Russia.
29. Sir George de Lacy Evans, 6*n,* p.166.
30. Brigadier-General Henry William Adams, 79*n,* p.163.
31. Captain William Whitaker Maitland, 49th Regt, 104*n,* p.165.
32. Captain Johnson Bourne, 17th Regt, 13*n,* p.158.
33. Miss Upton was the daughter of English civil engineer, William Upton, 25*n*, p.168.
34. HMS *Black Prince* (correctly named HMS *Prince*) was a 2,700-ton transport vessel built by C. J. Mare of Blackwall and launched on 12 April 1854. She was bought by the Admiralty for £105,000 from the

General Screw Steam Shipping Company in July 1854 and designated a storeship. She was used to transport troops and cargo to the Crimea. She was carrying 40,000 much-needed greatcoats and boots for the British Army in the Crimea when she was destroyed outside Balaklava harbour by a hurricane on 14 November 1854, losing 144 of the 150 men aboard. The wreck was discovered in 2010.

35. The *Resolute,* a transport ship, was sunk outside Balaklava harbour with 900 tons of gunpowder on board during the storm of November 1854.
36. William Howard Russell, 10*n,* p.167.
37. Captain Fitzhardinge Kingscote, 41st Regt. Born 1837, Kingscote, Gloucestershire, son of Colonel Thomas Henry Kingscote (CO Royal North Gloucestershire Militia) and Hon Harriott Mary Ann (daughter of Lt-Gen Benjamin Bloomfield, 1st Baron Bloomfield, GCB, GCH), of Kingscote House, Kingscote. Commissioned, 7 April 1854 (by purchase). Arrived in the Crimea aboard HMS *Jura,* 13 November 1854. Wounded severely (right hand amputated) during the final attack on the Redan, 8 September 1855. Transferred to half pay on reduction in the number of companies in the regiment, 1 October 1856. Retired as a major. Married to Agnes Grant Stuart, five sons and four daughters. JP County Mayo; Hon Major, Mayo Militia. Died 1900. His diary survives in the National Army Museum. His half-brother Nigel also served in the Crimea. He was a nephew by marriage (via his stepmother) to Lord Raglan.
38. Captain Johnson Bourne, 41st Regt, 13*n,* p.158.
39. Field Marshal Lord Raglan, 50*n*, p.161.
40. Brevet Lieutenant-Colonel Robert Nigel Fitzhardinge Kingscote, Scots Fusilier Guards. Commissioned as a lieutenant 27 October 1846 (by purchase). ADC to Lord Raglan. Brevet lieutenant-colonel, 17 July 1855. CB. He was later an MP. He was the half-brother of Captain Fitzhardinge Kingscote, 41st Regiment and the nephew of Lord Raglan.
41. HRH The Duke of Cambridge, 113*n,* p.165.
42. Field Marshal Lord Raglan, 50*n,* p.161.
43. The Tower is almost certainly a reference to the Malakoff, the major Russian defensive position on the south side of Sevastopol. It was a large structure sometimes called the White Tower (from the colour of the stone used in its construction), the Round Tower or the Round Fort. 34*n, p.*169.
44. Malakoff, 34*n*, p.168.
45. Funk Point, described as being on the extreme front of the Heights of Inkerman, near Sevastopol, probably close to Shell Hill on Mount Inkerman.
46. Captain William Aitchison, Scots Fusilier Guards, 112*n,* p.165.
47. Captain George Skipworth, 41st Regt, 33*n,* p.160.
48. Possibly William Allan's uncle, William Younger, partner in William Younger & Co, brewers, of Edinburgh.
49. General Pavel Petrovitch Liprandi (1796–1864), entered the service of the Imperial Russian Army as a volunteer in 1812 and was commissioned into the Pskov Musketeer Regiment the following year and saw action in the French retreat from Moscow to France. Transferred to Life Guards Grenadiers 1818; General Staff officer 1822. Served with distinction in the Russo-Turkish War of 1828–9. Commander of the fortress at Kinburn and CO Eletski Infantry Regt with which he served in Poland and was promoted to colonel. GOC 1st Brigade, 2nd Infantry then, in 1831, GOC assault column at the siege of Zamosc, Poland, awarded Cross of St George (3rd Class). ADC Czar Nicholas. Major-general 1839, GOC

King Frederick William III's Grenadier Regt; GOC Semenov Life Guards, 1842. Order of St Stanislaus (1st Class), 1844. Lieutenant-general, 1844. Chief of Staff of the Grenadier Corps. GOC 12th Infantry Division, Hungary 1849 and Crimea 1854–5 (second-in-command to Menshikov). Served in the defence of Sevastopol and was in command at the Battle of Balaklava.

50. The Mamelon (sometimes called the Mamelon Vert), was a key Russian defensive position overlooking the city of Sevastopol, the capture of which became one of the major objectives of the French siege forces.
51. Malakoff, 34*n*, p.168.
52. Captain Hugh Rowlands, 41st Regt, 29*n*, p.159.
53. Lieutenant-Colonel James Eman, 41st Regt, 3*n*, p.166.

4. Life in the Trenches

1. Lieutenant John William Swaby, 41st Regt, 2*n*, p.157.
2. Samuel Bamford Hamer of Hawnby, Yorkshire.
3. Lieutenant Hugh Charles Harriott, 41st Regt, 3*n*, p.157.
4. Captain Hugh Rowlands, 41st Regt, 29*n*, p.159.
5. Assistant-Surgeon James Lamont, 41st Regt. Appointed, 7 January 1853. Died of typhus, 5 January 1855. Unmarried. Son of William Lamont Esq, Grenada, West Indies.
6. Field Marshal Lord Raglan, 50*n*, p.161.
7. Captain Fitzhardinge Kingscote, 41st Regt, 28*n*, p.172.
8. Probably William Allan's uncle, Henry Johnson Younger, partner in William Younger & Co, brewers, of Edinburgh.
9. *Vivandières* were women who were attached to French regiments as sutlers (suppliers of provisions) or canteen keepers.
10. Assistant-Surgeon James Lamont, 41st Regt, 5*n*, p.173.
11. Surgeon William Abbott Anderson, 41st Regt. Third son of Lieut-Colonel Henry Anderson of Fort Amhurst, Chatham. He had previously been the assistant-surgeon to the 51st Regt. He died of typhus aboard a ship in Balaklava harbour, 3 January 1855 and was replaced by Assistant-Surgeon James Edward Scott, MD, from the Rifle Brigade.
12. William Ewart Gott (1827–79), husband of Anne Mary Aitchison, the cousin of William Allan. He was the grandfather of Lieutenant-General William Henry Ewart Gott, CB, CBE, DSO & Bar, MC (1897–1942) who was killed before taking command of the 8th Army in North Africa and was replaced by Lieutenant-General Bernard Montgomery.
13. Captain Hugh Rowlands, 41st Regt, 29*n*, *p*.159.
14. Surgeon William Abbott Anderson, 41st Regt, 11*n*, p.173.
15. Assistant-Surgeon James Lamont, 41st Regt, 10*n*, p.173.
16. Lieutenant Francis Charles Turner, 79th Regt. Born Edinburgh, *c*.1835, son of Major-General Turner, CB, Bombay Cavalry. Commissioned, 9 July 1852 (by purchase); lieutenant, 6 June 1854 (without purchase);captain, 15 June 1855 (by purchase). Served Alma, Balaklava and Sevastopol. Served India, 1858–9, present at siege and capture of Lucknow. Exchanged to 39th Regt, 1859. Retired 7 May 1867. Married Emma Leering, 1861. Lived at Glycine House, Hampton Court, 1872. Died 1905.
17. Major Henry Law Maydwell, 41st Regt, 40*n*, *p*.169.

18. Captain Edwin Richards, 41st Regt, 46*n*, p.161.
19. Gordon's Battery, 7*n*, p.169.
20. Mamelon, 50*n*, p.172.
21. Round Tower, 27*n*, p.168.
22. Malakoff, 34*n*, p.168.
23. HMS *Firefly*, a 550-ton wooden paddle-powered vessel, launched in 1832, armed with 5 guns. During the Crimean campaign she was commanded by Captain Henry Charles Otter and served in the Black Sea and in the Baltic. She was damaged by a Russian underwater mine on 9 June 1855. Lieutenant George Day received his VC decoration aboard HMS *Firefly*.
24. The *Loire* was a Dordogne-class troopship of the French navy, launched in 1855.
25. William Allan's old governess.
26. Gordon's Battery, 7*n*, p.169.
27. Captain Edward Every, 41st Regt, 128*n*, p.166,
28. Captain William Hunt, 41st Regt, 41*n*, p.160.
29. Consumption is an archaic term for tuberculosis.
30. Captain Charles Pelgué Bertram, 41st Regt, 15*n*, p.158.
31. Captain Hugh Rowlands, 41st Regt, 29*n*, *p*.159.
32. This was William Allan's aunt, Isabella Allan (née Younger), the wife of Lieutenant-Colonel George Allan.
33. Assistant-Surgeon Frederick Tydd Abbott, 41st Regt. Records show him to have been appointed, 7 April 1854, and to have arrived in the Crimea on 25 March 1855, but he is believed to have been present at the Alma, Little Inkerman and Inkerman and received the Crimea Medal with three clasps: Alma, Inkerman and Sevastopol.
34. Captain Henry Warter Meredith, 41st Regt. Plans were made for him to receive a grand reception when he returned to his home town of Wrexham. Unfortunately, Meredith's ill health prevented him arriving on the day of the festivities and he was unable to notify his father of this fact until after the activities had begun. These were then abruptly curtailed and a second reception was arranged for the following week. 14*n*, p.170.
35. Lieutenant-Colonel James Eman, 41st Regt, 3*n*, p.166.
36. Henry Pelham-Clinton, 5th Duke of Newcastle (1811–64). Served in Lord Aberdeen's government as Secretary of State for War and the Colonies (1852) and Secretary of State for War (1854–5) when he was forced to resign over the re-supply and conditions endured by the army in the Crimea. He later served as Secretary of State for the Colonies in Lord Palmerston's government (1859–64).
37.
38. Lamb – unidentified.
39. Captain Johnson Bourne, 17th Regt, 13*n*, p.158.
40. Presumably a transport vessel used during the war, no details of the *Cicero* have been located.
41. Probably the 3rd Parallel or Old Winter Advance. See sketch map on p.105.
42. Czar Nicholas I died of pneumonia on 2 March 1855. He had been czar since 1825 and was succeeded by Czar Alexander II.
43. Mamelon, 50*n*, p.172.
44. The Grand Crimean Central Railway was built by British contractors with work beginning on 8 February

1855, less than one week after the arrival of the materials and navvies at Balaklava. The first trains (horse-drawn) ran on the track on 23 February. In under seven weeks, seven miles of track had been laid. On 2 April 1855, the railway carried the first sick and wounded from the plateau before Sevastopol to the port of Balaklava; this was reckoned to be the first ever hospital train. It was completed and handed over to the Land Transport Corps in July 1855.

45. Major-General Sir John Lysaght Pennefather, GCB (1798–1872). The third son of Revd John Pennefather of Tipperary. Commissioned 7th Dragoon Guards, 14 January 1818; transferred to 22nd Regt, 8 April 1826; major, 22 March 1831; lieutenant-colonel, 18 October 1839. Served India (Battle of Meanee 1843, wounded, CB, Thanks of Parliament); half pay 1848–9; AQMG Cork District, 1849. Major-general, 20 June 1854, GOC 1st Brigade, 2nd Division, Crimea; temporary command of 2nd Division during the battle of Inkerman; GOC 2nd Division, November 1854–July 1855; invalided home, July 1855; GOC Malta, 25 September 1855; KCB 1855. GOC Aldershot Division 1860–5. Colonel 46th Regt, November 1854; Colonel 22nd Regt, 13 February 1860. Lieutenant-general, 9 May 1868. GCB 1867; Commander Sardinian Order of St Maurice & St Lazarus; General Officer Legion of Honour; Order of the Medjidie (2nd Class). Governor Royal Hospital, Chelsea 1870–2.
46. Lieutenant-Colonel James Eman, 41st Regt, 3*n*, p.166.
47. Field Marshal Lord Raglan, 50*n*, p.161.
48. Lieutenant Francis Charles Turner, 79th Regt, 16*n*, p.173.
49.
50. Round Tower, 36*n*, p.169.
51. Gordon's Battery, 7*n*, p.170.
52. Field Marshal Lord Raglan, 50*n*, p.161.
53. Malakoff, 34*n*, p.168.
54. Gordon's Battery, 7*n*, p.169.
55. Lieutenant-Colonel Richard Kelly, 34th Regt. Born Ireland, *c*.1815. Chief of the Irish clan O'Kelly. Commissioned 7 March 1834; brevet lieutenant-colonel, 12 March 1854; lieutenant-colonel, 9 March 1855. He was the officer commanding the guard in the trenches on 22 March 1855 when he was wounded and captured during the Russian attack on the Rifle Pits and held as a prisoner of war until after the fall of Sevastopol. *Légion d'honneur* (5th Class) 1857. Brevet-colonel 2 February 1858. CB July 1858, KCB 1860. Served Indian Mutiny (Mention in Despatches), Nepal 1859. Major-general. GOC Cork District; GOC Eastern District, 1877; lieutenant-general; general. Retired 1882. Colonel Royal Irish Regiment, 1886. Died Shrublands, Berkshire, July 1897.
56. Lieutenant Horace William Montagu, Royal Engineers. Commissioned, 1 January 1842; lieutenant 1 May 1845; captain 17 February 1854; major, 22 April 1855. He was captured by the Russians 24 March 1855 whilst engaged with the rest of his covering party in forcing back some of the enemy who had penetrated into the advanced trenches. Whilst a prisoner, he was allowed to visit the Russian Malakoff position to show its impregnability. He was exchanged in August and returned to his duties in the forward trenches and is believed to have given the French information about the Malakoff's defences before the final assault in September. Lieutenant-colonel 2 November 1855. Legion of Honour (5th Class); Order of the Medjidie (5th Class).
57. On the southern side of the city of Sevastopol were a number of defensive features which proved to be major obstacles to the Allies throughout the siege of 1854–5. The central feature, the Malakoff, was

flanked on the western side by the Redan (sometimes called the Great Redan) and on the east by the Little Redan. The name comes from the French term for an arrow- or tooth-shaped fortification (redent – the notches in a saw). The capture of the Redan became the focus of British activity for most of the siege.

58. Round Tower, 36*n*, p.169.
59. An archaic word for Muslim.
60. Mamelon, 50*n*, p.172.
61. Malakoff, 34*n*, p.168.
62. Captain Hugh Rowlands, 29*n, p*.159.
63. Redan, 56*n*, p.175.
64. Captain Robert Cary Barnard, 41st Regt, 24*n*, p.168.
65. Captain Robert Pratt, 41st Regt, 32*n*, p.160.
66. Lieutenant-Colonel James Eman, 41st Regt, 3*n*, p.166.
67. Captain Henry John Thomas, RA. Commissioned, 18 December 1835; captain, 11 November 1849.
68. Captain John Shiffner, 34th Regt. Born 1824, the son of the Revd George Shiffner of Hamsey, Sussex. Commissioned 34th Regt. Served Corfu and Ionian Islands (1845–8) and West Indies (1848–53). Landed in the Crimea 9 December 1854. He was injured whilst taking part in a Light Division horse race on 7 April 1855 'In taking a leap at a stone wall their [his and Captain Thomas, R.A.] horses missed, and horses and riders fell confusedly together ... very considerably contused.' He was killed in action during the assault on the Redan, 18 June 1855. His youngest brother, Bertie Shiffner, was commissioned into the same regiment, 20 July 1855 (without purchase).
69. T. Buckmaster & Co of 135 George Street, Edinburgh were tailors and army clothiers who had sent a representative out to the Crimea to take orders for the new officers' tunic that was introduced at this time to replace the more traditional coatee that had been worn in the early stages of the war. See illustration on page 56.
70. Unidentified.
71. Colonel William Bernard Ainslie, 93rd Regt. Commissioned, 28 September 1830. Lieutenant-colonel, 21 October 1853. CB. Commanded the famous 'Thin Red Line' at Balaklava, 25 October 1854 (Mentioned in Despatches). Served on the Kertch Expedition. Granted leave of absence 9 December 1855 until his retirement on half pay.
72. Emperor Napoleon III of France.
73. Round Tower, 36*n*, p.169.
74. Gordon's Battery, 7*n*, p.169.
75. Lieutenant-General Sir John Burgoyne, GCB, 44*n*, p.161.
76. Lieutenant-General Sir Harry David Jones, KCB, RE. Commissioned, 17 September 1808. Served Walcheren, 1809, Peninsular, 1810–14. Silver War Medal (5 clasps). Commanding Engineer for Montmatre, Paris, 1815. Brigadier-General Baltic operations 1854, commanded operations against Bomersund and the Aland Isles. Major-general, 12 December 1854. GOC Royal Engineers Crimea in succession to Burgoyne. Wounded in the forehead by grape shot, 18 June 1855. Granted local rank of lieutenant-general, 31 August 1855. KCB, 26 August 1855. Mentioned in General Simpson's despatch of 9 September 1855: 'I cannot sufficiently express my approbation of the conduct of the Royal Engineers under Lieutenant-General Sir Harry Jones who has conducted the siege operations from

the beginning of this year. For some time past he has been suffering on a bed of sickness, but the eventful hour of the assault would not permit him to remain absent; he was conveyed on a litter into the trenches to witness the completion of his arduous undertakings.' Hospitalised at Scutari suffering from sciatica on his way home to Britain October 1855. Member of the Council of War, Paris, January 1856 (which led to the drawing up of the peace treaty with Russia). Governor Royal Military College, Sandhurst, 1856. Hon DCL degree (Oxford), 1856. Cross Commander of the *Légion d'honneur*, 1856. Commander 1st Class Order of Savoy (Sardinia), August 1856; Member of the Commission into the Purchase System for Commissions, 1857. Sardinian War Medal. Chief Commissioner on the Royal Commission on Works of National Defence, 1859. Author of *Journal of Operations conducted by the Corps of Royal Engineers, Part II – from February 1855 to the Fall of Sebastopol, September 1855* (London, 1859). Lieutenant-general, 31 July 1860. Colonel Commandant Corps of Royal Engineers, 4 September 1860. Second son, Captain Arthur Trefusis Jones, died Lagos, 1861. Died 1866.

77. St George's Monastery was located on the top of the cliffs to the west of the town of Balaklava.
78. The location of these rifle pits can be seen in the sketch map on p.105, between the 3rd Parallel and the Quarries. They are labeled 'Egerton's Pit'.
79. Lieutenant-Colonel Egerton, 77th Regt. Born *c*.1813, the eldest son of General Sir Charles Bulkeley Egerton, GCMG, KCH, Colonel 89th Regt. Commissioned, 24 December 1829; lieutenant-colonel, 27 December 1850. Served Crimea from September 1854. Present at Alma, Inkerman and the siege of Sevastopol. Killed when shot through the upper lip by a rifle bullet which passed through his head whilst forming up troops to repulse a Russian assault before the Malakoff, 19 April 1855. Lord Raglan described him as an officer 'of superior merit, and conducted all his duties, whether in the camp or in the field, in a manner highly to his own honour, and greatly to the advantage of the public; and her Majesty's service could not have sustained a more severe loss; and it is so felt in the army and in the 77th, where he was much beloved, and is deeply lamented.' [Despatch 21 April, 1855] Buried, 21 April, alongside the Woronstov Road, Lord Raglan attending the funeral. He was recommended for a CB before his death. A marble memorial to him was placed in Chester Cathedral and a brass plaque in the Royal Garrison Church, Portsmouth.
80. Captain Audley Lemprière, 77th Regt. Born *c*.1834, the eldest son of Rear-Admiral G.O. Lemprière of Pelham House, Newton Valence, Hampshire. RMC Sandhurst. Commissioned, 10 December 1852 (without purchase). Served Crimea from September 1854, present at Alma, Inkerman and the siege of Sevastopol. Adjutant 77th Regt. Died of wounds received whilst repulsing the first Russian assault on the rifle pits before the Malakoff, 19 April 1855. He was shot through the lungs. A fellow officer described him as 'Very young, had just got his company and was about the smallest officer in the Army [under 5ft tall], a great pet of the Colonel's [Egerton, 45*n*, p.174] and termed by him "his child"; he was killed, poor fellow, at the first attack in the rifle pit. The Colonel, tho' wounded, snatched him up in his arms & carried him off declaring "they shall never take my child".' Lord Raglan described him as a 'very young, but promising officer'. [Despatch 21 April 1855] Buried 21 April, alongside the Woronstov Road, Lord Raglan attending the funeral. There are memorials to him in St Nicholas's Church, Chariton and St Mary's Church, Newton Valence. His uniform coatee, worn at the time of his death, is held by the National Army Museum.
81. Captain John William Trevor, 55th Regt. Commissioned, 7 June 1854. Embarked at Queenstown for the Crimea, 31 October 1854. Dangerously wounded in the elbow whilst with a working party in the rifle

pits before Sevastopol, 19 April 1855. Invalided to Britain, June 1855. Returned to duty Ireland, January 1856. Captain (without purchase), 30 April 1856. Exchanged to the 22nd Regt, 30 September 1859. Retired, 21 January 1868.

82. Captain Henry Charles Cunliffe-Owen, Royal Engineers. Born Switzerland, *c.*1822, son of Captain Charles Cunliffe-Owen, RN, and Mary Blosset. Commissioned Royal Engineers, 19 March 1839. Served in Cape Colony and saw active service 1845 and 1846–7, awarded medal with clasp. General Superintendant of the Great Exhibition of 1851. Served Crimea, severely wounded in the thigh by grape shot (left leg amputated), 19 April 1855. Part of his duties in the front line had been to try and locate a natural source of water. Invalided to Britain, May 1855. Brevet-major, 17 July 1855. CB, February 1856. Assistant Inspector-General of Fortifications, October 1856; Deputy Inspector-General of Fortifications, 1856–60; OC Royal Engineers Western District. Colonel. Married 1855, one son. Died at Plymouth, 1867. Memorial window St James's Church, Plymouth.
83. Lieutenant Charles Stuart Baynes, R.E. Commissioned, 27 June 1848. Severely wounded by rifle ball in the chest, 19 April 1855. Died of his wounds May 1855.
84. Captain Hugh Rowlands, 41st Regt, 29*n*, p.159.
85. Lieutenant-Colonel John Wilkie, 10th Hussars. Born, June 1817. Commissioned, 10th Hussars, 11 May 1838. OC 10th Hussars throughout the Crimean campaign including Alma, capture of Tchorgaun, battle of Tchernaya, siege of Sevastopol. Crimean Medal; Order of the Medjidie (5th Class); Turkish Crimea Medal. Colonel, 28 November 1854; major-general, 6 March 1868; lieutenant-general, 6 October 1876; general, 21 December 1878. Hon Colonel, 14th Hussars. He died at Knowehead, Lanarkshire, 30 April 1882.

5. On the Offensive

1. General François Certain de Canrobert (1809–1895). Commissioned, 1828. Served Algeria, 1835. *Légion d'honneur* for courageous conduct. Colonel CO 3rd Regiment, 1847. Commanded an expedition against Ahmed Sghir in 1848. Transferred to the Zouaves (1848-50)and saw active service against the Kabyles (1849) and at Bou Saada and Zaatcha (1849). For his valour on the latter occasion he received the rank of general of brigade and the commandership of the *Légion d'honneur*. He led the expedition against Narah in 1850. ADC to the president, Louis-Napoléon Bonaparte, and took part in the *coup d'état* of 2 December 1851. In the Crimean War he commanded a division at the Battle of Alma, where he was twice wounded. He succeeded to the chief command of the French army a few days after the battle following the death of Saint-Arnaud. Slightly wounded and had a horse killed under him at Inkerman. He eventually resigned his command, remaining in the Crimea in command of his old division almost up to the fall of Sevastopol. Created a Marshal of France and a Senator for Life. Grand Cross *Légion d'honneur*, and honorary GCB. Served in the Austro-Sardinian War and the Franco-Prussian War. Elected Senator for Lot in 1876 and for Charente in 1879 and again in 1885. He died at Paris, 1895. He married Leila-Flora MacDonald in 1863, great-granddaughter of the Jacobite heroine Flora MacDonald. They had one daughter and two sons.
2. Miss Florence Nightingale, OM, RRC (1820–1910). Appointed Superintendent of the Institute for the Care of Sick Gentlewomen in 1853, she travelled to Scutari in Turkey with a staff of 38 women volunteer nurses, arriving in November 1854. Her influence on the care of injured and sick soldiers was significant although there is now considerable debate as to her actual efficacy in reducing the death rate

at Scutari. It was not until after the war had ended that she effectively turned her attention to the sanitary conditions in military hospitals and thereby achieved any long-term improvements in the care of the sick.

3. Alexis Soyer (1810–58). A French chef who had established himself in London, he travelled to the Crimea to advise the authorities about cooking and the provisioning of hospitals. He introduced a training scheme for regimental cooks and designed a field stove that was in regular use by the British Army until well into the twentieth century.
4. Lola Montez (c.1820–61), Irish actress and courtesan, she was the mistress of King Ludvig I of Bavaria who made her Countess of Landsfeld. She visited the Crimea en route to Australia.
5. Captain Robert Pratt, 41st Regt, 32*n*, p.160.
6. Lieutenant James Augustus Lockhart, 41st Regt, 32*n*, p.168.
7. Stratford Canning, 1st Viscount Stratford de Redcliffe, KG, GCB, PC (1786–1880), was the British Ambassador to the Ottoman Empire, 1825–8 and 1841–58. He and his wife, Eliza Charlotte Alexander, visited the Crimea on two occasions during the war.
8. Lieutenant Stuart Baynes, R.E., 82*n*, p.178.
9. Captain George Peddie, 41st Regt. Commissioned 71st Regt, 10 February 1854. Transfered to 41st Regt, 2 March 1854; lieutenant, 8 December 1854 (without purchase); captain, 26 February 1856 (without purchase).
10. Major Green, 48th Regt. Commissioned, 12 January 1838; major, 13 December 1853 (by purchase).
11. Lieutenant Valentine Bennett, 33rd Regt. Third son of Valentine Bennett of Thomastown House, King's County. Commissioned, 17 November 1848 (by purchase); lieutenant, 26 March 1852 (by purchase). killed in action, 18 June 1855.
12. Ensign Richard Lloyd Edwards, 68th Regt. The eldest son of Richard Lloyd Edwards of Nanhoron, Pwllheli. Commissioned, 23 January 1852 (by purchase); lieutenant, 6 June 1854. KiA Sevastopol, 11 May 1855, aged 22. A letter, published in the *North Wales Chronicle,* 26 May 1855, reported: 'Last night, in the midst of an awful storm of rain and wind – so thick that no one could see a yard before him – a body of Russins came up on our left attack; but the sentries gave the alarm just in time, and Colonel Macbeth of the 68th Regiment, got his men into order, and received the first fire of the enemy, as they came up the trench, with perfect steadiness. There was a desperate struggle between the Russians and the men of the 68th outside the lines, in which the bayonet was freely used on both sides; but the enemy were repulsed by our fellows ... I much lament that Captain Lloyd Edwards, and six men of the 68th, were killed, and 22 men of the same regiment were wounded. We took some prisoners.' The *Morning Advertiser* reported: 'We have to regret the loss of poor Edwards of the 68th; he was a most promising young officer, and a universal favourite, from his kindness, spirit and good temper. He was, when found, lying on his face – the ball had gone right through his heart.' An additional prize was offered at the Royal London Eisteddfod of three guineas for the best 'Monody' (a poem lamenting a person's death), in Welsh or English, on the death of Captain Richard Lloyd Edwards.
13. Alexander Moncrieff of Culfargie and Barnhill, a qualified civil engineer and a lieutenant in the Forfarshire Militia. He visited the Crimea and was present during the first and second bombardments of Sevastopol. Whilst there he devised the idea of the protected barbette artillery mounting, perhaps better known as the 'Disappearing Gun' which, on being fired, recoiled into a sheltered position out of sight of the enemy. The design was eventually taken up by the Ordnance and Moncrieff spent eight

years in the Royal Arsenal, attached to the department of the Director of Artillery. Colonel Commandant Royal Artillery, JP; Member of the Institute of Civil Engineers, Fellow of the Royal Society; Knight of the Imperial Order of the Rose of Brazil; member of the Royal Scottish Archers; CB, 1880.

14. General François Certain de Canrobert, 1*n,* p.178.
15. General Aimable Jean Jacques Pélissier. Born at Maromme, Seine Inférieure, the son of an artisan, he attended the military college of La Flèche and the special school of St Cyr. Commissioned in the artillery, 1815. Appointed to the staff, 1819. ADC in the Spanish campaign, 1823, and in Morea, 1828–9. Served Algeria, 1830.Promoted *général de brigade,* 1845 and *général de division* 1850. Served Crimea, 1854. Succeeded Canrobert as C-in-C French forces, 16 May 1855. Captured the Malakoff, 8 September 1855. Marshal, 12 September 1855. Later named senator and created Duc de Malakoff in July 1856. French ambassador to London, 1858–9. GOC Army of Observation on the Rhine, 1859. Grand Chancellor *Légion d'honneur*, 1859. Governor of Algeria, 1860. Died 1864.
16. General Omar Pasha, 109*n,* p.165.
17. Field Marshal Lord Raglan, 50*n,* p.161.
18. Gordon's Battery, 7*n*, p.169.
19. Alexander Moncrieff, 13*n,* p.179.
20. Captain William Johnston, 41st Regt, 28*n,* p.159.
21. Lieutenant James Augustus Lockhart, 41st Regt, 32*n,* p.168.
22. Lieutenant Walter John Johnson, 41st Regt. Commissioned, 24 November 1854 (by purchase); lieutenant, 9 March 1855.
23. Colonel George V. Mundy, 33rd Regt. Commissioned, 27 February 1835; lieutenant-colonel, 12 December 1854. CB.
24. Field Marshal Lord Raglan, 50*n,* p.161.
25. Redan, 56*n*, p.175.
26. Malakoff, 34*n*, p.168.
27. Mamelon, 50*n*, p.172.
28. Major-General Sir John Lysaght Pennefather, GCB, 44*n,* p.175.
29. Lieutenant-Colonel James Eman, 41st Regt, 3*n,* p.167.
30. Round Tower, 36*n,* p.169.
31. William Howard Russell, 10*n,* p.167.
32. Captain Hugh Rowlands, 41st Regt, 29*n,* p.159.
33. Captain George Peddie, 41st Regt, 9*n,* p.179.
34. Captain Charles Pelgué Bertram, 41st Regt, 15*n,* p.158.
35. Redan, 56*n*, p.175.
36. Major (later lieutenant-colonel) Julius Edmund Goodwyn, 41st Regt. Commissioned, 5 January 1844 (by purchase); lieutenant, 6 June 1845 (by purchase); captain, 3 May 1850 (by purchase); major, 15 September 1854 (by purchase); lieutenant-colonel, 12 December 1854. Served Crimean campaign, wounded 18 June 1855. *Légion d'honneur,* 1856; CB, 1857. Brevet Colonel. GOC Brigade, India, 27 July 1866. Retired as a general and Colonel 1st Bn Gloucestershire Regt, 25 June 1881. Died, aged 66, 4 March 1890, 36 Brock Street, Bath.
37. Malakoff, 34*n*, p.168.
38. Mamelon, 50*n*, p.172.

39. Captain Robert Nicholl Dawson, R.E. Commissioned, 14 August 1854; lieutenant, 16 August 1854.
40. Lieutenant Thomas Graves Lowry, R.E. (Allan was mistaken in given him the initial 'R'). Killed leading an attack on the Quarries, aged 20, he was youngest son of Robert William Lowry of Pomeroy, County Tyrone and the brother of Captain Armar Graham Lowry and Lieutenant Edward Barnwell Lowry of the 41st Regt and Major Robert William Lowry and Lieutenant James Armar Lowry of the 47th Regt.
41. Captain Armar Graham Lowry, 41st Regt. Commissioned, 11 November 1853 (by purchase); captain, 9 September 1855. He had carried the Queen's Colour during the Battle of Inkerman. Later lieutenant-colonel. See endnote 30 (above) for family details.
42. Field Marshal Lord Raglan, 50*n,* p.161.
43. General Aimable Jean Jacques Pélissier, 15*n,* p.180.
44. Major-General Sir John Campbell, Bart. Born 1807, the second son of Lieutenant-General Sir Archibald Campbell, Bart, GCB, KCTS. Commissioned, 25 November 1821; lieutenant-colonel (38th Regt), 7 August 1840; colonel, 11 November 1851. Served Burma, 1823. CO 38th Regt. Brigadier-general commanding 1st Brigade, 4th Division, at the Alma and Inkerman. He displayed a courage amounting to rashness during the assault on the Redan, 18 June 1855, when he sent away his two ADCs before rushing out of the trench to cheer his men on in the assault and was killed almost immediately. There are memorials to him in Winchester Cathedral and St John's Church, Princes Street, Edinburgh. He married Helen Margaret, daughter of Colonel John Crow.
45. Colonel Lacy Walter Giles Yea, 7th Regt. Born 1808, Bristol, eldest son of Sir William Yea, Bart of Pyrland, Somerset. Commissioned 37th Regt, 6 October 1825. Exchanged to 5th Regt, 13 March 1827. Exchanged to 7th Regt, 13 March 1828. Lieutenant-Colonel, 9 August 1850. CO 7th Regt Crimean campaign. Present at the Alma, Inkerman and the siege of Sevastopol. Killed in action during the assault on the Redan, 18 June 1855. Lord Raglan wrote in his despatch of 19 June: 'Colonel Yea was not only distinguished for his gallantry, but had exercised his control of the Royal Fusiliers in such a manner as to win the affection of the soldiers under his orders, and to secure to them every comfort and accommodation which personal exertions could secure for them'.
46. Major-General Sir John Lysaght Pennefather, GCB, 44*n,* p.175.
47. Lieutenant-General Henry William Barnard, KCB. Born 1799 at Westbury, Oxfordshire, son of Revd William Henry Barnard (first cousin to Prime Minister George Canning). Commissioned, 9 June 1814. Major-General, 20.6.54. GOC Monmouth & South Wales District, 1854. Brigade commander and Chief of Staff to General Sir James Simpson. CB. *Légion d'honneur*. KCB. Died of cholera, India, 5 July 1857. Memorial Royal Garrison Church, Portsmouth.
48. General Sir James Simpson, GCB (1792–1868). Born Edinburgh son of David Simpson of Teviotbank. Commissioned Grenadier Guards, 3 April 1811 (he was the tallest officer in the British Army). Served Peninsular campaign, 1812–13, Belgium, 1815 (wounded at Quatre Bras). Lieutenant-colonel, 29th Regt 10 June 1826; brevet colonel, 28 June 1838. GOC Benares Division, India. Second-in-command to Sir Charles Napier in Sind, 1845. Commandant Chatham. GOC South West District. Local lieutenant-general, March 1855, Chief of Staff to Lord Raglan. Succeeded as C-in-C Crimea, 28 June 1855 (lieutenant-general and local general). Criticised for the assault on the Redan, 8 September 1855. General, 8 September 1855. GCB, 1855. Colonel 87th Regt. Resigned his command, 10 November 1855. Grand Cross *Légion d'honneur*; Military Order of Savoy; 1st Class Order of Medjidie. Colonel 29th Regt, 1863. Died, 18 April 1868. Married Elizabeth Dundas.

49. General Sir William Codrington, GCB (1804–84). Born 1804, second son of Admiral Sir Edward Codrington, victor of Navarino. Commissioned Coldstream Guards, 1821. Major-general, 20 June 1854. Appointed GOC 1st Brigade of the Light Division , at this time he had no active service experience whatsoever. Present at Alma (where he took part in the assault on the Great Redoubt) and Inkerman. GOC Light Division, 5 November 1854. KCB, 1855. Commander *Légion d'honneur*; knight grand cross Order of Savoy; Order of Medjidie (1st Class). Present during the siege of Sevastopol and planned the assault on the Redan, 8 September 1855. On 11 November 1855 he succeeded Sir James Simpson as C-in-C, a position which he retained until 12 July 1856. Lieutenant-general. Colonel 54th Regt. MP for Greenwich, 1857. Governor of Gibraltar, 1859–65. Colonel 23rd Regt, 1860. General, 1863. GCB, 1865. Colonel Coldstream Guards, 1875. Twice declined the rank of field-marshal. Died 1884.
50. Lieutenant-General Sir George Brown, GCB, KH, 36*n*, p.160.
51. Major-General James Bucknall Estcourt. Born 1802, second son of Thomas Grimston Bucknall Estcourt, Esq, of Estcourt, Gloucestershire. Commissioned 44th Regt, July 1820. Exchanged 43rd Regt, 1821. Married Caroline Carew, August 1837. Served Canada, 1838–9. Brevet lieutenant-colonel, 1839. Member of the British Boundary Commission to define the border between the USA and Canada, 1843. MP for Devizes, 1848–52. Appointed Judge-Advocate of the British Expeditionary Force to Turkey, 1853. Adjutant-General, 1853. Brigadier-general, March 1854. Present at the Alma, Inkerman, the siege of Sevastopol and the assault of 18 June 1855. Died of cholera, 24 June 1855. Would have been awarded the KCB had he survived.
52. Named after Lieutenant-Colonel Thomas Graham Egerton, 77th Regt (78*n*, p.177). See sketch map, p.105.
53. 8-gun Battery, also known as Dickson's Battery (after Lieutenant-Colonel Collingwood Dickson, who was awarded the VC for his action here on 17 October 1854). See sketch map p.105.
54. Captain Charles Pelgué Bertram, 41st Regt, 15*n*, p.158.
55. Lieutenant Hans S. St Vincent Marsh, 33rd Regt. Commissioned, 16 September 1851.
56. Brevet-Major Lumley Graham, 41st Regt. Born 1828, second son of Sir Sandford Graham, Bart, and Caroline Langston. Commissioned 43rd Regt, 13 August 1847; lieutenant, 28 February 1851; captain. Transfered to 48th Regt, 7 July 1854. Landed in the Crimea, 14 September 1854. Transfered to 41st Regt. Present at the battles of the Alma and Inkerman. Brevet major, 12 December 1854. Severely wounded in the Mamelon, in the French sector of the trenches before Sevastopol, 29 August 1855; loss of right arm. He was later an aide to General Eyre. Brevet lieutenant-colonel (for staff services); *Légion d'honneur* (1856); Order of Medjidie 5th Class and Turkish Crimea Medal. Half-pay 1856. Brevet lieutenant-colonel. Transferred to 19th Regt. Transfered 18th Regt 29 September 1865. Brevt colonel 14 October 1865. Retired as Brevet colonel and major 24 September 1869. Inherited the title of 4th Baronet Graham of Kirkstall on the death of his brother in 1875. Married to Augusta Barker, 1 January 1856, no children. In his final years he resided at Arlington Manor, Newbury. He died 25 October 1890. He translated *Tactical deductions from the War of 1870-71* by Albrecht Boguslawski and *The Battalion* by Hugo Von Helvig and wrote numerous articles on infantry tactics in battle. Buried Mortimer, West End, Reading.
57. Captain Hugh Rowlands, 41st Regt, 29*n*, p.159.
58. Captain Fitzhardinge Kingscote, 41st Regt, 28*n*, p.172.
59. Captain Frederick Cherburgh Bligh, 41st Regt, 18*n*, p.158.

60. Captain John William Wavell, 41st Regt. Born 1836. Commssioned, 14 December 1854. Served in the Crimea from June 1855. Passed Staff College, 1860. AAQMG South Africa, 1880. Colonel. Married Beatrice Matilda Byng. Three sons (eldest Major Arthur John Byng Wavell, MC, Welsh Regiment) and one daughter. Died 1891. He was a cousin to the father of Field Marshal Archibald Wavell.
61. Captain Hugh Rowlands, 41st Regt, 29*n*, p.159.
62. St George's Monastery, 76*n*, p.177.
63. Major-General Frederick Markham. Born 1805, son of Admiral John Markham and grandson of Archbishop William Markham of York. Commissioned 32nd Regt, 13 May 1824 (by purchase); lieutenant-colonel, 22 July 1842. Imprisoned for twelve months for acting as a second at a duel. Served Canada, 1837 (wounded three times), Punjab, 1848–9 (wounded). CB, 1849. Reward for Distinguished Service, 1853. ADC HM Queen Victoria, 1850. Author *Shooting in the Himalayas* (1854). Adjutant-General, India 1854. Major-General GOC Peshawar Division, November 1854. GOC 2nd Division, Sevastopol, 30 July 1855 (local lieutenant-general). Returned home on health grounds, September 1855. Died, 21 December 1855.
64. Lieutenant-General Sir Richard England, KCB, 90*n*, p.164.
65. Brigadier-General Henry Frederick Lockyer. Born 8 April 1796, Plymouth, the son of Thomas and Ann Lockyer. Commissioned 71st Regt. Served Peninsular War 1813–14, present at Nivelle, Nive, Orthes, Aire (severely wounded in left wrist and elbow) and Toulouse. Lieutenant-colonel, CO 97th Regt 26 October 1841 (without purchase); colonel; brigadier-general 2nd Brigade, 2nd Division, Crimea, November 1854. Local major-general, GOC Ceylon, September 1855; major-general, October 1858. Acting Lieutenant Governor of Ceylon, June–July 1860. Died aboard SS *Ripon*, October 1860. CB; KH; *Légion d'honneur*, 4th Class (1857). Died 30 August 1860. He married Ellia Ann Curry in 1819. Brother of Captain Nicholas Lockyer, RN, CB, of HMS *Albion* and Major Edmund Lockyer, 57th Regt.
66. Major-General Charles Ashe Windham, CB. Born 1810, third son of Vice-Admiral Windham, in Norfolk. Commissioned Coldstream Guards, December 1826; lieutenant-colonel 29 December 1846. Half pay 22 June 1849. Colonel, 20 June 1854. AQMG 4th Division, Crimea. Brigadier-general, 2nd Division. Led the final assault on the Redan, 8 September 1855. Major-general, 8 September 1855. Reward for Distinguished Service 22 June 1855. Commander of the Karabelnaia (British sector of Sevastopol), 1855. CB 5 July 1855. GOC 4th Division. Chief of Staff of the Army in the Crimea. Local lieutenant-general (Turkey) 1 January 1856. *Légion d'honneur* (3rd Class); Order of Savoy; Order of the Medjidie (2nd Class). Unattached 1858–9. MP East Norfolk, 1857. Served Indian Mutiny, 1857. Lieutenant-general, 1863. KCB, 1865. Colonel 46th Regt, 1861. GOC British Forces North America.
67. Lieutenant Charles Henry Evans, 55th Regt. Commissioned, 18 August 1854 (by purchase); lieutenant, 15 December 1854.
68. General Sir James Simpson, GCB, 48*n*, p.181.
69. Redan, 56*n*, p.175.
70. Malakoff, 34*n*, p.168.
71. Captain Horace W. Montagu, R.E., 55*n*, p.175.
72. Captain Hugh Rowlands, 41st Regt, 29*n*, p.159.
73. Captain Charles Pelgué Bertram, 41st Regt, 15*n*, p.158.
74. The great Russian fortress of Sweaborg and the city of Helsingfors on the Gulf of Finland were bombarded by the allied British and French fleets on 8 and 9 August 1855. Despite causing a great deal

of destruction, the naval guns failed to destroy the Russian defences and the operation could not be deemed a great success although contemporary news reports did suggest that the attack had rendered the harbour ineffective. Plans for the Allied fleet to return for a second bombardment were never implemented before hostilities came to an end. Revel was the Russian name for Tallinn, the capital of modern-day Estonia. Cronstadt was the port of St Petersburg, at the mouth of the river Neva; in the nineteenth century it was regarded as Russia's greatest naval station and was thought to be absolutely impregnable.

75. Brevet-Major Lumley Graham, 41st Regt, 56*n*, p.182.
76. Mamelon, 50*n*, p.172.
77. Captain Frederick Cherburgh Bligh, 41st Regt, 18*n*, p.158.
78. The Little Redan was a Russian defensive feature to the east of the Malakoff on the southern side of the city of Sevastopol.
79. Fort St Nicholas, 38*n*, p.169.
80. James Stewart. Unidentified.
81. Captain Philip Limborch Tillbrook, 50th Regt. Commissioned, 16 November 1849; captain, 18 October 1853.

6. The Fall of Sevastopol

1. Captain Edward Every, 41st Regt, 128*n*, p.166.
2. Lieutenant James Augustus Lockhart, 41st Regt, 32*n*, p.168.
3. Lieutenant-Colonel James Eman, 41st Regt, 3*n*, p.166.
4. The Light Company was positioned on the left of the regimental line and originally provided the regiment's skirmishers, or light infantry soldiers.
5. Redan, 56*n*, p.175.
6. Malakoff, 34*n*, p.168.
7. Captain Hugh Rowlands, 41st Regt, 29*n*, p.159.
8. These rifle pits were located west of the Quarries. See sketch map on p.105.
9. Captain Charles Pelugué Bertram, 41st Regt, 15*n*, p.158.
10. Brevet-Major Lumley Graham, 41st Regt, 56*n*, p.182.
11. Captain William Johnston, 41st Regt, 28*n*, p.159.
12. Captain John Younger Allan, 71st Regt, 124*n*, p.166.
13. Malakoff, 34*n*, p.168.
14. Redan, 56*n*, p.175.
15. Little Redan, 78n, p.184.
16. Captain Hugh Rowlands, 41st Regt, 29*n*, p.159.
17. General Aimable Jean Jacques Pélissier, 15*n*, p.180.
18. Captain Hugh Rowlands, 41st Regt, 29*n*, p.159.
19. Captain Edward Every, 41st Regt, 128*n*, p.166.
20. Captain John Edmund Harvey, 41st Regt. Commissioned, 14 August 1846 (by purchase); captain, 2March 1855 (by purchase).
21. Lieutenant James Augustus Lockhart, 41st Regt, 32*n*, p.168.
22. Captain Fitzhardinge Kingscote, 41st Regt, 28*n*, p.172.

23. Lieutenant Robert Eustace Maude, 41st Regt. Commissioned ensign, 22 September 1854 (by purchase); lieutenant, 11 January 1855. Slightly wounded in the leg during the final assault on the Redan, 8 September 1855.
24. Lieutenant James Alexander Hamilton, 41st Regt. Commissioned, 27 January 1854 (by purchase). Arrived in the Crimea, 13 November 1854, from Queenstown aboard HMS *Jura*. Lieutenant (without purchase), 6 November 1854; captain, 18 January 1856 (vice Skipwith). Adjutant, 9 February 1855. Slightly wounded in the assault on the Redan, 8 September 1855.
25. Private William Cuthbert (regimental number 3522), William Allan's servant.
26. Captain Edward Every, 41st Regt, 128*n,* p.166.
27. Lieutenant James Augustus Lockhart, 41st Regt, 32*n,* p.168.
28. Lieutenant-Colonel James Eman, 41st Regt, 3*n,* p.166.
29. Lieutenant-Colonel Julius Edmund Goodwyn, 41st Regt, 36*n,* p.180.
30. Lieutenant-Colonel Julius Edmund Goodwyn, 41st Regt, 36*n,* p.180.
31. Fort St Paul, a large fort located close to the dockyards.
32. Captain Hugh Rowlands, 41st Regt, 29*n,* p.159.
33. Captain George Skipwith, 41st Regt, 33*n,* p.160.
34. Alexander Moncrieff, 13*n,* p.179.
35. William Allan's aunt, Isabella Younger, the wife of Lieutenant-Colonel George Allan.
36. Captain Fitzhardinge Kingscote, 41st Regt, 38*n,* p.172.
37. Lieutenant-General Eduard Todleben (2828–84). Commissioned, 1836, into the engineers. Present at the siege of Silistria, 1853, then transferred to Sevastopol where, despite his low rank (lieutenant-colonel), he masterminded the construction of fortifications on the land side of the city. He personally conducted the defensive operations until he was wounded on 20 June 1855 by which time he was a lieutenant-general. He was eventually a full general GOC the department of engineers in the Russian Imperial Army. Governor of Bessarabia and Novorossiya. Created a hereditary count. Governor of Vilna. His memorial stands in Sevastopol and the town of Totleben in Pleven Province, Bulgaria is named after him.
38. Captain George Robert Fitzroy, 41st Regt, 17*n,* p.158.
39. Captain George Robert Fitzroy, 41st Regt, 17*n,* p.158.
40. Captain Fitzhardinge Kingscote, 41st Regt, 28*n,* p.172.
41. Brevet-Major Lumley Graham, 41st Regt, 56*n,* p.182.
42. Lieutenant Robert Eustace Maude, 41st Regt, 23*n,* p.184.
43. Captain Robert Pratt, 41st Regt, 32*n,* p.160.
44. Captain George Robert Fitzroy, 41st Regt, 17*n,* p.158.
45. William Allan can be seen wearing this medal in the photograph reproduced on page 18.
46. T. Buckmaster & Co, 68*n,* p.176.
47. Captain Charles Pelugué Bertram, 41st Regt, 15*n,* p.158.
48. Captain Fitzhardinge Kingscote, 41st Regt, 28*n,* p.172.
49. Ensign Richard Pack, 41st Regt. Commissioned, 2 February 1855; lieutenant, 18 January 1856.
50. Ensign Stanley Robert R. Smith, 41st Regt. Commissioned, 12 January 1855 (by purchase); lieutenant, 9 September 1855.
51. Captain Hugh Rowlands, 41st Regt, 29*n,* p.159.

52. Captain William Frederick Augustus Rooke, 47th Regt. Commissioned, 23 August 1844 (by purchase); lieutenant 13 July 1847; captain, 27 December 1851.
53. Lieutenant-Colonel Julius Edmund Goodwyn, 41st Regt, 36*n*, p.180.
54. Alexander Moncrieff, 13*n*, p.179.
55. Captain William Aitchison, Scots Fusilier Guards, 112*n*, p.165.
56. Captain William Aitchison, Scots Fusilier Guards, 112*n*, p.165.
57. Kinburn was a fortress on the south shore of the Dnieper river estuary which was bombarded by British and French warships on 17 October 1855. The battle is noted as an early success for ironclad warships. Despite sustaining a number of hits, the French warships were able to continue operating and the Russian forts were destroyed in under four hours.
58. Lieutenant William Johnston, 41st Regt, 28*n*, p.159.
59. Unidentified.
60. Brevet-Major Charles Nasmyth, 65*n*, p.162.
61. Captain Frederick Ball Dixon, 41st Regt. 29*n*, *p*.168.
62. Lieutenant-Colonel Julius Edmund Goodwyn, 41st Regt, 36*n*, p.180.
63. Probably John Gott (1830–1906) the brother-in-law of William Allan's cousin, Anne Mary Gott (née Aitchison). He later became the Bishop of Truro.
64. Lieutenant Henry George Charles Burningham, 3rd Regt, 22*n*, *p*.158.
65. Lieutenant-General Henry William Barnard, KCB, 47*n*, p.181.
66. Alexander Moncrieff, 13*n*, p.179.
67. The Russian supplies at Gheisk on the Sea of Azov were destroyed by a Royal Navy force led by Commander Sherard Osborn, RN, who wrote: 'I despair of being able to convey to you any idea of the extraordinary quantity of corn, rye, hay, wood, and other supplies so necessary for the existence of Russiau armies, both in the Caucasus and in the Crimea, which it has been our good fortune to destroy. ... During these proceedings we never had more than 200 men engaged. The enemy had ... from 3,000 to 4,000 men in Gheisk alone.' (http://home.wxs.nl/~pdavis, memoirs of naval surgeon William Loney, RN.)
68. Lieutenant-Colonel Julius Edmund Goodwyn, 41st Regt, 36*n*, p.180.
69. Lieutenant Edward L. Barnwell Lowry, 41st Regt. Commissioned ensign, 10 August 1854; lieutenant, 8 December 1854; captain, 14 June 1859. Served in the Crimea from 13 November 1854 (arrived aboard HMS *Jura*) where he was present at the siege of Sevastopol and took part in the final assault on the Redan, 8 September 1855, where he was slightly wounded. Crimea Medal with 1 clasp, Order of the Medjidie (5th Class), Turkish Medal. Lieutenant-colonel.
70. Ensign Henry Edward Byam, 41st Regt. Born 1835, Lyndhurst, Hampshire, second son of Lieutenant-General Edward Byam (Colonel 18th Hussars) and Elizabeth Augusta Byam (née Temple). Commissioned, 12 December 1854 (without purchase).
71. Lieutenant-Colonel Julius Edmund Goodwyn, 41st Regt, 36*n*, p.180.
72. Captain George Skipwith, 41st Regt, 33*n*, p.160.
73. Captain William Aitchison, Scots Fusilier Guards, 106*n*, p.165.
74. Unidentified.
75. Major-General Charles Ashe Windham, 66*n*, p.183.
76. Lieutenant & Adjutant Lionel Mordaunt Fraser, 41st Regt. Commissioned, 9 July 1852 (by purchase);

lieutenant, 2 February 1855. He later lived in the West Indies where he was Inspector General of Police and Inspector of Prisons for Trinidad. Author of *History of the West Indies, 1781–1839*.

77. Brevet-Major George Hyde Page, 41st Regt. Commissioned 55th Regt, 23 April 1844 (by purchase); lieutenant, 12 May 1843 (by purchase); lieutenant, 12 May 43. Served with distinction in the Maori War in New Zealand, 1846. Captain, 26 January 1855. Arrived Crimea March 1856. Brevet-major, 20 July 1855; brevet lieutenant-colonel; half-pay major, 25 April 1865. DQMG Australian Colonies, 2 March 1867, DQMG Cape of Good Hope, 8 April 1870. Retired as honorary lieutenant-general, 10 April 1885.
78. Surgeon James Edward Scott, MB, 41st Regt. Appointed assistant-surgeon Rifle Brigade, 11 June 1847. Served with the Rifle Brigade in South Africa 1852–3 (medal); surgeon, 9 February 1855; appointed surgeon 41st Regt (vice Anderson, deceased), 13 February 1855. Served Crimea. Staff surgeon (2nd Class), 21 November 1856; surgeon Rifle Brigade, 2 October 1857. MD. Honorary deputy surgeon-general on retiring, 6 December 1873. Married Martha Johnson of Portaferry, 5 May 1858. One son.
79. SS *Oneida*. A British vessel serving the troops at Sevastopol. No further details found.
80. *Jourdain*. A French vessel serving the troops at Sevastopol. No further details found.
81. Captain William Aitchison, Scots Fusilier Guards, 112*n*, p.165.
82. Lieutenant Edward L. Barnwell Lowry, 41st Regt, 69*n*, p.186.
83. Lieutenant Charles Vane Fitzroy, 41st Regt. Born 1836, son of Lieutenant-Colonel George Fitzroy of Grafton Regis, Northamptonshire. RMC gentleman cadet 1851. Commissioned, 6 June 1854; lieutenant, 8 December 1854 (without purchase); captain. Half pay, transferred to Rifle Brigade, 4 September 1857. Major. Retired. Died, Torquay, 1 May 1871. Brother of George Robert Fitzroy, 41st Regt and Coldstream Guards.
84. Major Richard Owen Francis Steward, 41st Regt. Commissioned, 29 September 1843; lieutenant, 26 September 1845; captain, 7 June 1850; major.
85. Lieutenant Edward L. Barnwell Lowry, 41st Regt, 69*n*, p.186.
86. Private William Cuthbert (regimental number 3522). Severely wounded on 8 September 1855, during the assault on the Redan, he became a prisoner of war and died in Sevastopol.
87. Lieutenant Charles Vane Fitzroy, 41st Regt, 83*n*, p.187.
88. Lieutenant Isaac King, 41st Regt. Lieutenant Royal Bucks Militia. Commissioned 41st Regt, 22 December 1854 (without purchase); lieutenant & adjutant 29 August 1856. Resigned as adjutant 31 December 1861. Retired as lieutenant, 18 December 1862.
89. Mrs Swaby, widow of Lieutenant John William Swaby, 41st Regt, who had been killed in action on 5 November 1854 (2*n*, p.157).
90. Captain William Aitchison, Scots Fusiliers Guards, 112*n*, p.165.
91. General Sir William Codrington, GCB, 49*n*, p.182.
92. Captain William Aitchison, Scots Fusiliers Guards, 112*n*, p.165
93. Major-General Alexander von Lüders (1790–1874). He served in the Imperial Russian Army during the Napoleonic Wars, the Russo-Turkish War (1828–9), Poland (1831), the Caucasian War (1843) and the Hungarian Revolution (1848). During the Crimean War he was GOC Army South in the Danube region. He was later a member of the Imperial Russian State Council.
94. Captain John Edmund Harvey, 41st Regt, 20*n*, p.184.
95. Brevet-Major George Hyde Page, 41st Regt, 77*n*, p.186.

96. Captain Frederick Cherburgh Bligh, 41st Regt, 18*n,* p.158.
97. Unidentified.
98. Brevet-Major George Hyde Page, 41st Regt, 77*n,* p.186.
99. Lieutenant-Colonel Robert Pratt, 41st Regt, 32*n,* p.160.
100. Lieutenant Charles Vane Fitzroy, 41st Regt, 83*n,* p.187.
101. Major Robert Cary Barnard, 41st Regt, 31*n,* p.168.
102. Captain William Aitchison, Scots Fusiliers Guards, 112*n,* p.165.
103. SS *Melbourne,* 4*n,* p.106.
104. Surgeon James Edward Scott, MD, 41st Regt, 78*n,* p.187.
105. Captain George Robert Fitzroy, 41st Regt, 17*n,* p.158.
106. Pioneer war photographer James Robertson (1813–88) was born in 1813. He trained as an engraver under Wyon (probably William Wyon) and worked as an engraver at the Imperial Ottoman Mint in Constantinople. He became involved in photography in 1853/4 when, in conjucntion with Felice Beato he opened a studio in Constantinople. In 1855 he and Beato travelled to Balaklava where they took over the photographic recording of the war from Roger Fenton and were present at the fall of Sevastopol. The partnership of Robertson & Beato was dissolved in 1867 and he gave up photography in the 1860s. He retired in 1881 and died in Japan 1888.
107. Roger Fenton, a pioneer war photographer, was born in Crimble Hall near Bury in 1819, the son of a banker and member of parliament. Despite obtaining an academic training in physics and mathematics and qualifying as a lawyer, he decided to pursue a career as an artist. He became interested in photography after visiting the Great Exhibition of 1851 and in 1855 went to the Crimean War to photograph troops for the publisher Thomas Agnew and with the support of Prince Albert. Many of his photographs were published in the *Illustrated London News.* He has been criticised for having avoided taking photographs of the more graphic and unpleasant aspects of the war. He gave up photography in 1862 and died in 1869.
108. Lieutenant-General Henry William Barnard, KCB, 47*n,* p.181.
109. Surgeon James Edward Scott, MD, 41st Regt, 78*n,* p.187.
110. Captain Henry Vansittart Pennefather, 41st Regt. Transferred from 22nd Regt, 3 August 1855.
111. Lieutenant W. H. Gardiner Cornwall, 41st Regt. Commissioned, 10 January 1855; lieutenant, 27 July 1855.
112. William John Hunt, a builder and surveyor of London, had been employed to build the Alpuka Palace to the design of architect Edward Blore, but there is no record of his being involved with the Orianda Palace. He was employed by Prince Woronstov between 1832 and 1852.
113. Lieutenant W. H. Gardiner Cornwall, 41st Regt, 111*n,* p.188.
114. Captain Henry Vansittart Pennefather, 41st Regt, 110*n,* p.188.
115. Captain John (Jack) Younger Allan, 124*n,* p.166.
116. Lieutenant Henry Stratton Bush, 41st Regt, 10*n,* p.157.
117. Lieutenant-Colonel Robert Pratt, 41st Regt, 32*n,* p.160.
118. General Sir William Codrington, GCB, 49*n,* p.182.
119. Fox Maule-Ramsay, 2nd Baron Panmure. Born Fox Maule, 22 April 1801, eldest son of 1st Baron Panmure and grandson of 8th Earl of Dalhousie. Whig MP for Perthshire, 1835–7; Under-Secretary of State for the Home Department, 1835–41; MP for Elgin Burghs, 1838–41; Vice-President of the

Board of Trade, 1841; MP for Perth, 1841–52; Secretary at War, 1846–52; President of the Board of Control, 1852; Secretary of State for War, 8 February 1855–21 February 1858; Keeper of the Privy Seal of Scotland, 1853–74. 2nd Baron Panmure, 1852; 11th Earl of Dalhousie, 1860. Lord Lieutenant of Angus, 1849–74. Married Montague Abercromby, daughter of 2nd Baron Abercromby, 1831, no children. Died, 6 July 1874.

120. Major Robert Cary Barnard, 41st Regt, 31*n,* p.168.

121. Lieutenant Charles Vane Fitzroy, 41st Regt, 83*n,* p.187.

122. Surgeon James Edward Scott, MD, 41st Regt, 78*n,* p.187.

123. Assistant-Surgeon Alexander Dudgeon Gulland, 41st Regt. Born Falkland, Scotland. Educated Edinburgh University; IRCS, 1854; MD, 1857. Army Medical Services, 23 June 1854. Joined 41st Regt as assistant-surgeon, 29 June 1855; supernumerary assistant-surgeon, 1 August 1856. Served siege of Sevastopol and Kertch Expedition. Assistant-surgeon Royal Artillery, 27 May 1858; staff surgeon, 16 October 1866. Joined 6th Regt, 16 November 1866. Served Jamaica, China 1860–2 (Taku Forts and Taiping Rebellion) and Hazara, 1868. Surgeon, 19 October 1872; brigade surgeon as surgeon-major, 27 November 1879; deputy surgeon-general, 14 June 1883; retired honorary surgeon-general, 1 October 1883. Married, his son Captain Alexander Falkland Gulland, 3 Bn East Kent Regt, died of wounds at Messines, 1917, aged 26 years. Died Cheltenham, 4 September 1924.

124. Lieutenant Isaac King, 41st Regt, 88*n,* p.187.

125. Lieutenant W. H. Gardiner Cornwall, 41st Regt, 111*n,* p.188.

126. Lieutenant Andrew Halliday Hall , 41st Regt. Commissioned, 15 December 1854; lieutenant, 9 March 1855.

127. SS *Great Britain* a passenger steamship designed by Isambard Kingdom Brunel for the Great Western Steamship Co and launched in 1843. The first iron screw-powered passenger ship she served the North Atlantic passenger service between Britain and the United States. Sold after running aground and refitted before being sold again to Antony Gibbs & Sons for the England–Australia passenger service. Used as a troopship during the Crimean War and the Indian Mutiny. In 1882 she was converted to sail power only and used as a bulk coal carrier. In 1886, she was sold to the Falkland Islands Company as a floating coal bunker. Abandoned on the Falkland Islands in 1937, she was salvaged and moved back to Britain in 1970 where she has been restored and is now an award-winning museum in Bristol.

128. General Aimable Jean Jacques Pélissier, 15*n,* p.180.

129. Major Robert Cary Barnard, 41st Regt, 31*n,* p.168.

130. Assistant-Surgeon Alexander Dudgeon Gulland, 41st Regt, 123*n,* p.189.

131. Captain George Peddie, 41st Regt, 9*n,* p.179.

132. Lieutenant Isaac King, 41st Regt, 88*n,* p.187.

133. Lieutenant Andrew Halliday Hall, 41st Regt, 126*n,* p.189.

134. Surgeon James Edward Scott, MD, 41st Regt, 78*n,* p.187.

135. Sir Charles Wood, Bart (1800–85), was a Liberal member of parliament. He served as Chancellor of the Exchequer, 1846–52; President of the Board of Control, 1852–55; First Lord of the Admiralty, 1855–58; Secretary of State for India, 1859–66. Created Viscount Halifax of Monk Bretton, 1866.

Chapter 7. Home

1. HMT *Transit*. Launched on 20 March 1855 as a screw-powered troopship. She was wrecked in the Strait of Banca on 10 July 1857.
2. Lieutenant-General Sir James Ferguson, KCB, 9*n,* p.157.
3. Captain Charles Pelgué Bertram, 41st Regt, 15*n,* p.158.
4. Captain Frederick Cherburgh Bligh, 41st Regt, 18*n,* p.158.
5. Lieutenant-Colonel Julius Edmund Goodwyn, 41st Regt, 36*n,* p.180.
6. Lieutenant-General Sir James Ferguson, KCB, 9*n,* p.157.
7. Mrs Jarvis, wife of Captain Jarvis, 11*n,* p.190.
8. Mrs Jenkins, unidentified.
9. Hart, ADC to Lieutenant-General Sir James Ferguson, Governor and C-in-C Gibraltar.
10. Brevet Major Frederick Cockayne Elton, 55th Regt. Born Whitestaunton, Somerset, son of Revd William Tierney Elton. Commissioned, 19 January 1849; lieutenant, 30 April 1852; captain, 29 December 1854; brevet major, 2 November 1855; major, 22 June 1858; brevet lieutenant-colonel. Served Crimean campaign, awarded Victoria Cross for a series of actions before Sevastopol during the spring and summer of 1855. Married Maria Jane Rynd of Ryndville, County Meath 1863. Died London, 24 March 1888.
11. Captain Jarvis. Presumably a member of the staff of the Governor-General of Gibraltar.
12. Surgeon James Edward Scott, MD, 41st Regt, 78*n,* p.187.
13. The identity of the 'two Johnsons' mentioned here is unclear. Lieutenant Walter John Johnson of the 41st Regt, commissioned, 24 November 1854 (by purchase) and promoted to lieutenant, 9 March 1855, landing in the Crimea on 30 May 1855. A second officer of the same surname does not appear in any list of the 41st Regt and may refer to an unidentified officer from another regiment with whom Allan was friendly.
14. Allan's original published letters became rather confusing with regard to the dates of the regiment's return home. The official dates were: Left Crimea, 17 June; Constantinople, 19 June; Malta, 26 June; Gibraltar, 3 July; Vigo, 9 July. The Transit arrived at Spithead on the evening of Saturday, 12 July. The ship docked at Portsmouth on Sunday, 13 July and the regiment disembarked on Monday, 14 July and was conveyed (for the first time ever) by train to Aldershot.
15. Lieutenant-Colonel Julius Edmund Goodwyn, 41st Regt, 36*n,* p.180.
16. Captain Armar Graham Lowry, 41st Regt, 41*n,* p.181.
17. Captain Fitzhardinge Kingscote, 41st Regt, 28*n,* p.172.
18. Captain George Robert Fitzroy, 41st Regt, 17*n,* p.158.
19. Lieutenant Henry Seymour Hill, 41st Regt. Born Corfu, 1835, son of Major Edward Eustace Hill. Commissioned, 7 June 1854 (without purchase); lieutenant, 8 December 1854 (without purchase); captain (without purchase), 15 April 1859; exchanged 13th Regt, 8 February 1861; exchanged 97th Regt, 19 October 1864; retired, 22 June 1870. Secretary of the Hospital for Diseases of the Heart, Soho, London. Married twice, two sons, two daughters. Died Kensington 1885.
20. Lieutenant Edward L. Barnwell Lowry, 41st Regt, 69*n,* p.182.
21. Lieutenant Richard Pack, 41st Regt, 49*n,* p.185.
22. Major Robert Cary Barnard, 41st Regt, 31*n,* p.168.
23. Captain Hugh Rowlands, 41st Regt, received a civic welcome in Caernarfon Castle, followed by a dinner.

The Mamaluke dress scimitar which he received from the people of Caernarfonshire is displayed in the Royal Welsh Museum, Brecon. (See also 29*n*, p.159 & 8*n*, p.170.)

24. Brigadier-General Sir Duncan Alexander Cameron (1808–88). Born, 19 December 1808. Commissioned 42nd Regt, 1825. GOC Highland Brigade Crimea. Later served GOC New Zealand. Local major-general (Crimea); lieutenant-general, 1868; general, 1874. Governor RMC Sandhurst, 1868–75. Died Blackheath, 7 June 1888.
25. Brigadier-General Charles Richard, Lord West, son of 5th Earl de la Warr. Commissioned 43rd Regt, 1833; lieutenant 15th Regt, 1835; captain 21st Regt, 1842; major, 1852; lieutenant-colonel, 1855; major-general, 1864. Served Sikh Wars and Crimean War. CB, 1855; *Légion d'honneur,* 1856. Succeeded to the titles of 6th Earl de la Warr, 6th Viscount Cantelupe and 12th Baron Delaware, 23 February 1869. KCB, 1871. Died, 1873.
26. Lieutenant-General Henry William Barnard, KCB, 47*n*, p.181.
27. Lieutenant-Colonel Julius Edmund Goodwyn, 41st Regt, 36*n,* p.180.
28. Almost certainly Colour-Sergeant William Davies (regimental number 2142), Light Company, 41st Regt.

Epilogue

1. This was almost certainly Lieutenant-General Henry Kent (1826–1921), son of Captain William Kent, RN. Commissioned 77th Regt, 8 August 1845 (by purchase); lieutenant, 23 August 1850; captain, 27 September 1854; major, 24 August 1858; lieutenant-colonel (by purchase), 12 June 1868. CO 77th Regt, 1868–80. Brevet colonel, 1873; major-general, 13 November 1883; lieutenant-general. Hon Colonel Royal East Middlesex Militia, 1890; Colonel Middlesex Regt, 1900. Served Crimea and India. Died Wimbledon, 1921.
2. Captain Hugh Rowlands, 41st Regt,29*n,* p.159 & 8*n*, p.170, 22*n,* p.190.

Appendix 1: Nominal Roll, 41st Regiment of Foot, September 1854–March 1856

Personal memoirs and letters from military campaigns, particularly those that date from before the Great War of 1914–18, were predominantly written by officers, as a result of which the majority of individuals named were fellow officers and rarely were the non-commissioned officers and men given any mention. In Allan's letters possibly the only private soldier to receive a mention was his servant, Private Cuthbert. It was therefore decided to include here as fully detailed a list of all the men who served in the Crimean campaign, officers, NCOs and other ranks, as a tribute to them all. As no such list existed it was necessary to create one from the various extant medal and muster rolls of the 41st Regiment of Foot between 1854 and 1856, all of which are held at the National Archives under the references WO100/29 (Medal Rolls) and WO12/5450– 5053 (Muster Rolls). These have been supplemented by information from the *Army List* and *Hart's Army List* and the Victoria Cross records held by the National Archives (WO32/7303).

The medal rolls in particular are a valuable source of information, not simply as a record of the names of the individuals concerned, but also which significant battles they served in – indicated by the award of clasps for Alma (A), Balaklava (B), Inkerman (I) and Sevastopol (S). By piecing together the information from various medal rolls, it is also possible to trace what happened to many of the men from the date when they landed in the Crimea with dates and places where they were wounded or killed. Sadly the Crimea War has gone down in history not as a celebration of glorious military successes and efficiency, but more as an example of military administrative ineptitude, particularly that of the supply and medical departments. A perusal of the medal rolls clearly indicate the enormous problem created by the large numbers of men who were treated for various illnesses at several hospitals and the horrific numbers who did not survive. Unfortunately, not all the names are annotated with extra details and one must assume that some gained no more than the Crimea Medal without any clasps, perhaps because they fell ill early in the campaign or because they were deemed to have served too far away from the actual front line to merit such an award. Some, however, may simply have been overlooked. They perhaps died early in the campaign and a detailed record of what happened to them has not survived.

The quarterly regimental muster rolls show each man's name and regimental number as well as in most cases when he arrived in the Crimea, when he was sent to hospital or back to England. The one weakness of these records is that each person entering up the details had his own variation of the spelling of names, particularly of Irish names, which leads to some confusion and may, indeed have resulted in some individuals appearing in this list more than once. There are also conflicting dates given for the same event e.g. one clerk may record the date of an individual going to hospital as the day he left the regimental camp, whereas another may give the following day's date as that when the individual went aboard the ship that was to transport him to hospital in Turkey.

The clarity of the writing in both the medal rolls and the muster rolls leaves much to be desired, both sets of documents having suffered from the effects of age and damp. Consequently, certain words have become at worst indecipherable and at best unclear. Where this has occurred, the entry has been shown with either a '?' or a '...?'.

Not all the officers who served with the 41st Regiment between September 1854 and December 1856 are recorded here as some remained at the depôt (either in Britain or Malta) throughout the campaign and their names have therefore been omitted.

The term 'Command', as in 'Command Balaklava', means that the individual was detached from the regiment and serving elsewhere.

Abbreviations:

CB — Companion of the Bath
CO — commanding officer
DCM — Distinguished Conduct Medal
DoW — died of wounds
KiA — killed in action
LoA — Leave of Absence
OC — officer commanding
PoW — prisoner of war

Medal clasps:

A — Alma
B — Balaklava
I — Inkermann*
S — Sevastopol

* Spelling as on the clasp

Name	Number	Clasps	Details
Lieutenant-Colonels			
Carpenter, George		AIS	Wounded (shot through right thigh) 5.11.54. DoW camp before Sevastopol 6.11.54, buried Cathcart's Hill Cemetery. CB.
Eman, James		AIS	Landed 14.9.54. DoW 10.9.55, buried Cathcart's Hill Cemetery. Married to Anne, c/o Elliott, Denmark Hill, Camberwell.
Goodwyn, Julius Edmund		AIS	Landed 14.9.54. Brevet lieutenant-colonel 9.3.55. To England 24.11.55. Recommended for the Victoria Cross by Major-General Charles Windham ' For good and active conduct at the salient of the Redan on the 8th September 1855.' – not approved. CB.
Pratt, Robert		S	Served Afghanistan 1842 (medal). Landed 18.5.55. Wounded 8.9.55. CB. Brevet lieutenant-colonel 41st Regt 9.9.55 (not CO).
Majors			
Barnard, Robert Cary			Commissioned 19.3.47; lieutenant 22.3.50. Adjutant 15.11.50. Sick Scutari October 1854. Not listed on the medal rolls. From Malta 14.10.55.
Maydwell, H.L.			To Provisional Battalion 22.12.54.
Graham, Lumley		AIS	Commissioned 43rd Regt 13.8.47 (by purchase); lieutenant 28.2.51. Served Cape Colony 1851–3 (medal); captain. Tfr to 48th Regt 7.7.54. Tfr to 41st Regt 1854. Brevet major 12.12.54. Staff officer, Turkey, 1855, ADC to Major-General Eyre. Severely wounded 29.8.55 (right arm amputated). Embarked for England 5.10.55. Major 25.3.56. Tfr to 19th Regt. Brevet lieutenant-colonel (for staff services). Tfr to 18th Regt 29.9.65. Brevet colonel 14.10.65. Retired as brevet colonel & major 24.9.69.
Steward, Richard Oliver Francis		AS	Commissioned 29.9.43 (by purchase); lieutenant 26.9.45 (by purchase); captain 7 June 1850 (by purchase); major 9.9.55. Sick Scutari 5.11.54. Embarked for England 19.10.55.
Captains			
Allan, William		AIS	Landed 14.9.54. To England 8.12.55. Lieutenant-Colonel, CO 41st Regt 25.5.77.
Bertram, Charles Pelgué		S	Landed 4.2.55. Proceeded to England 21.9.55. Brevet major.
Bligh, Frederick Cherburgh		AIS	Landed 14.9.54. Severely wounded 5.11.54. He returned to the Crimea on 12.7.55. Brevet major.
Bourne, Johnson		AIS	Landed 14.9.54. Proceeded to England 16.2.55. Rejoined 14.6.55. Retired by sale of commission 14.7.55.
Bush, Henry Stratton		AIS	Landed 14.9.54. Wounded 5.11.54. Awarded Sardinian Medal for action on 5.11.54. Brevet major.
Dixon, Frederick Ball		IS	Commissioned 21.1.53; lieutenant 6.6.54. Sick Scutari 20.9.54. Captain 6.3.55. Wounded 7.6.55.
Every, Edward		S	Landed 6.9.55. OC No 1 Company. KiA 8.9.55. Brother of Lieutenant O.H. Every, 90th Regt. Unmarried.
Hamilton, James Alexander		IS	Landed 13.11.54. Adjutant 9.2.55–17.1.56. Wounded 8.9.55.
Harvey, John Edmund			Transferred from 36th Regt 23.3.55. From Malta 14.10.55.
Johnston, William		AIS	Landed 14.9.54. Wounded 5.11.54. Adjutant 6.11.54 and temporary OC of two companies of the 41st Regt. Provost Marshal at Balaklava. Died Balaklava 8.10.55, buried Cathcart's Hill Cemetery.
Kingscote, Fitzhardinge		S	Commissioned 7.4.54 (by purchase). Landed 13.11.54. Captain 26.2.55. Severely wounded 8.9.55 (right hand amputated). Proceeded to England 5.10.55.
Lockhart, James Augustus		S	Landed 30.5.55. OC No 5 Company. KiA 8.9.55 by grape shot.
Lowry, Armar Graham		AIS	Landed 14.9.54.
Meredith, Henry Warter		AIS	Landed 14.9.54. Wounded 5.11.54. Brevet major.
Page, George Hyde			From Malta 7.12.55.
Peddie, George		S	Landed 13.11.54. Awarded the Sardinian Medal for his actions on 8.6.54. OC No 5 Company June 1855. OC No 6 Company, September 1855
Pennefather, Henry Vansittart.			Transfer from 22nd Regt 3.8.55. Staff officer, Malta, 1855.
Richards, Edwin		IS	Varna 20.9.54. KiA 5.11.54.
Rowlands, Hugh		AIS	Landed 14.9.54. Wounded (5.11.54 & 8.9.55). Victoria Cross 5.11.54. Town Major, Sevastopol, September–October 1855. Brigade Major 2nd Brigade 2nd Division, October 1855–March 1856. Awarded the Victoria Cross on the recommendation of Colonel Haly 'For rescuing Colonel Haly of the 47th Regiment from Russian soldiers, Colonel Haly having been wounded and surrounded by them and for gallant exertions in holding the ground occupied by his advanced picket, against superior numbers of the enemy, at the commencement of the Battle of Inkerman.' He also received a second Victoria Cross recommendation from

		Lieutenant-General Pennefather 'Distinguished on a hundred occasions in action and in the trenches. Particularly gallant & devoted in jumping out of the trenches under a terrific fire and rallying soldiers of the Light Division, beaten back by the Russians. Attack on the Redan 18 June 1855.' – not approved.
Skipwith, George	AIS	Landed 14.9.54. To England 1.12.55. Brevet major.
Lieutenants		
Baird, James	AIS	Landed 14.9.54. Former drum-major sergeant (regimental number 1587). Commissioned ensign 41st Regt 5.11.54; lieutenant 9.3.55. Wounded 9.6.55. Command Balaklava January–March 1856.
Byam, Henry Edward	S	Landed 16.6.55. To England 10.12.55.
Cornwall, W.H. Gardner		Commissioned 10.1.55; lieutenant 27.7.55.
Dixon, Augustus Frederick		Commissioned 19.2.55.
Fitzroy, Charles Vane	S	Landed 13.11.54. To England 6.10.55.
Fitzroy, George Robert	AI	Landed 14.9.54. Wounded 5.11.54. Transferred to Coldstream Guards 12.1.55.
Fraser, Lionel Mordaunt		Commissioned 9.7.52 (by purchase); lieutenant 2.2.55. Adjutant.
Hall, Andrew Halliday		Commissioned 15.12.54; lieutenant 9.3.55.
Harriott, Hugh Charles	AS	Landed 14.9.54. DoW Scutari 20.9.54.
Hill, Richard Seymour	S	Landed 13.11.54.
Johnson, Walter John	S	Commissioned 24.11.54 (by purchase); lieutenant 9.3.55. Landed 30.5.55.
Kennedy, Irving Francis		Commissioned 18.5.49 (by purchase); lieutenant 9.2.55. Landed 26.7.55. Attached to Land Transport Corps February–March 1856.
King, Isaac		Lieutenant Royal Bucks Militia. Commissioned 41st Regt (without purchase) 22 December 1854; lieutenant & adjutant 29 August 1856. Resigned as adjutant 31 December 1861. Retired as lieutenant 18 December 1862.
Lambert, Walter McClellan	S	Landed 4.2.55. Embarked for England 14.5.55.
Laughlin, Edward James	S	Commissioned 16.9.51. Served Gambia 1853. Lieutenant 6.1.54. Landed 11.6.55. Attached to Land Transport Corps March 1856.
Lowry, Edward L. Barnwell	S	Landed 13.11.54. Wounded 8.9.55.
Maude, Robert Eustace	S	Landed 6.9.55. Wounded 8.9.55 (shot through the leg). To England 6.10.55.
Nowlan, Henry James	S	Commissioned 11.8.54; lieutenant 8.12.54. Landed 4.2.55.
Pack, Richard		Commissioned 2.2.55.
Smith, Stanley Robert R.		Commissioned 12.1.55. (by purchase); lieutenant 9.9.55.
Stirling, John	IS	Sick at Scutari 20.9.54. KiA 5.11.54.
Swaby, John William	AIS	Landed 14.9.54. KiA 5.11.54.
Taylor, Alfred	IS	Varna 20.9.54. KiA 5.11.54.
Wavell, Arthur Henry		Commissioned 14 .12.54; lieutenant 9.3.55. Lieutenant-Colonel, 1st Battalion, The Welch Regiment (not CO), 1.7.81–22.5.82.
Wavell, John William	S	Landed 11.7.55.
Ensigns		
Fitzgerald, Lionel E.	AIS	Landed 14.9.54. Wounded 8.9.55. Commissioned from colour-sergeant (regimental number 1862) 16.11.55. To England 8.12.55 but died at Malta.
Surgeons		
Abbott, Frederick Tydd	AIS	Landed 14.9.54. Assistant-surgeon 7.4.54. Surgeon.
Anderson, William A.	AIS	Landed 14.9.54. Died aboard ship Balaklava 3.1.55, buried Cathcart's Hill Cemetery.
Scott, James Edward, MD	S	Assitant-Surgeon 11.6.47; surgeon 9.2.55. To England 8.12.55.
Assistant-Surgeons		
Gulland, Alexander Dudgeon	S	Assistant-surgeon 23.6.54. Joined 41st Regt 31.8.55.
Hungerford, Richard		Assistant-surgeon 26.5.54. Aboard ship from England 26.9.55–13.10.55. Landed 14.10.55.
Lamont, James, MD	AS	Assistant-surgeon 7.1.53. Landed 14.9.54. Sick Scutari 5.11.54. Died camp before Sevastopol 5.1.55.
Quartermaster		
Elliott, Archibald	IS	Commissioned 31.3.48. Quartermaster 21.7.48. Sick aboard ship 20.9.54. After Inkerman he was given temporary command of a company in the 41st Regt.

Name	No.		Notes
Paymasters			
Creagh, Thomas Miller		AS	Landed 14.9.54. LoA to England 5.11.54.
Grant, Alfred Elford			Quartermaster 3.8.49. Paymaster 27.7.55. Joined 24.9.55.
Sergeant-Majors			
Harris, John	1450	AIS	Landed 14.9.54. DoW 13.9.55 following assault on the Redan. Awarded DCM 7.2.55. Enlisted 21.11.40. Former labourer of Kingston, Somerset.
Ross, John	1696	AIS	Landed 14.9.54. Promoted 14.9.55 (former quarter-master sergeant)
Spence, John	1510	AIS	Landed 14.9.54. KiA 5.11.54, buried Cathcart's Hill Cemetery. Enlisted 2.2.41. Former labourer of Armagh.
Quartermaster-Sergeants			
Chapman, John	1954	AIS	Landed 14.9.54. Died in Smyrna (hospital) 24.3.55.
Finch, James Samuel	1909	AIS	Landed 14.9.54. Promoted from colour-sergeant 1.12.55.
Paymaster-Sergeants			
Crawford, William	2316	AIS	Landed 14.9.54. Awarded the Sardinian Medal for his action on 26.11.54. Corporal. Promoted sergeant. Promoted from sergeant 28.8.55.
Maitland, William	2646	AIS	Landed 14.9.54. Killed before Sevastopol 20.4.55.
Armourer-Sergeant			
Rooney, Thomas	2884	AIS	Landed 14.9.54.
Hospital-Sergeant			
Chipp, Henry	1827	AIS	Landed 14.9.54.
Orderly-Room-Sergeant			
Baird, John	1770	AIS	Landed 14.9.54. Served as orderly-room clerk since 1.7.52. Commissioned cornet Land Transport Corps 24.1.56.
Williams, James	2310	ABS	Landed 14.9.54. Command Balaklava 5.11.54. Promoted sergeant from corporal 10.10.55. Appointed orderly-room clerk 24.1.56.
Drum-Major-Sergeants			
Smith, Thomas	1786	AIS	Landed 14.9.54. Promoted corporal 18.3.55. Promoted from corporal 15.8.55. From St Michael.
Colour Sergeants			
Adams, Edward	1910	AIS	Landed 14.9.54. Promoted from sergeant 8.9.55.
Challen, Thomas	1829	AIS	Landed 14.9.54.
Davies, William	2142	ABS	Landed 14.9.54. Sick Scutari 5.11.54. Promoted from sergeant 7.7.55. Wounded 8.9.55. Awarded *Medaille Militaire* for action on 8.9.55.
Davis, Edwin	2431	AI	Landed 14.9.54. Promoted 1.12.55/30.7.55.
Dungan, Peter	1908	AIS	Landed 14.9.54. KiA before Sevastopol during the night of 22.8.55. Enlisted 21.2.44. Former labourer of Summerhill, Meath.
Fitzpatrick, John	1263	S	Sick Varna 20.9.54 & 5.11.54. Sent to England 6.7.55. Former carpenter of Almondsbury.
Johnson, William		AI	Landed 14.9.54.
Joiner, William	1920		Promoted from colour-sergeant 14.9.55. Reduced to colour-sergeant 1.12.55. To Malta 1.12.55.
Kelly, James	2798	AIS	Landed 14.9.54. Employed by the Commissariat January–March 1855. Promoted from sergeant 1.9.55. Wounded 8.9.55. Recommended for the Victoria Cross by Brevet Major Hugh Rowlands 'In charging gallantly into the Redan & zealously inducing other men to hold a position. 8 September 1855' – not approved. Awarded *Medaille Militaire* for action on 8.9.55. Employed by the Commissariat January–March 1855. Promoted from sergeant 31.7.55.
Madden, Ambrose	2195	AIS	Landed 14.9.54. Awarded the Victoria Cross 20.10.54. 'For having headed a party of men of the 41st Regiment and having cut off and taken prisoner one Russian officer and fourteen privates, three of whom he personally and alone captured.' Awarded *Medaille Militaire*. Embarked for Malta 19.3.55. Promoted to sergeant-major. Commissioned West India Regt 24.12.58. Died 1.1.63.
Price, George	2068	AIS	Landed 13.11.54. Sent to England from Scutari 7.9.55. Commissioned into the 9th Regt.
Smith, John	2026	AIS	Landed 14.9.54. Sent to England from Scutari 8.1.55. Awarded the *Medaille Militaire* for remarkable zeal in the field from the day of landing until June 1855.
Thomas, William	1410	AS	Landed 14.9.54. Command Balaklava 5.11.54. Promoted from sergeant 14.9.55.
Whitton, Joseph	1605	AIS	Landed 14.9.54. Promoted from sergeant 2.12.55.

Sergeants

Name	No.		Details
Armitage, William	2432	AIS	Landed 14.9.54. Promoted corporal 13.3.55. Promoted sergeant 5.1.56.
Armstrong, John	2617	AIS	Landed 14.9.54. To Scutari 11.1.56.
Atkinson, John	2650	AIS	Landed 14.9.54. Sent to Malta 16.4.55.
Austin, John	2398	AIS	Landed 14.9.54. Died before Sevastopol 2.3.55.
Bolger, David	2626	AIS	Landed 14.9.54. Sent to Malta 16.4.55.
Bond, Daniel	1180	S	Landed 13.11.54. Assistant provost sergeant January–March 1856.
Borrowdale, William	1538	AIS	Landed 14.9.54. Died before Sevastopol 8.5.55. Enlisted 3.11.34. Former tailor of ...?, Cumberland.
Brady, John	3645		Landed 30.5.55. Promoted corporal 10.10.55. Promoted sergeant 14.1.56.
Cadam, John	2336	AIS	Landed 14.9.54. Promoted from corporal 19.12.54. Proceeded to England 5.10.55.
Campbell, Andrew	2669	AIS	Landed 14.9.54. Promoted 5.2.55. Sent to Malta 16.4.55.
Challice, William	???6	S	Landed 4.2.55. Sent to England from Smyrna 24.6.55.
Chinn, Job	1636	IS	Sick Varna 20.9.54. Died aboard *Belgravia* 7.1.55. Enlisted 16.9.43. Former dyer of Coventry.
Chinn, William	1778	AIS	Landed 14.9.54. Died before Sevastopol 5.7.55.
Clarke, William	2015	AIS	Landed 14.9.54. Promoted corporal 6.2.55. Promoted sergeant. Proceeded to England 5.10.55.
Connell, Michael	2647	S	Landed 28.12.54. Died before Sevastopol 11.4.55.
Connolly, Hugh	2227	AIS	Landed 14.9.54. Promoted corporal 5.2.55. Promoted sergeant 10.10.55.
Corfield, George	1383	S	Landed 4.2.55. Command at Balaklava January–March 1854.
Creedon, John	2746	ABS	Command Balaklava 5.11.54. Promoted sergeant from corporal 14.1.56.
Cunningham, James	745	AIS	Landed 14.9.54. Sent to England from Scutari 23.3.55.
Dowling, Francis	2367	AIS	Landed 14.9.54. Promoted 5.2.55. Promoted sergeant from corporal 7.3.56.
Dunnigan, Patrick	2378	AIS	Landed 14.9.54. DoW before Sevastopol 15.9.55. Enlisted 21.2.44. Former labourer of BallyMcCormick, Longford.
Emerson, John	2436	AIS	Landed 14.9.54. KiA 8.9.55. Enlisted 25.2.48. Former labourer of Kilrush.
Evans, Charles	2630	AIS	Landed 14.9.54. Promoted corporal 1.2.55. Promoted sergeant from corporal 10.10.55.
Evans, John Robert	1998	AIS	Landed 14.9.54. Died before Sevastopol 1.4.55.
Farrell, John	3148	S	Landed 28.12.54. Promoted sergeant from corporal 14.1.56.
Ford, Daniel	2404	AIS	Landed 14.9.54. At Inkerman he picked up the Regimental Colour after Lieutenant Stirling had been killed and, after a fierce hand-to-hand struggle with the Russians, brought it back to safety. Awarded the DCM and a £10 gratuity. Sick Scutari 15.7.55. Retired as a sergeant-major in-pensioner at Chelsea Hospital.
Freeman, Allan	1608		Command Varna 1854. Died aboard *Columbo* 1.2.55.
George, John	2105		Died unknown date September 1854.
Gill, James	1335	AIS	Landed 14.9.54. Embarked for Malta 19.3.55.
Gready, Peter	3140	S	Landed 4.2.55. Promoted corporal 10.10.55. Promoted sergeant 14.1.56.
Green, Westropp	2442	AIS	Landed 14.9.54. Promoted corporal 10.10.55. Promoted sergeant 14.1.56.
Gruby, Edwin	1993	AIS	Landed 14.9.54. Commissariat January–March 1856.
Hare, Samuel	2907	S	Promoted sergeant from corporal 14.1.56.
Heath, William	1382		Landed from Malta 23.9.55.
Hennessey, Maurice	2842	AIS	Landed 14.9.54. Sick Scutari 2.5.55. Promoted sergeant from corporal 15.3.56.
Hicks, John	1261	ABS	Landed 14.9.54. Command Balaklava 5.11.54. Returned to England from Scutari 11.2.55.
Humphries, William	3345	AIS	Landed 14.9.54. According to the regimental history he died in the Crimea (circumstances unrecorded) and was buried in Cathcart's Hill Cemetery.
Hurley, Patrick	2698	AIS	Landed 14.9.54. DCM and £10 gratuity for action on 5.11.54. Promoted sergeant. Sent to England from Scutari 28.5.55.
Hynes, John	2978	AIS	Landed 14.9.54. Attached to Land Transport Corps January–March 1856
Jenn, James Abel	1598	AIS	Landed 14.9.54. Died Scutari 9.12.54.
Jennings, Patrick	2981	AIS	Landed 14.9.54.
Jones, David	1257	AS	Landed 14.9.54. Wounded 20.9.54. Sick Scutari 5.11.54. Awarded DCM and gratuity of £10 January 1855. Former pedlar of Carmarthen.
Jones, James	1997	AIS	Landed 14.9.54. Sent to England from Scutari 16.2.55.
Kehir, James	2420	AIS	Landed 14.9.54. At Inkerman, 5.11.54, he threw himself at several of the enemy who were attempting to get into the Sandbag Battery then rushed at the enemy with his bayonet and put them to flight. Severely wounded 5.11.54 (five places). Awarded the DCM and gratuity of £15. Sent to England from Scutari 11.7.55.
Lindsay, John	2123		Enlisted 21.5.45. Died Varna 28.9.54. Former labourer of Conwall, Donegal.
McCardle, Thomas	1698	S	Sick Varna 20.9.54 & 5.11.54.
McDonough, William	2140	ABS	Landed 14.9.54. Died before Sevastopol 24.4.55. Enlisted 25.6.45. Former clerk of Kilma...?

Morgan, William	1983	AS	Landed 14.9.54. Sick Scutari 5.11.54. Sent to England from Scutari 11.1.55. Former servant of Llandovery.
Morris, William	3129	AIS	Landed 14.9.54. Promoted corporal 5.2.55. Promoted sergeant from corporal 10.10.55.
O'Neill, James	2730	AIS	Landed 14.9.54. Severely wounded 8.9.55. To England 28.10.55. Recommended by Lieutenant-Colonel Goodwyn for the Victoria Cross 'Charged gallantly inside the Redan & holding a position there. Repelling two Russians at the 2 Gun Sand-bag Battery. 8 September 1855' – not approved. Awarded the *Legion d'Honneur* (5th Class) for actions on 5.11.54 and 8.9.55. Awarded MSM. Enlisted 1849. Discharged as colour-sergeant. Enlisted Rifle Brigade, sergeant. Served Fenian Raid, Canada (medal). First sergeant-major of London Rifle Brigade, sergeant instructor 1st Vol Bn, Suffolk Regt. Retired 1893 after 44 years service. Died 1913.
Oxborrow, George	3076	AIS	Landed 14.9.54. Promoted sergeant from corporal 10.10.55.
Penny, Henry	2969	AIS	Landed 14.9.54. Sick Scutari 14.3.55.
Pope, William	2447	AIS	Landed 14.9.54. Died aboard *Golden Fleece* 18.12.54.
Rees, Philip	2418	A	Landed 14.9.54. Wounded 20.9.54. Sick Scutari 5.11.54. Entry for clasp 'Sevastopol' ruled out on Medal Roll.
Ryan, William	2250	AIS	Landed 14.9.54. Sent to Malta 16.4.55.
Stennett, John	1631	AIS	Landed 14.9.54. Promoted corporal 5.2.55. Sick Scutari 29.4.55. Promoted sergeant 15.3.56.
Thomas, John	2054	AIS	Landed 14.9.54. Died before Sevastopol 14.2.55. Former potter of St Mary's.
Tilley, William	1498	AIS	Landed 14.9.54. Awarded DCM and gratuity of £5 January 1855. Promoted corporal 1.2.55. According to the regimental history, he died in the Crimea and was buried in Cathcart's Hill Cemetery.
Turnbull, Edwin	1999	AIS	Landed 14.9.54. Died Scutari 20.1.55.
Vincent, Thomas	1110	AIS	Landed 14.9.54. Served 1st Afghan War. Promoted corporal 6.2.55. Promoted sergeant from 10.10.55. Former smith of Bath. Short biography, *Vincent of the 41st,* by Geoffrey Moore, 1979.
Wall, John	2023	AIS	Landed 14.9.54. Promoted 25.3.55. KiA 8.9.55. Enlisted 17.9.44. Former labourer of Fownhope, Herefordshire.
Wallace, James	1482	S	Landed 6.9.55. To Renkioi 16.12.55.
Walsh(e), Henry	2549	AIS	Landed 14.9.54. Sick Scutari 2.11.54. Promoted sergeant from corporal 15.3.56.
Walsh, Thomas	2900	AIS	Landed 14.9.54. Promoted 5.2.55. KiA 8.9.55. Enlisted 12.7.50. Former servant of Fermoy.
Warren, Frederick	2857	AS	Landed 14.9.54. Sick Scutari 2.11.54.
Walhand, Joseph	2781	S	Landed 16.6.55. To England 19.1.56.
White, James	2693	AIS	Landed 14.9.54. Promoted 15.10.54. KiA 5.11.54.
White, Joseph	1672	AS	Landed 14.9.54. Sick Scutari 2.11.54.
Willan, William	2800	AIS	Landed 14.9.54. Died before Sevastopol 6.2.55. Enlisted 22.2.41. Former linen draper of Thornton.
Corporals			
Cadam, James	3906	S	On muster roll from 1.7.55. Promoted corporal 15.3.56.
Carroll, Thomas	3389	AIS	Landed 14.9.54. Promoted corporal 15.3.56.
Bell, William	2016	AIS	Landed 14.9.54. KiA 5.11.54. Enlisted 24.8.44. Former spinner of Manchester.
Bond, John	2480	AIS	Landed 14.9.54. Died Scutari 13.12.54.
Brunette, George	2850	AS	Landed 14.9.54. Died Balaklava 11.10.54. Enlisted 1.11.49. Former farmer of Inch.
Bubb, Thomas	1604	S	Landed 6.9.55. Born Stroud, Gloucestershire.
Burghall, William	2104	AIS	Landed 14.9.54. Awarded DCM and gratuity of £10 January 1855.
Burton, Thomas	2569	AIS	Landed 14.9.54. Died before Sevastopol 15.3.55.
Carroll, Michael	2424	AIS	Landed 14.9.54. Died Scutari 29.12.54. Former labourer of Dundalk.
Cassidy, Patrick	2488	AIS	Landed 14.9.54. Promoted 5.2.55. Died before Sevastopol 9.2.55. Enlisted 26.6.48. Former labourer of Clare.
Cobb, Samuel	1919	AIS	Landed 14.9.54. Died of fever Scutari 5.1.55.
Cochran, John	2019	AIS	Landed 14.9.54. Promoted corporal 14.1.56.
Collins, John	2228	S	Command Varna 20.9.54 & 5.11.54. Promoted 5.2.55. Died before Sevastopol 11.3.55. Enlisted 4.1.46. Former french polisher of Donaghadee.
Collins, Patrick	2924	AIS	Landed 14.9.54. Awarded the Sardinian War Medal for his action on 5.11.54.
Connors, Andrew	2602	AIS	Landed 14.9.54. Landed from Malta 4.10.55. Promoted corporal 14.1.56.
Cooper, William	1389	AIS	Landed 14.9.54. Died Balaklava 12.2.55.
Cranston, Robert	3070	S	Sick Varna 20.9.54. Sick Balaklava 5.11.54. Promoted corporal 14.1.56.
Crump, Samuel	2823	AI	Landed 14.9.54. Enlisted 4.5.49. Died camp Belbeck river. 25.9.54. Former carpet weaver of Kidderminster.
Dennis, William	2808	S	Landed 1.3.55. Promoted corporal 4.11.55.

Dunne, Michael	3637		Landed from Malta 10.3.56.
Edwards, Edwin	2046		Sick Scutari October 1854.
Edwards, William	1886	S	Sick Varna 20.9.54 & 5.11.54. Promoted corporal 14.1.56.
Farley, Robert	1477	AI	Landed 14.9.54.
Farmer, William	2742	AIS	Landed 14.9.54. Sick Scutari 24.1.55. Sent to England from Scutari 29.6.55.
Finn, Henry	1550	AIS	Landed 14.9.54. Promoted corporal 15.3.56.
Fitzpatrick, John	2309		Embarked for England 14.10.54. Former groom of Newry.
Gee, Daniel	1744	AIS	Landed 14.9.54. Died Scutari 20.1.55.
Goldrick, John	3431	AIS	Landed 14.9.54. Promoted 6.2.55. Sick Scutari 18.5.55.
Graine, Charles	1711	AB	Landed 14.9.54. Sick Balaklava 5.11.54.
Hackett, Patrick	2612	S	Landed 27.2.55. Landed from Malta 28.9.55. Proceeded to England 5.10.55.
Hart, John	1629	AIS	Landed 14.9.54. Listed as 'carpenter' November–December 1855.
Heary, Patrick	2218	AIS	Landed 14.9.54.
Hogan, Jeremiah	2771	AIS	Landed 14.9.54. Promoted corporal 14.1.56.
Horner, Charles	1104	AIS	Landed 14.9.54. Awarded DCM and gratuity of £5 January 1855. Promoted 1.2.55. Died in trench before Sevastopol 8.6.55. Enlisted 20.6.39.
Howley, Patrick	3758	S	Landed 6.9.55.
Jones, Thomas	1981	AIS	Landed 14.9.54. KiA 5.11.54. Enlisted 27.7.44. Former servant of Llandovery.
Jordan, Martin	2853	S	Sick Varna 20.9.54, Balaklava 5.11.54. Promoted corporal 15.3.56.
Kaine, William	3149	S	Landed from Provisional Battalion, Malta 19.5.55. Sent to England from Scutari 7.9.55.
Kelly, Thomas	2659	A	Landed 14.9.54. Sick Scutari 5.11.54. Died Scutari 28.11.54. Former baker of Oldcastle.
Kennedy, John	3582	S	Promoted corporal 14.1.56.
Lee, Francis	2670	AIS	Landed 14.9.54.
Lee, John	2161	AIS	Landed 14.9.54. Promoted 12.2.55. Killed in trench before Sevastopol 26.5.55. Former servant of ...?
Lemmon, Joseph	2401	S	Command Scutari 20.9.54 & 5.11.54. Promoted corporal 14.1.56.
Lunam, Patrick	3130	S	Landed 28.12.54.
Lynch, Denis	3084	AIS	Landed 14.9.54. Sick Scutari 7.9.55. Promoted corporal 11.12.55.
McLaughlan, Luke	3172	S	Landed 13.11.54. Sent to England from Scutari 15.5.55. Promoted corporal 14.1.56.
Maher, Michael	1877	AIS	Landed 14.9.54. Promoted corporal 14.1.56.
Mahony, Daniel	2757	S	
Malley, Patrick	3319		Landed 13.11.54. Promoted corporal 14.1.56.
Mara, Patrick	3120	AIS	Landed 14.9.54. Sent to England from camp 6.7.55.
Mason, Richard	1272	S	Sick Varna 20.9.54 & 5.11.54. Promoted corporal 19.12.54. Transferred to Land Transport 4.10.55.
Meads, James	2070	AS	Landed 14.9.54. Sick Balaklava. Sick Scutari 5.11.54. Sent to England from Scutari 21.8.55.
Meredith, Joseph	1944	AIS	Landed 14.9.54. Died Scutari 17.2.55.
Millard, William	3064	S	Landed 21.7.55. From Scutari 3.7.55. Promoted corporal 14.1.56.
Miller, James	3698	S	Landed 30.5.55. To Scutari 4.7.55. From Scutari 5.9.55. Promoted corporal 10.10.55.
Murray, Anthony	1887	AIS	Landed 14.9.54. Sent to England from Scutari 22.9.55.
Nelson, Charles	1801	AIS	Landed 14.9.54. For going out four times to rescue wounded men during the night of 18/19 June and being wounded, he was awarded the *Medaille Militaire*. Promoted corporal 14.1.56.
Nicholson, William	2226	AIS	Landed 14.9.54. Command Balaklava July–September 1855. Promoted corporal 10.10.55.
O'Dea, Martin	2584	AIS	Landed 14.9.54. To England 25.11.55.
O'Neil, James	2730		Promoted corporal 13.10.54.
Phillips, John	2083	AIS	Landed 14.9.54. Promoted 5.2.55.
Pottage, William	3007	AIS	Landed 14.9.54. Sent to Malta 16.4.55. Promoted corporal 15.10.54.
Putland, Henry	2959	AIS	Landed 14.9.54. Promoted 2.3.55. To England 16.1.56.
Richardson, John	3763	S	Landed 6.9.55. To Scutari 11.1.56.
Riches, Henry	1763	S	Command Varna 20.9.54 & 5.11.54. Promoted corporal 14.1.56.
Ritchie, Thomas	2834	AIS	Landed 14.9.54. Promoted corporal 14.1.56.
Shaughnessey, William	2377	AIS	Landed 14.9.54. KiA 5.11.54. Enlisted 9.1.47. Former labourer of Mohill.
Sheehan, Benjamin	3401	AS	Landed 14.9.54. Sick Scutari 5.11.54. DoW before Sevastopol 14.9.55. Enlisted 20.8.49. Former baker of Ballymona.
Smith, Andrew	2782	ABS	Landed 14.9.54. Command Balaklava 5.11.54. Promoted 16.3.55. Sent to Malta 16.4.55.
Soley, James	1883	AIS	Landed 14.9.54. Died before Sevastopol 1.2.55. Enlisted 13.2.44. Former stone sawyer of Cleiver, Windsor.
Starkey, Peter	2482	AIS	Landed 14.9.54. Awarded either the *Légion d'honneur* (5th Class) or the *Medaille Militaire* for action at Redan 8.9.55. Wounded 8.9.55. Recommend by Sergeant-Major Madden for the Victoria Cross 'Charged gallantly into

			the Redan & conspicuous in holding a position there. 8 September 1855' – not approved. Promoted corporal 5.1.56.
Stone, William	3203	AIS	Landed 14.9.54. From Scutari 4.7.55. Promoted corporal 14.1.56.
Stubbs, Samuel	2209	AIS	Landed 14.9.54. Promoted corporal 14.1.56.
Tanner, William	1789	AI	Landed 14.9.54. Promoted 3.3.55.
Targett, Henry	1252	AIS	Landed 14.9.54. Promoted corporal 12.10.54. Awarded DCM and gratuity of £10 January 1855. Died before Sevastopol 9.2.55. Enlisted 18.1.40. Former labourer of Weston.
Tompkins, George	1643	AIS	Landed 14.9.54. Sent Scutari sick from Sevastopol 29.7.55. From Scutari 3.10.55. Promoted corporal 14.1.56.
Troy, John	3242	S	Landed 13.11.54. Promoted corporal 15.3.56.
Tucker, Richard	2703	AI	Landed 14.9.54. Died aboard ship to Scutari 26.9.54.
Valentine, John	2138	AIS	Landed 14.9.54. Promoted corporal 29.12.54. DoW before Sevastopol 2.4.55.
Walsh(e), Patrick	2845	AI	Landed 14.9.54. Sent to England from Scutari 20.12.54.
Withers, John	3229	S	Landed 13.11.54. From Scutari 23.7.55. Promoted corporal 14.1.56.
Drummers			
Boobier, William	1720	AIS	Landed 14.9.54.
Brennan, John	3330	S	Landed 6.9.55.
Carberry, Michael	2858	AIS	Landed 14.9.54.
Casey, William	1881	AIS	Landed 14.9.54. Died aboard *Belgravia* 27.12.55.
Collins, Christopher	3332		Landed from Malta 23.1.56.
Duggan, John	3283		Landed from Malta 23.1.56.
Dunworth, William	2920	AIS	Landed 14.9.54.
Fitzgerald, John	3116	AIS	Landed 14.9.54. Sent to England from Scutari 26.6.55.
Fowler, John	1589	AIS	Landed 14.9.54.
Kean, Patrick	2919	AIS	Landed 14.9.54. Sick Scutari 6.11.54.
McNabb, John	1759	AIS	Landed 14.9.54. Promoted drum-major sergeant 17.1.55. Reduced to drummer 15.8.55.
Marshall, Robert William	1865	S	Sick Varna 20.9.54 & 5.11.54. Promoted ?.1.55. Sick Scutari 14.8.55.
Middleton, John	1798	AIS	Landed 14.9.54. Died before Sevastopol 25.2.55.
Middleton, Thomas	2348	AIS	Landed 14.9.54.
Molloy, Peter	3028	IS	Sick Varna 20.9.54.
Morrison, James	2993	AIS	Landed 14.9.54. Sent to England from Scutari 18.5.55.
Murphy, Patrick	3301		Landed from Malta 10.3.56.
Privates			
Adlum, Joseph	1518	AIS	Landed 14.9.54.
Ahern, Cornelius	3406	AIS	Landed 14.9.54. Deserted 27.7.55.
Aldridge, Daniel	3761	S	Landed 16.6.55. Sick Scutari 9.7.55. From Scutari 16.10.55.
Alford, Edward	3572	S	Landed 4.2.55.
Allchorn, Augustus	3293	S	Landed 13.11.54. Sick Scutari 29.4.55.
Allen, Christopher	3220	S	Landed 13.11.54. Died aboard *Arabia* en route to Scutari 24.1.55.
Allen, Henry	3901		Landed from Malta 10.3.56.
Allen, Joseph	3675	S	Landed 30.5.55.
Allen, Thomas	3745	S	Landed 30.5.55.
Allum, Samuel	3388	AIS	Landed 14.9.54. Promoted corporal 15.2.55. Reduced to private 10.10.55.
Ambulitt, Thomas	2117	AS	Landed 14.9.54. Sick Scutari 5.11.54.
Anderson, James	1666	AIS	Landed 14.9.54. Promoted corporal 1.2.55. Promoted sergeant. Reduced to private 10.10.55.
Anderson, Thomas	2792	IS	Command Varna 20.9.54. Died Scutari 22.1.55.
Andrews, George	1482	AIS	Landed 14.9.54. Died before Sevastopol 28.2.55.
Anton, John	3892		Landed from Malta 10.3.56.
Archard, William	3254	S	Landed 4.2.55. Sent to England from Scutari 26.6.55.
Armsby, George	3029	AIS	Landed 14.9.54.
Arnold, George	3802	S	Landed 6.9.55.
Ashmead, Richard	3746	S	Landed 16.6.55. Sick Scutari 19.7.55. From Scutari 3.10.55.
Asquith, Frederick	3263	S	Landed 13.11.54. Died before Sevastopol 27.1.55. Enlisted 21.3.54. Former labourer of Tadcaster.
Baker, Benjamin	3591	S	Landed from Malta 9.9.55. Attached to Land Transport Corps March 1856.
Ball, Patrick	3651	S	Landed 16.6.55.
Ball, William	3495	AIS	Landed 14.9.54. KiA 5.11.54.
Ballant, William	2568	S	Landed 4.2.55.
Banbury, George	2144	IS	Sick Varna 20.9.54. Sent to England from Scutari 28.4.55.
Banbury, William	3044	AIS	Landed 14.9.54.
Bannister, John	3261	S	Landed 13.11.54. Died Smyrna (hospital Turkey) 12.3.55.
Bannister, John	3653	S	Landed 30.5.55. KiA 8.9.55. Enlisted 4.11.54. Former labourer of St Mary's, Dublin.

Banton, William	1313	AIS	Landed 14.9.54. Sent to England from Scutari 1.1.55.
Barlow, John	3269	S	Landed 13.11.54. Sent to England from Scutari 22.9.55.
Barnes, Henry	2040	AIS	Landed 14.9.54. Sent to England from Smyrna 24.7.55.
Barnes, James	2912	A	Landed 14.9.54. Sick Scutari 5.11.54.
Barnes, Thomas	3708	S	Landed 6.9.55.
Barnett, Francis	3496	AIS	Landed 14.9.54. Sent to England from Scutari 11.1.55.
Barrett, Anthony	3829	S	Landed 6.9.55. Attached to Land Transport Corps January–March 1856.
Barrett, William	3407	AIS	Landed 14.9.54.
Barrett, William	3557	S	Landed 4.2.55. Sent to England from Smyrna 29.6.55.
Barrow, John	1958	AIS	Landed 14.9.54. Transferred to Land Transport Corps 17.12.55.
Barry, Edward	1223	AIS	Landed 14.9.54. Sent to Malta 16.4.55.
Bassley, George	3061		Sick at Scutari October 1854. Embarked for England from Scutari 11.11.54.
Bates, Robert	3547	S	Landed 4.2.55.
Baycock, William	3897		Landed from Malta 13.1.56.
Bayford, Thomas	2720	AIS	Landed 14.9.54. KiA 5.11.54. Enlisted 29.1.47. Former labourer of Farnham.
Beads, William	3285	S	Landed 28.12.54. Died 23.9.55. Enlisted 5.4.54. Former labourer of Kilough, King's County.
Bell, John	3339	S	Landed 28.12.54. Sent England from Scutari 28.4.55. Landed from Malta 10.3.56.
Benjamin, James	1323	AIS	Landed 14.9.54. KiA 5.11.54. Enlisted 22.5.40. Former labourer of Liverpool.
Bennett, Charles	3697	S	Landed 16.6.55. Sent England from Scutari 28.8.55.
Bennett, John	3705	S	Landed 6.9.55.
Berryman, William	3497	S	Command Varna 20.9.54 & 5.11.54. Sent to England from Scutari 23.4.55.
Birmingham, Patrick	3429	S	Sick Scutari 20.9.54 & 5.11.54. Died before Sevastopol 22.1.55.
Bishop, Joseph	1414	AIS	Landed 14.9.54. To Malta 8.12.55. Landed from Malta 10.3.56.
Blake, James	1899	AS	Command Scutari 5.11.54. Attached to Land Transport Corps January–March 1856.
Blake, Joseph	3045	AS	Landed 14.9.54. Sick Scutari 10.10.54. Sick Scutari 5.11.54. From Scutari 11.2.56.
Blake, William	2205	AS	Landed 14.9.54. Sick Scutari 5.11.54.
Blazey, Walter	3023	AIS	Landed 14.9.54. Died Scutari 7.2.55.
Boland, Denis	3243	S	Landed 13.11.54. To England 1.12.55.
Bolderston, David	3410	IS	Command Varna 20.9.54. Died Scutari 12.2.55.
Bolster, John	2665	AIS	Landed 14.9.54. KiA 5.11.54. Enlisted 31.10.48. Former servant of Mallow.
Bolter, Thomas	1199	AIS	Landed 14.9.54. Died before Sevastopol 9.8.55. Enlisted 28.10.39. Former needlemaker of Leicester.
Booth, George	3161	A	Landed 14.9.54. Sick Scutari 5.11.54. Died Scutari. 2.2.55. Enlisted 13.2.54. Former labourer of Durrab, King's County.
Booth, George	3411	IS	Command Varna 20.9.54. Died before Sevastopol 7.8.55.
Booth, William	3624	S	Landed 4.2.55. Sent to England from Scutari 31.7.55.
Boscombe, James	1322	AS	Landed 14.9.54. Sick Scutari 5.11.54. Sent to England from Scutari 31.3.55.
Bostock, William	1708	AIS	Landed 14.9.54. KiA 5.11.54. Enlisted 11.10.41. Former butcher of Nuneaton.
Bowles, Jacob	3747	S	Landed 16.6.55. Sent to England from Scutari 7.9.55.
Bourke, James	3065	AIS	Landed 14.9.54. Sent to England from Scutari 28.4.51.
Bourke, John	2430	AI	Landed 14.9.54. Died before Sevastopol 21.4.55.
Bourke, John	3024	AIS	Landed 14.9.54. Sick Scutari 14.8.55.
Bowen, George	1609	AIS	Landed 14.9.54. Died Scutari 30.1.55.
Bowles, Henry	1814	AIS	Landed 14.9.54.
Boycott, William	2060	AIS	Landed 14.9.54.
Boyde, Thomas	3375	ABS	Landed 14.9.54. Sick Scutari 5.11.54. Sent to England from Scutari 26.6.55.
Boyle, James	2830	AIS	Landed 14.9.54. Died before Sevastopol 12.10.55. Enlisted 28.5.49. Former labourer of Hilb...?, County Down.
Brace, Charles	2040	AS	Landed 14.9.54. Command Balaklava 5.11.54. Died Balaklava 3.4.55. Enlisted 11.9.44. Former labourer of Bishops Stortford.
Bracey, William	3289	S	Landed 13.11.54. Died Scutari 1.10.55.
Brackley, John	2267	S	Landed 30.5.55. Died before Sevastopol 24.2.55. Enlisted 18.4.46. Former labourer of Ballinalush.
Bradley, Stephen	2330	AS	Landed 14.9.54. Wounded 20.9.54. Sick Scutari 5.11.54.
Brady, Matthew	3089	AIS	Landed 14.9.54. Supposed to have died 5.10.55.
Bragg, John	3498	AIS	Landed 14.9.54. Sent to England from Scutari 28.9.55.
Bragg, William	3499	AIS	Landed 14.9.54. KiA before Sevastopol 4.9.55. Enlisted 7.12.49. Former labourer of Tiverton.
Brain, Thomas	3727	S	Landed 16.6.55. From Scutari 11.2.56.
Brayshaw, Hollings	3321	S	Landed 28.12.54. Died before Sevastopol 15.3.55.
Brennan, James	1782	AIS	Landed 14.9.54. Died Scutari 9.4.55.
Brennan, James	3454	S	Landed 28.12.54. Sent to England 6.7.55.
Brennan, John	2878	AIS	Landed 14.9.54. Promoted drummer. Reduced to private 23.11.55.
Brennan, James	3528		Landed 4.2.55. Transferred to 42nd Regt.
Brennan, John	3478	S	Landed 4.2.55.

Brennan, Maurice	3663	S	Landed 4.2.55. From Scutari 16.10.55.
Brennan, Michael	3286	S	Landed 13.11.54. Sent to England from Scutari 6.5.55.
Brennan, Patrick	2950	AIS	Landed 14.9.54. KiA 8.9.55. Enlisted 22.11.50. Former labourer of Ballymore.
Brennan, Patrick	3312	S	Landed 13.11.54. Sent to England from Scutari 11.7.55.
Brennan, Thomas	3306	S	Landed 4.2.55.
Bridgeman, Singeon	3475	S	Landed 6.9.55. To Scutari 25.10.55.
Brodie, Peter	2635	AIS	Landed 14.9.54. KiA 5.11.54. Enlisted 1.9.48. Former labourer of Campbeltown.
Brogan, John	3276	S	Landed 13.11.54. Sick Scutari 21.6.55. From Scutari 3.10.55.
Brooks, John	3884		Landed from Malta 10.3.56.
Brown, Charles	3500	AIS	Landed 14.9.54. Died before Sevastopol 11.1.55.
Brown, Denis	3131	AIS	Landed 14.9.54.
Brown, George	1735	A	Landed 14.9.54. Wounded 20.9.54. Sick Scutari 5.11.54. Sailed for England 11.11.54. Landed from Malta 10.3.56.
Brown, Jacob	3521	S	Landed 4.2.55. From Scutari 11.2.56.
Brown, Squire	3567	S	Landed 6.9.55.
Bryant, John	1380	S	Landed 18.5.55. Sick Scutari 3.7.55.
Bryant, William	1374	AIS	Landed 14.9.54. Awarded DCM and gratuity of £5 January 1855. Died before Sevastopol 9.2.55. Died before Sevastopol 4.5.55.
Bualy, Robert	2997	AIS	Landed 14.9.54. Attached to Land Transport Corps January–March 1856.
Buck, John	3196	AI	Landed 14.9.54. Transferred to 50th Regt.
Buckley, John	3830		Landed from Malta 10.3.56.
Burford, Richard	3748	S	Landed 16.6.55. Sick Scutari 21.6.55. From Scutari 3.10.55.
Burke, Cornelius	3878		Landed from Malta 10.3.56.
Burke, James	3065	AIS	Landed 14.9.54. KiA 5.11.54.
Burke, John	2430		DoW camp before Sevastopol. Enlisted 8.1.48. Former cordwainer of Cork.
Burke, John	3024		From Scutari 11.2.55. Former labourer of Boyle.
Burke, Patrick	3367	AIS	Landed 14.9.54. Former labourer of Crenin...?
Burke, Patrick	3434	AIS	Landed 14.9.54. Sent to Malta 16.4.55. Former labourer of Dun...?
Burnes, James	2433		KiA 5.11.54. Enlisted 22.11.47. Former labourer of Ballintoghen.
Burtonshall, Jesse	1818	AIS	Landed 14.9.54.Wounded 20.9.54.
Bush, John	1962	AIS	Landed 14.9.54. Died before Sevastopol 21.1.55.
Bushell, Michael	3173	ABS	Command Balaklava 5.11.54.
Bushell, Patrick	3046	AIS	Landed 14.9.54.
Bussley, Joseph	1704	S	Sick Scutari 30.7.55. Died 18.2.56.
Butler, Edwin	1710	AIS	Landed 14.9.54. Died Scutari 20.3.55.
Butler, Patrick	2938	AIS	Landed 14.9.54. Sent to england from Scutari 22.2.55.
Butler, Thomas	2186	AIS	Landed 14.9.54.
Butler, William	2901	AIS	Landed 14.9.54.
Butlin, Daniel	2999	S	Sick Varna 20.9.54. Sick Scutari 29.4.55. From Scutari 16.10.55.
Butterant, George	3655	S	Landed 6.9.55.
Byrne, Edward	3042	AIS	Landed 14.9.54. Sent to England 6.7.55.
Byrne, James	2655	AIS	Landed 14.9.54. Former labourer of Mountrath.
Byrne, James	3026	A	Landed 14.9.54. Wounded 20.9.54. Sick Scutari 5.11.54. Former groom of Kilmore.
Byrne, John	3272	S	Landed 13.11.54. Died before Sevastopol 23.11.54.
Byrne, John	3828		Left behind sick Scutari on passage from England. Deleted from list of those who landed 6.9.55. From Scutari 24.9.55. Returned to 3rd Regt as a deserter 27.9.55.
Byrne, John	3603	S	Landed 4.2.55. Sick Scutari from Sevastopol 31.8.55.
Byrne, Michael	3240	S	Landed 13.11.54. Sent to England from Smyrna 24.6.55.
Byrnes, Thomas	1953	AIS	Landed 14.9.54. Sent to England from Scutari 28.4.55.
Cahir, John	2814	AIS	Landed 14.9.54. Died beore Sevastopol 25.1.55. Enlisted 29.5.47. Former labourer of Tonghearara.
Callinan, Michael	3266	S	Landed 4.2.55. KiA 8.9.55.
Callis, William	3646		Landed 4.2.55.
Campbell, Peter	3099	IS	Sick Scutari 20.9.54.
Cannon, John	2100	S	Landed 4.2.55.
Caraghee, Peter	3224	S	Landed 13.11.54. Sent to England from Scutari 28.9.55.
Carney, Edward	2839	A	Landed 14.9.54. DoW 22.9.54. Enlisted 24.5.49. Former labourer of Galway.
Carlton, Christopher	3168	S	Landed 13.11.54. To Land Transport Corps 8.2.56.
Carr, Patrick	2191	S	Landed 6.9.55. Promoted to corporal. Reduced to private 1.11.55.
Carr, William	3032	S	Sick Malta 20.9.54 & Balaklava 5.11.54. Sent to England from Scutari 15.5.55.
Carroll, John	2149	AIS	Landed 14.9.54. Supposed to have died 5.10.55. Former carpenter of Wicklow.
Carroll, John	2484	AIS	Landed 14.9.54. Died Scutari 3.3.55. Former mason of Croom.
Carroll, John	3845		To Land Transport Corps 1.2.56.
Carroll, Michael	2685	AIS	Landed 14.9.54. Served Land Transport October–December 1855. To Land Transport Corps 1.2.56. Former labourer of Newtown.

Carroll, Owen	2588	AIS	Landed 14.9.54. Died before Sevastopol 22.3.55. Enlisted 2.9.48. Former labourer of Colesman's Well.
Carroll, Patrick	3073	AIS	Landed 14.9.54. KiA before Sevastopol 5.9.55.
Carroll, William	2573	AIS	Landed 14.9.54. Sent to England from Scutari 1.1.55.
Carter, Benjamin	2220	AIS	Landed 14.9.54. Promoted 12.3.55. Reduced to private.
Carter, John	3700	S	Landed 30.5.55.
Carter, William	3401	S	Landed 28.12.54. To Land Transport Corps 1.2.56.
Carver, William	3341	AIS	Landed 14.9.54. Died aboard *Arabia* en route to Scutari 26.1.55.
Casey, John	3141	S	Landed 13.11.54.
Cashman, John	3854		Landed from Malta 25.9.55.
Cashman, Timothy	3571	S	Landed 4.2.55. To England 16.1.56.
Cashmore, George	1620	AIS	Landed 14.9.54.
Cassidy, Matthias	2441	AIS	Landed 14.9.54. KiA 8.9.55. Enlisted 10.4.48. Former labourer of Clare.
Cassidy, Christopher	3279	S	Landed 4.2.55. Sick Scutari 15.8.55. From Scutari 16.10.55. To Land Transport Corps 1.2.56.
Cassidy, Michael	3660	S	Landed 4.2.55. Sick Scutari 25.2.55. From Scutari 11.2.56.
Casson, William	3180	S	Landed 30.5.55. Promoted to sergeant. Reduced to private. To England 5.10.55.
Caulfield, John	3644		To Land Transport Corps 1.2.56
Cavan, Bartley	3349	AIS	Landed 14.9.54. Sick Scutari 18.5.55.
Cavan, William John	3350	AIS	Landed 14.9.54. Sick Scutari 11.12.54. To Land Transport Corps 1.2.56.
Kavenagh, Andrew	1914	AIS	Landed 14.9.54. Sick Scutari 17.3.55. Landed from Malta 4.10.55.
Cavanagh, Thomas	3863	S	Landed 6.9.55.
Cavanagh, Patrick	2179	AIS	Landed 14.9.54. Sent to England from Scutari 22.6.55. Former carpenter of Cork.
Cavanagh, Patrick	1905	AIS	Landed 14.9.54. KiA 8.9.55. Enlisted 6.3.44. Former labourer of Trichonopoly.
Cavanagh, Patrick	3253	S	Died Scutari 26.1.55.
Chapman, Samuel	3867		Landed from Malta 4.10.55.
Chapman, William	3681	S	Landed 16.6.55. Proceeded to England 5.10.55.
Cheetham, George	2812	AIS	Landed 14.9.54.
Chegwin, Noah	2133	AIS	Landed 14.9.54. Sent to England from Scutari 26.2.55.
Chipp, Owen	2388	AIS	Landed 14.9.54.
Chiesa, Andrew	3364	S	Landed 28.12.54. Sent to Malta from Sevastopol 16.4.55.
Chisment, Joseph	1767	AIS	Landed 14.9.54.
Christopher, James	2637	AIS	Landed 14.9.54. Died Scutari 30.1.55.
Christy, Patrick	3525	S	Landed 4.2.55.
Church James	3749	S	Landed 30.5.55.
Cimamon, John	3307	S	Landed 28.12.54. Died before Sevastopol 2.3.55. Enlisted 17.4.54. Former labourer of Kilmagen.
Claffey, James	3626	S	Landed 4.2.55.
Clancy, Thomas	2894	AIS	Landed 14.9.54.
Clarke, John	3530	S	Landed 4.2.55.
Clarke, William	2015		Landed 14.9.54 (reduced from sergeant to private 15.8.54).
Clay, George	3074		Aboard ship 20.9.54. Sick Scutari 5.11.54.
Claypole, Joseph	3682	S	Landed 16.6.55.
Clarey, Edward	1757	AIS	Landed 14.9.54. Died Scutari 24.1.55.
Cleary, Patrick	2474	AIS	Landed 14.9.54. Sick Scutari 24.1.55.
Clements, Henry	2711	AIS	Landed 14.9.54.
Clieve, James	2325	S	Command Scutari 20.9.54 & 5.11.54. To Land Transport Corps 1.2.56.
Clifford, John	3750	S	Landed 6.9.55.
Cline, Bernard	3501	AIS	Landed 14.9.54. Sent to England from Scutari 11.7.55.
Clough, John	3382	AS	Landed 14.9.54. Wounded 26.10.54. Sick Scutari 5.11.54. DoW Scutari 3.1.55.
Clyde, William	2712	AIS	Landed 14.9.54.
Cockhran, Isaac	1113	A	Landed 14.9.54. Sick Scutari 5.11.54.
Cockroft, Thomas	3585	S	Landed 4.2.55. Sent to England from Scutari 29.6.55.
Coghlan, John	2804	AIS	Landed 14.9.54. KiA 5.11.54. Enlisted 26.5.49. Former labourer of Kinsale.
Coghlan, William	2653	AIS	Landed 14.9.54. Sent to England from Scutari 18.7.55.
Cokely, Jeremiah	2791	IS	Command Varna 20.9.54.
Cole, John	3050	AIS	Landed 14.9.54.
Cole, William	1938	AIS	Landed 14.9.54.
Coleman, Denis	2296	IS	Aboard ship 20.9.54. Died before Sevastopol 4.2.55.
Coles, John	3383	AIS	Landed 14.9.54. Sent to England from Scutari 2.6.55.
Colgan, John	3251	S	Landed 13.11.54. Died before Sevastopol 23.1.55.
Colgan, Richard	3207	S	Landed 13.11.54.
Collins, Archibald	2500	AIS	Landed 14.9.54.
Collins, Bartholomew	3278	S	Landed 13.11.54.
Collins, Edward	3532	S	Landed 4.2.55. KiA 8.9.55. Enlisted 3.7.54. Former labourer of Shurles.
Collins, John	2618	S	Landed 28.12.54. To Scutari 1.3.56.

Collins, Patrick	2924		
Collins, William	2723	AIS	Landed 14.9.54. Sick Scutari 11.12.54.
Collins, William	3244	S	Landed 13.11.54. Sick Scutari 14.8.55. Landed from Malta 4.10.55.
Comberford, Michael	3569	S	Landed 16.6.55. Sick Scutari 7.9.55. Landed from Malta 4.10.55. Promoted corporal 14.1.56. Reduced to private 13.3.56.
Condon, Daniel	3784		Landed from Malta 4.10.55.
Condon, David	2797	IS	Command Varna 20.9.54.
Conlan, Patrick	3602	S	Landed 4.2.55.
Conliff, Christopher	2224	AIS	Landed 14.9.54.
Conliff, William Arthur	2801	AIS	Landed 14.9.54.
Conlon, Michael	3634	S	Landed 30.5.55. DoW before Sevastopol 27.7.55. Enlisted 9.11.54. Former labourer of ...? County Clare.
Connell, Denis	2486	S	Landed 4.3.55.
Connell, John	2403		Landed 28.12.54.
Connell, John	3336	S	Landed 28.12.54. Sick Scutari 26.6.55. From Scutari 25.10.55.
Connell, Luke	2403	AIS	Landed 14.9.54. Sailed to England from Scutari 7.12.54.
Connolly, Hugh	2227	S	Landed 31.12.54.
Connolly, John	2473	AI	Landed 14.9.54.
Connolly, John	3502	S	KiA trenches before Sevastopol, 23.4.55. Enlisted 19.6.52. Former labourer of Killoughton.
Connolly, Michael	3871		Landed from Malta 10.3.56.
Connolly, Thomas	3702	S	Landed 30.5.55. Sent to England from Renkioi (hospital) 27.10.55 .
Connor, John	2473	AIS	Landed 14.9.54. Died before Sevastopol 25.3.55.
Connors, William	3088	AIS	Landed 14.9.54. Mentioned for distinguished service 8.9.55.
Conway, Bernard	3176	AIS	Landed 14.9.54. KiA 5.11.54. Enlisted 20.2.54. Former smith of Bally...?
Conway, Daniel	2628	AIS	Landed 14.9.54. Sent to England from Scutari 19.6.55.
Conway, James	3036	S	Landed 29.1.55.
Conway, Michael	3460	S	Landed 4.2.55.
Conway, Patrick	3849		Landed from Malta 10.3.56.
Cooke, James	3217	S	Landed 28.12.54. Died before Sevastopol 21.2.55. Enlisted 10.3.54. Former labourer of Kilbride.
Cooke, William	3742	S	Landed 30.5.55.
Coombes, John	3771	S	Landed 16.6.55. To Land Transport Corps 1.2.56.
Cooney, Edward	3423	AIS	Landed 14.9.54. Died before Sevastopol 11.2.55. Enlisted 29.11.49. Former mason of Huddersfield.
Cooney, Edward	3666	S	Landed 6.9.55. To Land Transport Corps 1.2.56.
Cooney, Peter	3466		Landed 13.11.54. Transferred 88th Regt 9.5.55.
Cooper, James	2139	AIS	Landed 14.9.54. KiA 5.11.54. Enlisted 20.12.44. Former labourer of Maisemore.
Cooper, John	3022	AS	Landed 14.9.54. Sick Scutari 5.11.54. Supposed to have died 5.10.55.
Cooper, William	3310	S	Landed 28.12.54.
Corbett, William	3880		Landed from Malta 10.3.56.
Corkery, James	2589	AIS	Landed 14.9.54. Died Scutari 4.3.55.
Corley, John	3298	S	Landed 4.2.55. Died before Sevastopol 8.5.55. Enlisted 18.4.54. Former labourer of Castlebar.
Corley, John	3729		Landed from Malta 10.3.56.
Cornellis, –	–		This man does not appear in any of the official records but is mentioned in the regimental history as the first man to enter the Redan on 8.9.55 for which he received a reward of £5. Wounded 8.9.55.
Corr, Charles	2416	AIS	Landed 14.9.54. Died Scutari 24.1.55.
Corr, William	2196	AIS	Landed 14.9.54. Sent to England from Scutari 2.1.55.
Cosgrove, Owen	3233	S	Landed 13.11.54. Sent to England from Scutari 18.7.55.
Costello, Coleman	3615	S	Landed 4.2.55.
Costello, Michael	3025	S	Sick Scutari 20.9.54 & 5.11.54. From Scutari 19.7.55.
Costello, Peter	3808	S	Landed 6.9.55. To Renkioi 25.1.56.
Costello, Thomas	3214	S	Landed 13.11.54.
Coughlan, Thomas	2415	AIS	Landed 14.9.54.
Counihan, Richard	2732	AIS	Landed 14.9.54.
Courtney, James	2529	A	Landed 14.9.54. Sick Scutari 5.11.54. Deserted 8.3.55.
Cowan, John	3191	S	Sick Varna 20.9.54 & 5.11.54. Sent to England from Scutari 18.7.55.
Cowen, Joseph	3260	S	Landed 13.11.54. Died aboard *Andes* 3.2.55.
Cox, David	3288	S	Landed 13.11.54. From Scutari 23.7.55. Missing from 8.9.55. Struck off strength 22.2.56. Enlisted 1.4.54. Former labourer of Hadenham, Buckingham.
Cox, George	1882	A	Landed 14.9.54. Sick Scutari 5.11.54, died 6.11.54.
Cox, Thomas	3849		Landed from Malta 10.3.56.
Cox, William	2031	A	Landed 14.9.54. Sick at Scutari 5.11.54. From Scutari 11.2.56.
Craig, John	2092	AIS	Landed 14.9.54. Died Scutari 6.2.55.
Cranch, David	2622	ABS	Landed 14.9.54. Command Balaklava 5.11.54.

Creedon, John	2746		Command Balaklava October/November 1854.
Creig, John	3450	S	Landed 13.11.54. KiA trenches before Sevastopol 18.6.55.
Creighton, John	770	AIS	Landed 14.9.54. Awarded DCM and gratuity of £5 January 1855. Died before Sevastopol 9.2.55. This man has the lowest regimental number suggesting he was the most senior private soldier to have served in the Crimea.
Cribley, George	3726	S	Landed 16.6.55.
Crick, George	3419	S	Landed 28.12.54. Sent to England from Scutari 30.11.55. Landed from Malta 10.3.56.
Cronan, Michael	3570	S	Landed 4.2.55.
Cronan, Patrick	3305	S	Landed 13.11.54.
Crossen, John	2578	AIS	Landed 14.9.54. Servant to General Sir Richard England (paid by 44th Regt 1.10.54-31.11.54). Sent to England 2.8.55.
Croughan, James	3205	S	Landed 13.11.54. Sick Scutari 20.12.54.
Croughan, John	1091	AIS	Landed 14.9.54. Sent to England from Abydos (hospital Turkey) 13.6.55.
Crowley, John	2860	AIS	Landed 14.9.54. Sent to England from Scutari 16.2.55.
Cuff, John	3047	AIS	Landed 14.9.54. KiA 5.11.54.
Culbert, John	2214	AIS	Landed 14.9.54. Missing 8.9.55. Mentioned for distinguished service 8.9.55. Struck off strength 22.2.56. Enlisted 19.12.45. Former servant of Dough, Antrim.
Cullanan, Michael	2491	A	Landed 14.9.54. Wounded 20.9.54. Sick Scutari 5.11.54.
Cullen, George	1930	AIS	Landed 14.9.54. Sent to England from Balaklava 10.11.55.
Cullen, Walter	2844	S	Sent to England from Smyrna 20.9.55.
Cummings, James	1837	AIS	Landed 14.9.54. Sent to England from Scutari 27.1.55.
Cummins, William	3104	AIS	Landed 14.9.54. Died camp before Sevastopol 5.4.55.
Cunningham, Michael	2282	AIS	Landed 14.9.54. Died Scutari 27.2.55.
Cunningham, Patrick	2247		Landed 13.11.54. To Land Transport Corps 1.2.56.
Cunningham, Patrick	3234	S	Landed 13.11.54. Died before Sevastopol 27.2.55.
Curbison, William	3531	S	Landed 4.2.55. KiA trenches before Sevastopol 3.4.55. 3.7.54. Former labourer of Birmingham.
Curley, Patrick	3594	S	Landed 4.2.55. Sent to England from Scutari 26.6.55.
Curran, John	2523	AIS	Landed 14.9.54. Sent to England 6.7.55.
Curry, Patrick			Transferred from 88th Regt 9.3.56 (regimental number 4720).
Curry, Thomas	3356	AIS	Landed 14.9.54.
Curtis, Thomas	3435	AS	Landed 14.9.54. Sick Scutari 5.11.54, died 27.11.54.
Cushen, Patrick	3092	AIS	Landed 14.9.54.
Cuthbert, William	3522		Landed 28.12.54. Servant to Captain William Allan 41st Regt. Missing from 8.9.55. According to Allan he had been severely wounded (both arms broken) and died of his wounds as a prisoner of war in Sevastopol.
Daily, James	3838	S	Landed 6.9.55.
Daily, John	2254	AIS	Landed 14.9.54. KiA 5.11.54.
Daily, William	3342	AIS	Landed 14.9.54. From Scutari 23.7.55. Mentioned for distinguished service 8.9.55. To England 1.11.55.
Dale, Thomas	3223	S	Landed 13.11.54. Died camp before Sevastopol 10.12.54.
Daley, David	3608	I	Sick Scutari 20.9.54.
Daley, Daniel	2510	S	Died Scutari 30.10.54.
Daley, Edward	3608	S	Landed 4.2.55.
Daley, Patrick	2487	AIS	Landed 14.9.54. Died Balaklava 16.10.55. Enlisted 26.6.48. Former labourer of Glanworth, County Cork.
Daniel, William	1714	AI	Landed 14.9.54.
Daniels, John	3408	AIS	KiA 5.11.54. Enlisted 4.11.43. Former labourer of Shelton.
Darling, Owen	2561	S	Sick Varna 20.9.54 & 5.11.54. From Scutari 4.7.55.
Darsey, Michael	3676	S	Landed 16.6.55. Sick Scutari 7.9.55. From Scutari 25.10.55.
Davey, Samuel	2124	AIS	Landed 14.9.54.
Davies, Daniel	1797	AIS	Landed 14.9.54. KiA 5.11.54. Enlisted 5.12.43. Former labourer of Abergavenny.
Davies, Griffith	2096	AIS	Landed 14.9.54. Sent to Malta 16.4.55.
Davies, James	1255	AIS	Landed 14.9.54. Promoted corporal. Reduced to private 3.10.55.
Davies, John	2112	AIS	Landed 14.9.54. Sick Scutari 30.7.55. Former servant of Pendergast.
Davies, John	2280	AIS	Landed 14.9.54. Former gardener of Manchester.
Davies, John	3568	S	Landed 14.2.55. To Scutari 3.5.55. To Scutari 11.1.56.
Davies, Lewis	2074	AIS	Landed 14.9.54. Died at Smyrna (hospital) 11.3.55. Enlisted 20.11.44. Former tailor of Llandovery.
Davies, Rees	2478	AIS	Landed 14.9.54.
Davies, Thomas	1831	AIS	Landed 14.9.54. Sick Scutari 2.5.55.
Davis, George	3877	S	Landed 3.9.55. To Scutari 11.1.56.
Davis, John	3743	S	Landed 4.2.55. From Scutari 16.6.55. Sick Scutari 7.9.55.
Daw, Joseph	3751	S	Landed 30.5.55. Sick Scutari 30.7.55. From Scutari 11.2.56.
Dawson, Arthur	3200	S	Landed 28.12.54. KiA 8.9.55.

Dawson, David	1633	AIS	Landed 14.9.54. Sent to England from Scutari 20.12.54.
Dealy, Joseph	3166	AIS	Landed 14.9.54.
Delaney, James	3631	S	Landed 4.2.55. Sent to England from Scutari 29.6.55.
Delaney, John	3326	S	Landed 28.12.54. Sent to England from Scutari 29.4.55.
Delaney, Thomas	3911		Landed from Malta 10.3.56.
Dempsey, John	3145	IS	Sick Scutari 20.9.54.
Denn, Patrick	3853		Landed from Malta 4.10.55. To Scutari 25.12.55.
Devine, James	3565	S	Landed 4.2.55. Sick Scutari 7.9.55.
Dibben, George	2399	S	Command Varna 20.9.54 & 5.11.54.
Dibley, William	3683	S	Landed 30.5.55.
Dickinson, William	3658	S	Landed 30.5.55.
Dillon, Andrew	3596	S	Landed 4.2.55.
Dillon, Charles	2985	AIS	Landed 14.9.54. Appointed drummer. Reverted to private 5.3.56.
Dilworth, James	2724	AIS	Landed 14.9.54. Sent to Malta 16.4.55.
Dixon, Richard	3287	S	Landed 28.12.54. Sick Scutari 12.6.55. From Scutari 3.10.55. To Scutari 25.10.55.
Dixon, Thomas	3657		Landed from Malta 10.3.56.
Dobson, William	3259	S	Landed 28.12.54. Sick Scutari 12.3.55. From Scutari 16.10.55.
Dodge, Thomas	3701	S	Landed 30.5.55. KiA trenches before Sevastopol 1.9.55.
Doherty, James	2520	ABS	Landed 14.9.54. Command Balaklava 5.11.54. From Smyrna 7.7.55.
Doherty, Simon	2122	AIS	Landed 14.9.54. Died before Sevastopol 3.9.55.
Dolohery, Michael	3372	S	Landed 20.8.55. From Corfu 20.8.55.
Donlan, William	3225	S	Landed 28.12.54.
Donley, John	3728	S	Landed 16.6.55. Sick Scutari 15.8.55. From Scutari 16.10.55. To Land Transport Corps 1.2.56.
Donnelly, Thomas	3318	S	Landed 28.12.54. Sent to England from Scutari 18.5.55.
Donnelly, Thomas	3586	S	Landed 4.2.55. From scutari 2.7.55. KiA 8.9.55.
Donnolly, Peter	2360	AIS	Landed 14.9.54. To Scutari 30.3.56.
Donoghue, Humphrey	3437	AIS	Landed 14.9.54. Sent to England from Scutari 26.6.55.
Donohoe, Matthew	3604	S	Landed 6.9.55.
Donohoe, Patrick	1097	AIS	Landed 14.9.54. Former labourer of Poonamalee.
Donohoe, Patrick	2468	AS	Landed 14.9.54. Sick Scutari 5.11.54. Former labourer of Rockhill.
Donohoe, Patrick	2558	AIS	Landed 14.9.54. Former servant of Mallow.
Donohoe, Patrick	3162	S	Died Scutari 10.4.55.
Donohoe, Thomas	3371	AIS	Landed 14.9.54. KiA 8.9.55.
Donovan, Daniel	2489	AS	Landed 14.9.54. Wounded severely 26.10.54. DoW 31.10.54.
Donovan, Patrick	1515	AIS	Sent to England from Scutari 22.2.55.
Donovan, William	2766	A	Landed 14.9.54. Died Balaklava Hospital 28.9.54. Enlisted 3.5.49. Former labourer of Kinsale.
Dooley, John	3857	S	Landed 6.9.55.
Doris, John	3169	AS	Landed 14.9.54. Command Balaklava 5.11.54. Sick Scutari 29.4.55. From Scutari 3.10.55.
Dowling, Francis	2367		
Downer, William	3694	S	Landed 30.5.55.
Downes, James	2361	AIS	Landed 14.9.54.
Downes, James	3589	S	Landed 30.5.55. From Scutari 11.2.56.
Downes, John	2629	AIS	Landed 14.9.54. Died before Sevastopol 18.1.55.
Dowsett, David	1841	AIS	Landed 14.9.54. Died Scutari 22.2.55.
Doyle, Denis	2624	S	Landed 6.9.55.
Doyle, Martin	2837	AIS	Landed 14.9.54. Sent to England from Scutari 22.9.55.
Draper, John	2000	AIS	Landed 14.9.54.
Driscoll, Jeremiah	1888	AIS	Landed 14.9.54.
Driscoll, Michael	2535	AIS	Landed 14.9.54. Missing since 8.9.55. Struck off strength 22.2.56.
Driscoll, Timothy	2515	AIS	Landed 14.9.54. Sent to England 6.7.55.
Drum, Francis	3715		
Drumgoul, Alexander	3368	AIS	Landed 14.9.54. Died camp before Sevastopol 16.4.55.
Drummond, James	3183	AIS	Landed 14.9.54. To Scutari 1.3.56.
Drummond, Richard	2865	AIS	Landed 14.9.54.
Dudley, Robert	2947	S	Aboard ship 20.9.54. Wounded severely 26.10.54. Sick Scutari 5.11.54. Sent to England from Scutari 10.1.55.
Duffy, Michael	3543	S	Landed 13.11.54. To Land Transport Corps 1.2.56.
Duffy, Thomas	2961	AIS	Landed 14.9.54. Sent to England from Scutari 22.2.55.
Duggan, Michael	3146	AIS	Landed 14.9.54. Promoted corporal 14.1.56. Reduced to private 11.3.56.
Duggan, Michael	3671	S	Landed 16.6.55.
Duigan, William	3165	S	Landed 13.11.54. Promoted corporal 10.10.55. Reduced to private 20.11.55.
Dunn, Edward	3035	AS	Landed 14.9.54. Sick Scutari 5.11.54.
Dunn, John	3607	S	Landed 4.2.55. KiA 8.9.55.
Dunne, John	3152	A	Landed 14.9.54. Sick Scutari 5.11.54.
Dunn, Michael	3855		Landed from Malta 10.3.56.
Dunne, Peter	3128	S	Landed 13.11.54.

Dunnegan, Richard	3815	S	Landed 30.5.55. Corporal. Sick Scutari 19.8.55. From Scutari 11.2.56. Reduced to private 13.3.56.
Dunning, Joseph	2908	AS	Landed 14.9.54. Sick Scutari 5.11.54. Died Scutai 3.2.55.
Durr, Timothy	3316	S	Landed 28.12.54. Died before Sevastopol 22.2.55. Enlisted 26.4.54. Former labourer of Boyle.
Dwyer, Michael	3490	S	Landed 4.2.55.
Dwyer, Patrick	3087	AI	Landed 14.9.54. From Scutari 16.10.55. To Land Transport Corps 1.2.56.
Dye, Samuel	2020	AIS	Landed 14.9.54. Sent to England from Scutari 16.5.55.
Dyson, Thomas	3462	S	Landed 13.11.54. Sick Scutari 29.4.55. From Scutari 25.10.55.
Eddy, Owen	2992	AIS	Landed 14.9.54. KiA trenches before Sevastopol 19.6.55. Enlisted 25.6.51. Former labourer of Kilemenan.
Edwards, Enoch	2648	AIS	Landed 14.9.54. Died before Sevastopol 3.3.55. Enlisted 26.9.48. Former labourer of Bryn Eglwys.
Edwards, George	2715	S	Sick Varna 20.9.54 & Balaklava 5.11.54.
Edwards, William	3597	S	Landed 4.2.55. To Land Transport Corps 1.2.56.
Egan, Denis	3155	S	Landed 13.11.54. Sent to England from Scutari 15.5.55.
Egan, Denis	3297	S	Landed 13.11.54.
Egan, John	2412	AIS	Landed 14.9.54. Sent to England from Scutari 13.8.55. Former labourer of Wair...?
Egan, John	3494	AIS	Landed 14.9.54. Former labourer of Dublin.
Elliott, Thomas	3686	S	Landed 30.5.55.
Ellis, John	2121	AIS	Landed 14.9.54.
Ellison, Amos	3302	S	Landed 28.12.54.
Embrow, Luke	3777	S	Landed 30.5.55. Sick Scutari 14.8.55. From Scutari 16.10.55.
Ennis, John	3257	S	Landed 28.12.54. Died before Sevastopol 13.3.55. Enlisted 3.4.54. Former labourer of Kill...?
Ennis, Michael	3150	AIS	Landed 14.9.54.
Ennis, Patrick	3335	S	Landed 28.12.54. Missing since 8.9.55. Struck off strength 22.2.56.
Etherington, Henry	3403	ABS	Landed 14.9.54. Sick Scutari 5.11.54. Sent to England from Scutari 23.3.55.
Eustace, Michael	3376	AIS	Landed 14.9.54. Proceeded to England 5.10.55.
Evans, Charles	2630		
Evans, David	1611	AIS	Landed 14.9.54. KiA 5.11.54.
Evans, Jonathan	2567	AIS	Landed 14.9.54. KiA 5.11.54. Enlisted 4.8.48. Former labourer of Llan...?
Evans, John	2364	S	Landed 13.11.54. Sick Scutari 30.7.55. From Scutari 20.10.55.
Evans, John	??43	AI	Landed 14.9.54.
Everson, John	2343	AI	Landed 14.9.54. Sent to England from Scutari 11.7.55 .
Ewins, Walter	2168	AIS	Landed 14.9.54. Wounded 20.9.54. Sent to England from Scutari 26.3.55.
Eylin, George	2847	ABS	Landed 14.9.54. Sick Balaklava 5.11.54. Promoted corporal 5.1.56. Reduced to private 1.2.56.
Fagan, James	3801	S	Landed 6.9.55. From Scutari 11.2.56.
Fahey, John	3661		Landed from Malta 10.3.56.
Fahey, Martin	3614	S	Landed 6.9.55.
Fahey, Martin	3552	IS	Landed 4.2.55. Sick Scutari 21.5.55. Sent to England from Scutari 26.6.55.
Fahey, Michael	3492		Landed 13.11.54. From Scutari 11.2.56.
Fallen, John	3687		Landed from Malta 10.3.56.
Fallon, Patrick	2376	AIS	Landed 14.9.54. Sent to England from Scutari 27.4.55.
Falsey, Patrick	3390	AIS	Landed 14.9.54. KiA 5.11.54. Enlisted 16.5.51. Former labourer of Mullough.
Fannin, Martin	3584	S	Landed 4.2.55. Sick Scutari 5.7.55. From Scutari 16.10.55.
Farley, Robert		S	KiA 8.9.55.
Farmer, John	2609	AIS	Landed 14.9.54. Sent to England from Scutari 15.5.55.
Farmer, Patrick	2658	AIS	Landed 14.9.54.
Farmer, William	2742		
Farrall, James	2397	S	Sick Varna 20.9.54 & 5.11.54. Died before Sevastopol 3.3.55. Enlisted 21.8.47. Former labourer of Killachee.
Farrall, Patrick	3503	AIS	Landed 14.9.54. Missing since 8.9.55. Struck off strength 22.2.56.
Farrell, John	3148		Landed 28.12.54.
Farrell, Lewis	3587	IS	Landed 16.6.55. Sent to England from Scutari 13.9.55.
Farrell, Patrick	3857		Landed from Malta 10.3.56.
Farrell, Timothy	3886		Landed from Malta 10.3.56.
Feehan, Peter	3337	S	Landed 28.12.54. Sick Scutari 24.6.55. From Scutari 3.10.55.
Feehely, James	3484	S	Landed 4.2.55.
Fenton, William	2307	AIS	Landed 14.9.54. Died Scutari 29.4.55.
Fenwick, George	3330	S	Landed 28.12.54. Sent Scutari sick from Sevastopol 29.7.55.
Feoney, Thomas	3021	AIS	Sent to Depot 7.12.54. Embarked for England 7.12.54.
Ferguson, Christopher	3476	S	Landed 28.12.54. Died Scutari 29.4.55. Enlisted 15.2.54. Former labourer of Kilbride.
Ferguson, John	3313	S	Landed 28.12.54.
Fermile/Fernoyle William	3613		Landed 4.2.55. AWOL 15.8.55. Struck off strength as deserter 15.10.55.

			William Allen noted that 'Fernoyle' was his batman who stole his money and was last heard of in Russia.
Finn, William	2571	AIS	Landed 14.9.54. KiA 5.11.54. Enlisted 22.8.48. Former labourer of Castletown.
Finnigan, Thomas	3504	AIS	Landed 14.9.54.
Finlass, John	2181	AIS	Landed 14.9.54. Sent to England from Scutari 10.1.55.
Fisher, Peter	2987	AIS	Landed 14.9.54.
Fiske, Noah	3436	S	Sick Varna 20.9.54 & 5.11.54. Sick Scutari 4.1.55.
Fitzgerald, Richard	2512	AIS	Landed 14.9.54. Sent to England from Scutari 22.3.55.
Fitzgerald, William	2902	AIS	Landed 14.9.54.
Fitzgibbon, Daniel	2922	ABS	Landed 14.9.54. Sick Scutari 5.11.54.
Fitzgibbon, James	2815	S	Sick Varna 20.9.54 & 5.11.54. KiA trenches before Sevastopol 9.5.55.
Fitzgibbon, John	3925		Landed from Malta 10.3.56.
Fitzharris, Moses	2313	AIS	Landed 14.9.54.
Fitzpatrick, John	2309		Landed from Malta 23.9.55. Sergeant. Reduced to private 10.10.55.
Fitzpatrick, John	2740	AIS	Landed 14.9.54. Died before Sevastopol 27.2.55. Former labourer of Grogan.
Flannigan, Michael	2956	A	Landed 14.9.54. Wounded 20.9.54. Sick Scutari 5.11.54.
Fleming, George	1747	AIS	Landed 14.9.54.
Flintoff, Thomas	3311	I	Landed 4.2.55. Sent to England from Scutari 18.7.55.
Fletcher, Henry	3384	AIS	Landed 14.9.54. Sick Scutari 18.5.55. from Scutari 3.10.55.
Flinn, Daniel	2462		Died Scutari 1.10.54.
Flood, James	2241	AIS	Landed 14.9.54.
Flood, John	2262	AIS	Landed 14.9.54. DoW before Sevastopol 16.10.55. Enlisted 18.4.46. Former labourer of Lancy, County Meath.
Flynn, Denis	3369	AIS	Landed 14.9.54. DoW before Sevastopol 9.9.55.
Foley, John	3133	S	Landed 4.2.55. Sick Scutari 21.6.55. From Scutari 3.10.55.
Foley, Michael	3790	S	Landed 6.9.55.
Forbes, Thomas	2011	S	Command Varna 20.9.54 & 5.11.54.
Foster, Thomas	3228	S	Landed 4.2.55.
Fowler, James	3111	AS	Landed 14.9.54. Wounded 20.9.54. Sick Scutari 5.11.54. To Land Transport Corps 1.2.56.
Fox, Martin	3847		Landed from Malta 10.3.56.
Foy, John	3326	I	Landed 4.2.55. Sent to England from Scutari 29.6.55.
French, John	1320	AIS	Landed 14.9.54. Sick Scutari 12.6.55.
French, Thomas	3440	AIS	Landed 14.9.54.
Frost, Frederick	3536	I	Landed 4.2.55. Sent to England from Scutari 22.9.55.
Fry, James	3752	S	Landed 16.6.55.
Gaffney, John	3273	S	Landed 28.12.54. Sick Scutari 26.12.54.
Gaffney, Michael	2699	IS	Command Varna 20.9.54.
Galey, William	3433	AIS	Landed 14.9.54. Sent to Malta 5.4.55.
Galvin, John	3873		Landed from Malta 10.3.56.
Gardiner, William	3883		Landed from Malta 10.3.56.
Gardner, Henry	3363	AIS	Landed 14.9.54. Died before Sevastopol 4.2.55.
Garlick, Francis	3770		Landed from Malta 10.3.56.
Garrard, Edward	1817	AI	Landed 14.9.54. Sick Scutari 5.11.54. Sent to England from Scutari 6.7.55.
Garvey, Michael	3211	S	Landed 13.11.54. To 28th Regt 9.11.55, being a deserter from that corps.
Garvey, Patrick	2437	AIS	Landed 14.9.54. Recommended for the Victoria Cross by Brevet Major Hugh Rowlands for 'Charging inside the Redan & conspicuous in holding a position against a superior number. 8 September 1855' – not approved. Awarded *Medaille Militaire* for action on 8.9.55.
Gatry, William	3433		
Gaynor, Patrick	3473	S	Landed 4.2.55.
Gee, George Pitts	2279	AS	Landed 14.9.54. Command Balaklava 5.11.54.
Gennaway, Thomas	3364	AI	Landed 14.9.54. Died before Sevastopol 19.8.55.
Geoghan, Joseph	3529	S	Landed 4.2.55.
Gibbons, Thomas	1314	S	Landed from Malta 6.9.55.
Gibson, Edwin	3419	S	Landed 6.3.55. Died before Sevastopol 24.3.55.
Giffany, Charles	2666	AIS	Landed 14.9.54. Sent to England 5.10.55.
Gill, Peter	3548	S	Landed from Malta 6.9.55.
Gilligan, Michael	3472	S	Landed 28.12.54.
Gleed, Richard	3722	S	Landed from Malta 6.9.55.
Gloster,Thomas	2446	A	Landed 14.9.54. Died Balaklava 27.9.54. Enlisted 20.5.48. Former mason of Cappermer.
Glynn, James	3379	AIS	Landed 14.9.54. Sent to England from Scutari 1.1.55.
Goldsworthy, William	2283	AIS	Landed 14.9.54. Died camp before Sevastopol 4.1.55.
Goligher, John	2093	AIS	Landed 14.9.54. Sent to England from Scutari 22.2.55.
Gordon, Samuel William	1781	AIS	Landed 14.9.54. Sent to England from Scutari 29.4.55.
Gould, John	3539	S	Died camp before Sevastopol 1.4.55.

Goulthorpe, William	3447	S	Landed 28.12.54. Died camp before Sevastopol 9.4.55.
Gouthrope, William	3814		Landed from Malta 10.3.56.
Grace, Michael	2754	AIS	Landed 14.9.54. Wounded 26.10.54. To England 28.10.55. Recommended for the Victoria Cross by Captain Lowry 'Charged gallantly into the Redan & conspicuous in holding a position there' – not approved.
Graham, John	3600	S	Landed 4.2.55.
Grahan, Bryan	3485	S	Landed 4.2.55.
Graine, Charles	1711	S	
Graney, Daniel	2765	IS	Sick Varna 20.9.54. Died before Sevastopol 7.11.54. Enlisted 21.4.49. Former groom of Newcastle.
Grange, Joseph	3769		Landed from Malta 10.3.56.
Gray, Edward	1628	AIS	Landed 14.9.54. Sent to England from Scutari 16.2.55.
Green, James	2347	AIS	Landed 14.9.54. Died camp before Sevastopol 14.4.55. Enlisted 1.3.47. Former labourer of Killurbet.
Green, John	3623	S	Landed 4.2.55. Sent to Malta 16.4.55.
Green, Thomas	2287	AS	Landed 14.9.54. Sick Scutari 5.11.54. Died aboard ship 8.1.55. Former servant of Kil...?
Green, Thomas	2532	AIS	Landed 14.9.54. Former labourer of Ballyduff.
Grier, John	3317	I	Landed 4.2.55. Sent to England from Scutari 18.7.55.
Gregg, William	3351	AIS	Landed 14.9.54. To England 28.10.55.
Gribble, Thomas	2697	AIS	Landed 14.9.54. Died Scutari 3.3.55.
Gridd, John			Landed 4.2.55. Died before Sevastopol 1.4.55.
Griffin, Charles	1247	AIS	Landed 14.9.54.
Griffiths, David	2032	AIS	Landed 14.9.54. Died hospital before Sevastopol 6.12.54. Former labourer of Swansea.
Griffiths, David	2708		Died Scutari 16.10.54. Former labourer of Wellington.
Griffiths, Thomas	2056	I	Sick Varna 20.9.54 & 5.11.54. Sent to England from Scutari 13.8.55.
Grimshaw, Thomas	3461	S	Landed 28.12.54.
Grimwood, George	2067	AIS	Landed 14.9.54.
Grogan, Patrick	3204	S	Landed 13.11.54. Supposed to have died 5.10.55.
Grogan, Peter	2297	AIS	Landed 14.9.54. Sent to Malta 5.4.55.
Gunn, Thomas	3738	S	Landed 16.6.55.
Hackett, John	3126	S	
Hackett, Michael	3844		Landed from Malta 4.10.55.
Hagan, Hugh	2661	S	Command Varna 20.9.54 & 5.11.54.
Hagerty, Matthew	2683	AIS	Landed 14.9.54. Died Scutari 27.1.55.
Hall, Benjamin	2821	AIS	Landed 14.9.54.
Hall, Charles	3334	S	Landed 28.12.54. Died camp before Sevastopol 16.4.55. Enlisted 8.4.54. Former labourer of Sporle.
Hall, William	3491	S	Landed 28.12.54. Died Scutari 26.3.55.
Hallaghan, David	3551	S	Landed 4.2.55. Promoted corporal 10.10.55. Reduced to private 16.1.56.
Hallard, James	——	S	Transferred from 14th Regt 5.9.55 (Regt No. 3819). Also known as Allan.
Hallard, John	3143	AIS	Landed 14.9.54.
Hallard, Patrick	3144	IS	Sick Scutari 20.9.54. Died before Sevastopol 22.2.55.
Hallem, James	3226	S	Landed 4.2.55. Proceeded to England 28.9.55.
Hallen, William	1697	ABS	Landed 14.9.54. Command Balaklava 5.11.54. Died Scutari 21.12.54.
Halward, Samuel	2790	AIS	Landed 14.9.54.
Hamill, John	1811	AIS	Landed 14.9.54. Sick Scutari 13.12.54. From Scutari 25.10.55.
Hammond, William	3365	AIS	Landed 14.9.54.
Hampton, Charles	3201	S	Landed 13.11.54.
Handwright, John	3417	AIS	Landed 14.9.54. Died Scutari 22.11.54.
Hanlon, Patrick	3839	S	Landed 6.9.55.
Hannan, Thomas	2958	A	Landed 14.9.54. Wounded 20.9.54. Sick Scutari 5.11.54.
Hanrahan, Roger	2720	AS	Landed 14.9.54. Wounded severely 26.10.54. Sick Scutari 5.11.54. Sent to England from Scutari 20.12.54.
Hanstan, Richard	2507	AIS	Landed 14.9.54.
Hardiman, David	1367	S	Command Varna October & November 1854. Landed 19.1.55.
Hare, Samuel	2907	AI	Landed 14.9.54.
Hargan, Peter	2389	AI	Landed 14.9.54. Sent to England from Scutari 29.6.55.
Harman, Thomas	3366	AI	Landed 14.9.54.
Hargon, Denis	2747		Died (details not known). Enlisted 17.4.49. Former labourer of Shandon.
Harrington, Charles	3080		Sick Scutari. Died Scutari 18.1.55.
Harrington, Joseph	3060		Sick Scutari 20.9.54 & 5.11.54.
Harris, Henry	3718		Landed from Malta 13.1.56. To Scutari 26.3.56.
Harris, John	3051	I	Command Varna 20.9.54 & 5.11.54. Sent to England from Scutari 13.9.55. Former labourer of Athlone.
Harris, Thomas	1889	AIS	Landed 14.9.54. Hospital orderly. Supposed to have died 5.10.55.
Harris, William	1726	S	Command Varna 20.9.54 & 5.11.54. To England 16.1.56. Former servant of Lampeter.

Harris, William	2674	AIS	Landed 14.9.54. Former labourer of Raglan.
Harris, William	2873	AIS	Landed 14.9.54. Sent to England from Scutari 2.6.55. Former labourer of Gloucester.
Harris, William Henry	1479	AIS	Landed 14.9.54. Died at Coolali (near Scutari) 10.2.55.
Harrison, James	3105	AIS	Landed 14.9.54. Sick Scutari 2.5.55. From Scutari 16.10.55. To Land Transport Corps 1.2.56.
Harrison, John	3881	S	Landed 6.9.55.
Harrison, Thomas	2705	AIS	Landed 14.9.54. Died before Sevastopol 8.8.55.
Hart, John	1629		Command Balaklava. Sick at Scutari. Died aboard ship at Scutari 24.2.55. Former labourer of Optley.
Hart, John	1893	S	Command Varna 20.9.54 & 5.11.54. Died aboard *Columbia* 24.2.55. Former cabinet maker of Maidstone.
Hart, Michael	1701	AIS	Landed 14.9.54. KiA 8.9.55.
Hartnady, Patrick	2582	AIS	Landed 14.9.54. Recommended (in conjunction with Private John Kennelly) for the Victoria Cross by Major-General Charles Windham. 'The first two men of the storming column of the 2nd Division who followed Major-General Windham across the ditch of the Redan on the 8th of September 1855' – not approved.
Harvine, John	1607	IS	Command Varna 20.9.54. Died Scutari 31.1.55.
Hastie, John	2444	AIS	Landed 14.9.54.
Haugh, Michael	3391	AIS	Landed 14.9.54. Supposed to have died 10.5.55.
Havey, Garrett	3409	AIS	Landed 14.9.54.
Hawes, John	3767		Landed from Malta 10.3.56.
Hawkins, Charles	2668	AIS	Landed 14.9.54.
Hayes, Daniel	2687	AI	Landed 14.9.54. Died at Smyrna (hospital) 13.3.55.
Hayes, James	2852	AIS	Landed 14.9.54. Died before Sevastopol 26.1.55. Enlisted 3.11.49. Former labourer of ...?
Hayes, Joseph	3107	AIS	Landed 14.9.54.
Hayes, Patrick	3404	AIS	Landed 14.9.54. To Land Transport Corps 1.2.56.
Hayes, Thomas	3649	S	Landed 6.9.55. Promoted corporal 29.12.55. Reduced to private 29.12.55.
Haynes, Samuel	3736	S	Landed 30.5.55. Sick Scutari 5.7.55.
Hayward, Edward	3069	IS	Sick Scutari 20.9.54. KiA 5.11.54.
Hayward, John	3735	S	Landed 30.5.55.
Healy, John	2271	AS	Landed 14.9.54. Sick Scutari 5.11.54. Sent to England from Scutari 22.3.55. Former labourer of Enfield.
Healy, John	3034	A	Sick Scutari 5.11.54. Former labourer of Ballyduff.
Heanlean, James	3505	AIS	Landed 14.9.54. Proceeded to England 5.10.55.
Heany, Martin	3274	S	Landed 13.11.54.
Heary, Nicholas	——		Transferred from 21st Regt 1.12.55 (regimental number 3513).
Heary, Patrick	2218		Landed 14.9.54. Sick attendant September–November 1854.
Hemmings, John	3685	S	Landed 30.5.55. Died camp before Sevastopol 15.6.55. Enlisted 17.11.54. Former labourer.
Henderson, Henry	3400	AIS	Landed 14.9.54. Sent to England from Scutari 20.12.54.
Henderson, William	3506	AIS	Landed 14.9.54. Died before Sevastopol 8.2.55.
Hennessey, John	2531	I	Sick Varna 20.9.54 & 5.11.54. Sent to England from Smyrna 24.7.55.
Hennessey, John	3848	S	Landed 6.9.55.
Hennessey, Michael	2871	AIS	Landed 14.9.54.
Henry, John	3446	S	Landed 4.2.55.
Henry, John	3508	S	Landed 13.11.54.
Herlihy, Cornelius	2563	A	Landed 14.9.54. Sick Scutari 5.11.54.
Herlihy, Patrick	2796	AS	Landed 14.9.54. Sick Scutari 5.11.54.
Hewins, John	3019	AIS	Landed 14.9.54. Sent to England from Scutari 20.12.54.
Hewitt, James	3373	AIS	Landed 14.9.54. Died camp before Sevastopol 23.4.55. Enlisted 27.12.52. Former labourer of Bodmin, Devon [sic].
Hickey, John	2291	AI	Landed 14.9.54. Sent to England from Scutari 27.8.55.
Hickey, John	3260	S	Landed 28.12.54. Died at Coolali (hospital Turkey) 1.6.55.
Hickey, Michael	360		Landed from Malta 4.10.55.
Higgins, Michael	3202	S	Landed 14.3.55.
Higgins, Myles	1850	AS	Landed 14.9.54. Sick Scutari 5.11.54. Missing since 8.9.55. Struck off strength 22.2.56.
Higgins, Patrick	2654	AIS	Landed 14.9.54. To Land Transport Corps 1.2.56.
Higgins, William	1772	I	Promoted sergeant from private 1.2.55. Reduced to private 22.3.55. Sent to England 6.7.55.
Hillard, William	3714	S	Landed 6.9.55. To Land Transport Corps 1.2.56.
Hillman, William	3753	IS	Landed 16.6.55. Died hospital before Sevastopol 2.7.55.
Hillson, John	1749	AIS	Landed 14.9.54. Mentioned for distinguished service 8.9.55. To England 28.10.55.
Hinds, John	3187	S	Sick Varna 20.9.54 & 5.11.54.
Hodgekins, Thomas	2182	AIS	Landed 14.9.54. KiA 8.9.55.

Hoey, Peter	2372	AS	Landed 14.9.54. Died of gunshot wounds in the trenches 18.10.54. Enlisted 28.5.47. Former labourer of Ballymacormick.
Holliday, John	3454	S	Landed 28.12.54. Died Scutari 17.2.55.
Hollis, John	2253	AIS	Landed 14.9.54. Died before Sevastopol 30.1.55.
Holmes, John	3177	A	Landed 14.9.54. KiA 20.9.54.
Holmes, William	3507	S	Sick Scutari 20.9.54 & 5.11.54. Sent to England from Scutari 31.3.55.
Holmes, William	3558	I	Landed 28.12.54. Sent to England from Scutari 29.6.55.
Hopkins, Patrick	3174	AIS	Landed 14.9.54. KiA 5.11.54. Enlisted 20.2.54. Former labourer of Ardagh.
Horan, Thomas	3458	S	Landed 28.12.54. Died camp before Sevastopol 14.6.55. Enlisted 12.5.54. Former shoemaker of Eglish.
Horogan, Denis	2767	A	Landed 14.9.54. Died in camp Alma 20.9.54. Enlisted 17.4.49. Former labourer of Shandon.
Houston, Francis	2098	AIS	Landed 14.9.54. Died Scutari 16.5.55.
Howard, John	2555	AS	Landed 14.9.54. Sick Balaklava 5.11.54.
Howell, Christon	3067	S	Command Varna 20.9.54 & 5.11.54.
Hughes, James	2680	S	Command Varna 20.9.54 & 5.11.54.
Hughes, John	3077	AIS	Landed 14.9.54. To England 28.10.55.
Hughes, John	3766	S	Landed 16.6.55. To England 25.11.55.
Hughes, Michael	2255	A	Landed 14.9.54. KiA 20.9.54. Enlisted 2.4.46. Former labourer of Mullingar.
Hughes, Patrick	2152	S	Sick Varna 20.9.54 & 5.11.54. Former servant, enlisted from Dublin.
Humphreys, James	3353	AIS	Landed 14.9.54. Died at Coolali (near Scutari) 21.1.55.
Hunt, James	3291	S	Landed 13.11.54.
Hunt, John	3508	I	Sick Varna 20.9.54 & 5.11.54. Sent to England from Scutari 24.8.55.
Hunter, William	2465	A	Landed 14.9.54. Died Balaklava 28.9.54. Enlisted 22.5.48. Former mason of Paisley.
Huntington, Thomas	3668	S	Landed 4.2.55.
Hutchinson, John	3509	AIS	Landed 14.9.54.
Hyatt, James	1721	IS	Sick Varna 20.9.54. Died at Scutari 24.1.55.
Hymns, John	3733	S	Landed 16.6.55. Sick Scutari 26.6.55. From Scutari 16.10.55.
Idens, John	1659	AI	Landed 14.9.54.
Irwin, Andrew	3386	AS	Landed 14.9.54. Sick Balaklava October 1854. Sick Scutari 5.11.54.
Jackson, Henry	3178	S	Landed 28.12.54.
James, Thomas	3762	S	Landed 30.5.55. Sick Scutari 15.8.55.
Janes, Henry	3290	S	Landed 13.11.54. Died Scutari 22.3.55.
Jarrey, Patrick	–	–	Not listed in the official records but mentioned in the regimental history as being recognised for distinguished service 8.9.55.
Jay, Thomas	3469	S	Landed 28.12.54. Sent to England from Scutari 6.5.55.
Jeffers, Patrick	3284	S	Landed 13.11.54. DoW before Sevastopol 8.9.55.
Jellicoe, James	2370	AIS	Landed 14.9.54. Died at Scutari 27.1.55.
Jenkins, Edward	2382	AIS	Landed 14.9.54.
Jenkins, John	1425	AIS	Landed 14.9.54. DoW Scutari 16.11.54.
Johnson, James	3510	AS	Landed 14.9.54. Wounded 20.9.54. Sick Scutari 5.11.54.
Johnston, Thomas	3324	S	Landed 4.2.55. To England 1.12.55.
Jones, David	2033	AIS	Landed 14.9.54. Died before Sevastopol 27.1.55. Enlisted 23.9.44. Former labourer of Dolgellau.
Jones, David	2033	ABI	Landed 14.9.54. Command Balaklava 5.11.54. Sent to England from Scutari 24.8.55. Former labourer of London.
Jones, George	1815	AI	Landed 14.9.54. Killed before Sevastopol 4.9.55. Former tailor, enlisted from St ... ?
Jones, George	2061	AIS	Landed 14.9.54. Died Scutari 13.4.55. Former labourer, enlisted from Apperly?
Jones, George	2917	S	Landed 13.11.54. Died before Sevastopol 15.3.55.
Jones, John	2235	IS	Command Varna 20.9.54. Awarded DCM and gratuity of £5 January 1855. Former labourer of Wrexham.
Jones, John	2539	AIS	Landed 14.9.54. Former sadler, enlisted from Cemaes.
Jones, John	3562	S	Landed 28.12.54.
Jones, Thomas	2422	AIS	Landed 14.9.54. Former labourer of Inneskerna.
Jones, Thomas	3511	AS	Landed 14.9.54. Sick Scutari 5.11.54. Supposed to have died 5.10.55. Former labourer of Shrewsbury.
Jones, William	1433	AIS	Landed 14.9.54. Sick Scutari 18.4.55. Former labourer of Llangarron.
Jones, William	2526	AS	Landed 14.9.54. Sick Scutari 5.11.54. Former labourer of Wrexham.
Jones, William	2807	AIS	Landed 14.9.54. Sent to Malta 16.4.55. Former labourer of Brason.
Joyce, Andrew	3812	S	Landed 6.9.55.
Joyce, Thomas	3182	ABS	Landed 14.9.54. Command Balaklava 5.11.54. To Land Transport Corps 1.2.56.
Joyce, Walter	2619	AIS	Landed 14.9.54. KiA 8.9.55.
Kamelly, James	3791		Landed from Malta 10.3.56.
Keagan, John	3405	AIS	Landed 14.9.54. Sick Scutari 30.7.55.
Kean, James	1623	AIS	Landed 14.9.54.
Kean, John	2864	AIS	Landed 14.9.54. KiA trenches before Sevastopol 23.4.55. Enlisted 21.1.51.

Name	No.		Notes
			Former linen bleacher of Killaney.
Keane, Martin	3020	AIS	Landed 14.9.54.
Keaney, Hugh	3690	S	Landed 16.6.55.
Kearnan, Michael	2305	AIS	Landed 14.9.54. Transfered to 88th Regt 1.2.56.
Kearney, Michael	2321	AIS	Landed 14.9.54.
Kearney, Patrick	2709	AIS	Landed 14.9.54.
Keary, James	3142	AIS	Landed 14.9.54. Sick Scutari 21.6.55. From Scutari 11.2.56.
Keary, Patrick	2984	AI	Landed 14.9.54. Killed before Sevastopol 1.9.55.
Keefe, Denis	2463	AIS	Landed 14.9.54. Killed before Sevastopol 16.6.55. Former labourer of Kilmean.
Keefe, Denis	2492		KiA trenches before Sevastopol 23.4.55. Enlisted 27.6.48. Former labourer of Gloucester.
Keefe, John	2452	AIS	Landed 14.9.54. Died before Sevastopol 9.3.55. Enlisted ?.5.48. Former labourer of Ballyarthur.
Keefe, John	2885	AS	Landed 14.9.54. Died Scutari 20.10.54. Former labourer of Mill Street.
Keefe, Owen	2729	AIS	Landed 14.9.54. Died aboard *Belgravia* 25.12.54. Enlisted 12.2.47. Former labourer of Michaels...?
Keefe, Timothy	2849	AIS	KiA 5.11.54. Enlisted 31.10.49. Former labourer of Drumaritte.
Keegan, Thomas	3620	S	Landed 4.2.55. Died camp before Sevastopol 14.5.55. Enlisted 22.9.48. Former groom of Dublin.
Kegan, Martin	2327	AIS	Landed 14.9.54.
Keen, John	3768	S	Landed 16.6.55. Missing since 8.9.55. Struck off strength 22.2.56.
Keenah, John	3209	S	Landed 13.11.54.
Kelsher, Edward	2903	AIS	Landed 14.9.54.
Kelly, Andrew	2793	AS	Landed 14.9.54. Wounded 20.9.54. Sick Scutari 5.11.54.
Kelly, Andrew	3281	S	Landed 28.12.54. To Land Transport Corps 1.2.56.
Kelly, James	3163	AIS	Landed 14.9.54.
Kelly, John	2594	AIS	Landed 14.9.54. Former labourer of Tullamore.
Kelly, John	3043	AIS	Landed 14.9.54. Died at Scutari 8.1.55. Former labourer of Athlone.
Kelly, John	3164	AIS	Landed 14.9.54.
Kelly, John	3246	S	Landed 13.11.54.
Kelly, Michael	2263	IS	Sick Varna 20.9.54. Sent to England from Scutari 16.2.55.
Kelly, Patrick	3083	AIS	Landed 14.9.54.
Kelly, Patrick	3135	S	Landed 28.12.54.
Kelly, Richard	2832	AIS	Landed 14.9.54. Died Smyrna (hospital) 14.3.55.
Kelly, Thomas	3049	AIS	Landed 14.9.54. Former labourer, enlisted Killigan.
Kelly, Timothy	3103	AIS	Landed 14.9.54.
Kelly, William	2651	AS	Landed 14.9.54.Sick Scutari 5.11.54.
Kemp, Richard	2752	I	Sick Varna 20.9.54 & 5.11.54. Sent to England from Scutari 18.7.55
Kennedy, Henry	3264	S	Landed 13.11.54. Died in camp before Sevastopol 8.12.54. Enlisted 27.3.54. Former labourer of Tullabush.
Kennedy, James	3122	S	Sick Varna 20.9.54 & 5.11.54.
Kennedy, Jason	2838	AIS	Landed 14.9.54. DoW camp before Sevastopol 26.4.55.
Kennedy, John	3040	AIS	Landed 14.9.54. Wounded 20.9.54.
Kennedy, John	3451	S	Landed 13.11.54. Died at Scutari 23.2.55.
Kennedy, Philip	2928	S	Sick Varna 30.9.54 & 5.11.54.
Kennedy, Timothy	3820		Landed from Malta 23.9.55.
Kennedy, William	1095	AIS	Landed 14.9.54. KiA 5.11.54. Enlisted 13.5.39. Former labourer of Secunderabad.
Kennedy, William	2308	AIS	Landed 14.9.54. Died before Sevastopol 20.1.55. Former labourer of Fernaugh.
Kennelly/Kenealy, John	3420	AIS	Landed 14.9.54. Wounded 8.9.55. Recommended (in conjunction with Private Patrick Hartnady) for the Victoria Cross by Major-General Charles Windham: 'The first two men of the storming column of the 2nd Division who followed Major-General Windham across the ditch of the Redan on the 8th of September 1855' – not approved. Mentioned for distinguished service 8.9.55. Awarded *Medaille Militaire* for action on 8.9.55.
Kennelly, John	3582		Landed 4.2.55.
Kenney, William	3215		Landed from Malta 10.3.56.
Kenny, Edward	2208		Sick Scutari October & November 1854.
Kenny, John	3193	AIS	Landed 14.9.54.
Kent, Nicholas	2644	A	Landed 14.9.54. Sick Scutari 5.11.54.
Keough, James	3124	AIS	Landed 14.9.54.
Keough, Patrick	3192	S	Landed 13.11.54. Supposed to have died 5.10.55.
Keough, Peter	3457	S	Landed 28.12.54.
Kereford, James	2314	AIS	Landed 14.9.54. PoW since 5.11.54. Struck off strength 22.2.56.
Kieley, Thomas	3824	S	Landed 6.9.55.
Kiernan, Thomas	3308	S	Landed 13.11.54.

Kilcriest, Thomas	2395	AIS	Landed 14.9.54.
Kilkelly, Patrick	3267	I	Landed 4.2.55. Sent to England from Scutari 18.7.55.
Kilkenny, Patrick	3706	S	Landed 16.6.55. Sick Scutari 3.7.55. To Scutari 11.1.56.
Kilmurray, James	2335	AIS	Landed 14.9.54.
Kilroy, John	3188	AI	Landed 14.9.54.
Kilson, William	3483	S	Landed 28.12.54.
King, Bernard	3221	S	Landed 13.11.54. Sent to England from Scutari 27.1.55.
Kingdom, George	3439	AIS	Landed 14.9.54.
Kinsella, Edward	2318	AIS	Landed 14.9.54. Died before Sevastopol 12.5.55.
Knight, Daniel	3798		Landed from Malta 23.9.55.
Knight, George	2553	AS	Landed 14.9.54. Died before Sevastopol 1.10.54. Enlisted 29.7.41. Former travelling stationer of Castlebar.
Knights, Charles	2566	A	Landed 14.9.54. Sick Scutari 5.11.54.
Knowler, George	3821	S	Landed 6.9.55. Drummer. Reduced to private 23.10.55.
Knowler, William	2855	AIS	Landed 14.9.54.
Knowles, George	1864	AIS	Landed 14.9.54. Sent to England from Scutari 24.4.55.
Lacey, James	2266	AS	Landed 14.9.54. Sick Scutari 5.11.54. Sent to England from Scutari 24.9.55.
Lacey, John	2354		Landed 12.10.54. Sick Scutari 5.11.54. To depot at Varna 1.9.55. Present in Crimea, October 1855. Sick Varna January 1856. Sick Scutari February 1856. From Scutari 11.2.56.
Lahiff, Patrick	3607	IS	Sick Varna 20.9.54. Died in camp before Sevastopol 24.12.54.
Lally, James	3132	S	Landed 28.12.54.
Lamb, William	2965	AS	Landed 14.9.54. Sick Scutari 5.11.54. Command Balaklava July–August 1855.
Landrigan, William	3630		Landed from Malta 10.3.56.
Lane, John	1545	S	Command Varna 20.9.54 & 5.11.54.
Langham, James		S	Landed 4.2.55. DoW before Sevastopol 12.10.55.
Langley, Adam	3117	AIS	Landed 14.9.54. To England 1.12.55.
Langley, Joseph	1783	S	Sick Scutari 20.9.54 & 5.11.54. Sent to England from Scutari 31.3.55.
Latty, Joseph	2392	AIS	Landed 14.9.54. Bandsman. Served No. 6 Company. Killed 15.11.55 when an explosion occurred in the siege train depot. Enlisted 2.8.47. No former occupation of Mullingar.
Laugham, Samuel	1210		Landed with draft from depot *c.*December 1854 with the rank of sergeant. Reduced to private 9.2.55. Died 12.10.55. Enlisted 7.11.39. Former frame-work knitter of Banbridge, Middlesex.
Lavell, John	3031	AIS	Landed 14.9.54. Sent to England from Scutari 1.1.55.
Lawler, Michael	2773	AIS	Landed 14.9.54. Sick Scutari 15.7.55. To Scutari 27.8.55. From Scutari 11.2.56.
Lawler, Patrick	2440	A	Landed 14.9.54. Wounded 20.9.54. Died Scutari 16.10.54.
Lawlor, John	3343	AIS	Landed 14.9.54. Died Scutari 31.1.55.
Lawler, John	2783	AI	Landed 14.9.54. Sent to England from Scutari 2.1.55. Former sergeant, reduced to private October 1854. Former labourer of Quism.
Lawrence, Henry	3705	S	Landed 16.6.55. KiA 8.9.55.
Leary, Charles	3062	AIS	Landed 14.9.54.
Lee, John	2161		Former servant of Narboro.
Lee, John	3068	AIS	Landed 14.9.54. From Smyrna 3.7.55. Died Scutari 19.12.54. Former bricklayer of Ross.
Lee, John	3112	IS	Sick Varna 20.9.54. Former labourer of Castlereagh.
Lefevre, Joseph	1685	A	Landed 14.9.54. KiA 20.9.54. Enlisted 19.7.43. Former labourer of Belganon.
Lenehan, Cornelius	3523	S	Landed 4.2.55.
Lenehan, John	3907	S	Present in Crimea after 1.7.55.
Lester, Robert	883		Landed from Malta 10.3.56.
Leonard, Martin	2784	AIS	Landed 14.9.54.
Levinge, Christopher	2393	AIS	Landed 14.9.54. Died camp before Sevastopol 31.5.55. Enlisted 11.8.47.
Levinge, Frederick James	3346	AS	Landed 14.9.54. Sick Scutari 5.11.54. Proceeded to England 5.10.55.
Lewis, Charles	3755	IS	Landed 16.6.55. To Scutari 27.8.55. Sent to England from Scutari 7.9.55.
Lewis, David	3227	I	Landed 13.11.54. Sent to England from Scutari 29.6.55.
Lewis, Howel	3642	S	Landed 16.6.55. Proceeded to England 5.10.55.
Lewis, John	2147		Sick Varna October & November 1854.
Lewis, Matthew	1924	IS	Sick Scutari 20.9.54. Died Scutari 20.11.54.
Lewis, Thomas	3231	S	Landed 13.11.54.
Lewis, William	3097	AIS	Landed 14.9.54. Sick attendant July–September 1855.
Light, Charles	3360	AS	Landed 14.9.54. Wounded severely 26.10.54. Sick Scutari 5.11.54. Sent to England from Scutari 10.1.55.
Lillis, John	2906	S	Command Varna 20.9.54 & 5.11.54.
Lillis, Thomas	2688	AIS	Landed 14.9.54. KiA 5.11.54.
Lines, Thomas	3138	S	Landed from Malta 6.9.55.
Llewellyn, William	1074	AIS	Landed 14.9.54. Died Scutari 3.2.55.
Lloyd, Evan	1975	AIS	Landed 14.9.54. Sick Scutari 3.7.55. From Malta 6.9.55.

Lloyd, John	3268	S	Landed 13.11.54. Died before Sevastopol 3.3.55.
Lloyd, Thomas	3357	AIS	Landed 14.9.54. Died aboard *Australia* 30.1.55. Enlisted 20.6.45. Former baker of Liverpool.
Load, James	3776	S	Landed 16.6.55.
Loader, John	3692	S	Landed 16.6.55.
Lock, Henry	3740	IS	Landed 16.6.55. Died hospital before Sevastopol 8.8.55.
Long, Charles	3736	S	Landed 18.5.55. KiA 8.9.55. Enlisted 3.1.55. Former labourer of Hatling, Sto...?
Long, Patrick	3378	AI	Landed 14.9.54. Sent to England from Scutari 13.8.55.
Longbottom, Jeremiah	3185	S	Landed 13.11.54. KiA 8.9.55.
Loughran, Thomas	1904	AIS	Landed 14.9.54. Sick Scutari 12.6.55.
Lowry, Patrick	3545	I	Landed 4.2.55. Sent to England 6.7.55.
Lowther, John	3621	S	Landed 30.5.55.
Lunam, Patrick	3130		Landed 28.12.54.
Lusk, Thomas	2213	AIS	Landed 14.9.54.
Lusk, William	3908	S	In public employ July–August 1855.
Lynch, Francis	3512	AIS	Landed 14.9.54. Awarded DCM and gratuity of £5 January 1855. Sent to England from Scutari 28.4.55.
Lynch, James	2304	AIS	Landed 14.9.54. Died before Sevastopol 29.1.55. Enlisted 11.10.48. Former shoemaker of Ball...?
Lynch, James	2593	AIS	Landed 14.9.54. Sent to England from Scutari 30.10.55. Former labourer of Killand.
Lynch, John	2337	AIS	Landed 14.9.54.
Lynch, Michael	3241	S	Landed 13.11.54. Sick Scutari 15.3.55. From Scutari 3.10.55.
Lyons, John	3118	AS	Landed 14.9.54. Sick Scutari 5.11.54. Former labourer. To England 1.12.55.
Lyons, John	3392	AIS	Landed 14.9.54. Former labourer, enlisted from ...?
McAlpine, Allen	3513	AIS	Landed 14.9.54. Transfered to 79th Regt 6.1.56.
McAuliffe, Charles	2564	AIS	Landed 14.9.54.
McAuliffe, Jeremiah	2652	AIS	Landed 14.9.54.
McBryde, Patrick	2811	AIS	Landed 14.9.54. Died 15.9.55. Enlisted 19.5.49. Former labourer of Innisheen, Dundalk.
McCabe, John	3190	AS	Landed 14.9.54. Sick Scutari 5.11.54.
McCaffrey, Niel	3459	S	Landed 13.11.54.
McCarthy, Andrew	2407	AIS	Landed 14.9.54.
McCarthy, Charles	3737	S	Landed 6.9.55. From Malta 6.9.55.
McCarthy, John	2455	AIS	Landed 14.9.54. KiA 5.11.54. Enlisted 1.6.48. From PoW 26.10.55. Former labourer of Dunagh.
McCarthy, Patrick	2802	AIS	Landed 14.9.54.
McCarthy, Patrick	3139	S	Landed 28.12.54. In hospital July–September 1855. To Scutari 25.10.55.
McCarthy, Thomas	2350	AIS	Landed 14.9.54.
McCarthy, Timothy	3662	S	Landed 6.9.55. From Malta 6.9.55. To Renkioi 26.9.55. From Scutari 11.2.56.
McCormick, Andrew	3156	S	Landed 13.11.54. To Land Transport Corps 1.2.56.
McCormick, Michael	3300	S	Landed 28.12.54. Sick Scutari 2.5.55. From Scutari 24.9.55.
McCullough, John	3514	AS	Sick Scutari 5.11.54. Sent to England from Scutari 31.3.55.
McDade, John	3197	AI	Landed 14.9.54 (omitted from original listing). To England 28.10.55.
McDermot, John	3486	S	Landed 13.11.54. Sent to England 6.7.55.
McDermot, Luke	3222	S	Landed 28.12.54.
McDonald, John	2294	AIS	Landed 14.9.54. KiA 5.11.54.
McDonald, John	3096		To Scutari 16.8.55. From Scutari 25.10.55.
McDonald, Joseph	3030	S	Landed 13.5.54. KiA 8.9.55. Enlisted 5.2.53. Former labourer of Holbeck, Leeds.
McDonald Peter	3652	S	Landed 16.6.55.
McDonnel, Thomas	3277	S	Landed 13.11.54. Sent to England from Scutari 3.5.55.
McDonnell, John	3096	S	Sick Scutari 20.9.54 & 5.11.54. Sick Scutari 15.8.55.
McEvoy, John	3230	S	Landed 13.11.54. From Scutari 23.7.55.
McGee, George	3157	S	Landed 13.11.54. Proceeded to England 5.10.55.
McGee, Patrick	3136		Landed 13.11.54.
McGiff, James	3205	S	Landed 13.11.54.
McGoldrick, William	3039	AIS	Landed 14.9.54. Wounded 20.9.54. KiA trenches before Sevastopol 18.5.55.
McGrath, James	3443		Sick Scutari September, October & November 1854. Landed 4.2.55. To England 16.1.56.
McGrath, James	3643	S	Landed 27.4.55. To Scutari 15.9.55.
McGrath, Lawrence	3605	S	Landed 4.2.55.
McGuiness, John	2998		Landed 14.9.54. Died in camp 16.9.54.
McGuire, Michael	3633	S	Landed from Malta 6.9.55.
McGuire, Patrick	3354	AI	Landed 14.9.54.
McInerry, James	3094	AIS	Landed 14.9.54.
Macintosh, Paul	1777		Sick at Varna September, October & November 1854. Died Scutari of diarrhoea January 1855.

Mackay, Francis	2425	AIS	Landed 14.9.54. Awarded DCM and gratuity of £5 January 1855. Died before Sevastopol 8.2.55. Enlisted 10.12.47. Former labourer of Dumfries.
McKenna, Patrick	3672	S	Landed from Malta 6.9.55.
McKenna, James	2230	AIS	Died in camp before Sevastopol 29.12.54. Enlisted 2.1.46. Former ...? of Donagh.
McKeough, James	2334	AIS	Landed 14.9.54. Proceeded to England 5.10.55.
Macland, George	3879		Landed from Malta 15.10.55.
McMahon, James	2946	AIS	Landed 14.9.54. Sent to England from Scutari 22.2.55.
McMahon, John	2445	AIS	Landed 14.9.54. Proceeded to England 5.10.55.
McMahon, Matthew	3195	AB	Landed 14.9.54. Command Balaklava 5.11.54. To Scutari 16.8.55.
McMahon, Owen	3216		Landed 13.11.54.
McMahon, Terence	2429	IS	Command Varna 21.9.54.
McMahon, Thomas	2736	AIS	Landed 14.9.54. DoW before Sevastopol 8.10.55. Enlisted 12.4.49. Former labourer of Quinn, County Clare.
McManomy, Patrick	3772	S	Landed from Malta 6.9.55.
McMullen, Hugh	2760	AIS	Landed 14.9.54. Died Scutari of gelatic 14.1.55.
McNamara, Henry	3628	S	Landed 30.5.55.
McNamara, James	2490	A	Landed 14.9.54. Sick Scutari of 5.11.54.
McNamara, Michael	3086	AIS	Landed 14.9.54.
McPherson, Thomas	3012	AIS	Landed 14.9.54.
McQuade, Bernard	2656	AIS	Landed 14.9.54. Died before Sevastopol 9.3.55. Enlisted 12.10.48. Former labourer of Drum...?
McQuade, Thomas	1951	AIS	Landed 14.9.54. Recommended for the Victoria Cross by Captain Lowry 'For reconnoitering to the front on an occasion of alarm & panic in the trenches. Night of 12 June 1855' – not approved. He was, however, awarded the French *Medaille Militaire*.
McReady, John	3515	AIS	Landed 14.9.54. KiA before Sevastopol during the night of 22.8.55.
Macken, Denis	1505		Sick Varna 20.9.54 & 5.11.54. Died Malta 4.12.54.
Madden, John	3638	S	Landed 6.9.55. From Malta 6.9.55.
Madigan, John	2749	AIS	Landed 14.9.54. KiA 8.9.55. Enlisted 17.4.49. Former labourer of Ballygr...? Cork.
Madigan, Michael	2448	AIS	Landed 14.9.54. Sent to England from Scutari 1.1.55.
Magee, Patrick	3136	S	Landed 13.11.54. To England 20.10.55.
Maguire, George	3153	AIS	Landed 14.9.54. Sick Scutari November 1854. From Scuatari 10.3.55.
Maguire, William	3296		Landed 28.12.54. To Scutari 11.9.55.
Mahon, John	3160	AI	Landed 14.9.54. From Scutari 19.9.55.
Mahon, Owen	3216	S	Landed 13.11.54. Died Scutari 22.1.55.
Mahoney, Daniel	2551	AIS	Landed 14.9.54. KiA inside the Redan when he was shot in the head 8.9.55. Described as 'an enormous Grenadier' in the regimental history. Enlisted 11.7.48. Former labourer of Mallow.
Mahoney, Daniel	2757	AI	Landed 14.9.54. Former weaver of Kinsale.
Mahoney, John	2756	AIS	Landed 14.9.54.
Mahoney, John			From 30th Regt 6.1.56 (regimental number 4039).
Mahoney, Michael	2598	ABS	Landed 14.9.54. Sick Scutari 5.11.54. To Scutari 4.7.55. Sent to England from Scutari 24.8.55.
Maitland, Charles	3862		From Malta 23.9.55. To Renkioi 16.10.55.
Malone, John	2948	AS	Landed 14.9.54. Sick Scutari 5.11.54. Proceeded to England 5.10.55.
Malone, John	???8	S	Died Abydos (hospital in Turkey) 14.12.54.
Malone, Michael	3894		Landed from Malta 10.3.56.
Malowney, John	3455		Landed 28.12.54. To England 5.10.55.
Manning, John	2351	AIS	Landed 14.9.54. Proceeded to England 5.10.55.
Mannion, Edward	3057	AS	Landed 14.9.54. Sick Scutari 5.11.54. Died Scutari 21.1.55.
Mannix, William	3593	S	Landed 4.2.55. Died 19.10.55. Enlisted 29.8.54. Former labourer of Scakill, County Clare.
Mansell, Daniel	3079	AIS	Landed 14.9.54. Died of fever Scutari 19.1.55.
Manuel, John	3053	S	Sick Varna 20.9.54 & 5.11.54. Died Synope (hospital) 11.4.55.
Mara, Michael	3090	AIS	Landed 14.9.54.
Marchant, Cornelius	3731	S	Landed 16.6.55. Promoted to corporal 14.1.56. Reduced to private 14.3.56.
Marchant, Patrick	3248	S	Landed 13.11.54. Sent to England from Scutari 30.3.55.
Marsden, William	2963	AIS	Landed 14.9.54. KiA 8.9.55.
Marshall, William	1865		Sick at Varna September, November & December 1854. Landed 19 12.54.
Martin, Christopher	2918	S	Died 26.9.55.
Martin, James	2390	AB	Landed 14.9.54. Command Balaklava 5.11.54.
Martin, John	2435	AS	Landed 14.9.54. KiA by gunfire before Sevastopol 26.10.54. Enlisted 25.2.48. Former labourer of Ballincarry.
Martin, John	3212	S	Landed 13.11.54. Sent to England from Scutari 30.3.55.
Martin, Michael	2385	A	Landed 14.9.54. Command Balaklava 5.11.54.
Martin, William	2353	I	Sick Scutari 20.9.54. From Scutari 26.2.56.
Maryon, William	2813	AIS	Landed 14.9.54. Sent to England from Scutari 30.3.55.

Mason, Thomas	3003	AIS	Landed 14.9.54. Died Scutari 18.1.55. Enlisted 9.7.51. Former ship's carpenter of Hunfleet.
Matthews, George	3556	S	Landed 4.2.55. Sent to England from Scutari 15.5.55.
Matthews, John	2276	AIS	Landed 14.9.54. Sent to England from Scutari 11.5.55.
Matthews, Joseph	3782	S	Landed 30.5.55.
Maxfield, Charles	3347	AI	Landed 14.9.54. Died Scutari 8.2.55. Enlisted 3.3.43. Former labourer of Langannon.
May, Henry	3756	S	Landed 16.6.55. To Scutari 15.10.55.
Maywise, George	????	AI	Landed 14.9.54.
Mealy, Patrick	2964	IS	Sick Scutari 20.9.54. KiA 5.11.54.
Mee, Michael	3255	S	Landed 13.11.54. Sent to England from Scutari 30.3.55.
Meehan, Alexander	3664	S	Landed 6.9.55. From Malta 6.9.55.
Meehan, John	2521	AS	Landed 14.9.54. Sick Scutari 5.11.54. Died Scutari 25.2.55.
Meekins, William	3540	S	Landed 4.2.55. Sent to England from Scutari 21.8.55.
Megson, John	3870		From Malta 23.9.55. Died 19.10.55. Enlisted 20.4.55. Former stone mason of Beverley.
Merrifield, John	2237		To Renkioi 24.1.56.
Messling, Charles	1995	AIS	Landed 14.9.54.
Miers, George	3348	AIS	Landed 14.9.54.
Miles, John	1235	AIS	Landed 14.9.54. Died at Smyrna (hospital) 3.3.55. Enlisted 20.3.39. Former labourer of Bradford.
Miles, George	3713	S	Landed 30.5.55.
Millott, Thomas	3689	S	Landed 16.6.55. KiA 8.9.55. Enlisted 4.10.54. Former labourer of St Pauls, Dublin.
Mills, Edward	3054	S	Landed 28.12.54. Sent to Malta 15.4.55.
Mitchell, John	2038	AIS	Landed 14.9.54. Sent to Malta 5.4.55.
Mitchell, John	3206	S	Landed from Malta 6.9.55.
Moan, James	1940	AI	Landed 14.9.54. AWOL since 15.8.55, struck off as deserter 16.10.55.
Moharty, Owen	2586	AIS	Landed 14.9.54. Died aboard *Golden Fleece* 7.2.55.
Mohur, Thomas	2727	AI	Landed 14.9.54. To Scutari 31.7.55.
Molloy, John/James	3806	S	Landed 16.6.55. From Scutari 24.8.55.
Molloy, Peter	3028		Hospital October 1854. Sick Scutari November 1854.
Moloney, Jeremiah	2524	S	Died before Sevastopol 26.1.55. Enlisted 18.7.48. Former labourer of Glin...?
Moloney, Patrick	3095	AIS	Landed 14.9.54.
Monaghan, Christopher	2219	AIS	Landed 14.9.54. Died before Sevastopol 17.3.55.
Monaghan, James	3037	IS	Sick Varna 20.9.54.
Monaghan, Michael	3922	S	Died 1.11.55. Enlisted 23.2.54. Former labourer of Bowbridge, Dublin.
Montfort, John	3258	S	Landed 13.11.54. Died of diarrhoea aboard *Belgravia* 2.1.55.
Moore, John	3650	S	Landed 30.5.55. To Renkioi 27.9.55.
Moore, Martin	3516	IS	Sick Varna 20.9.54. Died Scutari 22.12.54.
Moore, Michael	3137	S	Landed 13.11.54.
Moran, Martin	2974	AIS	Landed 14.9.54. KiA 5.11.54.
Moran, Peter	3832	S	Landed from Malta 6.9.55.
Morgan, Christopher	3471		Landed 28.12.54. Transferred 88th Regt 13.5.55.
Morgan, John	2631	AIS	Landed 14.9.54. Died before Sevastopol 23.1.55.
Morgan, Morgan	2119	AIS	Landed 14.9.54.
Morgan, William	1356	AIS	Landed 14.9.54. Died aboard *Gomelza* 4.2.55. Former labourer of Madley.
Morgans, Richard	2062	AIS	Landed 14.9.54. Died Scutari 4.1.55. Enlisted 5.1.49. No previous occupation of Chatham.
Moriarty, George	3475	S	Landed 4.2.55.
Morrisey, Edward	2689	AIS	Landed 14.9.54. To England 28.10.55.
Morrison, John	3636	S	Landed 16.6.55. To Scutari 15.8.55.
Morrow, William	3524	S	Landed 4.2.55. From Scutari 3.7.55. KiA 8.9.55. Enlisted 10.7.54. Former labourer of Clan...?, Longford.
Moss, John	3804	S	Landed from Malta 6.9.55.
Moss, Thomas	2701	A	Landed 14.9.54. Command Scutari 5.11.54. From Scutari 5.10.55.
Moss, William	3888		Landed from Malta 10.3.56.
Moynihan, Jeremiah	3855	S	Landed from Malta 6.9.55.
Mulcahy, John	3872	S	Landed from Malta 6.9.55.
Mulcahy, William	2786	AIS	Landed 14.9.54. To England 10.11.55.
Mullally, Patrick	3245	S	Landed 13.11.54.
Mulligan, Laurence	2381	AIS	Landed 14.9.54. Sent to England from Scutari 27.1.55.
Munday, James	2338	AIS	Landed 14.9.54. Sent to England from Smyrna 24.7.55.
Munday, Moses	3809	S	Landed from Malta 6.9.55.
Munroe, Thomas	3856		Landed from Malta 23.9.55. To Land Transport Corps 1.2.56.
Murphy, Garrett	2684	AIS	Landed 14.9.54.
Murphy, James	2439	AIS	Landed 14.9.54. Died aboard ship 18.3.55. Former labourer of Tulla
Murphy, James	2581	IS	Sick Scutari 20.9.54. Sent to England from Scutari 16.2.55. Former labourer of Dunamore.

Murphy, Jeremiah	3387	AI	Landed 14.9.54.
Murphy, John	1230	AIS	Landed 14.9.54. KiA 5.11.54. Enlisted 13.12.39. Former labourer of Hougha...?
Murphy, John	2892	AIS	Landed 14.9.54. Employed at HQ 5.11.54. Paymaster-Sergeant 2.3.55. Reduced to private 28.8.55. Proceeded to England 5.10.55. Former clerk, enlisted from Cork.
Murphy, Martin	3295	S	Landed 13.11.54.
Murphy, Michael	2312	AI	Landed 14.9.54. Former labourer of Gorey.
Murphy, Michael	2572	AIS	Landed 14.9.54. From Smyrna 3.7.55. Former labourer of Templemore.
Murphy, Michael	3344	AIS	Landed 14.9.54. Former labourer of Limerick.
Murphy, Michael	3635	S	Landed 30.5.55.
Murphy, Patrick	3295	AI	Landed 14.9.54. KiA 5.11.54.
Murphy, Patrick	2427	IS	Sick Varna 20.9.54. Died Scutari 7.4.55. Former labourer of Kilmaley.
Murphy, Patrick	2868	A	Landed 14.9.54. Sick Scutari 5.11.54. Former labourer of Dumore.
Murphy, Patrick	3093	AIS	Landed 14.9.54. KiA 5.11.54. Former labourer of Limerick.
Murphy, Samuel	2332	AIS	Landed 14.9.54. KiA 8.9.55. Enlisted 20.11.46. Former labourer of Carmen, Wicklow.
Murphy, Thomas	2798	AIS	Landed 14.9.54. KiA 5.11.54. Enlisted 21.5.49. Former labourer of Ballynamore.
Murray, Charles	2726	S	Sick Scutari 20.9.54 & 5.11.54.
Murray, John	3320		Landed 28.12.54. From Scutari 24.9.55.
Murtough, Michael	3134	AIS	Landed 14.9.54. Sick Scutari October–December 1854. To Scutari 11.9.55.
Murtough, Nicholas	2273		Sick Scutari 20.9.54 & 5.11.54.
Murtough, Thomas	3181	S	Landed 13.11.54.
Mutlow, John	3734	S	Landed from Malta 6.9.55.
Myles, William	2876	AI	Landed 14.9.54. From Scutari 11.2.56.
Nally, William	3154	ABS	Landed 14.9.54. Command Balaklava 5.11.54.
Naughton, Denis	3101	AIS	Landed 14.9.54. Wounded 20.9.54. To England 25.1.56.
Navan, John	2738	AIS	Landed 14.9.54.
Neal, Absolom	3773	S	Landed 30.5.55. To Scutari 10.7.55. From Scutari 3.10.55.
Neal, George	3778	S	Landed 30.5.55. Sent to England from Scutari 7.9.55.
Neal, James	3853		Landed from Malta 23.9.55.
Neill, Henry	3425	AS	Landed 14.9.54. Sick Scutari 5.11.54. PoW since 8.9.55.
Nettles, Robert	2772	AIS	Landed 14.9.54. Died before Sevastopol 17.2.55. Enlisted 13.5.38. Former labourer of Pall...?
Nettles, William	1693	AIS	Landed 14.9.54. Died before Sevastopol 12.3.55.
Newton, John/James	3395	A	Landed 14.9.54. Command Balaklava 5.11.54. From Scutari 11.2.56.
Neylon, Bryan	2930	AIS	Landed 14.9.54. Died before Sevastopol 13.3.55. Enlisted 9.11.50. Former labourer of ...?
Noden, George	1989	AIS	Landed 14.9.54. Sent to England from Scutari 11.7.55.
Noonan, James	2248	AIS	Landed 14.9.54. Died 28.12.55. Enlisted 13.3.46. Former labourer of Kilboggan.
Norman, Robert	2443	AIS	Landed 14.9.54. Died before Sevastopol 13.3.55.
Norris, Alexander	3441	AIS	Landed 14.9.54. Sent to England from Scutari 26.3.55.
Nowlan, William	2341	AIS	Landed 14.9.54. Died before Sevastopol 6.8.55. Enlisted 9.2.47. Former labourer of Kilcoleman, Mayo.
Nowland, Patrick	1164	S	Landed 13.11.54.
Nugent, James	2691	AIS	Landed 14.9.54. Died Scutari 4.6.55.
Nugent, John	3786	S	Landed 30.5.55. Died camp before Sevastopol 15.6.55. Enlisted 3.8.53. Former groom of ...?
Nugent, William	3679	S	Landed 30.5.55. To England 25.2.56.
O'Brien, John	2456	AIS	Landed 14.9.54.
O'Brien, Patrick	3085	AIS	Landed 14.9.54. KiA 5.11.54.
O'Brien, Robert	3229	S	Landed 28.12.54. Died Scutari 6.3.55.
O'Brien, Thomas	3648	S	Landed 16.6.55. To Renkioi 8.2.56.
O'Brien, Timothy	3711		Landed from Malta 10.3.56.
O'Connell, Denis	2494	AIS	Landed 14.9.54. Sent to England from Scutari 22.12.54.
O'Connor, John	3641	S	Landed 16.6.55. To Scutari 7.7.55. From Scutari 10.2.56.
O'Halloran, Edward	3385	AIS	Landed 14.9.54. Died camp before Sevastopol 2.4.55.
O'Halloran, Martin	2434	AIS	Landed 14.9.54. DoW before Sevastopol 22.9.55. Enlisted 25.2.48. Former labourer of Clare Castle.
O'Hara, Patrick	3270	S	Landed 13.11.54.
O'Keefe, John	2574		Sick Scutari September–December 1854. Embarked Scutari for England 25.12.54.
O'Leary, Patrick	2432	AIS	Landed 14.9.54. Sent to England from Scutari 20.1.55 (regimental number 2432 duplicated with Sergeant Armitage).
Olliver, William	3412	AIS	Landed 14.9.54. KiA 5.11.54.
O'Maly James	3377	AIS	Landed 14.9.54. Proceeded to England 5.10.55.
O'Neil, Owen	3610	S	Landed 4.2.55.
O'Neil(l), Timothy	2601	AIS	Landed 14.9.54. Died camp before Sevastopol 22.4.55.
O'Rielly, Patrick	3223	S	Landed 28.12.54.
Pace, James	3696	S	Landed 30.5.55. To England 26.1.56.

Parker, Andrew	3827		Landed from Malta 10.3.56.
Palmer, Joseph	1863		Command Varna 20.9.54 & Balaklava 5.11.54.
Parker, Leonard	1928	AS	Landed 14.9.54. Sick Scutari 5.11.54. Sent to Malta 5.4.55.
Parkins, James	3056	AIS	Landed 14.9.54.
Passey, William	2359	ABS	Landed 14.9.54. Command Balaklava 5.11.54.
Pearce, James	1773	AIS	Landed 14.9.54.
Peeke, John	2301	AIS	Landed 14.9.54.
Peer, John	3765	S	Landed 16.6.55. To Scutari 4.7.55. Sent England from Scutari 18.7.55.
Pender, John	3170	A	Landed 14.9.54. Wounded 20.9.54. Sick Scutari 5.11.54. Sent home to Depot 11.11.54.
Penny, Joseph	1891	AIS	Landed 14.9.54. Died before Sevastopol 19.1.55. Enlisted 12.2.44. Former labourer of Wakefield.
Peppered, John	3677	S	Landed 30.5.55. From Scutari 24.9.55.
Perkins, Henry	3517	AI	Landed 14.9.54.
Perry, John	1990	AIS	Landed 14.9.54. KiA 5.11.54. Enlisted 2.8.44. Former labourer of Brinckley.
Perry, Michael	1875	AIS	Landed 14.9.54. Died Scutari 23.11.54.
Perry, Patrick	2991	S	Sick Varna 20.9.54 & 5.11.54. From Smyrna 3.7.55. KiA 8.9.55. Enlisted 31.3.51. Former groom of Ballybuggan, Dublin.
Petley, Thomas	1792	S	Command Varna 20.9.54 & 5.11.54.
Phelps, George	1239	AIS	Landed 14.9.54. KiA by gunfire before Sevastopol 6.12.54.
Phillips, Daniel	3559	S	Landed 16.6.55.
Phillips, Michael	2458	AIS	Landed 14.9.54. PoW since 5.11.54. From PoW 26.10.55. Enlisted 1.6.48. Former labourer of Chindegan.
Philpott, David	2605	AIS	Landed 14.9.54.
Philpott, Richard	3396	AIS	Landed 14.9.54. DoW before Sevastopol 9.9.55. Enlisted 5.4.53. Former labourer of Southampton.
Pickering, Thomas	3325	S	Landed 28.12.54. Died before Sevastopol 18.3.55.
Pickerell, John	3467		Landed from Malta 4.10.55. To Scutari 25.12.55.
Pilkington, Michael	2457	AIS	Landed 14.9.54.
Pitman, James	2718	AIS	Landed 14.9.54. Died Scutari 5.6.55.
Pottow, Henry	1771	AIS	Landed 14.9.54. Died of dysentry Scutari 18.1.55. Enlisted 9.10.43. Former labourer of Belguam (India?).
Pound, John	3720	S	Landed 30.5.55. From Scutari 24.9.55 .
Power, John	3839	S	Landed from Malta 6.9.55.
Power, Martin	3413	AIS	Landed 14.9.54.
Power, Michael	3866		Landed from Malta 10.3.56.
Pratley, Edward	3725	S	Landed from Malta 6.9.55. KiA 8.9.55. Enlisted 3.1.55. Former labourer of Leafield.
Pratley, John	2076	AIS	Landed 14.9.54. Died before Sevastopol 18.2.55.
Price, John	3358	AIS	Landed 14.9.54. Sent to England from Scutari 29.6.55.
Pringle, William	3186	AB	Landed 14.9.54. Command Balaklava 5.11.54. To Scutari 20.7.55. From Scutari 3.10.55.
Purcell, Robert	2587	AIS	Landed 14.9.54. KiA 5.11.54. Enlisted 1.9.48. Former labourer of Kilburn.
Puskiss, Alexander	3699	S	Landed 16.6.55. Sick attendant August–September 1855. KiA 8.9.55. Enlisted 27.11.54. Former labourer of Southampton.
Putland, Samuel	1845	A	Landed 14.9.54. KiA 20.9.54.
Quigley, Patrick	2406	S	Landed 27.2.55. Sick bay attendant October–December 1855.
Quinn, John	2640	AIS	Landed 14.9.54. Sent to England from Scutari 6.5.55.
Quinn, Michael	2498	AIS	Landed 14.9.54. Sent to Malta 5.4.55.
Rainbird, William	3329	S	Landed 28.12.54. From Scutari 24.8.55. To England 16.1.56.
Read, Alfred	3414	AIS	Landed 14.9.54.
Redington, James	2345	AS	Landed 14.9.54. Sick Scutari 5.11.54. Sent to England from Scutari 19.6.55.
Redmond, Thomas	3370	AIS	Landed 14.9.54. Sent to England from Scutari 30.8.55.
Reed, Daniel	3537	S	Landed 28.12.54.
Reeves, Richard	1890	S	Sick Varna 20.9.54 & 5.11.54. KiA 8.9.55. Enlisted 5.2.44. Former carpet weaver of New Church, Worcester.
Regan, Denis	2940	AI	Landed 14.9.54.
Regan, James	3194	S	Landed 28.12.54. KiA before Sevastopol 30.7.55.
Reid, William	2794	AIS	Landed 14.9.54.
Reilly, Patrick	3175	IS	Sick Varna 20.9.54. To Land Transport Corps 1.2.56.
Reilly, Philip	2194	AIS	Landed 14.9.54. Sent to England from Scutari 28.3.55.
Reilly, Robert	3237	S	Landed 13.11.54. Died in hospital before Sevastopol 6.12.54.
Reilly, Thomas	3882		Landed from Malta 10.3.56.
Reilly, Timothy	3038	AIS	Landed 14.9.54. KiA 5.11.54.
Remmer, James	3659	S	Landed 4.2.55. From Smyrna 3.7.55. Died before Sevastopol 8.8.55. 2.11.54. Former labourer of Easingwold, York.
Rendall, Andrew	2095	AIS	Landed 14.9.54. KiA 5.11.54. Enlisted 6.11.44. Former labourer of Leith.
Rennie, James	3577	S	Landed 4.2.55. Sent to England from Scutari 22.6.55.
Renshaw, Thomas	2292	AIS	Landed 14.9.54.

Renshaw, William	1688	AI	Landed 14.9.54. From Scutari 11.2.56.
Reynolds, Bernard	3235	S	Landed 13.11.54. Shot before Sevastopol 20.3.55.
Reynolds, Patrick	3625	S	Landed 4.2.55. Killed before Sevastopol during the night of 22.8.55.
Reynolds, William	1963	AIS	Landed 14.9.54. Proceeded to England 5.10.55.
Rice, James	3861	S	Landed from Malta 6.9.55.
Rice, Patrick	3518	IS	Command Varna 20.9.54. Died Scutari of dysentry 5.1.55.
Richards, William	1980	IS	Sick Scutari 20.9.54. KiA 5.11.54. Enlisted 9.7.44. Former groom of Rhaeadr.
Richardson, Henry	3549	S	Landed 4.2.55. Died camp before Sevastopol 3.5.55.
Richardson, Michael	2302	AIS	Landed 14.9.54. To England 28.10.55.
Rickard, John	1332	AIS	Landed 14.9.54. Sent to England from Scutari 1.1.55.
Rielly, Thomas	3533	S	Landed 13.11.54.
Rielly, Thomas	3555	S	Landed 4.2.55. Employed by Land Transport September 1855.
Riggs, William	3668		Landed from Malta 10.3.56.
Rigsby, William	1808	AIS	Landed 14.9.54. KiA before Sevastopol 26.8.55.
Ring, John	2464	S	Command Varna 20.9.54 & 5.11.54. Employed by Land Transport September 1855. To Land Transport Corps 1.2.56.
Riorden, Daniel	3426	AI	Landed 14.9.54.
Ritchie, Matthew	2829	AIS	Landed 14.9.54. Reduced from corporal 4.9.55. To England 19.1.56.
Robb, William	2776	AIS	Landed 14.9.54. From Scutari 24.8.55.
Roberts, Roberts	2017		Sick Scutari, embarked for England 14.10.54.
Robinson, Arthur	3442	A	Landed 14.9.54. Sick Scutari 5.11.54. Died Scutari January 1855.
Robinson, Daniel	3421	S	Command Varna 20.9.54 & Balaklava 5.11.54. Sent to England from Scutari 27.1.55 (reported in press to have died at Scutari of diarrhoea 14.1.55).
Robinson, Thomas	1192	AIS	Landed 14.9.54. KiA 8.9.55. Former labourer of Leicester.
Robinson, Thomas	3392	AIS	Landed 14.9.54. Sent to England from Scutari 27.1.55. Former carpenter of Carlow.
Rodway, Edward	1779	IS	Sick Scutari 20.9.54.
Roe, James	3428	AIS	Landed 14.9.54. From Smyrna 3.7.55. KiA 8.9.55.
Roe, John	1650	AS	Landed 14.9.54. Command Balaklava 5.11.54. From Scutari 23.7.55.
Rogan, Martin	2979	AIS	Landed 14.9.54. Mentioned for distinguished service 8.9.55. Died before Sevastopol 19.10.55. Enlisted 19.2.51. Former labourer of Ballina, County Mayo.
Rogers, Thomas	3779	S	Landed 16.6.55.
Rogerson, Martin	3444	S	Landed 28.12.54. Recommended for the Victoria Cross by Captain Lowry 'For bringing in wounded men from the glacis of the Redan, under heavy fire, and when one of the party had already been wounded. 18 June 1855' – not approved. He was awarded the *Medaille Militaire* for his gallantry on this occasion when he was wounded. To Land Transport Corps 1.2.56.
Rooney, John	3468	S	Landed 28.12.54. To England 28.10.55.
Rooney, Patrick	3601	S	Landed 4.2.55.
Root, John	1931	IS	Command aboard ship 20.9.54.
Rosengrave, John	3171	AIS	Landed 14.9.54.
Rosell, Thomas	3292	S	Landed 28.12.54. Died camp before Sevastopol 11.5.55.
Roughan, Michael	2585	AIS	Landed 14.9.54. Died before Sevastopol 24.2.55.
Rushton, George	3576	S	Landed 4.2.55. From Scutari 2.7.55. Died before Sevastopol 2.8.55. Enlisted 7.8.54. Former labourer of Colne, Lancaster.
Ryan, James	3397	AIS	Landed 14.9.54. Died before Sevastopol 11.7.55. Enlisted 1.4.47. Former labourer of Clough, Queen's County.
Ryan, James	3797	S	Landed from Malta 6.9.55.
Ryan, Patrick	3678	S	Landed 30.5.55.
Ryan, William	3612	S	Landed 4.2.55. Sent to Malta 16.4.55.
Ryder, Edmund	2778	AIS	Landed 14.9.54. Died Scutari 28.11.54.
St John, James	3158	S	Landed 13.11.54.
Sally, Patrick	2614	AIS	Landed 14.9.54. Died before Sevastopol 15.2.55. Enlisted 6.9.48. Former groom of Dublin.
Sands, Robert	3448	S	Landed 4.2.55. From Scutari 23.7.55.
Sargeant, John	2048		Command Varna September–December 1854.
Savage, Charles	3739	S	Landed 30.5.55. From Scutari 5.10.55. To Land Transport Corps 1.2.56.
Saxby, William	3792	S	Landed from Malta 6.9.55.
Scaly, James	3127	AIS	Landed 14.9.54. Died in camp before Sevastopol 24.12.54. Enlisted 9.2.54. Former labourer of Tullamore.
Scanlon, Francis	3609	S	Landed 30.6.55. To Land Transport Corps 1.2.56.
Scanlon, Thomas	3609		Landed 4.2.55.
Scott, Robert	3415	AIS	Landed 14.9.54. PoW since 8.9.55. From PoW 16.10.55.
Scrivin, John Cox	3438	A	Landed 14.9.54. Sick Scutari 5.11.54.
Scrivins, William	3781	S	Landed 30.5.55. To Renkioi 16.12.55.
Sealy, Christopher	3764	S	Landed 30.5.55.
Searle, John	3519	S	Sick Varna 20.9.54 & 5.11.54. Sent to England from Scutari 22.6.55.
Seerey, Nicholas	3147	S	Landed 13.11.54.

Selman, Daniel	2058	AIS	Landed 14.9.54. Died in camp before Sevastopol 6.1.55. Enlisted 14.10.44. Former labourer of Cricklade.
Seymour, William	2899	AS	Landed 14.9.54. Died in camp before Sevastopol 13.10.54. Enlisted 12.7.50. Former labourer of White Church.
Shanley, Michael	2352	AI	Landed 14.9.54. Reduced from corporal.
Sharkey, Michael	3063	S	Sick Scutari 20.9.54 & 5.11.54. Sent to England from Scutari 20.1.55.
Shaughnessy, John	2890	AIS	Landed 14.9.54. Sent to England from Scutari 10.1.55.
Shaughnessey, Patrick	2409	AIS	Landed 14.9.54. Promoted corporal. Reduced to private 15.12.55.
Shaw, William	2114	AS	Landed 14.9.54. Sick Scutari 5.11.54. Sent to England from Scutari 22.6.55.
Shea, John	3232	S	Landed 13.11.54.
Shears, James	3361	AIS	Landed 14.9.54. Sent to Malta 16.4.55.
Sheedy, John	3091	S	Sick Varna 20.9.54 & 5.11.54. Sent to England from Scutari 18.7.55.
Sheehan, Benjamin	3401		From Scutari 5.6.55.
Sheehan, Edmund	2731	AIS	Landed 14.9.54.
Sheehan, John	2293	AIS	Landed 14.9.54.
Sheehan, Patrick			Transferred from 9th Regt 12.10.55 (regimental number 3608).
Sheehy, James	2627	AIS	Landed 14.9.54. Awarded DCM and gratuity of £5 January 1855. Proceeded to England 5.10.55.
Sheet, George	3673		Landed from Malta 19.10.55.
Sheill, James	2342	AIS	Landed 14.9.54. Sent to Malta 16.4.55.
Shelly, Patrick	1927		Sick Varna 20.9.54 & 5.11.54.
Shields, Thomas	3890		Landed from Malta 10.3.56.
Shippard, George	3850	S	Landed from Malta 6.9.55.
Shisk, Thomas	2799	AIS	Landed 14.9.54. Doed before Sevastopol 27.1.55. Enlisted 21.5.49. Former labourer of Goughall.
Shortle, William	3684	S	Landed 16.6.55. To Scutari 15.8.55. From Scutari 3.10.55.
Sinclair, John	3826	S	Landed from Malta 6.9.55.
Singleton, James	2952	AS	Landed 14.9.54. Sick Scutari 5.11.54. Died camp before Sevastopol 5.6.55.
Skinner, John	1462	AIS	Landed 14.9.54. Wounded 20.9.54. KiA 5.11.54. Enlisted 14.12.40. Former labourer of Whitealuk.
Skinner, Robert	3541	S	Landed 4.2.55. Groom to Colonel Herbert.
Slattery, Thomas	2896	AIS	Landed 14.9.54. Promoted corporal 24.1.55. Sergeant. Reduced to private 6.11.55.
Sloane, Daniel	2810	AIS	Landed 14.9.54.
Smiley, Robert	2252		Sick Varna. Embarked Scutari for England 25.11.54.
Smith, Charles	3732	S	Landed 30.5.55. To Scutari 25.10.55.
Smith, James	1844	IS	Command Varna 20.9.54. Former shoemaker of Coventry.
Smith, James	3078	AIS	Landed 14.9.54. Sent to England from Scutari 21.1.55. Former labourer of West ...?
Smith, James	3102	AIS	Landed 14.9.54. Sent to England from Smyrna 24.7.55. Former labourer of ...?
Smith, John	3606	S	Landed 4.2.55. From Scutari 5.9.55. Missing from 8.9.55, presumed dead. Struck off strength 22.2.56. Enlisted 31.8.54. Former bricklayer of Leeds.
Smith, John	3807		Landed from Malta 6.9.55.
Smith, Patrick	3048	AIS	Landed 14.9.54.
Smith, Ralph	3704	S	Landed 30.5.55. To England 1.12.55.
Smith, Robert	3355	AI	Landed 14.9.54. From Scutari 24.9.55.
Smith, Samuel	1813	AIS	Landed 14.9.54. Died before Sevastopol 29.1.55.
Smith, Thomas	1994	AIS	Landed 14.9.54. Former bricklayer, enlisted from Sudbury.
Smith, Thomas	2090	AIS	Landed 14.9.54. Sent to England from Scutari 2.1.55. Former miner of ...?
Smith, Thomas	3744	S	Landed 30.5.55. Sailed from Scutari for England 21.7.55.
Smith, Thomas	3544	S	Landed 4.2.55. Died before Sevastopol 14.5.55. Sent to England from Scutari 31.7.55.
Smith, William	3465	S	Landed 4.2.55. Sent to Malta 16.4.55.
Smullen, Charles	2497	AIS	Landed 14.9.54.
Smullen, Patrick	2405	AIS	Landed 14.9.54. Died before Sevastopol 1.9.55.
Spain, Michael	3669	S	Landed 30.5.55.
Spilsbury, James	1748	AS	Landed 14.9.54. Command Balaklava 5.11.54.
Stafford, James	3721	S	Landed 30.5.55. From Scutari 11.2.56.
Stagg, James	3362	AIS	Landed 14.9.54. Died before Sevastopol 17.4.55.
Stagg, William	3741	S	Landed 16.6.55. To Scutari 9.9.55.
Stevens, James	3294	S	Landed 13.11.54.
Stevens, John	3280	S	Landed 13.11.54. Died before Sevastopol 22.8.55. Enlisted 10.4.54. Former labourer of Tynnan, Wexford.
Stevens, John	3098	AIS	Landed 14.9.54. Sent to Malta 16.4.55.
Stewart, James	1430	AIS	Landed 14.9.54.
Stones, John	3179	S	Landed 28.12.54.
Stones, John	3869		Landed from Malta 4.10.55.
Strapp, John	2881	AIS	Landed 14.9.54.

Sullivan, Jeffrey	2597	AIS	Landed 14.9.54. Died before Sevastopol 14.3.55. Enlisted 12.5.47. Former labourer of Coolclough.
Sullivan, John	2616	AS	Landed 14.9.54. Sick Scutari 5.11.54. Died before Sevastopol 25.4.55.
Sullivan, John	3128	AI	Landed 14.9.54. Sent Scutari sick from Sevastopol 16.9.55. From Scutari 11.2.56.
Sullivan, John	3488		Landed 4.2.55. DoW before Sevastopol 25.4.55.
Sullivan, Maurice	2745	AIS	Landed 14.9.54. Died Scutari 26.12.54.
Sullivan, Patrick	3674		Landed from Malta 10.3.56.
Sully, Henry	2113	AIS	Landed 14.9.54. Died Scutari 8.12.54.
Summersby, Thomas P.	1937	AIS	Landed 14.9.54. Sent to England from Scutari 10.1.55.
Sunderland, John	2320	S	Sick Varna 20.9.54 & 5.11.54. Sent to England 6.7.55.
Sutcliffe, James	3018	AIS	Landed 14.9.54. Sent Scutari sick from Sevastopol 15.8.55. From Scutari 24.9.55.
Sutcliffe, William	3619	S	Landed 4.2.55.
Swan, John	3639	S	Landed from Malta 6.9.55. To Land Transport Corps 1.2.56.
Sweeney, James	3380	AIS	Landed 14.9.54. Died before Sevastopol 21.1.55.
Sweeney, Timothy	2173	AIS	Landed 14.9.54. Sent to England from Scutari 19.6.55.
Swingler, Absolam	2156	AIS	Landed 14.9.54. Died before Sevastopol 23.3.55. Enlisted 30.6.45. Former ...? of Leicester.
Taggett, John	3058	AIS	Landed 14.9.54.
Talkington, Henry	1294		Embarked Scutari for England 15.10.54.
Tavenner, Edward	3418	AI	Landed 14.9.54.
Taylor, John	2595	AIS	Landed 14.9.54. Servant to Capt Thompson, ADC. Command Scutari. Sent to England from Scutari 31.12.54. Landed from Malta 16.10.55. Former labourer of Kil...?
Taylor, John	3359	AIS	Landed 14.9.54. Died at Coolali 4.2.55. Former labourer of Reading.
Thomas, Elijah	2671	IS	Sick Scutari 20.9.54. Sent to England from Scutari 16.2.55.
Thomas, John	2053	AIS	Landed 14.9.54. Sent to England from Scutari 27.1.55. Former tailor of Newcastle.
Thomas, John	2750	S	Sick Scutari 20.9.54 & 5.11.54. Sent Scutari sick from Sevastopol. 15.8.55. From Scutari 15.10.55. Former labourer of Arm...?
Thomas, Joseph	2695	AS	Landed 14.9.54. Sick Scutari 5.11.54. From Scutari 24.8.55.
Thompson, James	2936	AIS	Landed 14.9.54. From Smyrna 3.7.55.
Thompson, Keeran	3125	S	Landed 13.11.54.
Thornton, Edwin	3480	S	Landed 28.12.54. Died before Sevastopol 1.4.55.
Tighe, Patrick	3238	S	Landed 4.2.55.
Tiplady, Thomas	3340	S	Landed 4.2.55. Died before Sevastopol 28.2.55. Enlisted 2.5.54. Former labourer of Middleton.
Tipler, William	2387	AIS	Landed 14.9.54.
Toohey, Martin	3680	S	Landed 16.6.55.
Trimble, Patrick	3210	S	Landed 13.11.54.
Trowbridge, Samuel	3402	AIS	Landed 14.9.54. Died Scutari 13.1.55.
Troy, Martin	3843	S	Landed from Malta 6.9.55.
Truston, Martin	2259	AIS	Landed 14.9.54. Sent to England from Scutari 1.1.55.
Turnbull, Joseph	3710	S	Landed from Malta 6.9.55.
Turner, Charles	2806	AS	Landed 14.9.54. Sick Scutari 5.11.54. Died Scutari 27.1.55.
Turner, Henry	1355	AIS	Landed 14.9.54.
Turner, James	2789	AIS	Landed 14.9.54. Died before Sevastopol 29.3.55.
Tynan, James	3189	IS	Sick Varna 20.9.54. Sent to England from Scutari 2.6.55.
Underwood, Thomas	3422	AI	Landed 14.9.54.
Underwood, Thomas	3726	S	Landed from Malta 6.9.55.
Varo, Edward	3557	S	Landed 28.12.54. From Smyrna 3.7.55.
Wade, Patrick	2882	AIS	Landed 14.9.54. Died Scutari 21.11.54.
Walker, George	3560	S	AWOL 2.3.56.
Walker, John	3560		Landed 4.2.55.
Walker, William	3072	AIS	Landed 14.9.54.
Wall, Cornelius	3759	S	Landed from Malta 6.9.55.
Wall, James	1730	S	Sick Scutari. Command Balaklava July–September 1855. Former miner of Wellington.
Wall, James	3106	AIS	Landed 14.9.54. Former labourer of Kilfecle.
Wallace, William	3430	AIS	Landed 14.9.54. Died camp before Sevastopol 28.12.54.
Walsh, James	3374	AIS	Landed 14.9.54. Sent to Malta 5.4.55.
Walsh, James	3617		Landed from Malta 10.3.56.
Walsh, John	3823		Landed from Malta 10.3.56.
Walsh, Maurice	2525	S	Sent Scutari sick from Sevastopol 15.8.55.
Walsh, Michael	3236		Landed 13.11.54. Transferred 30.6.55.
Walsh, Michael	3851		Landed from Malta 10.3.56.
Walsh, Patrick	2845	S	Landed 13.11.54. Landed from Malta 6.9.55.
Walsh, William	2245	ABS	Landed 14.9.54. Command Balaklava 5.11.54. KiA 8.9.55. Enlisted

			5.3.46. Former labourer of Sligo.
Walshe, Patrick	3817		Landed from Malta 10.3.56.
Walton, William John	3424	AS	Landed 14.9.54. Wounded 20.9.54. Sick Scutari 5.11.54. Sick Scutari 18.?.55. From Scutari 11.2.56.
Ward, Patrick	3875		Landed from Malta 10.3.56.
Warren, John	1452	A	Landed 14.9.54. Died Balaklava 26.9.54. Enlisted 20.11.49. Former labourer of London.
Warren, Thomas	3780	S	Landed 30.5.55. Sent Scutari sick from Sevastopol 3.7.55 .
Warrington, James	3656	S	Landed 30.5.55. Sent Scutari sick from Sevastopol 24.8.55. From Scutari 20.9.55.
Watkins, William	3416	AIS	Landed 14.9.54. Sent to Malta 16.4.55.
Waud, Charles	2907	IS	Sick Varna 20.9.54.
Wavell, William	3695	S	Landed 30.5.55. KiA trenches Sevastopol 22.6.55.
Wealsh, John	2504	AIS	Landed 14.9.54. Died Smyrna (hospital) 31.3.55.
Welsh, Morris	2525	AI	Landed 14.9.54. To Scutari 16.8.55. From Scutari 11.2.56.
Welsman, Robert	1350	AIS	Landed 14.9.54. Awarded DCM and gratuity of £5 January 1855. Sent to England from Scutari 16.2.55.
White, Edward	3014	S	Landed 13.11.54. Died aboard *Ripon*.
White, James	3793	S	Landed from Malta 6.9.55.
White, John	1399	AIS	Landed 14.9.54. Sent to England from Scutari 2.3.55.
White, John	3716	S	Landed from Malta 6.9.55. Supposed to have died 5.10.55.
White, Matthew	3082	AS	Landed 14.9.54. Sick Scutari 5.11.54.
White, Thomas	2803	AI	Landed 14.9.54. Former labourer of Ballymoan.
White, Thomas	3113	IS	Sick Scutari 20.9.54. Died Balaklava 14.1.55. Former labourer of Coventry.
Whitsey, Francis	3394	AS	Landed 14.9.54. Sick Scutari 5.11.54. Died Scutari 29.11.54.
Whittle, William	2649	AIS	Landed 14.9.54. KiA 5.11.54. Enlisted 10.10.48. Former labourer of Northam. This soldier is also recorded as being a PoW and was struck off the strength 22.2.56.
Williams, Edward	1996	AIS	Landed 14.9.54. To Renkioi 8.2.56.
Williams, Griffith	2120	AIS	Landed 14.9.54. KiA 5.11.54.
Williams, John	1725	AS	Landed 14.9.54. Sick Scutari 5.11.54. To Scutari 20.7.55. From Scutari 5.9.55. Former mason of Hereford.
Williams, John	1967	AIS	Landed 14.9.54. Former weaver of Launceston.
Williams, John	3445	S	Landed 4.2.55. Sent Scutari sick from Sevastopol 20.9.55.
Williams, Thomas	1600	AIS	Landed 14.9.54. Awarded DCM and gratuity of £5 January 1855. From Scutari 5.7.55. Former labourer of Hardington.
Williams, Thomas	2108	AIS	Landed 14.9.54. KiA 5.11.54. Enlisted 20.3.45. Former weaver of St Harmon.
Williams, Thomas	3110	AS	Landed 14.9.54. Sick Scutari 5.11.54. To Land Transport Corps 1.2.56. Former labourer of Loughreagh.
Williams, Thomas	3398	AIS	Landed 14.9.54. Died before Sevastopol 18.2.55. Former miner of Brecon.
Williams, William	3774	S	Landed 16.6.55. Died hospital before Sevastopol 7.8.55.
Willis, Joseph	3564	S	Landed 4.2.55. From Smyrna 3.7.55. To Scutari 25.10.55.
Willoughby, George	3489	S	Landed from Provisional Battalion, Malta 19.5.55. Promoted sergeant from corporal 10.10.55. Reduced to private 28.2.56.
Wilson, James	2223	AIS	Landed 14.9.54.
Wilson, John	3108	IS	Sick Scutari 20.9.54. Died before Sevastopol 26.3.55. Former labourer of Newcastle.
Wilson, John	3520	AIS	Landed 14.9.54. Died before Sevastopol 30.7.55. Enlisted 6.4.40. Former labourer of Elkington, Northampton.
Wilson, John Charles	2197	AIS	Landed 14.9.54. Sent Scutari sick from Sevastopol 21.6.55. From Scutari 11.2.56.
Wilson, Joseph	1866	AIS	Landed 14.9.54. Died before Sevastopol 9.8.55. Enlisted 18.1.44. Former labourer of ...? Chester.
Wilson, Joseph	2051	AIS	Landed 14.9.54. Died Scutari 26.11.54. Former labourer of Taunton.
Wilson, Matthew	2215	AIS	Landed 14.9.54. Died before Sevastopol 17.2.55. Enlisted 24.10.45. Former servant of ...?town.
Winch, William	1584	AIS	Landed 14.9.54.
Wisely, Thomas	3588	S	Landed 4.2.55. Sent to England from Scutari 11.5.55.
Wood, George	3114	S	Landed 13.11.54. Sent to England from Scutari 22.3.55. Returned to the Crimea from Malta 10.3.56.
Wood, John	1719	S	Command Varna 20.9.54 & 5.11.54. Died before Sevastopol 8.3.55.
Wood, Squire	3487	S	Landed 13.11.54.
Wood, William	3184	AS	Landed 14.9.54. From Scutari 2.7.55. Sent Scutari sick from Sevastopol 7.9.55.
Woodrough, Thomas	3381	AIS	Landed 14.9.54. Died before Sevastopol 6.5.55.
Woods, George	2722	AIS	Landed 14.9.54. KiA 5.11.54.
Woodward, James	3198	S	Landed 13.11.54. From Scutari 2.7.55. KiA 8.9.55.
Woodward, John	3199	S	Landed 13.11.54. Died Scutari 8.3.55. Enlisted 20.2.54. Former shoemaker of St Werburgh, Derby.

Woolford, Jesse	3691		Landed from Malta 23.9.55. Promoted corporal. Reduced to private 4.11.55.
Woolford, Joseph	3693		Landed from Malta 4.10.55. Corporal. Reduced to private 9.10.55.
Workman, James	3720		Landed from Malta 10.3.56.
Wormington, William	1729	AS	Landed 14.9.54. Sick Scutari 5.11.54. Sent Scutari sick from Sevastopol 2.8.55. To England 16.1.56.
Wright, John	3303		Landed 13.11.54.
Wright, Jones	2298	ABS	Landed 14.9.54. Command Balaklava 5.11.54.
Wrigley, Henry	2042	AIS	Landed 14.9.54. Died Scutari 15.2.55.
Yates, William	1251	AIS	Landed 14.9.54. Sent to England from Scutari 22.3.55.

Appendix 2: Official Strength and Casualties of the 41st Regiment during the Crimean Campaign

The 41st Regiment published its official statistics for the Crimean Campaign in D.A.N. Lomax's seminal work *The History of the 41st Regiment*. A comparison of these figures with the details incorporated into the Nominal Roll shows significant discrepancies in the casualty totals, caused by different methods of recording the same event e.g. is 'KiA' the same as 'Died before Sevastopol' or does the latter include those men who died of wounds/disease? Similarly, 'Landed from Malta' includes men arriving in the Crimea for the first time as well as those men who had been invalided to Malta, but who were latter returned to active service. It has not been possible therefore to compare many of the figures quoted by Lomax with those collated into the composite Nominal Roll. Even those figures that appear to be comparable were calculated on different dates (Lomax gave a start date of 15 April 1855 and a cut off date of 9 September 1855, whereas the Nominal Roll has been compiled from a start date of 14 September 1854 and a cut off date of 10 March 1856).

	Lomax up to 9.9.55	*Nominal Roll up to 10.3.56*
Actual strength which landed at Scutari, 15 April 1854, in sergeants, drummers and rank and file	863	
Actual strength which landed at Calamita Bay, 14 September 1854, in sergeants, drummers and rank and file (approximate)		819
Total of NCOs and men received from England and Malta, exclusive of the above	521	
Total of sergeants, drummers and rank and file, 41st, who served in the Crimea	**1,384**	**1,505**
Men killed or died during the campaign	387	370
Men invalided home or became non-effective	246	
Men remaining in the Crimea	794	
Total	**1,427**	
Officers killed (in action)	6*	6
Officers wounded (including those who died of wounds)	13	15
NCOs and men killed (in action)	110	103
NCOs and men wounded (including those who died of wounds)	426	
Total losses in action	555	
Total invalided	246	
Total casualties during the campaign	**801**	

NB – Lomax notes that 'the casualties deducted from the strength sent out to the East will not give the number remaining in the Crimea on 9 September 1855, as men at Scutari cannot be included as in the Crimea. Authority for above, *Parliamentary Returns, 1856*.'

* Lomax states that 'This is accurate, but very misleading. The 41st lost thirteen officers during the war:
(a) Killed in action – 6, viz: Captains Richards, Every and Lockhart; Lieutenants Swaby, Taylor and Stirling.
(b) Died of wounds – 4, viz: Lieutenant-Colonels Carpenter and Eman; Lieutenant Harriott and Ensign Fitzgerald.
(c) Died of disease – 3, Captain Johnston, Surgeon Anderson and Assistant-Surgeon Lamont.